English Fundamentals

Form C

Twelfth Edition

Donald W. Emery
Late of The University of Washington

John M. Kierzek
Late of Oregon State University

Peter Lindblom
Miami-Dade Community College

Lesson 21 pgs. 204 + 205
using verbs correctly: Principal Parts: Tense

Longman

New York   San Francisco   Boston
London   Toronto   Sydney   Tokyo   Singapore   Madrid
Mexico City   Munich   Paris   Cape Town   Hong Kong   Montreal

Vice President and Editor-in-Chief: Joseph Terry
Senior Acquisitions Editor: Steven Rigolosi
Associate Editor: Barbara Santoro
Senior Marketing Manager: Melanie Craig
Supplements Editor: Donna Campion
Production Manager: Ellen MacElree
Project Coordination and Electronic Page Makeup: Electronic Publishing Services Inc., NYC
Cover Design Manager: Nancy Danahy
Cover Designer: Suzanne Harbison
Manufacturing Buyer: Roy Pickering
Printer and Binder: Hamilton Printing Company
Cover Printer: Phoenix Color Corp.

Library of Congress Cataloging-in-Publication Data

Emery, Donald W. (Donald William), 1906-
    English fundamentals. Form C / Donald W. Emery, John M. Kierzek, Peter Lindblom.—
12th ed.
        p. cm.
    Includes index.
    ISBN 0-321-09636-3
    1. English language—Gammar—Problems, exercises, etc. I. Kierzek, John M., 1891-
II. Lindblom, Peter D., 1938- III. Title.

PE1112 .E473 2002
428.2—dc21   2002024681

Please visit our website at http://www.ablongman.com

ISBN 0-321-09636-3

1 2 3 4 5 6 7 8 9 10—HT—05 04 03 02

Contents

Part 3

Sentence Building 125
Lessons, Practice Sheets, and
Exercises

Part 4

Punctuation 163
Lessons, Practice Sheets, and
Exercises

Preface

The twelfth edition of *English Fundamentals* builds upon the foundation of eleven successful editions to provide quality instruction in English. As the book has flourished through the years, it has retained in each subsequent edition the tried and true presentations that have made the book a success for so many years. In each new version there have been changes and refinements to keep the book on pace with contemporary students. This new book closely resembles the previous versions, but it also changes in ways that will make students' experiences with it richer and more rewarding. With these changes, however, the purpose and the audience have not changed since the first edition. All students who want to improve their ability to use English in writing and speaking can profit from this twelfth edition.

Organization of the Text

Certain important qualities have always been characteristic of *English Fundamentals:* clear, effective instruction in the fundamental principles of English; carefully crafted exercises designed to illustrate those principles; and a comprehensive testing system to diagnose problems and measure progress. The first lessons introduce students to the basic system of the language and provide carefully chosen examples of verb connections, basic sentence patterns, and the internal workings of the sentence. Simplified presentations make the book accessible both for developmental students and for those who have advanced in their study of the language. Because the first sections are cumulative, building step by step a foundation in the operating principles of the language, these early lessons should be studied first. Once the foundation is laid, the order for studying the remaining units is flexible. Work on spelling and capitalization, for example, can be undertaken at almost any point, even during study of another unit.

Building on the foundation of the early lessons, subsequent lessons explore the more complex structures and relationships of the language. Students examine the function of various clauses and phrases, first learning to recognize their structures, and then learning to use them through drills on sentence combining, embedding, and transformation. The drills are proven methods for helping students to develop flexibility and sophistication in their writing and to recognize effective, correct constructions when they revise.

The last instructional section surveys college writing. Students study the writing process, with special emphasis on techniques of invention, and then learn to apply that process to a wide range of writing assignments typical of college courses. These assignments range from personal essays to academic papers, with an additional focus on paragraph development. The section includes an examination of essay tests and test-taking. To accommodate the interests of a wide range of students, the examples and exercises throughout the book come from a number of disciplines, including science and business.

The text concludes with a set of twenty progress tests and three appendixes. The first appendix contains eleven sentence-combining exercises, each containing five or six units.

These exercises are in addition to the embedding, combining, and transformation drills found in the exercises attached to each lesson. These additional drills encourage the students to try out a variety of sentence-building strategies by combining the short sentences in each unit in as many ways as possible. The sentence-combining drills also require the students to review punctuation rules as they combine the sentences and properly punctuate the new, longer sentences. The second appendix offers diagnostic tests to analyze students' abilities in spelling, punctuation, sentence structure, and usage. The third appendix contains the answer key to the practice sheets. The book concludes with an index to help students use the text for references to specific concepts.

New to This Edition

The instructional material in all lessons has been significantly rewritten to make the concepts more accessible to the students. Explanations have been simplified, and examples have been updated to accommodate a wider range of students.

Over the past three editions, the number of practice sheets and exercises requiring active writing has increased so that there are now forty-five pages that ask students to write or rewrite sentences to reinforce the concepts taught in the lessons. The result is that every major concept is covered by drills that require both recognition and production. These new drills use sentence-combining, embedding, transformation, and rewriting to encourage the students to use the concepts taught in each lesson.

Practice Sheets

The twelfth edition continues the use of practice sheets. After every lesson there is at least one easily understood worksheet that provides examples of and practice with the concept introduced in that lesson. The sentences in the practice sheets are usually shorter and somewhat simpler than those in the exercise worksheets that follow. Thus, the practice sheets provide a starter exercise, a warm-up for students to begin work on each new concept. The practice sheets also allow teachers to use the book with students whose reading levels might require simplified material.

An answer key for every practice sheet may be found in Appendix C. Its presence allows students to use *English Fundamentals* independently as a drill and practice book. Students in composition classes who, for example, need extra work on punctuation for compound sentences can find that section in the index, read the instruction and commentary, work through the practice sheets, and correct their work by referring to the answer key in Appendix C.

Variety in Exercises

In the minds of some, English texts that focus on the fundamentals of the language often limit student work to recognition, identification, and correction—a sort of fill-in-the-blanks scheme that doesn't require much actual writing. *English Fundamentals* requires such work as is necessary to build certain skills but also incorporates a large number of exercises that require active production of sentences. Students will practice sentence combining and reducing independent clauses to various dependent clauses and phrases. They will learn to embed independent clauses in sentences and will rewrite sentences. They will transform active expressions to passive ones and vice versa, and change from direct to indirect quotation, and from indirect to direct. They will write sentences to practice using various constructions. Research has shown, and we are convinced, that such active manipulation of the structures of language will greatly improve students' ability to write effectively and correctly.

Optional Testing Program

The twelfth edition, like the eleventh, offers additional tests. The Optional Testing Program consists of thirty tests sent to instructors on request. These tests are printed in a separate volume with perforated pages. The tests differ from the progress tests in the text in that they generalize, focusing on major concepts (for example, introductory subordinate elements) rather than specific constructions. The tests first ask for recognition of correct forms, then ask for generation of the new structure out of the basic parts. There is an answer key provided with the tests so that, in addition to use in evaluation, they can be used as higher-level practice exercises.

Text Specific Supplements

A complete Answer Key (0-321-09638-X) is available to accompany *English Fundamentals*. Please see your Longman sales representative for details.

The Longman Basic Skills Package

In addition to the book-specific supplements discussed above, a series of other skills-based supplements are available for both instructors and students. All of these supplements are available either free or at greatly reduced prices.

For Additional Reading and Reference

The Dictionary Deal.   Two dictionaries can be shrinkwrapped with any Longman Basic Skills title at a nominal fee: *The New American Webster Handy College Dictionary* (a paperback reference text with more than 100,000 entries) and *Merriam Webster's Collegiate Dictionary*, tenth edition (a hardback reference with a citation file of more than 14.5 million examples of English words drawn from actual use). For more information on how to shrinkwrap a dictionary with your text, please contact your Longman sales representative.

Penguin Quality Paperback Titles.   A series of Penguin paperbacks is available at a significant discount when shrinkwrapped with any Longman Basic Skills title. For a complete list of titles or more information, please contact your Longman sales consultant.

Newsweek Alliance.   Instructors may choose to shrinkwrap a 12-week subscription to *Newsweek* with any Longman text. For more information on the Newsweek program, please contact your Longman sales representative.

Electronic and Online Offerings

The Longman Writer's Warehouse.   The innovative and exciting online supplement is the perfect accompaniment to any developmental writing course. Developed by developmental English instructors specially for developing writers, The Writer's Warehouse covers every part of the writing process. Also included are journaling capabilities, multimedia activities, diagnostic tests, an interactive handbook, and a complete instructor's manual. The Writer's Warehouse requires no space on your school's server; rather, students complete and store their work on the Longman server, and are able to access it, revise it, and continue working at any time. For more details about how to shrinkwrap a free subscription to The Writer's Warehouse with this text, please consult your Longman sales representative. For a free guided tour of the site, visit **http://longmanwriterswarehouse.com.**

The Writer's ToolKit Plus. This CD-ROM offers a wealth of tutorial, exercise, and reference material for writers. It is compatible with either a PC or Macintosh platform, and is flexible enough to be used either occasionally for practice or regularly in class lab sessions. For information on how to bundle this CD-ROM free with your text, please contact your Longman sales representative.

GrammarCoach Software. This interactive tutorial helps students practice the basics of grammar and punctuation through 600 self-grading exercises in such problems areas as fragments, run-ons, and agreement. IBM only. 0-205-26509-X

The Longman English Pages Web Site. Both students and instructors can visit our free content-rich Web site for additional reading selections and writing exercises. From the Longman English pages, visitors can conduct a simulated Web search, learn how to write a resume and cover letter, or try their hand at poetry writing. Stop by and visit us at **http://www.ablongman.com/englishpages.**

The Longman Electronic Newsletter Twice a month during the spring and fall, instructors who have subscribed freceive a free copy of the Longman Developmental English Newsletter in their e-mailbox. Written by experienced classroom instructors, the newsletter offers teaching tips, classroom activities, book reviews, and more. To subscribe, visit the Longman Basic Skills Web site at **http://www.ablongman.com/basicskills**, or send an e-mail to **Basic Skills@ablongman.com**.

For Instructors

Electronic Test Bank for Writing. This electronic test bank features more than 5,000 questions in all areas of writing, from grammar to paragraphing, through essay writing, research, and documentation. With this easy-to-use CD-ROM, instructors simply choose questions from the electronic test bank, then print out the completed test for distribution. CD-ROM: 0-321-08117-X. Print version: 0-321-08486-1.

Competency Profile Test Bank, Second Edition. This series of 60 objective tests covers ten general areas of English competency, including fragments; comma splices and run-ons; pronouns; commas; and capitalization. Each test is available in remedial, standard, and advanced versions. Available as reproducible sheets or in computerized versions. Free to instructors. Paper version: 0-321-02224-6. Computerized IBM: 0-321-02633-0. Computerized Mac: 0-321-02632-2.

Diagnostic and Editing Tests and Exercises, Fifth Edition. This collection of diagnostic tests helps instructors assess students' competence in Standard Written English for purpose of placement or to gauge progress. Available as reproducible sheets or in computerized versions, and free to instructors. Paper: 0-321-11730-1. CD-ROM: 0-321-11731-X.

ESL Worksheets, Third Edition.   These reproducible worksheets provide ESL students with extra practice in areas they find the most troublesome. A diagnostic test and post-test are provided, along with answer keys and suggested topics for writing. Free to adopters. 0-321-07765-2

Longman Editing Exercises.   54 pages of paragraph editing exercises give students extra practice using grammar skills in the context of longer passages. Free when packaged with any Longman title. 0-205-31792-8 Answer key: 0-205-31797-9

80 Practices.   A collection of reproducible, ten-item exercises that provide additional practices for specific grammatical usage problems, such as comma splices, capitalization, and pronouns. Includes an answer key, and free to adopters. 0-673-53422-7

CLAST Test Package, Fourth Edition.   These two 40-item objective tests evaluate students' readiness for the CLAST exams. Strategies for teaching CLAST preparedness are included. Free with any Longman English title. Reproducible sheets: 0-321-01950-4 Computerized IBM version: 0-321-01982-2 Computerized Mac version: 0-321-01983-0

TASP Test Package, Third Edition.   These 12 practice pre-tests and post-tests assess the same reading and writing skills covered in the TASP examination. Free with any Longman English title. Reproducible sheets: 0-321-01959-8 Computerized IBM version: 0-321-01985-7 Computerized Mac version: 0-321-01984-9

Teaching Writing to the Non-Native Speaker.   This booklet examines the issues that arise when non-native speakers enter the developmental classroom. Free to instructors, it includes profiles of international and permanent ESL students, factors influencing second-language acquisition, and tips on managing a multicultural classroom. 0-673-97452-9

Using Portfolios.   This supplement offers teachers a brief introduction to teaching with portfolios in composition courses. This essential guide address the pedagogical and evaluative use of portfolios, and offers practical suggestions for implementing a portfolio evaluation system in a writing class. 0-321-08412-8

[NEW] The Longman Guide to Classroom Management.   Written by Joannis Flatley of St. Philip's College, the first in Longman's new series of monographs for developmental English instructors focuses on issues of classroom etiquette, providing guidance on dealing with unruly, unengaged, disruptive, or uncooperative students. Ask your Longman sales representative for a free copy. 0-321-09246-5

[NEW] The Longman Instructor's Planner.   This all-in-one resource for instructors includes monthly and weekly planning sheets, to-do lists, student contact forms, attendance rosters, a gradebook, an address/phone book, and a mini almanac. Ask your Longman sales representative for a free copy. 0-321-09247-3.

For Students

Researching Online, **Fifth Edition.**   A perfect companion for a new age, this indispensable new supplement helps students navigate the Internet. Adapted from *Teaching Online,* the instructor's Internet guide, *Researching Online* speaks directly to students, giving them detailed, step-by-step instructions for performing electronic searches. Available free when shrinkwrapped with this text. For more information, contact your Longman Sales Representative.

Ten Practices of Highly Successful Students. This popular supplement helps students learn crucial study skills, offering concise tips for a successful career in college Topics include time management, test-taking, reading critically, stress, and motivation. 0-205-30769-8

Thinking Through the Test, **by D.J. Henry.** This special workbook, prepared specially for students in Florida, offers ample skill and practice exercises to help student prep for the Florida State Exit Exam. To shrinkwrap this workbook free with your textbook, please contact your Longman sales representative.

[NEW] The Longman Writer's Journal. This journal for writers, free with any Longman English text, offers students a place to think, write, and react. For an examination copy, contact your Longman sales consultant. 0-321-08639-2

[NEW] The Longman Writer's Portfolio. This unique supplement provides students with a space to plan, think about, and present their work. The portfolio includes an assessing/organizing area (including a grammar diagnostic test, a spelling quiz, and project planning worksheets), a before and during writing area (including peer review sheets, editing checklists, writing self-evaluations, and a personal editing profile), and an after-writing area (including a progress chart, a final table of contents, and a final assessment). Ask your Longman sales representative for ISBN 0-321-10765-9.

For information on other supplements that are available with this text, please see your Longman sales representative.

Acknowledgments

Our thanks go to all those who offered advice and suggestions for improving this and previous editions: Edwin J. Blesch, Jr., Nassau Community College; Ladson W. Bright, Cape Fear Community College; James Vanden Bosch, Calvin College; Bernadine Brown, Nassau Community College; Kitty Chen Dean, Nassau Community College; Patricia Derby, Chabot College; Neil G. Dodd, East Los Angeles College; Loris D. Galford, McNeese State University; Harold J. Herman, University of Maryland; William T. Hope, Jefferson Technical College; Sue D. Hopke, Broward Community College; Clifford J. Houston, East Los Angeles College; George L. Ives, North Idaho College; Edward F. James, University of Maryland; Thomas Mast, Montgomery College; Walter Mullen, Mississippi Gulf Coast Community College; Mary E. Owens, Montgomery College; Crystal Reynolds, Indiana State University; Bill Sartoris, Camden College; Albert Schoenberg, East Los Angeles Community College; Ines Shaw, North Dakota State University; Barbara Stout, Montgomery College; and Robert S. Sweazy, Vincennes University Junior College.

Donald W. Emery
John M. Kierzek
Peter Lindblom

Basic Sentence Patterns

Lessons, Practice Sheets, and Exercises

Lesson 1   *The Simple Sentence; Subjects and Verbs*

While you might find it difficult to produce a satisfying definition, you probably know that the sentence is a basic unit of written or oral expression. Thus, if you were asked, you might define a sentence as "an orderly arrangement of words that makes sense." If you wished to be more specific and more formal, you might say a sentence is "a self-contained grammatical unit, usually containing a subject and a verb, that conveys a meaningful statement, question, command, or exclamation."

You need to understand the basic construction of the sentence in order to write and speak effectively and correctly. In the first few lessons of this book, you'll examine the parts that make up a sentence and the distinctive characteristics of a few types of sentences that serve as the basic structures of more complicated units.

To begin, be sure you can recognize the two indispensable parts of a sentence:

1. The **subject:** the unit about which something is said.
2. The **predicate:** the unit that says something about the subject.

Although the predicate usually includes other modifying words and phrases, the indispensable part of a predicate is the verb, the word (or words) that says what the subject does or is. Here are a few things to remember about the subject–verb relationship:

1. In a sentence that reports a specific action, the verb is easily recognized. For instance, to find the subject and verb in *The rusty bumper on the front of my truck rattles noisily,* ask the question, "What happens?" The answer, *rattles,* gives the verb. Then, by asking the question "Who or what rattles?", you will find the subject, *bumper.* Notice that neither "front rattles" nor "truck rattles" makes the basic statement of the sentence.

2. Some sentences do not report an action. Instead, the sentence says something about the *condition* of the subject. It points out a descriptive quality of the subject or says that something else resembles or is the same thing as the subject. In this kind of sentence, you must look for verbs like *is, are, was, were, seem,* and *become.* Such types of verbs are often called *describing (linking) verbs.* They are words that are almost impossible to define because they lack the concrete exactness and action of verbs like *rattle, throw, smash,* and *explode.*

1

In a sentence using a describing verb, the subject usually reveals itself easily. For example, in the sentence "The long first chapter seemed particularly difficult," the verb is *seemed*. The question "Who or what seemed?" provides the subject, *chapter*. The other possible choices—*long, first, particularly,* and *difficult*—do not make sense as answers to the question "Who or what seemed?".

3. Very often the subject of a sentence has material between it and its verb:

   The *price* of potatoes *is* high. [The subject is *price,* not *potatoes.*]
   Each of my sisters *is* tall. [The subject is *each,* not *sisters.*]
   Only *one* of these watches *works.* [The subject is *one,* not *watches.*]

4. Most modern English sentences place the subject before the verb, but in some sentences, the verb precedes the subject:

   Behind the house *stood* [verb] an old *mill* [subject].
   Under the table *sat* [verb] a large *cat* [subject].

   A very common type of sentence with the verb–subject arrangement uses *here* or *there* preceding the verb:

   There *are* [verb] three willow *trees* [subject] in our yard.
   Here *is* [verb] the *list* [subject] of candidates.

5. Casual, informal language often combines short verbs and subjects with apostrophes representing the omitted letters:

   I'm (I am)   It's (It is)   You've (You have)   They're (They are)

For your first practice work you'll be using only a single subject for each sentence. Within this limitation the subject is always a noun or a pronoun. Before the first practice, it would be wise to review a few facts about nouns, pronouns, and verbs so that you can recognize them easily.

Nouns

A **noun** is a word that names something, such as a person, place, thing, quality, or idea. If the noun names just any member of a group or class, it is called a *common noun* and is not capitalized:

man, city, school, relative

A noun is a *proper noun* and is capitalized if it refers to a particular individual in a group or class:

Albert Lawson, Toledo, Horace Mann Junior High School, Aunt Louise

Most nouns have two forms; they show whether the noun is naming one thing (singular number) or more than one thing (plural number, which adds *s* or *es* to the singular): one *coat,* two *coats;* a *lunch,* several *lunches.* Proper nouns are rarely pluralized, and some common nouns have no plural form, for example, *honesty, courage, ease,* and *hardness.* (Lesson 28 examines in detail the special spelling problems of plural nouns.)

Nouns often follow *the, a,* or *an,* words that are called **articles.** A descriptive word (an adjective) may come between the article and the noun, but the word that answers the question "What?" after an article is a noun:

Article	$\left(\begin{array}{c}\textit{optional}\\\textit{adjective}\end{array}\right)$	*noun*
A (or The)	happy	girl.

Another way to identify nouns is to recognize certain suffixes. A **suffix** is a unit added to the end of a word or to the base of a word (see Supplement 1).* Here are some of the common suffixes found in hundreds of nouns:

age [break*age*]; ance, ence [resist*ance*, insist*ence*]; dom [king*dom*]; hood [child*hood*]; ion [prevent*ion*]; ism [national*ism*]; ment [move*ment*]; ness [firm*ness*]; or, er [invest*or*, los*er*]; ure [expos*ure*]

Pronouns

A **pronoun** is a word that substitutes for a noun. There are several classes of pronouns. (See Supplement 2.) The following classes can function as subjects in the basic sentences that you will examine in these early lessons:

Personal pronouns substitute for definite persons or things: *I, you, he, she, it, we, they.*

Demonstrative pronouns substitute for things being pointed out: *this, that, these, those.*

Indefinite pronouns substitute for unknown or unspecified things: *each, either, neither, one, anyone, somebody, everything, all, few, many,* and so on.

Possessive pronouns substitute for things that are possessed: *mine, yours, his, hers, its, ours, theirs.*

Verbs

A **verb** is a word that expresses action, existence, or occurrence by combining with a subject to make a statement, to ask a question, or to give a command. One easy way to identify a word as a verb is to use the following test:

Let's _____

　　　(*action word*)

*In some lessons of this book you will find notations referring you to a supplement that appears at the end of the lesson. Read the supplement *after* you have thoroughly studied the lesson. The lesson contains the essential information that is vital to your understanding of subsequent lessons and exercises. The supplement presents material that has relevance to some points of the lesson. The supplements at the end of this lesson are found on page 4.

Any word that will complete the command is a verb: "Let's *leave.*" "Let's *buy* some popcorn." "Let's *be* quiet." This test works only with the basic present form of the verb, not with forms that have endings added to them or that show action taking place in the past: "Let's *paint* the car" (not "Let's *painted* the car").

Supplement 1

Hundreds of nouns have distinctive suffix endings. The definitions of some of these suffixes are rather difficult to formulate, but you can quite readily figure out the meanings of most of them: *ness,* for instance, means "quality or state of" (thus *firmness* means "the state or quality of being firm"); *or* and *er* show the agent or doer of something (an *investor* is "one who invests").

A unit added to the beginning of a word is called a **prefix.** Thus, to the adjective *kind,* we add a prefix to derive another adjective, *unkind,* and a suffix to derive the nouns *kindness* and *unkindness.* An awareness of how prefixes and suffixes are used will do far more than aid you in your ability to recognize parts of speech: Your spelling will improve and your vocabulary will expand.

Supplement 2

Two classes of pronouns, the **interrogative** and the **relative,** are not listed here. Because they are used in questions and subordinate clauses but not in simple basic sentences, they will not be discussed until later lessons.

Another type of pronoun that you use regularly (but not as a true subject) is the **intensive** or **reflexive** pronoun, the "self" words used to add emphasis:

You *yourself* made the decision.

or to name the receiver of an action when the doer is the same as the receiver:

The boy fell and hurt *himself.*

The first example is the intensive use; the second is the reflexive. Pronouns used this way are *myself, yourself, himself* (not *hisself*), *herself, itself, ourselves, yourselves,* and *themselves* (not *themself, theirself,* or *theirselves*).

The "self" pronouns are properly used for only these two purposes. They should not be substituted for regular personal pronouns:

Mary and I [not *myself*] were invited to the dance.
Tom visited Eric and me [not *myself*] at our ranch.

A fourth type of pronoun is the **reciprocal** pronoun that denotes a mutual relationship, for example *one another, each other:*

We try to help *each other* with our homework.

Practice Sheet 1

Subjects and Verbs

NAME _____ SCORE _____

Directions: In the space at the left, copy the word that is the verb of the italicized subject.

_____ 1. The *line* for movie tickets was very long.

_____ 2. *Few* of the office workers arrived early today.

_____ 3. *Those* were three of my favorite songs.

_____ 4. There goes our last *chance* at a victory in this series.

_____ 5. Her great *love* for the music becomes more apparent every day.

_____ 6. Only *two* of the senators answered the roll today.

_____ 7. In that back closet hangs my old *raincoat*.

_____ 8. In her hand was a $325 softball *bat*.

_____ 9. *More* than a hundred students signed that petition.

_____ 10. From the back of the auditorium came a wonderfully shrill *whistle*.

_____ 11. *All* but one of the players attended the spring mini-camp.

_____ 12. On that top shelf there's an old baseball *cap*.

_____ 13. The *packages* are now ready for the shipping company.

_____ 14. *None* of the men knew the way to the country store.

_____ 15. All the people from the branch office *attended* yesterday's meeting.

_____ 16. A heavy *rain* pounded the corn crop unmercifully last night.

_____ 17. At the top of the tallest tree in the valley sat a lone *bald eagle*.

_____ 18. A *man* from the office across the hall walked into my office.

_____ 19. *Some* of those jokes seemed quite cruel.

_____ 20. The *opportunity* for revenge came almost immediately.

5

Directions: In the space at the left, copy the word that is the subject of the italicized verb.

_____ 1. Every one of our students *enjoyed* that presentation very much.

_____ 2. High above us *soared* the space shuttle on its way to the space station.

_____ 3. Most of Mr. Jackson's assets *are* in high grade bonds.

_____ 4. Robertson's record of community service *is* certainly impressive.

_____ 5. Close to my sister's elementary school *runs* a beautiful river.

_____ 6. Here *are* the last two payments on my car loan.

_____ 7. None of the programs on television tonight *sound* exciting.

_____ 8. A shipment of desperately needed supplies *arrived* early this morning.

_____ 9. Several of his new friends *came* to the park this morning for a baseball game.

_____ 10. At the side of the handsome rock star *stood* a grim-faced body-guard.

_____ 11. The lure of great wealth *drew* thousands to the gold fields.

_____ 12. Many of those self-taught programmers *go* on to great success.

_____ 13. The happy ending to that film *surprised* many people in the audience.

_____ 14. And with that fumble *died* our last hope of victory.

_____ 15. The absence of those two commission members *doomed* that vote.

_____ 16. There *were* several new developments in the mayor's campaign today.

_____ 17. The work of those volunteers in that emergency *amazed* everyone.

_____ 18. All of those volunteers in the effort on behalf of the homeless *deserve* our deepest gratitude.

_____ 19. Higher interest rates *make* life difficult for many new homeowners.

_____ 20. Some of the best sources for that paper *are* not available in our library.

NAME _____ SCORE _____

Directions: In the first space at the left, copy the subject of the sentence. In the second space, copy the verb.

_____   1. Even the less difficult of the two problems was too hard for
_____   Mark.
_____   2. An important letter from the governor's office arrived today.
_____
_____   3. In that last file folder was the most important item of informa-
_____   tion.
_____   4. Some of my father's friends presented a new program to the
_____   city council.
_____   5. Only the fastest runners in the race completed the entire course
_____   ahead of Charles.
_____   6. In the corner of the stable slept a tired old man.
_____
_____   7. Even the slowest of those workers finished ahead of the people
_____   in my group.
_____   8. The test scores of the students in that history class far exceeded
_____   the scores of students in the other classes.
_____   9. Jackie's feeling of excitement ran quickly through the entire
_____   group.
_____   10. A few of the team's former players made a contribution to the
_____   scholarship fund.
_____   11. The detective's investigation produced no new clues.
_____
_____   12. At the head of the long line into the cafeteria stood three mem-
_____   bers of the track team.
_____   13. Many of the brightest members of my high school class went to
_____   the nearby state university.
_____   14. There's some money left in last year's entertainment budget.
_____
_____   15. A small group of enthusiastic rooters goes to all the team's
_____   games.
_____   16. In the basement of that old cabin there is a leaky water pipe.
_____
_____   17. A rose bush with many blooms on it grew out of that old pile
_____   of twigs.
_____   18. None of my teammates have jobs for this summer vacation.

_____ 19. Yesterday's heroes get little credit from today's players.

_____ 20. Yesterday was the toughest day of practice in the entire season up to this point

_____ 21. Yesterday after class I went back to my room for a long study session.

_____ 22. Here are two members of the firm's first management team.

_____ 23. That dilapidated building on Second Street burned to the ground yesterday.

_____ 24. After a great start Jim's grades began a decline around mid-term.

_____ 25. Her best season as a hitter was 1998.

_____ 26. He's the last person in that first group of applicants.

_____ 27. On the front page of yesterday's paper were two very informative articles.

_____ 28. Each of those two calculators produced a different answer to that problem.

_____ 29. Every member of the baseball team reports for weight training in the gym at 7:00 A.M.

_____ 30. From the last row of the bleachers rose a great, loud cheer for Jenkins' home run.

_____ 31. The deep pounding sounds of the drum shook the rafters in that small room.

_____ 32. At the first sound of thunder, all the golfers left the course as quickly as possible.

_____ 33. Under that pile of dirty clothes, I found my lost library book.

_____ 34. During her lunch hour my boss goes to the gym for a workout.

_____ 35. None of the proofreaders found the errors in this morning's paper.

_____ 36. During my first night as an usher at the stadium, two people got in a terrible argument about the location of their seats.

_____ 37. They're certainly the best horses in the entire racing stable.

_____ 38. There goes my little sister with her two new friends.

_____ 39. The low price of that set of golf clubs surprised my father.

_____ 40. Several of the better students in the class finished the test ahead of time.

In Lesson 1 you learned how to recognize a verb. Every verb has a **base** or **infinitive.** This form of the verb "names" the verb. But verbs change their form according to various conditions, three of which are person, number, and tense. You should learn these forms because they occur in nearly every sentence that you speak or write.

Person specifies the person(s) speaking ("first" person: *I, we*); the person(s) spoken *to* ("second" person: *you*); and the person(s) or thing(s) spoken *about* ("third" person: *he, she, it, they*).

Number shows whether the reference is to *one* thing (*singular* number) or to more than one thing (*plural* number).

Tense refers to the time represented in the sentence, whether it applies to the present moment (I *believe* him) or to some other time (I *believed* him, I *will believe* him).

To demonstrate these changes in form, you can use a chart or arrangement called a *conjugation.* In the partial conjugation that follows, three verbs are used: *earn, grow,* and *be.* The personal pronoun subjects are included to show how the person and number of the subject affect the form of the verb.

Indicative Mood
Active Voice*

	Singular	*Plural*
	Present Tense	
1st Person	I earn, grow, am	We earn, grow, are
2nd Person	You earn, grow, are	You earn, grow, are
3rd Person	He earns, grows, is**	They earn, grow, are
	Past Tense	
1st Person	I earned, grew, was	We earned, grew, were
2nd Person	You earned, grew, were	You earned, grew, were
3rd Person	He earned, grew, was	They earned, grew, were
	Future Tense	
1st Person	I shall earn, grow, be	We shall earn, grow, be
2nd Person	You will earn, grow, be	You will earn, grow, be
3rd Person	He will earn, grow, be	They will earn, grow, be

Indicative mood indicates that the verb expresses a fact as opposed to a wish, command, or possibility. *Active voice* indicates that the subject of the verb is the *doer*, rather than the receiver, of the action of the verb.

**The pronoun *he* is arbitrarily used here to represent the third-person singular subject, which may be any singular pronoun *(she, it, who, nobody)*; singular noun *(girl, neighbor, elephant, misunderstanding, Alice, Christopher Robert Klein III)*; or word groups constituting certain types of phrases or clauses that will be studied in later lessons.

Present Perfect Tense

1st Person	I have earned, grown, been	We have earned, grown, been
2nd Person	You have earned, grown, been	You have earned, grown, been
3rd Person	He has earned, grown, been	They have earned, grown, been

Past Perfect Tense

1st Person	I had earned, grown, been	We had earned, grown, been
2nd Person	You had earned, grown, been	You had earned, grown, been
3rd Person	He had earned, grown, been	They had earned, grown, been

Future Perfect Tense

1st Person	I shall have earned, grown, been	We shall have earned, grown, been
2nd Person	You will have earned, grown, been	You will have earned, grown, been
3rd Person	She will have earned, grown, been	They will have earned, grown, been

Notice that in the past tense, *earn* adds an *ed* ending, but *grow* changes to *grew*. This difference illustrates **regular** and **irregular** verbs, the two groups into which all English verbs are classified. *Earn* is a regular verb, *grow* is an irregular verb. (Lesson 21 discusses irregular verbs in more detail.)

Notice also that some verb forms consist of more than one word *(will earn, have grown, had earned, will have been)*. In such uses, *will, had,* and *have* are called **auxiliary verbs.** More auxiliary verbs are examined in Lesson 5.

With the "naming" words (nouns and pronouns) and the "action" words (verbs), you can construct true sentences:

Janice arrived.
He laughed.
Power corrupts.

But to make sentences more varied and complete, you need modifiers or "describing" words (adjectives and adverbs) and prepositional phrases.

Adjectives

An **adjective** is a word that describes or limits—that is, gives qualities to—a noun. Adjectives are found in three different positions in a sentence:

1. Preceding a noun that is in any of the noun positions within the sentence

   The *small* child left. He is a *small* child. I saw the *small* child. I gave it to the *small* child.

2. Following a describing (linking) verb and modifying the subject

   The child is *small*. Mary looked *unhappy*. We became *upset*.

3. Directly following the noun (less common than the two positions described above)

   He provided the money *necessary* for the trip. The hostess, *calm and serene*, entered the hall.

Certain characteristics of form and function help you to recognize adjectives. There are several suffixes that, when added to other words or roots of other words, form adjectives. Here again, an understanding of the meaning of a suffix can save trips to the dictionary. For instance, in the hundreds of adjectives ending in *able (ible),* the suffix means "capable of" or "tending to"; thus *usable* means "capable of being used" and *changeable* means "tending to change."

able, ible [read*able,* irresist*ible*]; al [internation*al*]; ant, ent [resist*ant,* diverg*ent*]; ar [lun*ar*]; ary [budget*ary*]; ful [meaning*ful*]; ic, ical [cosm*ic,* hyster*ical*]; ish [fool*ish*]; ive [invent*ive*]; less [blame*less*]; ous [glamor*ous*]; y [greas*y*]

One note of warning: Many other words in English end with these letters, but you can easily see that they are not employing a suffix. T*able,* fer*ment,* arr*ive,* d*ish,* and pon*y,* for instance, are not adjectives. (See Supplement 1 for more information on adjectives.)

Adjectives Used in Comparisons

Nearly all adjectives, when they are used in comparisons, can be strengthened or can show degree by changing form or by using *more* and *most:*

great trust, *greater* trust, *greatest* trust
sensible answer, *more sensible* answer, *most sensible* answer

The base form (*great* trust, *sensible* answer) is the **positive degree.** The second form (*greater* trust, *more sensible* answer) is the **comparative degree:** it compares two things. The third form (*greatest* trust, *most sensible* answer) is the **superlative degree** and distinguishes among three or more things. (See Supplement 2.)

Adverbs

Another modifier is the **adverb,** a word that modifies anything except a noun or a pronoun. Most adverbs modify verbs (She walked *quickly*). Other adverbs modify adjectives and other adverbs (The *very* old man walked *quite slowly*). Some adverbs modify whole sentences (*Consequently,* we refused the offer).

Adverbs tell certain things about the verb, the most common being:

1. **Manner:** John performed *well.* We worked *hard.* The child laughed *happily.* I would *gladly* change places with you.
2. **Time:** I must leave *now.* I'll see you *later. Soon* we shall meet *again.*
3. **Frequency:** We *often* go on picnics, *sometimes* at the lake but *usually* in the city park.
4. **Place:** *There* he sat, alone and silent. *Somewhere* we shall find peace and quiet.
5. **Direction:** The police officer turned *away.* I moved *forward* in the bus.
6. **Degree:** I could *barely* hear the speaker. I *absolutely* refuse to believe that story.

The most frequently used adverbs answer such questions as "How?" (manner or degree), "When?" (time or frequency), and "Where?" (place or direction).

Adverbs of a subclass called **intensifiers** modify adjectives or adverbs but not verbs. For example, a *very* good meal, his *quite* surprising reply, *too* often, *somewhat* reluctantly, and so on.

Many adverbs change form the way adjectives do, to show degree:

to drive *fast,* to drive *faster,* to drive *fastest*

to perform *satisfactorily,* to perform *more satisfactorily,* to perform *most satisfactorily*

See Supplement 2 for details on some common irregular intensifiers.

Prepositions

A **preposition** is a word that introduces a phrase and shows the relationship between the object of the phrase and some other word in the sentence. Notice that many prepositions show a relationship of space or time. Here are some common prepositions; those in the last column are called *group prepositions:*

about	beside	inside	through	according to
above	besides	into	throughout	because of
across	between	like	till	by way of
after	beyond	near	to	in addition to
against	by	of	toward	in front of
around	down	off	under	in place of
at	during	on	until	in regard to
before	except	out	up	in spite of
behind	for	outside	upon	instead of
below	from	over	with	on account of
beneath	in	since	without	out of

A preposition always has an object; with its object and any modifiers, the preposition makes a **prepositional phrase.** You can easily illustrate the function of prepositions by constructing sentences like the following:

After breakfast I walked *to* town *without* my friend. [Objects: *breakfast, town, friend.*]

On account of the rain, I canceled my plans *for* a game *of* tennis *at* the park *with* John. [Objects: *rain, game, tennis, park, John.*]

The trees *outside* the window *of* the kitchen are full *of* blossoms *during* the spring. [Objects: *window, kitchen, blossoms, spring.*]

Supplement 1

Besides what could be called true adjectives, there are other classes of words that modify nouns. If you concentrate on the *functions* of the various kinds of words, however, you can safely classify as adjectives all words that precede nouns and limit their meaning. Such adjectives include articles, numerals, and possessives (*an* apple, *the* weather, *my three* roommates); modifiers that can be used also as pronouns (*these* people, *some* friends, *all* workers); and nouns that modify other nouns (*basketball* players, *summer* days, *crop* failures).

Many words can be used as adjectives or as pronouns; the position of a word within the sentence determines which part of speech it is.

Several [*adj.*] classmates of mine [*pron.*] read this [*adj.*] report.
Several [*pron.*] of my [*adj.*] classmates read this [*pron.*].

Supplement 2

A few commonly used modifiers form their comparative and superlative degrees irregularly:

good *(adj.)*,	better,	best
well *(adv.)*,	better,	best
bad *(adj.)*,	worse,	worst

NAME _____ SCORE _____

Directions: In each space at the left, write one of the following numbers to identify the part of speech of each italicized word:

1. Noun   3. Verb   5. Adverb
2. Pronoun   4. Adjective   6. Preposition

_____ 1. The choir sang *beautifully,* and we *applauded* them vigorously.

_____ 2. There was much applause *after* the soloist's *beautiful* song.

_____ 3. *Everyone* admired the *craftsmanship* in that beautiful table.

_____ 4. *These* can be bought quite *inexpensively* at the discount store.

_____ 5. *Mine* is an *inexpensive* model of that particular car.

_____ 6. *During* the storm the water *rose* rapidly in the streets.

_____ 7. The beautiful *rose* in the silver vase came from *my* brother.

_____ 8. The *silver* in that coin is not worth *very* much.

_____ 9. The net *worth* of that company has increased *significantly* in the last year.

_____ 10. *Under* a cushion of the couch, I *found* two quarters.

_____ 11. The *thick* pads of the vaulting pit *cushioned* the vaulter's fall.

_____ 12. An enormous *thunderhead* rose high *over* the mountains.

_____ 13. There is a *considerable* difference between my grade and *his.*

_____ 14. The townspeople *piled* sandbags *along* the river's edge as protection against the rising waters.

_____ 15. The deep mud on the track *barely* slowed the *powerful* horses.

_____ 16. Outside the *house* the rain fell *steadily.*

_____ 17. My friends waited for *me outside* the classroom.

_____ 18. *Few* of the people chose the new version *of* that program.

_____ 19. A *few* people *chose* the new version of this program.
_____

_____ 20. *That* was a very *easy* assignment.
_____

_____ 21. *That* assignment was very *easy*.
_____

_____ 22. We *easily* finished the work *before* noon.
_____

_____ 23. The two women *lost* their *way* on that back road.
_____

_____ 24. On the end of the dock there is a *cleat with* a line on it.
_____

_____ 25. "Tie the line *securely around* the cleat," said Mark.
_____

_____ 26. The *accident tied* up traffic for about two hours.
_____

_____ 27. John *accidentally* sent the E-mail to the *entire* staff.
_____

_____ 28. *We walked* a very long way that afternoon.
_____

_____ 29. *Half* of that vast *fortune* is more than enough for anyone.
_____

_____ 30. We had walked *almost* half way by *noon*.
_____

_____ 31. Beth's *enthusiasm* for her new job is *commendable*.
_____

_____ 32. We often *commend* her for her *enthusiastic* attitude.
_____

_____ 33. *This* is the only *workable* plan.
_____

_____ 34. We *will work* very *hard* on that project.
_____

_____ 35. I sometimes *question* that manager's *intelligence*.
_____

_____ 36. His fellow *managers* would *unquestionably* disagree.
_____

_____ 37. I'm *impressed* by the strength of *those* sales figures.
_____

_____ 38. Our new secretary *certainly* made a favorable *impression* on all of us.
_____

_____ 39. This new varnish gives the deck a *much harder* finish.
_____

_____ 40. Our hitters will certainly *try harder* next time.
_____

Exercise 2   *Parts of Speech*

NAME _____   SCORE _____

Directions: In each space at the left, write one of the following numbers to identify the part of speech of each italicized word:

1. Noun   3. Verb   5. Adverb
2. Pronoun   4. Adjective   6. Preposition

_____ 1. John *has performed* very *well* in every performance of that rather obscure
_____   play.
_____ 2. Janice's company *will provide* the funds *necessary* for building the new
_____   building on the campus.
_____ 3. The *most economical* solution to that problem will cost about $200,000.
_____
_____ 4. *Most* of the tickets to the play *were bought* well in advance of opening
_____   night.
_____ 5. I must go now; I *will meet* you *later* in the afternoon for a cup of coffee.
_____
_____ 6. *Lack* of support from two important senators *doomed* that bill.
_____
_____ 7. A deep *feeling* of gloom filled the *losing* team's locker room.
_____
_____ 8. The speaker stepped *timidly* to the microphone with a copy of his speech
_____   *in* his hand.
_____ 9. Of all the proposals, *yours* is easily the *best*.
_____
_____ 10. The *solution* to that puzzle appears *quite* difficult.
_____
_____ 11. Jim *puzzled* over the first question on the test for several anxious *moments*.
_____
_____ 12. The *vine on* the fence *produced* several exotic blooms last week.
_____
_____ 13. The *produce* market down the street *sells* fresh strawberries for $3.75 a
_____   pint.
_____ 14. The *products* from that factory on the east side of town *sell* extremely well
_____   in Southeast Asia.
_____ 15. *Extreme* conditions outdoors in January forced cancellation of the *annual*
_____   cross-country skiing expedition.
_____ 16. Long before the arrival *of* the president's motorcade, *most* of the children
_____   had left the parade route.
_____ 17. The *audience* did not find the first two skits in the program *very* amusing.
_____
_____ 18. Please stand *up* and speak very *clearly.*
_____

17

———— 19. The group walked slowly *up* the *steep* hill and down into the valley.

———— 20. *George talked* to Melanie on the phone for almost fifteen minutes yesterday.

———— 21. The men left work early today, but *they* had already *finished* their project.

———— 22. We *worked* for several weeks on that report *for* the vice president.

———— 23. *At* 5:00 A.M. the first *shift reported* for work in the mine.

———— 24. The instructor *shifted* our next test from tomorrow *morning* to a date later in the month.

———— 25. The boss gave the *others their* instructions early this morning.

———— 26. Of the three books by that author, the *last* was by far the *best.*

———— 27. The police *booked* the three men on suspicion of *robbery.*

———— 28. The small child ran *eagerly* across the yard *after* the small brown dog.

———— 29. That backpack must be yours; I *left mine* in the back of my car.

———— 30. The *clever* one-act play is *more* successful than any of the short stories by that writer.

———— 31. If you are *clever* in your interpretation of that poem, you will receive a better grade *from* the teacher.

———— 32. The small rat *cleverly worked* his way through the maze as the psychology students watched.

———— 33. That book *contains psychological* studies of several important people in the history of South America.

———— 34. *On account of* last year's losses in the stock market, my uncle *has cancelled* his European vacation.

———— 35. My *recommendation* for the new position in data processing is a young woman *from* a local college.

———— 36. I *can recommend* several restaurants in town, but Mario's is *certainly* the best for Italian food.

———— 37. *Many* of the students from the college eat at Mario's *regularly.*

———— 38. After lunch we drove down *through* that beautiful canyon *near* Highway 66.

———— 39. Only a *few* of the club's members from last year *will be* active in the coming year.

———— 40. The answers to *some* of those questions in the test are not printed in the *textbook.*

Directions: Each of the words below is labeled as a noun, verb, adjective, or adverb. In the spaces following each word, write related words for the part of speech indicated. Do not use adjectives ending in *-ing* or *-ed*.

Example:
wide (adj.)   _____*width*_____ (n.)   _____*widen*_____ (v.)

1. advise (v.)   _____ (n.)   _____ (adj.)

2. alertness (n.)   _____ (v.)   _____ (adv.)

3. allowable (adj.)   _____ (n.)   _____ (v.)

4. beautify (v.)   _____ (n.)   _____ (adv.)

5. brightly (adv.)   _____ (n.)   _____ (v.)

6. complete (v.)   _____ (n.)   _____ (adv.)

7. construct (v.)   _____ (n.)   _____ (adj.)

8. defiance (n.)   _____ (v.)   _____ (adj.)

9. delicate (adj.)   _____ (n.)   _____ (adv.)

10. different (adj.)   _____ (n.)   _____ (v.)

11. dull (adj.)   _____ (n.)   _____ (v.)

12. enjoy (v.)   _____ (n.)   _____ (adj.)

13. happiness (n.)   _____ (adj.)   _____ (adv.)

14. haste (n.)   _____ (v.)   _____ (adv.)

15. invent (v.)   _____ (n.)   _____ (adj.)

16. noise (n.)   _____ (adj.)   _____ (adv.)

17. obscure (adj.)   _____ (n.)   _____ (v.)

18. romanticize (v.)   _____ (n.)   _____ (adj.)

19. sadness (n.)   _____ (v.)   _____ (adv.)

20. security (n.)   _____ (v.)   _____ (adv.)

Exercise 2A   *Subjects and Verbs*

NAME _____   SCORE _____

Directions: In the first space at the left, copy the word that is the subject of the sentence. In the second space, copy the verb. Many of the verbs consist of more than one word.

_____ 1. There has never been a greater need for compromise.

_____ 2. At the head of the lake stands a small fishing camp.

_____ 3. By Friday noon I'll have finished the last of my final exams.

_____ 4. You will never have another chance at a bargain like this one.

_____ 5. Few of those suggestions for new products have been workable.

_____ 6. Within a very few hours the newspapers will have published the entire story.

_____ 7. You'll probably be delighted with the low price of that new car.

_____ 8. Most of the visitors to the island went home after a few weeks.

_____ 9. On the platform beside the speaker sat several local dignitaries.

_____ 10. Because of the threat of a thunderstorm, hundreds of season ticket holders stayed away from the game.

_____ 11. And thus began a long series of rather strange developments.

_____ 12. There had been no advanced warning of the tornado.

_____ 13. Jane had never before taken a test of that type.

_____ 14. There's only one appointment available in Tuesday morning's schedule.

_____ 15. The homecoming game will be the highlight of the weekend.

_____ 16. In his long tenure in office the governor has vetoed only three bills.

_____ 17. The first thing on the agenda was a report of Mrs. Levin's committee.

_____ 18. Three of my cousins arrived yesterday for the holidays.

_____ 19. One of the new students made a very interesting presentation.

_____ 20. She's the most talented of our physicists.

_____ 21. Mr. Black has on more than one occasion provided legal services at no cost for an indigent client.

_____ 22. On the inside cover of the book is a short biography of the author.

_____ 23. The windstorm leveled a small grove of trees out in back of the barn.

_____ 24. Not a single rookie lineman survived the final cut to forty-nine players.

_____ 25. She's always been one of our most consistent performers in the high jump.

_____ 26. The increase in our appropriation will provide funds for several new services.

_____ 27. The first patches of crabgrass appeared in my lawn last week.

_____ 28. From far away up in the mountains came the mournful howling of a timber wolf.

_____ 29. His portrait, along with those of his two children, hangs in the National Gallery.

_____ 30. By the end of next month, we will have finished most of the remodeling.

_____ 31. The opening-day attendance at the county fair is usually about twelve thousand.

_____ 32. With elaborate ceremony the rotund little mayor handed our tour leader a key to the city.

_____ 33. The original document has remained in the lawyer's office since Grandfather's death in 1961.

_____ 34. All of us in the neighborhood have noticed the increased traffic on Travers Boulevard.

_____ 35. Nearly half of the apartments in the huge building are now vacant.

_____ 36. Ahead of the stragglers stretched the long, uninviting expanse of prairie.

_____ 37. One of the clerks reluctantly stamped my permit.

_____ 38. The presence of the National Guard prevented further looting.

_____ 39. On the receptionist's desk were several pictures in ornate frames.

_____ 40. The three grandsons, with their wives and children, often return to the original farm.

Lesson 3 — *Basic Sentence Patterns with Intransitive Verbs*

As you know from Lesson 1, the sentence, a combination of subject and predicate arranged to make a statement, is the basic unit of written and oral communication. There are just five sentence types or patterns, and learning to recognize those five patterns can help you to become a more effective communicator. In this lesson and the following lesson, we will look at the five patterns so that you can learn to use them in your writing.

The nature of the verb is the key to recognizing sentence patterns. There are two types of verbs, transitive and intransitive. The prefix *trans* means across, and the letters *it* come from the Latin word meaning to *go,* so *transit* means to go across. The additional prefix *in* means *not,* so *intransit* means not to go across. (Don't confuse the Latin word with the colloquial *in-transit,* which means in the act of going somewhere.)

When an **intransitive verb** is used, the verb does not transfer its action to an object. In the sentence "John spoke softly," the action is *spoke* and the actor is *John.* The action does not "go across" to a noun that receives that action. The verb is intransitive. Some intransitive verbs do not express an action; they simply connect or link the subject to a noun that renames the subject or to an adjective that modifies the subject. These types of intransitive verbs are called **linking verbs.** In the following sentences there is no action:

> *John* is a *genius.*
> *John* is *brilliant.*

The subject *John* is simply linked by the verb to a word that identifies or modifies it.

In our system, Sentence Patterns 1 and 2 use intransitive verbs. Sentence Patterns 3, 4, and 5 use transitive verbs and are addressed in Lesson 4.

Sentence Pattern 1

Sentence Pattern 1 contains an intransitive verb and is the only sentence pattern that does not require a word to complete the sense of the action. Some activity takes place in each of these sentences, but no completer is needed because the action of the verb is not transferred to anything.

> The child *runs.*
> The tree *fell.*
> The customer *complained* loudly.
> The professor *walked* into the room unexpectedly.

The action of the verb is complete within itself. Pattern 1 sentences nearly always contain modifiers that tell how, when, and where the action occurred:

> Yesterday the neighborhood children played noisily in the vacant lot.

Notice that the material associated with the verb is all adverbial: "When?" *Yesterday.* "How?" *Noisily.* "Where?" *In the vacant lot.* The important characteristic of a Pattern 1 sentence is that there is no noun answering the question "What?" after the verb. The best way to recognize an intransitive verb is to spot the lack of a noun answering the question "What?" after the verb.

In some Pattern 1 sentences, the purpose of the statement is simply to say that the subject exists. Usually some adverbial material is added to show the place or the time of the existence:

The glasses *are* in the cabinet.
Flash floods often *occur* in the spring.
There *were* several birds around the feeder.

Before you study the remaining sentence patterns, we need to define a term that identifies an important part of the sentences in the four remaining patterns. As you know, the two parts of any sentence are the subject and the predicate. The central core of the predicate is the verb, but the predicate also often includes words that complete the thought of the sentence. Words that follow the verb and complete the thought of the sentence are called **complements.** Complements can be nouns, pronouns, or adjectives, but all serve the same purpose in the sentence: they complete the idea or sense of the sentence.

Sentence Pattern 2

Pattern 2 includes two closely related kinds of sentences. The purpose of the first type of Pattern 2 sentence is to rename the subject, to say that the subject is the same as something else. In the sentence "John is a genius," the noun *genius* is called a **subjective complement** because it completes the verb and renames the subject. (See Supplement.) The intransitive linking verb used in Pattern 2 sentences is often a form of *be.*

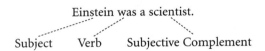

Einstein was a scientist.

Subject   Verb   Subjective Complement

Note that both words, *Einstein* and *scientist,* refer to the same thing. There is no action; rather, a connection is established between the subject and the verb.

In the second type of Pattern 2 sentence, the subjective complement is an adjective, a word that describes rather than renames the subject. For example, in the sentence "The child is clever," the subject is joined by the verb to an adjective, again called a subjective complement. Comparatively few verbs serve the linking function. For convenience, you can think of them in three closely related groups:

1. *Be,* the most commonly used linking verb, and a few others meaning essentially the same thing: *seem, appear, prove, remain, continue,* and so forth

John *is* a talented musician.
The performer *seemed* nervous.
He *remained* calm.
His words *proved* meaningless.

2. *Become,* and a few others like it: *turn, grow, work, get, wear,* and so forth

   Later she *became* an accountant.
   Soon he *grew* tired of the game.
   Billy *turned* red from embarrassment.

3. A few verbs referring to the senses (*look, smell, taste, feel, sound*), which can be followed by adjective subjective complements that describe the condition of the subject

   The roses *look* beautiful in that vase.
   This milk *tastes* sour.

The ability to recognize Pattern 2 sentences will help you understand a few troublesome usage problems that will be examined in a later lesson—to understand why, for instance, careful writers use "feel bad" rather than "feel badly": "*I feel* bad about the election results."

Supplement

A note about grammatical terminology is needed here. A noun following a linking verb and renaming the subject is sometimes called a *predicate noun* or a *predicate nominative;* and an adjective following a linking verb and describing the subject is sometimes called a *predicate adjective.*

> subjective complement (n.) = predicate noun
> predicate nominative
> subjective complement (adj.) = predicate adjective

NAME _____ SCORE _____

Directions: Each of the following sentences is a Pattern 2 sentence containing a noun (or a pronoun) subjective complement. In the space at the left, copy the subjective complement.

_____ 1. The purpose of Stonehenge still remains a mystery.

_____ 2. Some of us, after all, are still suspects in this case.

_____ 3. This seems a good time for a short rest and a cool drink.

_____ 4. Many of the mercenaries turned traitor.

_____ 5. Yours was not an entirely fair judgment.

_____ 6. Ms. Stone, at one time, had been the dean of our College of Fine Arts.

_____ 7. The oldest house on Maple Street is ours.

_____ 8. This purchase will, in the long run, prove a wise investment.

_____ 9. A four-wheel-drive truck will be an absolute necessity on these rugged roads.

_____ 10. Chemistry 103 is one of the prerequisites for Chemistry 462.

_____ 11. To everyone's surprise, Jerry became a moderately successful farmer.

_____ 12. In the run-off election the incumbent emerged the winner.

_____ 13. Townsend gradually became a power in local politics.

_____ 14. One of Alice's grandfathers had been a pilot on a Mississippi River steamboat.

_____ 15. The board's usual meeting time is the first Tuesday of each month.

_____ 16. Seaview soon became one of the most popular resorts on the coast.

_____ 17. Lucy's German-speaking cousin proved a real help on our tour.

_____ 18. The quartet's concert will, undoubtedly, be the highlight of the concert season.

_____ 19. After this emotional experience, he became a believer in miracles.

_____ 20. The two of them have remained close friends for nearly thirty years.

Directions: Each of the following sentences is a Pattern 2 sentence containing an adjective subjective complement. In the space at the left, copy the subjective complement.

_____ 1. The young man's suggestion seemed perfectly innocuous.

_____ 2. Ms. Allen is very well qualified for the job.

_____ 3. Our air has grown foul with smog and fumes.

_____ 4. The long search for a replacement proved ineffectual.

_____ 5. The only cooking oil in the cabin has turned rancid.

_____ 6. A few of the natives seemed suspicious of the explorer's intentions.

_____ 7. Your ill-tempered criticisms are unworthy of you.

_____ 8. Our basketball team remained undefeated for the rest of the season.

_____ 9. Jill's parents now feel much better about her choice of profession.

_____ 10. The meal will be ready soon.

_____ 11. During the testimony the suspect looked uncomfortable.

_____ 12. You're much too young for this job.

_____ 13. I certainly felt conspicuous in that group of much younger tennis players.

_____ 14. To me, your plan sounds workable.

_____ 15. I've always been shy in the presence of strangers.

_____ 16. The host's embarrassment was painfully clear to all of us.

_____ 17. At this high altitude one gets tired after the slightest exertion.

_____ 18. That last victory was vital to the team.

_____ 19. After that successful ascent she became quite bold in her selection of climbing sites.

_____ 20. A few old members became *active* again.

Exercise 3   *Sentence Patterns with Intransitive Verbs*

NAME _____   SCORE _____

Directions: Circle the subject and underline the verb in each of the following sentences. If the sentence is a Pattern 2 sentence, copy the subjective complement in the space at the left. If the sentence is a Pattern 1 sentence, leave the space blank.

_____ 1. The car ahead of ours suddenly swerved to the right.

_____ 2. After the three review sessions I felt ready for the final examination.

_____ 3. Grandfather has always been an extremely stubborn person.

_____ 4. On the western horizon was the dim outline of the San Carlos mountain range.

_____ 5. I'm not really happy about the outcome of the election.

_____ 6. The surface of the freshly painted cabinet felt smooth.

_____ 7. There surely is some explanation for the man's peculiar behavior.

_____ 8. Parts of the medieval ramparts still stand in the oldest part of the city.

_____ 9. The only remaining umbrella in the coatroom is undoubtedly yours.

_____ 10. In spite of the damaging evidence, the prisoner appeared unworried.

_____ 11. Only a few of our tomatoes have ripened.

_____ 12. Some of our tomatoes certainly look ripe.

_____ 13. Tony's Diner had become the unofficial headquarters for our sales people.

_____ 14. The price of basic foodstuffs remained steady for several months.

_____ 15. Behind the main house stood a small guest house.

_____ 16. We worked without a break until nearly midnight.

_____ 17. A lug on the left front wheel had worked loose.

_____ 18. She's been one of our most loyal volunteer workers.

_____ 19. After two years of hard work and study, Jean became the purchasing officer's chief assistant.

_____ 20. Among the missing are three riders in the final group in the race.

_____ 21. Three riders in the final group in the race have been lost for about three hours.

_____ 22. Those dogs become restless at the slightest sound.

_____ 23. After two lazy weeks at the beach, I felt almost guilty about my lack of activity.

_____ 24. Belinda is one of Professor Bellini's most promising sopranos.

_____ 25. Next month at this time we shall be on the high seas.

_____ 26. From the hills behind the house came the high-pitched shriek of a red-tailed hawk.

_____ 27. All of us in the office have become quite tired of your practical jokes.

_____ 28. The weather will probably turn much cooler after this welcome rainfall.

_____ 29. The print on the old newspaper had faded badly.

_____ 30. In late autumn the evenings get quite chilly.

_____ 31. Here are your assignments for the next two weeks.

_____ 32. After the meeting with the attorneys, Ben seemed even more despondent.

_____ 33. These figures are, of course, only educated guesses.

_____ 34. This class looks unusually alert this morning.

_____ 35. Most of the snow will have melted before the end of the month.

_____ 36. With tears in his eyes, the old man turned away.

_____ 37. In the hot weather most of the milk at our campsite turned sour.

_____ 38. To us naive rookies the whole procedure looked quite simple.

_____ 39. Coral reefs are really calcareous skeletons of coral.

_____ 40. The last of the buses had already left for the airport.

In Sentence Pattern 2 the intransitive verb links the subject to a noun or adjective that completes the idea of the sentence: "Maria is our pitcher"; "Maria is brilliant." When a **transitive verb** is used, the action expressed by the verb "goes across" to some noun that receives the action. That noun is called the **direct object** and is the receiver of the action expressed in the verb. In the sentence "John watched a movie," the action (the verb) is *watched,* and the actor (the subject) is *John.* The receiver of the action (the direct object) is *movie.* The direct object can be found by asking the question "What?" after the subject and verb have been found. "John watched what? John watched a movie."

Sentence Pattern 3

In Pattern 3 sentences the verb is a transitive verb. It does not link or connect; instead, it identifies an action and transfers that action to a receiver or object of the action (the direct object). The subject–verb combination of the sentence does not complete a thought unless there is an object to receive the action named in the verb. For example, in the sentence "The child hits the ball," the subject–verb combination (*child hits*) does not make a complete statement. A complete statement requires that the child hit *something.*

The direct object is always a noun or a noun equivalent, such as a pronoun:

I broke my glasses. What names the activity? *Broke* is the verb. Who broke? *I* is the subject. I broke what? *Glasses.* Thus, *glasses* is the direct object.

Someone saw us. What names the activity? *Saw.* Who saw? *Someone* saw. Someone saw what? *Us* is the direct object.

We need to draw a contrast between a Pattern 2 sentence and a Pattern 3 sentence. Although both patterns require a complement, in a Pattern 2 sentence such as "The child is a genius," the subject is either renamed or modified by the subjective complement. In the sentence "Someone saw us," it is clear that *someone* and *us* are not the same. *Us* is the receiver of the action *saw* and simply cannot be taken to be the same as the *someone* who saw. In both Pattern 2 and Pattern 3 sentences, the thought of the sentence is not complete without a complement, but in Pattern 3 the subject acts upon the complement, the direct object.

Sentence Pattern 4

Pattern 4 sentences also contain a direct object. But because Pattern 4 sentences use verbs such as *give* or *show,* the sentences need a **second** complement to complete their thought. After a transitive verb such as *shows, gives,* or *tells,* the direct object (the receiver of the action) answers the question "What?" and an **indirect object** answers the question "To whom?" or "For whom?" Thus, "She sang a lullaby," is a Pattern 3 sentence, but "She gave the children a gift," is a Pattern 4 sentence.

In the sentence "The parents give the child a present," you can easily see that two complements are used. The sentence mentions the thing that is given (*present*, the direct object) and the person to whom the direct object is given (*child*, the indirect object). Although the indirect object usually names a person, it can name a nonhuman thing, as in "We gave your *application* a careful reading."

Other verbs that are commonly used this way and therefore produce a Pattern 4 structure are *allow, assign, ask, tell, write, send, pay, grant,* and so on. Nearly all sentences using such verbs can make essentially the same statement by using a prepositional phrase, usually beginning with the preposition *to* or *for*. When the prepositional phrase is present in the sentence, it is a Pattern 3 sentence.

> The postman brought me a letter. [Pattern 4; *me* is an indirect object.]
>
> The postman brought a letter to me. [Pattern 3; *me* is the object of a preposition.]
>
> Mother bought us some candy. [Pattern 4]
>
> Mother bought some candy for us. [Pattern 3]

Sentence Pattern 5

Pattern 5 sentences regularly use verbs such as *consider, call, think, find, make, elect, appoint,* and *name*. There are two closely related types of Pattern 5 sentences. Each type begins like a Pattern 3 sentence:

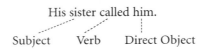

But the nature of the verb *called* allows the use of a second complement answering the question "What?" after *called him*. His sister called him what?

> His sister called him a genius.

The reference of the two nouns following the verb is a key to the difference between this type of sentence and a Pattern 4 sentence. In a Pattern 4 sentence the two noun complements refer to different things, but in a Pattern 5 sentence they refer to the same thing.

> Mother made us some fudge. [Pattern 4; *us* and *fudge* refer to different things.]
>
> This experience made John an activist. [Pattern 5; *John* and *activist* are the same thing.]

Thus, there are two complements in Pattern 5 sentences. The one closer to the verb is the direct object. The second complement is called the **objective complement.** In the first type of Pattern 5 sentence, the objective complement is a noun that *renames* the direct object. In the second type of Pattern 5 sentence, the objective complement is an adjective that *describes* the direct object.

> His sister called him a genius.
> His sister called him brilliant.

Because the objective complement renames or describes the direct object, we can use a handy test to help us recognize Pattern 5: The insertion of *to be* between the complements will give us an acceptable English wording.

We appointed Jones [to be] our representative.
I thought this action [to be] unnecessary.

Sometimes the word *as* is used between the direct object and the objective complement in Pattern 5 sentences:

We appointed Jones as our representative.

Some adjective objective complements are very important to the meaning of the verb. Thus, it is sometimes effective to place these objective complements immediately after the verb and before the direct object:

Usual order: He set the caged animals [D.O.] free [O.C.].
Variation: He set free [O.C.] the caged animals [D.O.].

Supplement

With one special kind of verb, there is a problem of distinguishing between a direct object and the object of a preposition. Here are two examples:

Harry jumped off the box.
Harry took off his raincoat.

The first sentence is Pattern 1. *Off* is a preposition, *box* is the object of the preposition, and the prepositional phrase is used as an adverbial modifier because it tells *where* Harry jumped. The second sentence is Pattern 3. The verb, with its adverbial modifier *off*, is the equivalent of the transitive verb *remove. Raincoat* is the direct object.

There is another way to distinguish between the adverbial use and the prepositional use of such a word as *off* in the preceding examples. When the word is a vital adverbial modifier of the verb, it can be used in either of two positions: following the verb or following the direct object.

Harry took off his raincoat.
Harry took his raincoat off.

When the word is a preposition, the alternate position is not possible: "Harry jumped the box off" is not an English sentence. Here are some other examples of verbs with adverbial modifiers. Notice that in each case you can easily find a transitive verb synonym for the combination:

Give up [*relinquish*] her rights.
Leave out [*omit*] the second chapter.
Put out [*extinguish*] the fire.
Make over [*alter*] an old dress.
Make up [*invent*] an excuse.

SUMMARY OF VERBS USED IN DIFFERENT SENTENCE PATTERNS

1. **Verbs that serve a linking function and commonly form Pattern 2 sentences:**

   be, seem, appear, prove, remain, continue, become, turn, grow, work, get, wear, look, smell, taste, feel, sound

2. **Verbs that commonly produce Pattern 4 sentences:**

   allow, assign, ask, tell, write, send, pay, grant

3. **Verbs that commonly produce Pattern 5 sentences:**

   consider, call, think, find, make, elect, appoint, name

Practice Sheet 4

Complements of Transitive Verbs

NAME _____ SCORE _____

Directions: Each of these sentences is a Pattern 3 sentence. Circle the subject and underline each verb. In the space at the left, copy the direct object.

_____ 1. The three children timidly crossed the makeshift bridge.

_____ 2. After his speech, not one member of the audience applauded him.

_____ 3. According to legend, garlic possesses valuable medicinal properties.

_____ 4. An armed guard at the gate keeps out unwanted visitors.

_____ 5. Mr. Thorpe will not tolerate any insolence in his classroom.

_____ 6. Every morning you will sweep out the front hall.

_____ 7. At the fair we saw some fascinating agricultural exhibits.

_____ 8. All of the teacher's noticed Mary's improvement in reading.

_____ 9. Nearly every evening Jaspar played a few games of checkers with the old man.

_____ 10. Someone had turned off the warning light at the intersection.

_____ 11. Our club will appreciate your prompt response to this appeal for donations.

_____ 12. Dozens of the neighborhood parents have cleaned up the debris-cluttered vacant lot.

_____ 13. Your next test will cover the material in the first three chapters of your text.

_____ 14. In spite of her age, Martha plays a spirited game of tennis.

_____ 15. Bob picked up one of the coins from the pavement.

_____ 16. Last night on television, we saw part of a most interesting travelogue.

_____ 17. I shall file this bit of information for future reference.

_____ 18. Rachel had read only two of Shakespeare's plays.

_____ 19. Your niece made an excellent impression on the interviewing committee.

_____ 20. The boys sampled nearly every one of the prize-winning cookies.

Directions: The following are Pattern 3, 4, or 5 sentences. Circle each subject and underline each verb. Identify the italicized complement by writing one of the following in the space at the left.

D.O. [direct object]   I.O. [indirect object]   O.C. [objective complement]

_____ 1. One of your mother's friends mailed *me* a picture of your new boat.

_____ 2. The representatives of the two factions will talk over their *problems* at a meeting next week.

_____ 3. The teacher called me the silver-tongued *orator* of Sherwood High.

_____ 4. The frightened shepherds left their flocks *untended.*

_____ 5. We left the *auditorium* before the final speeches.

_____ 6. Aunt Louise left her *nephew* nearly a million dollars.

_____ 7. You never again will hear this famous *quartet* in concert.

_____ 8. One of the children had brought the *teacher* a bouquet of wildflowers.

_____ 9. I don't consider your criticism *valid.*

_____ 10. The coach's pep talk gave *the team* new encouragement.

_____ 11. The coach's pep talk made the team more *aggressive.*

_____ 12. A garage owner showed *us* the best route across the desert.

_____ 13. Some commentators interpreted Farwell's statement as a *bid* for the nomination.

_____ 14. You've sampled nearly every *one* of the dozens of flavors of ice cream.

_____ 15. The rioters set *free* most of the political prisoners.

_____ 16. The committee hereby names you the presiding *officer.*

_____ 17. One of the interviewers will probably ask *you* some questions about your previous employment.

_____ 18. The speaker gave us *nothing* except platitudes.

_____ 19. Grandfather brought *each* of the youngsters a bag of popcorn.

_____ 20. Chet made up a flimsy *excuse* for his absence.

Exercise 4   *Complements*

NAME _____   SCORE _____

Directions: Circle the subject and underline the verb in each of the following sentences. Identify the italicized word by writing one of the following in the space at the left:

S.C. [subjective complement]   D.O. [direct object]
I.O. [indirect object]   O.C. [objective complement]

If the italicized word is *not* used as one of the complements, leave the space blank.

_____   1. The losing candidate had promised his *constituents* many favors.

_____   2. At the height of the storm my garage door came *loose.*

_____   3. After long and serious contemplation, Louise turned down Mr. Foster's job *offer.*

_____   4. Mr. Foster had offered *Louise* a responsible position in his travel agency.

_____   5. After only a few minutes of the strenuous work, I took off my heavy *jacket.*

_____   6. Dr. Russell's arguments against our proposal showed *us* his true intentions.

_____   7. After breakfast Mother usually reads every *page* of the local newspaper.

_____   8. Ms. Shaw then read the *class* two of Shakespeare's sonnets.

_____   9. Peter had never before looked through a *telescope.*

_____   10. Patricia looked quite *unhappy.*

_____   11. Peter then looked up the *meaning* of the word in his dictionary.

_____   12. Your gaudy necktie seems somewhat *out-of-place* in this sedate office.

_____   13. The three women wore almost identical *costumes.*

_____   14. The three women's costumes were almost *identical.*

_____   15. Jim had never before eaten an *artichoke.*

_____   16. Here is a small *donation* for your favorite charity.

_____   17. At times the children drove me nearly *wild* with their noisy games.

_____   18. She's one of the youngest *members* of our faculty.

_____   19. Mr. Walters proposed several new *items* for next week's agenda.

_____   20. That success made James *famous* all over the campus.

Directions: Using appropriate forms of the verb indicated, write original sentences illustrating the following patterns:

  Sentences 1–5: Pattern 2
  Sentences 6–10: Pattern 3
  Sentences 11–15: Pattern 4
  Sentences 16–20: Pattern 5.

1. become _____

2. seem _____

3. taste _____

4. appear _____

5. grow _____

6. grow _____

7. break _____

8. build _____

9. catch _____

10. watch _____

11. tell _____

12. give _____

13. send _____

14. write _____

15. assign _____

16. call _____

17. elect _____

18. make _____

19. appoint _____

20. name _____

In this lesson you will examine a few more forms and uses of verbs, including some additional auxiliary verbs. With these forms and those that you have already examined, you will be acquainted with nearly all of the verb forms that the average speaker and writer will ever use.

In Lesson 2 you examined the partial conjugation of three verbs: *earn, grow,* and *be.* You may want to refer to that conjugation (pages 9–10) as we discuss a few more points about changes in verb form.

Third-person singular verbs in the present tense end in *s* (or *es*): *earns, teaches, is, has.* Notice that on nouns, the *s* (*es*) ending shows a plural form, whereas on verbs it shows a singular form:

dogs, noses	(plural nouns)
wags, sniffs	(singular verbs)

If you review the conjugation of the verb *be* in Lesson 2, you will notice the verb is completely irregular. Unlike any other verb in the language, it has three forms (*am, is,* and *are*) in the present tense and two forms (*was* and *were*) in the past tense.

In general, the tenses are used as follows:

Present:	Action occurring at the present moment.
	He *earns* a good salary.
Past:	Action occurring at a definite time before the present moment.
	Last year he *earned* a good salary.
Future:	Action occurring at some time beyond the present moment.
	Next year he *will earn* a good salary.
Present perfect:	Action continuing up to the present moment.
	So far this year he *has earned* ten thousand dollars.
Past perfect:	Action continuing to a fixed moment in the past.
	Before leaving for college, he *had earned* ten thousand dollars.
Future perfect:	Action continuing to a fixed moment in the future.
	By next Christmas he *will have earned* ten thousand dollars.

In Lesson 21 you will be reminded of a few usage problems involving tenses.

Principal Parts

We noted in Lesson 2 that *earn* is a regular verb and *grow* is an irregular verb. We customarily make use of three distinctive forms, called the **principal parts** of the verb, to show the difference between regular and irregular verbs. The following are the principal parts:

- *Base* or *infinitive*, the "name" of the verb, used in the present tense with *s* (*es*) added in the third person singular
- *Past*, the form used in the simple past tense
- *Past participle*, the form used in the three perfect tenses

In all regular verbs, the past and the past participle are alike, formed simply by the addition of *ed* to the base form (or only *d* if the base word ends in *e*). Thus, *earn* becomes *earned*. Irregular verbs are more complicated because for nearly all of them, the past tense and the past participle are not spelled alike. Thus, the past tense of *grow* is *grew*, and the past participle of *grow* is *grown*. Following are the three forms of some irregular verbs illustrating spelling changes and endings:

Base	*Past*	*Past Participle*
be	was, were	been
become	became	become
bite	bit	bitten
break	broke	broken
catch	caught	caught
do	did	done
eat	ate	eaten
put	put	put
ring	rang	rung
run	ran	run
see	saw	seen

(You will study more principal parts of verbs and the usage problems associated with them in Lesson 21.) Both regular and irregular verbs add *ing* to their base form to produce the **present participle.** The present participle is often used with auxiliary verbs.

Auxiliary Verbs

In the sample conjugation in Lesson 2, you observed the use of *shall/will* and *have* as auxiliary verbs in the future tense and the perfect tenses. Another important auxiliary is *be*, used with the present participle (the *ing* form of the main verb) to produce what is called the **progressive form.** As an example of its use, suppose someone asks you what you are doing in your English class. You probably would not reply, "Right now, we *review* parts of speech." Instead, you probably would say, "Right now, we *are reviewing* parts of speech," to show that the action is not fixed in an exact moment of time but is a continuing activity. This very useful type of verb occurs in all six tenses:

We are reviewing.
We were reviewing.
We shall be reviewing.
We have been reviewing.
We had been reviewing.
We shall have been reviewing.

Another type of auxiliary verb includes *may, might, must, can, could, would,* and *should.* *May, can,* and *might* are used to suggest possibility. *Can* sometimes also suggests capability.

I may go to town tomorrow.   (If certain conditions exist.)
I might go to town tomorrow.   (If certain conditions exist.)
I can go to town tomorrow.   (I am able to go.)

Must indicates an obligation.

I must go to town.

Could is used to indicate ability, possibility, or permission in the past tense.

I could have gone to town.   (If I had wanted to go.)

These words are called **modal auxiliaries,** and they are used the way *will* and *shall* are used:

I *should study* this weekend.
I *should have studied* last weekend.

Occasionally, *do* acts as a modal auxiliary and combines with the base form of a main verb to make an "emphatic" form: "But I *did* pay that bill last month." In Lesson 6 you will examine the much more common use of the *do* auxiliary in questions and negatives.

Other variations of some modals and "time" auxiliaries make use of *to* in the verb phrase.

Mr. Nelson *has to retire* [must retire] early.
You *ought to eat* [should eat] more vegetables.
I *used to be* a secretary.
Jim *was supposed to be here* at ten o'clock.
I *am to depart* for Miami early in the morning.
I *am going to depart* for Miami early in the morning.
We *meant to leave* much earlier today.

Here are a few other points to remember about auxiliary verbs:

1. *Have, be,* and *do* are not used exclusively as auxiliaries; they are three of the most commonly used main verbs:

I *have* a brown pen. [Main verb]
I *have* lost my brown pen. [Auxiliary]
He *is* a good speaker. [Main verb]
He *is* becoming a good speaker. [Auxiliary]
He *did* a good job for us. [Main verb]
Yes, I *did* embellish the story somewhat. [Auxiliary]

2. When the verb unit contains auxiliaries, there may be short adverbial modifiers separating parts of the whole verb phrase:

We *have* occasionally *been* sailing.
He *has,* of course, *been telling* the truth.

3. In a few set expressions following introductory adverbs (usually adverbs of time), the subject is placed within the verb phrase between an auxiliary and the main verb:

Only lately *have* I *learned* to drive.
Rarely *do* we *turn on* the television set.

NAME _____ SCORE _____

Directions: Each of these sentences contains at least one auxiliary verb. (Some have two; some three.) Copy the auxiliary verb(s) in the first space at the left. In the second space, write 1, 2, 3, 4, or 5 to identify the sentence pattern.

_____ _____   1. In the gathering darkness we could barely find the path back to the camp.

_____ _____   2. Ms. Robinson has been writing a musical comedy since last fall.

_____ _____   3. Since the concert I have become quite enthusiastic about the student choir.

_____ _____   4. The company could not have been happier with our proposal.

_____ _____   5. By tomorrow our broker will have found us a new house.

_____ _____   6. The swim club should have elected Jim Stone as its president.

_____ _____   7. The boys had searched the premises thoroughly without any problems.

_____ _____   8. By any standard, the judges should have named her the best performer in the finals.

_____ _____   9. My father has been much happier since his return from the camping trip to Montana.

_____ _____   10. The passage of time will provide many answers to your perplexing questions.

_____ _____   11. The winner of the marathon must have been training for many months.

_____ _____   12. Next year PBS will carry live coverage of a number of outstanding jazz concerts.

_____ _____   13. You should have been resting this afternoon for the game.

_____ _____   14. Young golfers have never found this course easy.

_____ _____   15. Our beautiful cousin will be leaving for home tomorrow after a two weeks' visit.

_____ _____   16. The new teacher has been evaluating our work on that difficult project.

_____ _____   17. The cheerleaders have been working hard in preparation for the homecoming game.

_____ _____   18. At exactly 2 P.M. the president will hand me my diploma.

_____ 19. Our final efforts today should make the foreman glad.
_____

_____ 20. Because of the change in his grip, Mark should be driving the
_____ golf ball about twenty yards farther.

_____ 21. In our next show we will be singing selections from several
_____ Broadway musicals.

_____ 22. In the past few weeks we have not sung well at all.
_____

_____ 23. Our latest practice sessions, however, have been very encouraging
_____ to the director.

_____ 24. In addition to his academic success, Jorge Lopez has become one
_____ of the school's outstanding athletes.

_____ 25. Their past experiences have made them quite optimistic about
_____ better attendance later in the season.

_____ 26. Recently I have been buying myself at least one DVD per week.
_____

_____ 27. Without much effort Mary Jones has been making herself a
_____ leader in various student organizations.

_____ 28. Yesterday could not have been a more beautiful day for planting
_____ the new fruit trees.

_____ 29. The snow on the ski slopes has been piling higher and higher for
_____ the last three days.

_____ 30. Under the circumstances you should consider yourself very
_____ lucky.

_____ 31. Her open, honest approach to the issues has impressed many of
_____ the voters positively.

_____ 32. The girl's success in gymnastics will certainly bring her grand-
_____ parents great joy.

_____ 33. We might have started earlier in our get-out-the-vote campaign.

_____ 34. With a little persistence she could have found the spare key under
_____ the flower pot.

_____ 35. All of us should have been helping Juanita with her English lessons.
_____

_____ 36. With a little more information we might have been wiser in our
_____ choices.

_____ 37. Someone should have given you my message earlier today.
_____

_____ 38. Everyone will call him a great success after this victory.
_____

_____ 39. The team might very well consider you as a replacement for the
_____ manager.

_____ 40. By tomorrow afternoon the women should have returned from
_____ their trip down the river.

Exercise 5   *Complements*

NAME _____   SCORE _____

Directions: In the space at the left, write one of the following to identify the italicized word:

    S.C. [subjective complement]   I.O. [indirect object]

    D.O. [direct object]   O.C. [objective complement]

If the italicized word is not a complement, leave the space blank. Circle every auxiliary verb.

_____ 1. She might very well be *one* of the year's outstanding legislators.

_____ 2. Our new plan for recruiting students has been working *well*.

_____ 3. The platoon leader formulated a daring *plan* for escape.

_____ 4. Our policy of early retirement proved a great *boon* to workers in their fifties.

_____ 5. Lately many people have become *interested* in land as an investment.

_____ 6. Janice flew her new *plane* from Cleveland to Detroit.

_____ 7. In this class you must keep yourself *alert* for a pop quiz at any time.

_____ 8. *There* on the left-hand side of the road was a beautiful small waterfall.

_____ 9. *Fundamental* to your understanding of the whole process is a firm grasp of the two basic principles.

_____ 10. The seniors left a large *collection* of old lecture notes on the hard drive of the computer in the fraternity house.

_____ 11. Aunt Miriam left my *sister* a fine antique vase.

_____ 12. Nordstrom's leaping catch of the line drive by Jones left the spectators *speechless* with amazement.

_____ 13. In the old days kids always kept their spending *money* in a cookie jar.

_____ 14. Away from its mother a newborn fawn keeps very *still*.

_____ 15. Because of the friendship of the two children, the relationship between the two families remained very *cordial*.

_____ 16. The librarian can probably find *us* some new materials on that subject.

_____ 17. We walked directly through the *center* of town to the auditorium.

———— 18. You will find some of the most interesting *people* in the world on this campus.

———— 19. Two miles down the valley we found a clear, cold *spring*.

———— 20. No one has ever called our candidate a really original *thinker*.

———— 21. Toward the end of the speech his voice sounded quite *strained*.

———— 22. The captain handed *each* of the other officers a copy of the order.

———— 23. The president postponed our *appointment* until tomorrow.

———— 24. This next song has always been a *favorite* of mine.

———— 25. The highway patrol always monitors the emergency *channel*.

———— 26. Some outdoorsmen consider rattlesnake meat a tasty *dish*.

———— 27. You will work *better* after a short rest.

———— 28. The ice on the trees gave the city *square* a festive air.

———— 29. The city council voted Jean Morgan its outstanding *member*.

———— 30. The fire department's response to our call was exceptionally *fast*.

———— 31. The court order saved *me* the trouble of another trip to Washington.

———— 32. The referees made very few *mistakes* this past season.

———— 33. An attitude like yours will make the job even more *tedious*.

———— 34. One of those two people should be a good *choice* for a seat on the County Commission.

———— 35. This morning the mail carrier brought *Alicia* a summons for jury duty.

———— 36. The instructor assigned my *class* that difficult first chapter from that Victorian novel.

———— 37. At first I considered knitting a very simple *task*.

———— 38. All of the club members expended a great *deal* of effort in the political campaign.

———— 39. He has told *everyone* in town the story of my embarrassing social blunder.

———— 40. With a soft laugh Mark held the tiny *baby* close to his chest.

Any long piece of writing made up exclusively of basic sentences would be too monotonous to read. You should think of the basic sentences not as models for your writing but as elementary units, important because they are the structures from which more effective sentences develop. In this lesson, we shall look at two alterations of basic sentence patterns:

1. Sentences that use passive verbs
2. Sentences in the form of a question

Lessons 7 through 11 will then show how basic sentences can be combined and certain elements can be reduced to subordinate clauses and phrases to produce varied, well-developed sentences.

Passive Voice

In Lesson 2 you examined a partial conjugation of the verb *earn*. The forms listed there are in the active voice, which means that the subject is the doer of the action. A more complete conjugation would include the passive voice. In the passive voice, the subject is not the doer of the action, but the verb is always transitive. Passive verb forms make use of the auxiliary verb *be* combined with the past participle of the verb, as shown in the following illustration of the third-person singular in the six tenses:

> This amount is earned.
> This amount was earned.
> This amount will be earned.
> This amount has been earned.
> This amount had been earned.
> This amount will have been earned.

The present and past tenses of progressive verbs can also be shifted to the passive voice, giving us forms in which *be* is used in two auxiliary capacities in the same verb form:

> These cars *are being sold* at a loss.
> These cars *were being sold* at a loss.

Because only transitive verbs have passive forms, only sentence patterns 3, 4, and 5 can be altered to the passive voice. When the idea of a Pattern 3 sentence in the active voice is expressed with a passive verb, there is no direct object (complement) in the sentence:

Active Voice: Children play games.

Passive Voice: Games are played [by children].

If the doer of the verb's action is expressed in a sentence using a passive verb, the doer must occur as the object of the preposition *by*. When a Pattern 4 sentence is altered to form a passive construction, the indirect object that follows the active verb becomes the subject of the passive verb:

Active Voice: John gave Allen a model plane.

Passive Voice: Allen was given a model plane [by John].

Here the passive verb is followed by a complement, *plane,* which we continue to call a direct object in spite of the fact that it follows a passive verb.

Notice also how a Pattern 5 sentence can be given a different kind of expression by means of a passive verb:

Active Voice: The parents consider the child a genius.
The parents consider the child clever.

Passive Voice: The child is considered a genius [by the parents].
The child is considered clever [by the parents].

In these sentences the direct object becomes the subject, but the passive verb requires a complement (*genius, clever*). Because the complement renames or describes the subject, it is called a subjective complement.

The passive voice serves a real purpose in effective communication: It should be used when the *doer* of the action is unknown or is of secondary interest in the statement. In such a situation, the writer, wishing to focus attention on the *receiver* of the action, places that unit in the emphatic subject position. The passive verb form makes this arrangement possible. Thus, instead of some vague expression such as "Somebody should wash these windows," we can say, "These windows *should be washed."*

Sometimes the passive voice is described as "weak." Admittedly, some writers do get into the habit of using the passive form when there is little justification for it. In most narrative writing, the doer of the action is logically the subject of the verb. "The fullback crossed the goal line" would certainly be preferred to "The goal line was crossed by the fullback," a version that gives the same information but tends to stop any action suggested by the sentence. The passive voice also lends itself to a kind of muddied, heavy-footed writing that produces prose like this:

> It *is* now *rumored* that the secretary of defense *has been informed* that contingent plans *have been made to.* . . .

The writer of such a sentence, however, probably finds the passive voice effectively hides the identity of the person who is spreading the rumor, who has informed the secretary of defense, or who has made the plans. This use of the passive voice creates an impersonal, bureaucratic language very popular in many institutions.

You should practice with passive constructions so you can use this important device when it is called for. Equally important, if a criticism of your writing mentions doubtful uses of the passive, you need to be able to recognize passive verbs in order to change them when it is necessary.

Questions

In the sentence types you examined in earlier lessons, you noted the normal positioning of the main sentence parts: the subject first, followed by the verb, followed by the complement, if any. In questions, however, other arrangements are possible. As we study these new structures, we must first recognize the fact that there are two kinds of questions:

1. Questions answered by "Yes" or "No"
2. Questions answered by information

Questions Answered by "Yes" or "No"

In the following paired sentences, the first sentence is a statement and the second sentence a related question. These sentences demonstrate how the structure of a Yes/No question differs from that of a statement.

1. John is happy.   Is John happy?
2. You were there.   Were you there?
3. You see Ms. Locke often.   Do you see Ms. Locke often?
4. You heard the announcement.   Did you hear the announcement?

Notice from these examples that if the verb is *be* in the present or past tense, the subject and the *be* form (*am, are, is, was,* or *were*) reverse positions. With other one-word verbs in the present or past tense, the proper form of the auxiliary *do* is used, followed by the subject and the base form of the main verb.

   If the verb already has an auxiliary, the subject follows the auxiliary verb. If there are two or more auxiliaries, the subject follows the first one.

5. You have seen the movie.   Have you seen the movie?
6. They will arrive later.   Will they arrive later?
7. The house is being painted.   Is the house being painted?
8. He should have been told.   Should he have been told?

When the verb is *have* in the present tense, two versions of the question are possible: the subject–verb reversal and the *do* auxiliary. (See Supplement 1.)

9. You have enough money.   Have you enough money?
10. You have enough money.   Do you have enough money?

Questions Answered by Information

Some questions ask for information rather than for a "Yes" or "No" response. These questions make use of words called **interrogatives,** words that stand for unknown persons, things, or descriptive qualities. The most commonly used interrogatives are these:

pronouns: *who (whom), which, what*
adjectives: *whose, which, what*
adverbs: *when, where, why, how*

The interrogative pronoun *who,* which stands for an unknown person or persons, has three forms:

1. *Who,* when it is used as a subject or a subjective complement
2. *Whose,* when it is used as a possessive modifier of a noun
3. *Whom,* when it is used as an object

(In a later lesson you will learn that these three forms of *who* have another important use in subordinate clauses. And the choice between *who* and *whom* as a problem of usage is discussed more extensively in Lesson 24.)

In questions using these interrogatives, the normal arrangement of the main sentence parts is retained only when the interrogative is the subject or a modifier of the subject. (Here again we shall use paired statements and related questions to demonstrate these structures.)

1. *My brother* [S.] paid the bill.   *Who* [S.] paid the bill?
2. *Five cars* [S.] were damaged.   *How* many cars [S.] were damaged?

In all other situations the subject–verb position is altered as it is with Yes/No questions. The interrogative word, or the unit containing the interrogative word, stands at the beginning of the sentence to signal that a question, not a statement, is forthcoming:

I studied *geometry* [D.O.] last night.
What [D.O.] did you study last night?

You saw *Jim* [D.O.] at the party.
Whom [D.O.] did you see at the party?

She is Mother's *cousin* [S.C.].
Who [S.C.] is she?

We can use Bill's *car* [D.O.].
Whose car [D.O.] can we use?

You spent fifteen *dollars* [D.O.].
How much money [D.O.] did you spend?

You [S.] called *Bob* [D.O.] a *thief* [O.C.].
Who [S.] called Bob a thief?
Whom [D.O.] did you call a thief?
What [O.C.] did you call Bob?

When the interrogative unit is the object of a preposition, two arrangements of the question are often possible:

1. The entire prepositional phrase may stand at the beginning.
2. The interrogative may stand at the beginning with the preposition in its usual position.

The speaker was referring *to the mayor.*
To whom was the speaker referring?
Whom was the speaker referring to?

(See Supplement 2.)

Supplement 1

The type of verb also determines the structuring of sentences that are negative rather than positive. The positioning of the negator *not* (or its contraction *n't*) depends on the presence or absence of an auxiliary verb. Sentences using *be* or *have* must be considered special cases.

1. If the verb is *be* in the present tense or in the past tense, used either as the main verb or as an auxiliary verb, the *not* follows the *be* form:

   I *am not* pleased with the report.
   He *was not* [wasn't] available.
   They *were not* [weren't] invited.

2. With other one-word verbs in the present or past tense, the proper form of the auxiliary *do* is used followed by the negator and the base form of the main verb:

   I *do not* [don't] expect a reward.
   He *does not* [doesn't] attend regularly.
   We *did not* [didn't] respond.

3. If the verb already has an auxiliary, the negator follows the auxiliary. When there are two or more auxiliaries, the *not* follows the first one:

   We *could not* [couldn't] see very well.
   I *may not* have understood him.
   They *will not* [won't] refund my money.
   This cake *ought not* to have been baked so long.

4. When *have* in the present tense is the main verb, two negative forms are possible:

   I *have not* [haven't] enough time to play.
   I *do not* [don't] have enough time to play.

Supplement 2

At the informal language level, another version—"*Who* was the speaker referring to?"—is often found, despite the traditional demand for the objective case for the object of a preposition. The formal level of both spoken and written English would call for: "*To whom* was the speaker referring?"

NAME _____ SCORE _____

Directions: These are Pattern 3, 4, or 5 sentences. In the first space at the left write the pattern number. In the second space, write the passive form that is used when the italicized word in the sentence is made the subject.

Example:

___4___
will be sent

Later I will *send* you a copy of the bulletin.

_____

1. People on the neighboring farm could see the *flames.*

_____

2. We will allow *you* another chance.

_____

3. Somebody will meet the *candidate* at the airport.

_____

4. Some legislators are considering a tax *hike.*

_____

5. The teacher is keeping the test *questions* a secret.

_____

6. The teacher will show us the test *questions* tomorrow.

_____

7. We would appreciate your *cooperation* in this venture.

_____

8. The college will gladly send *you* an updated catalogue.

_____

9. Some people do not consider that comedian's *act* funny.

_____

10. You should have paid the taxi *driver* without any argument.

Directions: The purpose of this exercise is to contrast the structure of a question with that of a statement. In the space at the left, copy the word from the question that serves the function of the italicized word in the statement.

_____   1. What will we serve for dessert?
        We will serve apple *pie* for dessert.

_____   2. What will our dessert be?
        Our dessert will be apple *pie*.

_____   3. How many people does the county employ?
        The county employs nearly three hundred *people*.

_____   4. Which of the two guides can we rely on?
        We can rely on the *older* of the two guides.

_____   5. Whom has Martha selected as her maid of honor?
        Martha has selected her *sister* as her maid of honor.

_____   6. How much money did you spend on your trip?
        I spent four hundred *dollars* on my trip.

_____   7. How old is your grandfather?
        My grandfather is sixty-five years *old*.

_____   8. Whom will you invite to the party?
        I'll invite my *neighbors* to the party.

_____   9. Who will the guests at the party be?
        The guests at the party will be my *neighbors*.

_____ 10. How many fish did you catch?
        I caught four *fish*.

_____ 11. Whose car did you borrow?
        I borrowed *Joan*'s car.

_____ 12. Whom has the chancellor appointed as chairwoman?
        The chancellor has appointed *Dr. Lewis* as chairwoman.

_____ 13. What have you two been arguing about?
        We have been arguing about *politics*.

_____ 14. To whom should I address this card?
        You should address this card to *Aunt Letty*.

_____ 15. How much did the old man pay you?
        The old man paid me twenty *dollars*.

NAME _____   SCORE _____

Directions: Each of the following sentences uses a passive verb. Underline each verb. Rewrite each sentence using an active form of the verb. (You will have to supply a logical subject for the active verb if the sentence does not provide one.) If your rewrites are correctly done, your first four sentences will be Pattern 3, your next three will be Pattern 4, and your final three will be Pattern 5.

1. By 6:00 P.M. every season ticket had been delivered by special couriers.

   _____

2. Every page of your paper must be checked very carefully for errors and misspelled words.

   _____

3. That famous novel was written by Alec's grandfather many years ago.

   _____

4. Our new delivery system was developed by two consultants from a small company in Utah.

   _____

5. The men should have been shown the new contract long before the day for the vote.

   _____

6. Most patients are given only one dose of that powerful medication by their doctors.

   _____

7. Each member of the staff was given a slightly different version of that report by the secretary.

   _____

8. That article is considered a successful presentation.

   _____

9. Marge was elected chair of the committee by the members of the class.

   _____

10. Ken's work on that project was judged barely adequate by the project managers.

   _____

Directions: The italicized word in each question is a complement or the object of a preposition. In the space at the left, write one of the following to identify the italicized:

    D.O. [direct object]   O.C. [objective complement]
    S.C. [subjective complement]   O.P. [object of preposition]
    I.O. [indirect object]

_____ 1. Which *one* of these watches should I buy for my sister?

_____ 2. When will the college authorities make this information *available* to the student body?

_____ 3. *Whom* do the police suspect?

_____ 4. *What* will the withholding tax on my new salary be?

_____ 5. How *hot* do the August days get here in the desert?

_____ 6. How much money does your nephew owe *you*?

_____ 7. How much *money* does your nephew owe you?

_____ 8. *Whom* should our union send to the regional meeting?

_____ 9. *Which* of these amendments did you vote for?

_____ 10. How *tall* will this bush grow?

_____ 11. *Who* will the supervisor's replacement be?

_____ 12. *Whom* will the boss name as the supervisor's replacement?

_____ 13. How deep should we make this *ditch*?

_____ 14. How *deep* should this ditch be made?

_____ 15. How many *people* have you told this ridiculous story to?

_____ 16. What *salary* did the old man promise you?

_____ 17. What salary did the old man promise *you*?

_____ 18. *Whom* in the chain of command do you report to?

_____ 19. What will you allow *me* on my old Chevrolet?

_____ 20. *Whom* do you consider the best manager in the league?

_____ 21. Whom do you consider the best *manager* in the league?

_____ 22. How *accurate* are the weather forecasts on TV?

_____ 23. To *whom* am I indebted for the doubtful honor?

_____ 24. What *kind* of student has your oldest son become?

_____ 25. How much has your group leader told *you* about the campaign?

Clauses and Phrases
Lessons, Practice Sheets, and Exercises

Lesson 7   *Coordination: Compound Sentences*

To begin to study sentences that build on the simple patterns discussed in the previous lessons, let's examine a student writer's description of a snowstorm. Each sentence is numbered for later reference.

(1) The first really serious snowfall began at dusk and had already spread a treacherous powdering over the roads by the time the homeward-bound crowds reached their peak. (2) As the evening deepened, porch and street lights glowed in tight circles through semisolid air. (3) The snow did not fall in a mass of fat, jovial flakes; it squatted in a writhing mist of tiny particles and seemed less snow than a dense, animated fog. (4) Through the night the wind rose, worrying the trees as a puppy shakes a slipper. (5) It rushed round the corners of buildings and tumbled over roofs, from which it snatched armfuls of snow to scatter in the streets. (6) Save for the occasional grumble of a sanitation truck sullenly pushing its plow, all sound stopped. (7) Even the wind was more felt than heard. (8) Day did not dawn. (9) The world changed from charcoal gray to lead between six and seven, but the change was one from night to lesser night. (10) The snow still whirled. (11) Drifts had altered the neat symmetry of peaked roofs into irregular mountain ranges ending in sheer cliffs four or five feet above the leeward eaves. (12) The downwind side of every solid object cast a snow shadow that tapered away from a sharp hump until it merged into the surrounding flat pallor. (13) Along the street, windshield wipers, odd bits of chrome, startling blanks of black glass, and isolated headlights decorated large white mounds. (14) Men and women shut off their alarm clocks, stretched, yawned, looked out of their windows, paused in a moment of guilt, and went back to bed. (15) Snow had taken the day for its own, and there was no point in arguing with it.

The fifteen sentences of this paragraph are all made up of groups of related words called clauses. A **clause** is a group of words that always contains a subject and a verb in combination. Recalling the scenes, actions, and responses associated with the event, the author has created a series of clauses (subject–verb combinations): the snowfall began, the snowfall had spread a powdering, the homeward-bound crowds reached their peak, the evening deepened, lights glowed, and so on.

Although it may not be apparent when you first read the paragraph, the entire passage is based on short, simple sentences of the patterns studied in the preceding lessons. The writer's problem was to combine or alter these short statements in order to put them into their most pleasing and effective form. Presenting all of them as basic sentences would communicate the author's ideas but in a form that, in addition to being monotonous, would not give proper emphasis to the most important ideas. Only two sentences (8 and 10) are retained as one-subject, one-verb basic sentences. Some of the sentences (3, 9, and 15) combine two basic sentences, giving each clause equal force. Two sentences (1 and 5) join more than one verb to the same subject. Sentence 13 joins four subjects to the same verb, and Sentence 14 has two subjects joined to six verbs.

In the next several lessons we shall be examining the word groups—independent clauses, subordinate clauses, and phrases—that are the language tools allowing a writer to apply various strategies to produce effective sentences.

Compounding Sentences

A sentence, as you learned in Lesson 1, is a word group containing a subject and a verb. From this definition, and from the one already given for a clause, it would seem that a sentence and a clause are identical. And this is true for one kind of clause, the **independent clause** (also called the *main clause* or *principal clause*). The independent clause can stand by itself as a sentence. Every example sentence and every exercise sentence that you have worked with thus far in this book has been made up of one independent clause. We call a sentence consisting of only one independent clause a **simple sentence.**

One means of combining or altering short, simple sentences is called *compounding,* joining grammatically equal parts so that they function together. We can join two or more subjects, verbs, complements, or modifiers by using a **coordinating conjunction.** (**Conjunctions** are words that join words, phrases, or clauses; conjunctions that join grammatically equal units are called *coordinating.*) The three common coordinating conjunctions are *and, but,* and *or;* other coordinators are *nor, for, yet,* and *so.* With the use of a coordinating conjunction, we can join two very short sentences and create a longer, more readable sentence.

Dad read the notice. I read the notice.
Dad *and* I read the notice. [Compound subjects]

Marge enjoys golf. Marge enjoys tennis.
She enjoys golf *and* tennis. [Compound direct objects]

I studied very hard. I failed the test.
I studied very hard *but* failed the test. [Compound verbs]

I found the lecture interesting. I found the lecture instructive.
I found the lecture interesting and instructive. [Compound objective complements]

I can see you during your lunch hour. I can see you after five.
I can see you during your lunch hour or after five o'clock. [Compound prepositional phrases]

Compounding is often used with two (sometimes more than two) independent clauses; the result is a common type of sentence called the **compound sentence.** We can create compound sentences in two ways.

Clauses Joined by a Coordinating Conjunction

Any of the coordinating conjunctions already mentioned can be used to join two independent clauses. The normal punctuation is a comma before the conjunction:

I had reviewed the material, and I did well on the test.

It is important to distinguish this sentence from a nearly synonymous version using a compound verb:

I had reviewed the material and did well on the test.

In this version, the sentence is not a compound sentence because there is no separate subject for the second verb. It is a simple sentence with a compound verb and should be written without a comma.

Clauses Joined by a Semicolon

Sometimes the two independent clauses stand side by side with no word tying them together:

No one was in sight; I was alone in the huge auditorium.

Often the second of the two clauses joined by a semicolon begins with an adverbial unit that serves as a kind of tie between the clauses. This adverbial unit may be:

1. A simple adverb

Currently we are renting an apartment; later we hope to buy a house.
These were last year's highlights; now we must look at plans for next year.

2. A short phrase

I cannot comment on the whole concert; in fact, I slept through the last part of it.

3. A conjunctive adverb

Your arguments were well presented; *however,* we feel that the plan is too expensive.

The most common conjunctive adverbs are *therefore, however, nevertheless, consequently, moreover, otherwise, besides, furthermore,* and *accordingly.* These words, often followed by a comma, should be used cautiously; they usually contribute to a heavy, formal tone. To lessen this effect, writers often place them, set off by commas, within the second clause:

Your arguments were well presented; we feel, *however,* that the plan is too expensive.

Because adverbial units like *later* and *therefore* are *not* coordinating conjunctions, the use of a comma to join the two clauses is inappropriate. This error is often called a *comma splice* or a *comma fault.* The important thing to remember is that when independent clauses are joined by a coordinating conjunction, the use of a comma is the custom. When there is no coordinating conjunction, the comma will not suffice; the customary mark is the semicolon. We will study these punctuation rules thoroughly in Lesson 17.

NAME _____   SCORE _____

Directions: The 25 sentences here illustrate three sentence types:

   Type 1. The sentence is a simple sentence with the subject having two verbs joined by a coordinating conjunction. Normal punctuation: none.

   We worked all day on the car but could not find the trouble.

   Type 2. The sentence is a compound sentence with two independent clauses joined by a coordinating conjunction: *and, but, or, nor, for, yet,* or *so.* Normal punctuation: a comma before the conjunction.

   We worked all day on the car, and now it runs well.

   Type 3. The sentence is a compound sentence but does not use one of the coordinating conjunctions to join the independent clauses. (The second clause often contains an adverbial unit.) Normal punctuation: a semicolon.

   We worked all day on the car; now it runs well.

In each of the following sentences a ^ marks a point of coordination. If the sentence is type 1, write 0 in the space at the left. If the sentence is type 2, write C (for comma) in the space. If the sentence is type 3, write S (for semicolon) in the space.

_____0_____ 1. The dean met with the student delegation ^ and accepted its recommendation with great pleasure.

_____C_____ 2. The dean met with the student delegation for an hour ^ but he did not accept its recommendation.

_____0_____ 3. The dean did not meet with the student delegation ^ instead she left campus for a meeting.

_____S_____ 4. Some may find his jokes corny ^ I, however, never fail to be amused by them.

_____0_____ 5. During the past year Martha held several jobs ^ for a short time she was a wrangler at a dude ranch.

_____C_____ 6. I predict great success for her ^ for she is an intelligent and hard-working woman.

_____C_____ 7. Sometimes those students arrive early for class ^ but most of the time they are a moment or two late.

_____S_____ 8. *Epidendron radicans* is the name of a beautiful flowering orchid ^ sometimes it has a hundred blossoms at one time.

_____C_____ 9. Few people can cope with a great deal of ambiguity ^ and they are usually frustrated by even small amounts of it.

61

_____ 10. Some can cope with ambiguity ∧ most, however, are frustrated by it.

_____ 11. Joe's dad has lived in Maple Ridge for years ∧ and is, in fact, one of the oldest residents.

_____ 12. They watched a television special filmed in Hawaii ∧ and became quite depressed when the snow piled up outside.

_____ 13. Some of the team members tried to organize a ski trip ∧ but finally gave up because of the great expense involved.

_____ 14. For years Georgette had wanted to move to Alaska ∧ she finally spent a few months there this year.

_____ 15. The moderate climate of California attracts hordes of visitors every year ∧ and many of them decide to settle there permanently.

_____ 16. We should go sailing tomorrow ∧ for the weather will be cool and clear.

_____ 17. My cousins waited at the station for over an hour ∧ but never did see the train to the city.

_____ 18. The train is usually late ∧ but seldom is it a full hour behind schedule.

_____ 19. That doctor advocates moderate exercise for people of all ages ∧ and provides suggested programs of exercise for everyone.

_____ 20. The doctor advocates moderate exercise for people of all ages ∧ and he suggests jogging for all but a few people.

_____ 21. My brother will call Norman ∧ and John, no doubt, will call June.

_____ 22. Earlier today I called Norman and John ∧ but found neither of them at home.

_____ 23. That particular car has an automatic transmission ∧ but it can be ordered with a five speed instead.

_____ 24. Most tennis players have difficulty with their backhand ∧ Art, however, calls his backhand his best stroke.

_____ 25. My mother plays tennis very poorly ∧ but still enjoys herself on the court.

NAME _____   SCORE _____

Directions: The 25 sentences here illustrate three sentence types:

Type 1. The sentence is a simple sentence with the subject having two verbs joined by a coordinating conjunction. Normal punctuation: none.

We worked all day on the car but could not find the trouble.

Type 2. The sentence is a compound sentence with the two independent clauses joined by a coordinating conjunction—*and, but, or, nor, for, yet* or *so*. Normal punctuation: comma before the conjunction.

We worked all day on the car, and now it runs well.

Type 3. The sentence is a compound sentence without one of the coordinating conjunctions joining the independent clauses. (The second clause often begins with an adverbial unit.) Normal punctuation: a semicolon.

We worked all day on the car; now it runs well.

In each of the following sentences a ^ marks a point of coordination. If the sentence is type 1, write 0 in the space at the left. If the sentence is type 2, write C (for comma) in the space. If the sentence is type 3, write S (for semicolon) in the space.

_____C_____ 1. I have tried this experiment with five different classes ^ and the results have been exactly the same.

_____0_____ 2. Our agents can choose coverage from many insurance companies ^ and can objectively recommend the best policy for your needs.

_____S_____ 3. We should have time to finish our discussion this afternoon ^   my flight doesn't leave until 5 P.M., you know.

_____S_____ 4. To the east is the unbroken green carpet of the Amazon Jungle ^ to the west are the awesome snow-capped peaks of the Andes.

_____C_____ 5. You may finance the purchase with ten payments on easy terms ^ or you may prefer to pay cash and receive a 5 per cent discount.

_____0_____ 6. You may finance the purchase with ten payments on easy terms ^ or pay cash and receive a 5 per cent discount.

_____S_____ 7. Slowly add the beaten eggs and stir the sauce constantly ^ otherwise the mixture will curdle.

_____0_____ 8. I saw this movie last month in St. Louis ^ but would not mind seeing it again with you.

63

_____ C _____ 9. Federal marshals picked up the three escapees and returned them to the penitentiary ∧ and Centerville once again slipped back into its sleepy routine.

_____ S _____ 10. Glenn stammered slightly, looked at the ceiling, and blushed furiously ∧ obviously he did not know the correct answer.

_____ S _____ 11. In my day engineering students carried wooden slide rules ∧ nowadays they appear in class with their pocket electronic calculators.

_____ S _____ 12. In the winter of 1776–1777 hunger, disease, and cold plagued the American army ∧ by December Washington had lost half of this men.

_____ C _____ 13. Lumber prices went up 40 percent in less than ten months ∧ and by the end of the year construction costs had risen an average of 18 per cent.

_____ O _____ 14. At their first Thanksgiving feast in 1621, the Pilgrims not only prepared turkey and venison ∧ but also served steamed clams and boiled lobsters.

_____ C _____ 15. Foulweather Bluff is aptly named ∧ for many a fishing boat has been wrecked here during the winter gales.

_____ O _____ 16. For the fraternity members Homecoming weekend meant a round of games and parties ∧ for us pledges it meant added house duties.

_____ O _____ 17. All first-year students must prepare a tentative schedule of courses ∧ and have it approved by their advisers.

_____ S _____ 18. The General Assembly will debate the embargo issue tomorrow ∧ however, the prospect of an early compromise solution is remote.

_____ C _____ 19. Dean Willis did not acknowledge our petition ∧ nor did he grant our representatives an interview.

_____ O _____ 20. Dean Willis neither acknowledged our petition ∧ nor granted our representatives an interview

_____ S _____ 21. The company's expenditures for research and engineering were $83.9 million, up from $76.3 million in 2001 ∧ we anticipate a further increase next year.

_____ C _____ 22. This evolving mixed economy has served the Western world well, on the whole ∧ but there are other ways of producing and distributing commodities.

_____ S _____ 23. Some scholars say that Stonehenge was a temple for sun worship ∧ others believe it was used as a sepulcher.

_____ C _____ 24. Not only are these assignments fun for the students ∧ but their brevity makes the teacher's job of correcting papers quite simple.

_____ S _____ 25. As a retired worker, you should study carefully these facts and figures ∧ you may find that your property is dangerously underinsured.

Directions: Combine the short sentences in each numbered item into one longer sentence.

1. Alice loves to listen to jazz.
   She occasionally enjoys a little country and western music.

   _____

2. We were all forced to work late on Thursday night.
   Therefore I had little time to study for Friday morning's test.

   _____

3. The traffic into the stadium was backed up for several blocks.
   We still made it to our seats in time for the kickoff.

   _____

4. We are thinking of going to the library tonight.
   We might do our research over the Internet instead.

   _____

5. Jackie did not find a new phone number for that customer.
   She did not find a new address.

   _____

6. Walt and his two friends finished baseball practice.
   Then they went to a nearby restaurant for supper.

   _____

7. Maria got up quite early this morning.
   She needed to study for another hour for her history test.

   _____

8. Lightning struck very close to the parking garage.
   Several car alarms went off noisily.

   _____

9. John needs to leave an hour early for the airport.
   Otherwise he might get caught in that rush hour traffic on I-50.

   _____

10. I could not find any No.2 pencils for tomorrow's test.
    I will need to stop at the store on my way to school.

    _____

Lesson 8   *Subordination: Adverb Clauses*

To this point you have had practice with the simple sentence (one independent clause) and the compound sentence (two or more independent clauses). Basic as these sentences are to your thinking and writing, you need to move beyond these structures in order to make your writing flexible and effective. Often you can improve the precision of your statements if you use slightly more complex structures.

"Rain began to fall, and we stopped our ball game" is a perfectly correct sentence. But notice these slightly altered versions of that sentence:

> When rain began to fall, we stopped our ball game.
> After rain began to fall, we stopped our ball game.
> Because rain began to fall, we stopped our ball game.

These three, in addition to lessening the singsong tone of the compound sentence, are more informative. The first two tell the time at which the game was stopped—and notice that *when* and *after* point out slightly different time frames. The third version gives a different relation between the two statements; it tells not the time of, but the reason for, stopping the game.

If, instead of writing the compound sentence, "Rain was falling, and we continued our ball game," you write "Although rain was falling, we continued our ball game," you have refined your thinking and your expression. Your readers now interpret the sentence exactly as you want them to: They now know that the ball game was continued in spite of the fact that rain was falling.

The process by which a statement is reduced to a secondary form to show its relation to the main idea is called **subordination.** The grammatical unit that expresses a secondary idea as it affects a main idea is the **subordinate,** or **dependent, clause,** which we define as a subject–verb combination that cannot stand alone as a sentence. A subordinate clause works in a sentence in the same way that a single part of speech—an adverb, an adjective, or a noun works. Instead of a single word—quickly, quick, quickness—used as an adverb, an adjective, or a noun, a group of words is used. A sentence made up of one independent clause and at least one dependent clause is a **complex sentence.**

Adverb Clause

The **adverb clause** works in exactly the same way a one-word adverb works; it provides information by modifying a verb, an adjective, or another adverb. The most common types of adverb clauses modify verbs. In fact, they answer direct questions about the action: When? (time); Where? (place); Why? (cause); and How? (manner). The role of the adverb clause is shown by the conjunction that introduces the adverb clause. The conjunction—the structural signal of subordination—is not an isolated word standing between the two clauses. It is part of the subordinate clause. In such a sentence as, "We left the house after the rain stopped," the unit "the rain stopped" could stand alone as an independent clause.

But the clause is made dependent by the inclusion of the conjunction *after*. The dependent clause "after the rain stopped" establishes the time when "we left the house." Thus, the clause works as an adverb of time in the same way that the one-word adverbs work in the following sentences:

> We left the house *early.*
> We left the house *late.*
> We left the house *yesterday.*

Various types of adverb clauses and their most common conjunctions are listed here with examples.

Time (*when, whenever, before, after, since, while, until, as, as soon as*):

> The baby cried *when the telephone rang.*
> The cat ran out *before Lou could shut the door.*
> *After the bell rings,* no one can enter.
> I've known Palmer *since he was in high school.*
> You should not whisper *while Dr. Fuller is lecturing.*
> You may leave *as soon as your replacement arrives.*

Place (*where, wherever*):

> We parted *where the paths separated.*
> I shall meet you *wherever you want me to.*

Cause (or **Reason**) (*because, since, as*):

> I walk to work every day *because I need the exercise.*
> *Since she could not pay the fine,* she could not drive the car.
> *As you are the senior member,* you should lead the procession.

Purpose (*so that, in order that*):

> We left early *so that we could catch the last bus.*
> They died *that their nation might live.*
> They came to America *in order that they might find freedom.*

Manner (*as, as if, as though*):

> Stan acted *as if the party was boring him.*
> Please do the work *as you have been instructed.*

Result (*so . . . that, such . . . that*):

> Jerry arrived *so late that he missed the concert.*
> The workmen made *such a racket that I got a headache.*

Condition (*if, unless, provided that, on condition that*). This kind of adverb clause gives a condition under which the main clause is true:

Sit down and chat *if you are not in a hurry.*
He will not give his talk *unless we pay his expenses.*
She will sign the contract *provided that we pay her a bonus.*
If I were you, I would accept the offer.
If you had told me earlier, I could have helped.

There is an alternate arrangement for certain kinds of conditional clauses. In this arrangement, *if* is not used; instead, a subject–verb inversion signals the subordination. Sentences like the last two preceding examples sometimes take this form:

Were I you, I would accept the offer.
Had you told me earlier, I could have helped.

Concession (*although, though, even if, even though, since*). This clause states a fact in spite of which the main idea is true:

Although she is only nine years old, she plays chess.
Our car is dependable *even though it is old.*

Comparison (*than, as*). Two distinctive characteristics of the adverb clause of comparison should be noted. First, part or all of the verb, although it is needed grammatically, is usually not expressed. Second, when an action verb is not expressed in the subordinate clause, the appropriate form of the auxiliary *do* is often used even though the *do* does not occur in the main clause:

Gold is heavier *than iron* [is].
Your computer is not as new *as mine* [is].
Her theme was better *than any other student's in the class* [was].
Ellen earned more bonus points *than her brother* [did].

Adverb clauses may also modify adjectives and adverbs. In this type of clause, the conjunction *that* is sometimes unexpressed.

Jim slept *as late as possible.* [Modifies the verb *slept*]
We are sorry *that you must leave early.* [Modifies the adjective *sorry*]
I am sure *(that) he meant no harm.* [Modifies the adjective *sure*]
The car is running better *than it did last week.* [Modifies the adverb *better*]

Elliptical Clause

Ellipsis means *omission,* to *leave something out.* A clause that leaves some parts understood or unexpressed is called an **elliptical clause.** There are many types of elliptical clauses. You should be aware of them because they can lend variety to your writing. In the following examples, brackets enclose the parts of the clauses that may be unexpressed. (See Supplement.) Note that all the types of adverb phrases (time, place, cause, purpose, manner, result, condition, concession, and comparison) may be elliptical.

While [I was] *walking home,* I met Mr. Jones.
When [he is] *in Cleveland,* he stays with us.
Call your office *as soon as* [it is] *possible.*

Adjustments will be made *whenever* [they are] *necessary.*
Mary, *although* [she is] *a talented girl,* is quite lazy.
If [you are] *delayed,* call my secretary.
Your ticket, *unless* [it is] *stamped,* is invalid.

A Note on Sentence Variety

Although some adverb clauses—those of comparison, for instance—have a fixed position within the sentence, many adverb clauses may be placed before, inside, or following the main clause:

When they deal with the unknown, Greek myths are usually somber.
Greek myths, *when they deal with the unknown,* are usually somber.
Greek myths are usually somber *when they deal with the unknown.*

Notice that no comma is used in the third example above. Usually a comma is not needed when the adverbial clause is the final element of the sentence, as the third example below also illustrates.

Although he did not have authority from Congress, President Theodore Roosevelt ordered construction of the Panama Canal.

President Theodore Roosevelt, *although he did not have authority from Congress,* ordered construction of the Panama Canal.

President Theodore Roosevelt ordered construction of the Panama Canal *although he did not have authority from Congress.*

You should practice various arrangements to relieve the monotony that comes from reliance on too many "main-subject-plus-main-verb" sentences.

Supplement

Occasionally an elliptical adverb clause of comparison must be recast because the exact meaning is unclear when parts of the clause are unexpressed. Here are two sentences that are ambiguous in the shortened forms of the clauses:

Mr. Alton will pay you more *than Stan.*

Probable Meaning: Mr. Alton will pay you more than [he will pay] Stan.
Possible Meaning: Mr. Alton will pay you more than Stan [will pay you].

Parents dislike homework as much *as their offspring.*

Probable Meaning: Parents dislike homework as much as their offspring [dislike homework].
Possible Meaning: Parents dislike homework as much as [they dislike] their offspring.

SUMMARY OF ADVERB CLAUSES

1. Function: to modify a verb, an adjective, or an adverb
2. Position: fixed for some types (She sold more tickets *than I did*); others may be at the beginning, in the interior, or at the end of main clause
3. Subordinators: conjunctions, most of which show adverbial relationships such as time (*when, since, while*), cause (*because, as*), and so on
4. Special structures:
   a. An adverb clause modifying an adjective subjective complement and subordinated by *that* sometimes has the subordinator *that* unexpressed:

      I'm sure *(that) you are wrong.*

   b. Elliptical clauses:

      Mary is older than I (am).
      If (you are) unable to attend, call me.
      While (she was) preparing lunch, Mary cut her finger.

Practice Sheet 8

Adverb Clauses

NAME _____ SCORE _____

Directions: Identify each of the italicized adverb clauses by writing one of the following numbers in the space at the left:

1. Time	4. Purpose	7. Condition	10. Modification of an
2. Place	5. Manner	8. Concession	adjective or adverb
3. Cause	6. Result	9. Comparison	

_____ 1. We waited at the airport *until the last plane from Nashville had arrived.*

_____ 2. *Because we encountered two time-consuming traffic delays,* we were late for the opening of the play.

_____ 3. *If you are in line by eight o'clock,* you'll very likely get good seats for the concert.

_____ 4. Peculiar things happen around here *whenever there is a full moon.*

_____ 5. Our star basketball center is limping *as though she might have reinjured her ankle.*

_____ 6. No one else in the club worked harder *than you did.*

_____ 7. *Had we more time,* we could do a thorough job on the repairs.

_____ 8. The conspirators usually met at midnight *where the railroad tracks cross the old Fairmont Road.*

_____ 9. *Unless you hear to the contrary,* you will present your report at the June meeting.

_____ 10. The ticket sales were so small *that the promoters went heavily into debt.*

_____ 11. This year's county fair did not draw as many people *as last year's did.*

_____ 12. You can usually find Glen present *wherever free food is being served.*

_____ 13. Barbara gets herself into awkward situations *because she is too trustful of people.*

_____ 14. I have not talked with Janet *since she started her new job.*

_____ 15. Tim couldn't buy his date any popcorn, *since he had spent all of his money on the theater tickets.*

_____ 16. The children usually behave quite well *when we have company in the house.*

_____ 17. The maintenance crews start their work *as soon as the offices close.*

_____ 18. *Although exhausted from the long climb,* we felt very proud of our achievement.

_____ 19. This car gets better mileage *than yours.*

_____ 20. *If I were you,* I'd never speak to him again.

_____ 21. The tenor sang so poorly *that the audience hissed him.*

_____ 22. The guard at the gate will admit you *if you have a membership sticker on your windshield.*

_____ 23. Jane went home early *because the bright sun had given her a headache.*

_____ 24. We stayed at the airport *until Marie's plane had left.*

_____ 25. Mr. Reeves recognized his old basketball coach *though he had not seen him in thirty years.*

_____ 26. Has any one of your team members seen Terry *since he returned?*

_____ 27. *Since our funds were running low,* we hitchhiked to the baskeball tournament.

_____ 28. *Although he has never had a lesson,* Jerry plays the piano quite well.

_____ 29. The family stopped their traveling *wherever the men could find work.*

_____ 30. No one worked harder at the picnic *than Alice Dow.*

_____ 31. I certainly would accept Dean Liston's offer *if I were you.*

_____ 32. We can have our picnic *wherever you want to.*

_____ 33. *Before we left,* our host served us a light lunch.

_____ 34. Jack is now as tall *as his older brother was two* years ago.

_____ 35. *Had we spent less time at the museum,* we could have returned home in time for dinner.

_____ 36. *While driving to work this morning,* I planned my next vacation trip.

_____ 37. Recently Terry has been behaving *as if he resented our presence.*

_____ 38. In her new job Rachal earned more in four months *than she made all year at her old job*

_____ 39. Ben complains so much that people *don't enjoy his company.*

_____ 40. All the petty problems of everyday life fade away *when I am skiing.*

NAME _____   SCORE _____

Directions: Each sentence contains an adverb clause. Underline each adverb clause. In the space at the left, write one of the following number to identify the type clause.

1. Time	4. Purpose	7. Condition	10. Modification of an
2. Place	5. Manner	8. Concession	adjective or adverb
3. Cause	6. Result	9. Comparison	

_____   1. The children go to the zoo quite often because they love animals.

_____   2. After I took a thirty-minute nap, I felt full of energy again.

_____   3. Even though they were somewhat frightened by the darkness, the girls ventured into the cave.

_____   4. I will sit here and read this novel until the rain passes over.

_____   5. The A grade on my term paper made me so happy that I almost cried.

_____   6. Mrs. Johnson's 1987 Dodge runs as well as any late model.

_____   7. Unless Charley calls us, we won't know the exact time of his arrival.

_____   8. The little girl hid her diary where no one else could find it.

_____   9. Because I had always enjoyed his music, I bought a ticket to the Dave Brubeck concert.

_____   10. As I was walking down the street, I saw an old man in a leather coat.

_____   11. The weather was so cold and rainy that I decided to stay home all day.

_____   12. You probably lost your glasses when you opened your purse for your wallet.

_____   13. If you can't assemble the new cabinet, read the directions again.

_____   14. Few bank robbers were more skillful than Willy Sutton.

_____   15. Many of my fellow students can't study unless they are listening to loud rock music.

_____   16. I'll meet you wherever it will be convenient for you.

_____   17. I have more work now than I can manage.

_____   18. The witness fidgeted nervously and acted as if he might faint at any moment.

_____   19. Although she is very beautiful, I am not interested in dating her.

_____ 20. Edward R. Murrow had more impact on television newscasting than anyone else.

_____ 21. Unless we hear otherwise, we shall expect you day after tomorrow.

_____ 22. Surprisingly, some very old cars are worth more than new ones.

_____ 23. In these days of inflation we must look for bargains wherever we shop.

_____ 24. We are saving money so that we can take a long vacation trip.

_____ 25. Her beauty leaves me breathless whenever I see her.

_____ 26. We made little headway through the pile of books even though we worked all day.

_____ 27. Our manager, Ms. Jordan, smiled broadly because she was very pleased with the report.

_____ 28. Since the children are quite young, they must be accompanied by adults on the field trip.

_____ 29. All the people in the class used the cameras as they had been taught.

_____ 30. Since they expected a hard freeze during the night, the men checked the antifreeze in all the cars.

_____ 31. Since the new manager took over the job, the morale of the office staff has improved greatly.

_____ 32. I finished the dishes and made the beds while you were at the grocery store.

_____ 33. All the others in the camp slept later than Marilyn.

_____ 34. Although the managers usually work very long hours, last Friday they left at noon.

_____ 35. Please notify the Coast Guard if we have not returned by sundown.

_____ 36. After Marie had sanded the car, she painted it a glossy black

_____ 37. The boys stood in line for five hours so that they could buy tickets for tomorrow's game.

_____ 38. If you can register early, you will have a better selection courses.

_____ 39. Breathing is more difficult at very high elevations than at sea level.

_____ 40. The plants blossomed perfectly because the nurseryman had given them special fertilizer.

Directions: Rewrite the sentence or sentences in each numbered item as a complex sentence using an adverbial clause; use the subordinating conjunction that properly establishes the relationship between the two sentences or clauses. Note that certain coordinating conjunctions have direct equivalents in subordinating conjunctions.

1. We hurried home from the park, for a thunderstorm was building up in the west. (Cause)

    _____

2. We had already sold all of the tickets for opening night of the show; therefore we were unable to supply tickets for the people in the president's party. (Cause)

    _____

3. We had already sold almost all the tickets for opening night of the show, but we were able to find a few individual seats for the president's party. (Concession)

    _____

4. You need to find two more sources for your paper, or you will not have enough material to develop your thesis. (Condition)

    _____

5. The workmen made an enormous racket with the circular saw, and I got a terrible headache. (Result)

    _____

6. Marge stared at her test paper in a certain way. She had never seen any of the questions before. (Manner)

    _____

7. We found a very good place to pitch our tent. The ground is high and dry, and there is a very nice view of the lake. (Place)

    _____

8. On Monday we got up very early and went to the ticket office to be sure to get tickets for the play-off game. (Purpose)

    _____

9. All the people in the building were leaving for lunch. At that time the fire alarm went off in the building. (Time)

    _____

10. The people in the stands stood and sang the National Anthem, and then the umpire called out, "Play ball."

    _____

Lesson 9 *Subordination: Adjective Clauses*

Just as a single-word adjective modifies a noun or pronoun, clauses that begin with *who, whom, whose, which,* or *that* can modify nouns or pronouns. A clause that modifies a noun or pronoun is called an **adjective or relative clause.** An adjective clause gives information about the noun in the same way that the one-word adjectives do. Both one-word adjectives and adjective clauses can be seen as basic sentences that have been worked into a main clause.

> I looked into the sky. The sky was blue.
> I looked into the blue sky.

> I looked into the sky. The sky was filled with towering cumulous clouds.
> I looked into the sky, which was filled with towering cumulous clouds.

In Item 1 the sentence, "The sky was blue," becomes the one-word adjective *blue* and modifies the noun *sky*. In Item 2 the sentence, "The sky was filled with towering cumulous clouds," cannot become a one-word adjective; therefore, the sentence becomes an adjective or relative clause opened by the word *which*. The clause modifies the word *sky* in the sense that it provides us with information about the sky.

Adjective Clauses

Nearly all of the adjective clauses you read, write, or speak use *who, whose, whom, which,* or *that* to tie the adjective clause to the noun it modifies. These words, in spite of the fact that they join one clause to a word in another clause, are not conjunctions. They are pronouns that have a connective or *relating* function; thus they are called **relative pronouns.** (See Supplement.) Relatives can function *within* the adjective clause as subjects, direct objects, or objects of prepositions.

It is helpful to think of an adjective clause as a simple sentence that is incorporated within another sentence. The relative pronoun, by substituting for a noun, refers ("relates") the clause directly to the word being modified. Because the relative pronoun is the word signaling the subordination, the pronoun, sometimes preceded by a preposition, always begins the adjective clause.

Examine the following paired units. Every "A" unit has two simple sentences; the second repeats a noun from the first sentence. The "B" sentence shows how the second idea has been reduced to an adjective clause and has become part of the first sentence. Notice that the normal position of an adjective clause is immediately following the noun or the pronoun it modifies.

A. This is a well-built truck. *The truck* will save you money.
B. This is a well-built truck *that* will save you money.
   [The clause modifies *truck. That* is the subject in the adjective clause.]

79

A. Alice has a new boyfriend. *The new boyfriend* [or *He*] sings in a rock group.
B. Alice has a new boyfriend *who* sings in a rock group.
   [*Who* is the subject in the clause that modifies *boyfriend*.]

A. Here is the book. I borrowed *the book* [or *it*] yesterday.
B. Here is the book *that* I borrowed yesterday.
   [*That* is the direct object in the adjective clause.]

A. The firm hired Chet Brown. The boss had known *Chet Brown* [or *him*] in Omaha.
B. The firm hired Chet Brown, *whom* the boss had known in Omaha.
   [*Whom* is the direct object in the adjective clause.]

A. May I introduce Dick Hart? I went to college *with Dick Hart* [or *him*].
B. May I introduce Dick Hart, with *whom* I went to college?
   [The clause modifies *Dick Hart*. Notice that the preposition *with* stands at the beginning of the clause with its object *whom*. At the informal level of language usage, the preposition in this structure is sometimes found at the end of the clause. See Supplement 2 of Lesson 6 on page 51.]

A. She is a young artist. I admire the young *artist's* [or *her*] work.
B. She is a young artist *whose* work I admire.
   [*Work* is in this position because, although it is the direct object of *admire*, it cannot be separated from its modifier, the relative adjective *whose*, which must be placed at the beginning of the adjective clause.]

We also use the adverbs *when* and *where* as relatives. *When* and *where* introduce adjective clauses in combinations meaning "time when" and "place where." The following examples show that the subordinator is really the equivalent of an adverbial prepositional phrase. (The "B" sentences are complex sentences combining the material of the two "A" sentences.)

A. Beth and I recalled the time. We considered ourselves rebels *at that time*.
B. Beth and I recalled the time *when* we considered ourselves rebels.

A. This is the spot. The explorers came ashore at this spot.
B. This is the spot *where* the explorers came ashore.

These clauses are logically considered adjective clauses because they immediately follow nouns that require identification, and the clauses give the identifying material. If you remember "time-when" and "place-where," you will not confuse this type of adjective clause with other subordinate clauses that may use the same subordinators.

Note: In certain adjective clauses, the relative word is unexpressed; the meaning is instantly clear without it: the food *(that) we eat,* the house *(that) he lived in,* the man *(whom) you saw,* the time *(when) you fell down,* and so on.

Restrictive and Nonrestrictive Adjective Clauses

Depending on their role in a sentence, adjective clauses are restrictive or nonrestrictive. A **restrictive clause** provides identification of the noun it modifies. A **nonrestrictive clause** provides information that is not essential for identification. Thus, in the sentence "The man who owns that car just walked up," the man is identified by the clause *who owns that car*. But in the sentence "John Williams, who owns that car, just walked up," the clause *who* *owns that car* does not identify John Williams (he is identified by his name); the clause tells us something additional, it adds information about John Williams.

Restrictive Clauses

The restrictive adjective clause is not set off by commas because it is essential to the identification of the word being modified.

> The grade *that I received on my report* pleased me.
> Anyone *who saw the accident* should call the police.

Without the modifying clauses (*that I received on my test; who saw the accident*), the nouns are not identified. What grade and what anyone are we talking about? But when we add the modifiers, we identify the *particular* grade and the *particular* anyone. In other words, this kind of clause restricts the meaning of a general noun to one specific member of its class.

Nonrestrictive Adjective Clauses

The nonrestrictive adjective clause does require commas. Although the clause supplies additional or incidental information about the word that it modifies, the information is not needed for identifying the noun. (Don't, however, get into the habit of thinking that a nonrestrictive clause is unimportant; unless it has some importance to the meaning of the sentence, it has no right to be in the sentence.) Nonrestrictive modifiers are usually found following proper nouns (*Mount Everest, Philadelphia, Mr. Frank Smith*); nouns already identified (the oldest *boy* in her class, her only *grandchild*); and one-of-a-kind nouns (Alice's *mother,* the *provost* of the college, the *writer* of the editorial).

The following examples contrast restrictive and nonrestrictive adjective clauses. (See Supplement.)

> I visited an old friend *who is retiring soon.* [Restrictive]
> I visited my oldest and closest friend, *who is retiring soon.* [Nonrestrictive]

> The man *whose car had been wrecked* asked us for a ride. [Restrictive]
> Mr. Ash, *whose car had been wrecked,* asked us for a ride. [Nonrestrictive]

> A small stream *that flows through the property* supplies an occasional trout. [Restrictive]
> Caldwell Creek, *which flows through the property,* supplies an occasional trout. [Nonrestrictive]

> She wants to retire to a place *where freezing weather is unknown.* [Restrictive]
> She wants to retire to Panama City, *where freezing weather is unknown.* [Nonrestrictive]

Supplement

A few distinctions in the use of *who, which,* and *that* in adjective clauses are generally observed. *Which* refers only to things; *who* refers to people; and *that* refers to things or people. *That* is used only in restrictive clauses; in other words, a "that" adjective clause is not set off by commas. Because *which* is the relative pronoun that must be used in a nonrestrictive clause modifying a thing, there is a convention that *which* should not introduce a restrictive adjective clause. This convention is generally, but by no means always, observed. People tend to use *which* in their writing when *that* would be better.

SUMMARY OF ADJECTIVE CLAUSES

1. Function: to modify a noun or a pronoun
2. Position: follows the noun or pronoun that it modifies
3. Subordinators:
   a. relative pronouns (*who, whom, which, that*), which function within the adjective clause as subjects, direct objects, or objects of prepositions
   b. relative adjectives (*whose, which*)
   c. relative adverbs (*when, where*)
4. Special problem: Adjective clauses that are vital to the identification of the nouns being modified are restrictive and do not require commas. Clauses not necessary for identification are nonrestrictive and are set off by commas.

NAME _____ SCORE _____

Directions: Each italicized unit is an adjective clause. In the space at the left, copy the word the clause modifies. Be prepared to explain in class why some of the clauses are set off by commas and some are not.

Bench   1. Someone has already bought the antique bench *that I saw earlier.*

veg.   2. Can you suggest any vegetables *that might grow in this rocky soil?*

spot   3. We looked for a quiet spot *where we could study.*

_____ 4. Luke then drove to Mobile, *where shipyard workers were being hired.*

concert   5. The popular conductor will retire after next Wednesday's concert, *which is already sold out.*

hat   6. The hat *she wore at the wedding* attracted much attention.

Jeff O'Neal   7. Jeff O'Neal is one old-timer *who will never be forgotten in this town.*

_____ 8. Jeff O'Neal is one old-timer *whom this town should honor.*

_____ 9. The park will be named for Jeff O'Neal, *who played an important role in the town's early days.*

_____ 10. Here is a picture of Jeff O' Neal, *whose granddaughter still lives in the family home.*

_____ 11. How do you like the tie *I'm wearing?*.

_____ 12. Have you ever met the woman *against whom you will be playing in the semifinal round?*

_____ 13. Bert recently received a letter from Larry Benham, *with whom he roomed in college.*

_____ 14. Those *who arrive late* will not be seated until the first intermission.

_____ 15. Laura is one of those people *who are rarely on time.*

Directions: Each sentence contains one adjective clause. Underline the adjective clause and copy the word it modifies in the space at the left.

_____ 1. The flight on which our party was booked was canceled at the last minute.

_____ 2. Uncle Theo, who is usually very cautious when money is involved, lent Edith the down payment.

_____ 3. The meat that was served to us was so tough that I could hardly cut it.

_____ 4. Can you explain the error that caused our plan to fail?

_____ 5. I had known very little about meteors until I read the book you recommended.

_____ 6. I'm afraid that the person who told you that story imagined nine-tenths of it.

_____ 7. Did you get the name of the person whose car ran into yours?

_____ 8. The police are looking for anyone who was in the area when the fire broke out.

_____ 9. In front of the theater was a block-long line, at the very end of which we saw our two friends.

_____ 10. These con men can always find someone who's trusting, greedy, and foolish.

_____ 11. Two police officers were stationed where they could observe everyone who went through the turnstile.

_____ 12. Although three couples whom she had invited did not show up, Sylvia considered her party a success.

_____ 13. Any contribution you can make will be appreciated.

_____ 14. The new senator offered four amendments, only one of which the committee accepted.

_____ 15. As Director of Human Resources, you must often make decisions that are painful.

NAME _____   SCORE _____

Directions: Each of these sentences contains an adjective clause. None of the clauses is set off by commas. Put parentheses around each adjective clause and set off the nonrestrictive clause with commas. (Note: In some sentences, an adverb clause that relates to the adjective clause should be included in the parentheses.) In the first space at the left, write the word the clause modifies. In the second space, write R for restrictive clauses and Non for nonrestrictive clauses.

_____ _____   1. Ellen's grandfather wouldn't hire a man who smoked cigarettes while he was on the job.

_____ _____   2. The woman whom you just met is active in state and national politics.

_____ _____   3. Later Jerry met Mac Winn who is active in local politics.

_____ _____   4. Dr. Lang's lecture series for which no fee was charged drew large crowds.

_____ _____   5. Lloyd grew up in an area where there were several good ski slopes.

_____ _____   6. Lloyd later moved to Aspen where there are excellent ski slopes.

_____ _____   7. Students whose schedules were approved before the semester began will not be penalized.

_____ _____   8. Josh Field is one of the three men who founded our firm.

_____ _____   9. Josh Field who was one of the founders of our firm died in 1997.

_____ _____   10. Josh Field was a man whom everybody admired.

_____ _____   11. Here is a picture of Josh Field whose daughter is still active in the firm.

_____ _____   12. The tie you're wearing is hardly appropriate for this somber occasion.

_____ _____   13. I am sure that Leffingham is one politician for whom no reasonably intelligent person would vote.

85

_____ 14. This is a bad time of the year for anyone who is allergic to bee
_____ stings.

_____ 15. Dean's new roommate is a fellow whose parents now live in
_____ Spain.

_____ 16. Luke won't register for a course that meets before he has his mid-
_____ morning coffee.

_____ 17. Luke is registered for Speech 201 which meets daily at two
_____ o'clock.

_____ 18. Carrots are the only vegetables Junior willingly eats.
_____

_____ 19. The delegates should be housed in a hotel that is closer to the
_____ Convention Center than this one is.

_____ 20. The delegates are housed in the Windsor Hotel which is close to
_____ the Convention Center.

_____ 21. On Friday the theater will put on sale the few seats that remain
_____ unsold.

_____ 22. I am quite sure that the person to whom you gave the money was
_____ not my uncle.

_____ 23. Here is a portrait of Governor Schuyler, for whom the academy
_____ is named.

_____ 24. Mrs. Kane kept all of the letters that her son had sent her when
_____ he served in the Navy.

_____ 25. That novel was written at a time when miners lived precarious
_____ lives.

_____ 26. Kate remained in New Haven until 1997 when she received her
_____ degree in mathematics.

_____ 27. These goblets are cheaper than those you bought in Ireland.
_____

_____ 28. Jack usually has in his briefcase a crossword puzzle that he works
_____ on while riding the bus.

_____ 29. We must arrive home before eight so that Aunt Flora can see a
_____ TV drama to which she is addicted.

_____ 30. Jenkins told us about an incident he had observed while he was
_____ walking home.

Directions: The two sentences in each item can be combined into one sentence by changing the second sentence into an adjective clause. Be sure to punctuate the adjective clauses correctly.

1. Here is John Marks. He is the new Director of Communications for candidate Richards.

   _____

2. In 1903 the Wright brothers made the first powered airplane flight on Kill Devil Hill, which is near Kitty Hawk, North Carolina.

   _____

3. I keep my climbing ropes and other gear in my office. There all the gear is protected from excess humidity

   _____

4. For Christmas, my parents gave me a beautiful watch. It had belonged to my grandmother.

   _____

5. We wrote a letter of encouragement to Representative Olson. His views on the environment seem carefully thought out.

   _____

6. The grassy, open spot on the top of that hill is the place. My brothers and I used to watch for shooting stars.

   _____

7. That clock keeps exceptionally accurate time. It resets itself daily to the Naval Observatory's Atomic clock.

   _____

8. That little Italian restaurant is one of my favorite places to eat. It is located in an older section of town.

   _____

9. Yesterday in the mail I received a check. The check was for a mail-in rebate on my new scanner.

   _____

10. Hank Johnson has left the auto dealership. He sold me my new car last fall.

    _____

Lesson 10   *Subordination: Noun Clauses*

An adverbial clause such as *after the rain stopped* can work to set the time of the main verb just as the single-word adverb *yesterday* does. The adjective clause *whom I knew well* can modify our understanding of a noun in the same way the single-word adjective *tall* does. **A noun clause works in a similar way: It does the work of a regular noun.**

Noun Clauses

A **noun clause** is a group of words containing a subject–verb combination and a subordinating word. The subordinating words that serve to introduce noun clauses are conjunctions (*that, if, whether*); pronouns (*who, whom, what, which, whoever, whatever, whichever*); adjectives (*whose, which, what*); and adverbs (*when, where, why, how*). Remember that the subordinating word is part of the clause and always stands at or near the beginning of the clause.

Jill now wonders *if her answer was the correct one.*
[Noun clause subordinated by the conjunction *if.*]

All of us hope *that you'll return soon.*
[Noun clause subordinated by the conjunction *that.*]

I do not know *who he is.*
[Noun clause subordinated by the pronoun *who* used as the subjective complement within the clause.]

I know *what I would do with the extra money.*
[Noun clause subordinated by the pronoun *what* used as the direct object within the clause.]

Tell me *whom Mary is feuding with now.*
[Noun clause subordinated by the pronoun *whom* used as the object of the preposition *with.*]

You must decide *which car you will use today.*
[Noun clause subordinated by the adjective *which* modifying the direct object *car.*]

Why Morton left school still puzzles his friends.
[Noun clause subordinated by the adverb *why.*]

As you can see from these examples, a noun clause, like a noun, can be a subject, direct object, subjective complement, object of a preposition, or appositive (see page 91). You can understand the uses of the noun clause if you think of it as a clause equivalent to a "something" or a "someone" in one of these noun slots:

Subject (S)

The *girl* opened the window. [Single-word noun as S.]
Whoever came in first opened the window. [Noun clause as S.]
His *story* is very convincing. [Noun as S.]
What he told us is very convincing. [Noun clause as S.]

Copyright © 2003 by Pearson Education, Inc.

Subjective Complement (S.C.)

This is his *story*. [Single-word as S.C.]
This is *what he told us*. [Noun clause as S.C.]

Direct Object (D.O.)

Mr. Allen announced *his resignation*. [D.O. with adj.]
Mr. Allen announced *that he would resign*. [Noun clause as D.O]
Can you tell me your *time* of arrival? [Single-word as D.O.]
Can you tell me *when you will arrive*? [Noun clause as D.O.]

Object of a Preposition (O.P.)

Give the package to the *man*. [Single-word as O.P.]
Give the package to *whoever opens the door*. [Noun clause as O.P.]

Note that the choice between *who/whoever* and *whom/whomever* depends on its use in the clause. This rule creates apparently awkward and sometimes tricky choices:

Give the book to whomever you see first. [*whomever* is the object of the verb see]
Give the book to whoever answers the door. [*whoever* is the subject of the verb answers.]

(See Supplement 1.)

In noun clauses used as direct objects, the conjunction *that* is often unexpressed because the meaning is usually clear without it.

I know *that you will be happy here*.
[Noun clause subordinated by the conjunction *that*.]

I know *you will be happy here*.
[Noun clause with subordinating word omitted.]

This omission of the subordinating word creates an ellipsis, a construction similar to an elliptical adverbial clause. In adverbial clauses, the subject and part of the verb (the auxiliaries) are omitted. In this construction, only the subordinating word is omitted.

Most of the noun clauses that you read and write will be used as subjects, direct objects (the most common use), subjective complements, or objects of prepositions. However, two rather special uses should be noted, the *delayed* noun clause and the *appositive* noun clause.

Delayed Noun Clause

One common use of a noun clause is as a delayed subject. The signal for this construction is the word *it* standing in the subject position, with the meaningful subject being a noun clause following the verb:

It is unfortunate *that you were delayed*.

Although the sentence begins with "It" and the clause follows the verb, the clause is the real subject. The meaning of the sentence is "That you were delayed is unfortunate."

A related noun clause use puts the word *it* in the direct object slot with a noun clause following an objective complement. This use, which is encountered less frequently than the delayed subject, gives us a clause that we can call a delayed direct object:

We think it unlikely *that Jones will be reelected*.

Appositive Noun Clause

To understand the other special noun clause, you must know what an appositive is. An **appositive** is a noun unit inserted into a sentence to rename another noun that usually immediately precedes the appositive. A simple example occurs in the following sentence:

> Senator Jones, a dedicated environmentalist, objected.

Because any noun unit can be used as an appositive, noun clauses sometimes function in this position. Some noun clause appositives are separated from the noun they are renaming by at least a comma, sometimes by a heavier mark:

> There still remains one mystery: *how the thief knew your name.* [The noun clause renames the preceding noun, *mystery.*]

A rather special type of appositive noun clause, subordinated by *that* and following such nouns as *fact, belief, hope, statement, news,* and *argument,* is usually not set off by any mark of punctuation:

> You cannot deny the fact *that you lied under oath.*
> Your statement *that the boss is stupid* was undiplomatic.

(See Supplement 2.)

Supplement 1

You have probably already noticed that the pronouns, adjectives, and adverbs that subordinate noun clauses are essentially the same words that are used in questions (Lesson 6). The two uses are alike in the important fact that they always stand at the beginning of the clause. The two uses differ in that, as interrogatives, the words bring about the subject–verb inversion, whereas in noun clauses the subject–verb position is the normal one:

> *Whom* will the mayor appoint?
> [This sentence is a direct question; it calls for an answer. *Whom* is the D.O. of the main verb.]
>
> *I* wonder *whom the mayor will appoint.*
> [This sentence is a statement, not a direct question. Notice that a question mark is not required. *Whom* is the D.O. within the noun clause.]

Supplement 2

Because an appositive is a renamer, it represents a reduced form of a Pattern 2 sentence in which the subject and a noun subjective complement are joined by a form of *be.* The writer of the sentence "Senator Jones, a dedicated environmentalist, objected" could have written two simple sentences, the second one repeating a noun used in the first:

> Senator Jones objected.
> Senator Jones [or He] is a dedicated environmentalist.

The adjective clause offers the writer one device for compressing this information into one sentence:

Senator Jones, who is a dedicated environmentalist, objected.

The appositive represents a further compression:

Senator Jones, a dedicated environmentalist, objected.

If you think of the appositive as a renamer of the preceding noun (the two nouns could be joined by a form of *be*), you have a handy test to help you recognize any noun clause appositive use:

There still remains one mystery: *how the thief knew your name.*
[Test: The mystery *is* how the thief knew your name.]

You can't deny the fact *that she has real talent.*
[Test: The fact *is* that she has real talent.]

Your contention *that the witness lied* has some merit.
[Test: The contention *is* that the witness lied.]

If you remember a few points about the form, function, and positioning of adjective and noun clauses, you should have little difficulty in distinguishing between them. Although certain kinds of noun clauses in apposition may, at first glance, look like adjective clauses, a few simple tests clearly show the difference:

The news *that you brought us* is welcome. [Adjective clause]
The news *that Bob has recovered* is welcome. [Noun clause]

If you remember that an adjective clause is a describer and that an appositive noun clause is a renamer, you can see that in the first sentence the clause describes—in fact, identifies—the noun *news,* but it does not tell us what the news is. In the second sentence the clause does more: It tells us what the news is. Remember the *be* test. "The news is *that you brought us . . .*" does not make sense, but "The news is *that Bob has recovered . . .*" does; therefore, the second clause is a noun clause in apposition.

Another test that can be applied to these two types of sentences is based on the fact that in adjective clauses, but not in noun clauses, *which* can be substituted for *that."* The news *which* you brought us . . ." is acceptable English; the clause, in this case, is an adjective clause. But because we can't say "The news *which* Bob has recovered . . ." the clause is a noun clause; it cannot be an adjective clause.

SUMMARY OF NOUN CLAUSES

1. Function: to work as a noun within the main clause
2. Positions: subject (or delayed subject), renaming subjective complement, direct object (or delayed direct object), object of preposition, or appositive
3. Subordinators:
   a. conjunctions: *that, if, whether*
   b. pronouns: *who, whom, which, what,* and . . . *ever* forms, standing for unknown persons or things
   c. adjectives: *whose, which, what*
   d. adverbs: *when, where, why, how*
4. Special problem: Some noun appositive clauses closely resemble adjective clauses. They differ in that, in addition to describing the noun, the appositive clause renames the noun:

   The remark *that Jim made* (adjective clause) was unwise.
   The remark *that Mr. Smith cannot be trusted* (appositive noun clause) was unwise.

NAME _____   SCORE _____

Directions: Identify the use of each italicized noun clause by writing one of the following abbreviations in the space at the left:

    S.   [subject or delayed subject]   S.C.   [subjective complement]
    D.O. [direct object or delayed   O.P.   [object of preposition]
           direct object]   Ap.   [appositive]

_____   1. It seems fair *that the finder of the wallet should keep the money.*

_____   2. The highway department has not yet decided *which route the new highway will follow.*

_____   3. The clever swindler sold the phony stock to *whoever was gullible enough to believe him.*

_____   4. Because of the good condition of the car, no one believes *that it has 90,000 miles on it.*

_____   5. The players were excited about *what the coach told them.*

_____   6. My best estimate is *that very few people will flunk the test.*

_____   7. *Whoever finds the most Easter eggs* will receive a live bunny as a prize.

_____   8. Did he really ask *if I would lend him $200?*

_____   9. All the students were discussing *how they might best study for the exam.*

_____   10. Please return the package to *whoever gave it to you.*

_____   11. The forecaster considers it unlikely *that the weather will be cloudy again tomorrow.*

_____   12. *What course of action the legislature will take* is not clear now.

_____   13. The finished picture will contain *whatever you see in the viewfinder.*

_____   14. His suggestion *that we burn all the leaves* is not a wise one in this dry weather

_____   15. For his school expenses James depends on *whatever he earns during the summer vacation.*

_____   16. Our main problem right now is *that we must get the snow off the roof without delay.*

_____   17. We could not sway Jane's opinion *that she is the best choice for president of the senior class.*

_____   18. *Whoever is now using my prescription sunglasses* could damage his eyes.

_____   19. Can you show us *where copies of property deeds are kept?*

_____   20. Mr. Stanton's response to our proposal was not *what we had expected.*

95

Directions: Each of the following sentences contains one noun clause. Put parentheses ( ) around each noun clause. In the space at the left, write one of the following to identify the use of the noun clause:

S.	[subject or delayed subject]	S.C.	[subjective complement]
D.O.	[direct object or delayed direct object]	O.P.	[object of preposition]
		Ap.	[appositive]

Remember that a noun clause may be part of another subordinate clause or may include another subordinate clause within it.

_____ 1. We should concern ourselves with how these developments will affect future students at the college.

_____ 2. It is conceivable that almost 75 percent of our graduates will enter some business.

_____ 3. The president was surprised by the fact that the mail contained no complaints about his decision.

_____ 4. The reason for our early arrival is that we left home this morning before the sun had risen.

_____ 5. When Mr. Jordan heard that Sue had applied for a job, he called the bank president for a recommendation.

_____ 6. What happened at graduation makes a very funny story.

_____ 7. Many of the students were happy about what happened at graduation.

_____ 8. I'm afraid that what happened at graduation might prove embarrassing to the school.

_____ 9. I know that anyone you recommend will do a good job for us.

_____ 10. The office staff will offer help to whoever gets the job.

_____ 11. Everyone I've talked to seems interested in whatever will reduce taxes.

_____ 12. You can be sure that whoever takes the job will earn every penny he makes.

_____ 13. Our decision is that if a player misses practice she may not play in the next game.

_____ 14. The only suggestion Barbara made was that we should undertake a cake sale as a fund-raising project.

_____ 15. What do you think of Barbara's suggestion that we should undertake a cake sale as a fund-raising project?

_____ 16. Until I saw the redwoods, I never realized how truly awesome a single tree could be.

_____ 17. What I discovered yesterday is extremely important to the success of the experiment.

_____ 18. Whoever called me about the apartment should be here shortly.

_____ 19. It now seems highly unlikely that we can get away early for the holiday.

_____ 20. The reason for the delay is that we are waiting for the caterer to deliver the box lunches.

Exercise 10   *Noun Clauses*

NAME _____   SCORE _____

Directions: Each of the following sentences contains one noun clause. Put parentheses around each noun clause and identify its use by writing one of the following in the space at the left.

S.	[subject or delayed subject]	S.C.	[subjective complement]
D.O.	[direct object or delayed direct object]	O.P.	[object of preposition]
		Ap.	[appositive]

_____ 1. The teacher told Stan that he would very likely receive a passing grade.

_____ 2. Our greatest fear now is that the dam on the south fork of the river might collapse.

_____ 3. Do you believe what Judy said about her brother's income?

_____ 4. One of your troubles is that you are too gullible.

_____ 5. Whatever you say from now on will only get you into deeper trouble.

_____ 6. Some players think it possible that the rules will be changed next year.

_____ 7. Mr. Chandler has never revealed who gave him the information for that important story.

_____ 8. The rumor that Andy won the lottery has been spreading around town lately.

_____ 9. I will never believe that Andy won the lottery.

_____ 10. The real culprit is whoever started the completely unfounded rumor.

_____ 11. All of us are pleased with what you have accomplished.

_____ 12. It is now clear that others knew the location of the treasure.

_____ 13. But all of you know I'm right.

_____ 14. Will someone show me how this contraption works?

_____ 15. What you have just been told must never be passed on to anyone else.

_____ 16. If you thought that the traffic would be heavy, why didn't you leave earlier?

_____ 17. The idea that Martin would someday be the CEO of a major company never occurred to any of his high school friends.

_____ 18. Whoever installed that outdoor light did an excellent piece of work.

_____ 19. Our chances of winning the conference championship depend on how well the relay team performs this afternoon.

_____ 20. Elsa's fondest hope is that she will find a job in Paris after she graduates.

Directions: Combine the following pairs of word groups into a single sentence by joining the second to the first as a noun clause.

1. The only question is (something). Why you decided to move into that apartment in the first place.

   _____

2. Your friends will have only one question. Why you decided to move into that apartment in the first place.

   _____

3. Please give this message to (someone). Whoever comes to the door when you knock.

   _____

4. (Something) was not clear from that phone call. Whether you still want to meet for lunch.

   _____

5. (Someone) should be a little embarrassed. Whoever did the proofreading on that first page in the paper.

   _____

6. That announcement did not surprise anyone. (The announcement was that) Jim is leaving next week for a new job.

   _____

7. Did you know (something)? We were having lunch downtown at the time.

   _____

8. Some staff members think (something) is possible. This policy will be changed soon.

   _____

9. The teacher told Marcia (something). She needs to study harder for the next test.

   _____

10. (Something) was very fortunate. The people in that car were wearing seat belts.

    _____

Exercise 10A

Subordinate Clauses

NAME _____   SCORE _____

Directions: The italicized material in each of these sentences is a subordinate clause. In the space at the left, write one of the following to identify the clause.

> Adv. [adverb clause]   Adj. [adjective clause]   N. [noun clause]

_____ 1. The park ranger warned the group *that he would not be responsible for their safety if they continued the climb.*

_____ 2. Ms. Strom explained to the children that the birds *that they had spotted in the fir tree* were starlings.

_____ 3. *If you can tell us the name of the capital of Zimbabwe,* you'll win a year's supply of detergent.

_____ 4. Andy's poor grades in mathematics partially explain *why he never became an engineer.*

_____ 5. The car was registered in the name of a local entrepreneur *whom the FBI had been seeking.*

_____ 6. The evening celebration was not entirely successful *because the noisy fireworks made a few of the children hysterical.*

_____ 7. The advertisement reported that a handsome reward would go to *whoever finds the missing briefcase.*

_____ 8. Our governor is a forgiving man; he recently appointed to the Board of Regents a woman *who once called him incompetent.*

_____ 9. Mr. Benson beamed when the photographer told him *that he looked quite youthful for a man of sixty-five.*

_____ 10. Time relationships sometimes become confused for people *as they grow older.*

_____ 11. *As his hostess told Tim the Latin names for the flowers,* he busily wrote them in his notebook.

_____ 12. "Anyone can see *why experts call this painting a masterpiece,*" said the pompous guide.

_____ 13. The food was greasy and overcooked *although the half-starved hikers considered it very tasty.*

_____ 14. The carpet *that your store sent me* is not what I ordered.

_____ 15. The story *she told us* left us speechless.

99

_____ 16. During "show-and-tell" time in the lower grades, children sometimes report on family events *that should be kept secret.*

_____ 17. After the trial period the boss and her three assistants will decide *what your salary will be.*

_____ 18. "I think your concluding paragraph will be more effective *if you make it shorter by about half,*" said the teacher.

_____ 19. Official announcements from the White House have been enthusiastic, *although a few spokespersons remain cautious.*

_____ 20. Home owners in the Mud Lake area worry about what could happen if fire breaks out *while the water pressure is low.*

_____ 21. The three children were discussing an important matter: *what kind of dessert their mother should serve them.*

_____ 22. At a press conference tomorrow a representative of the search committee will announce *who the five finalist are.*

_____ 23. A recently hired night watchman is apparently the person *who had turned the burglar alarm off.*

_____ 24. An accountant *whom Peter knew only casually* came forth with the bail money.

_____ 25. We finally found a place *where we could store our goods.*

_____ 26. We are looking for a whitewater river *where we can do some exciting kayaking.*

_____ 27. My son will drive you *wherever you need to go this afternoon.*

_____ 28. *After looking in several stores for a shirt of that color,* I finally found it in that little store right down the street from my office.

_____ 29. *If we don't go home this weekend,* we might not get another chance for several weeks.

_____ 30. Pamela doesn't know *if she will be able to finish that paper by tomorrow morning.*

Directions: In each pair of word groups, use the first group as a main clause and add the second to the first by making it an adjective clause, an adverb clause, or a noun clause. Rewrite enough of the two word groups to make the new sentence clear. Identify the subordinate clause you have created by writing one of the following in the space at the left:

Adv. [adverb clause]   Adj. [adjective clause]   N. [noun clause]

_____   1. Jensen was delighted.
             He landed a big contract.

_____   2. Not everyone in the class knew (something).
             The due date for the paper had been changed.

_____   3. Andrew always remembers with great fondness that spot.
             (The spot is) where he proposed to his wife.

_____   4. By noon it was certain.
             The game would be rained out.

_____   5. The weight was so heavy (that something happened).
             I dropped it with a crash in the middle of the floor.

_____   6. You need to follow the steps in the instructions (in a certain way).
             Exactly as I have written them.

_____   7. Please give this message to anyone.
             Who comes to the meeting from my office.

_____   8. Please give this message to (someone).
             Whoever comes to the meeting from my office.

_____   9. The person is sitting at the first desk on your right.
             The person can help you with your problem.

_____ 10. We might need to cut down that tree.
             Lightning struck it last night.

Directions: In place of the *someone* or *something* in the first sentence, put a noun clause formed from the idea of the second sentence or phrase. The suggested subordinating word is provided in parentheses.

> *Example:*   *Someone* should turn on the heat. (whoever)
> The person who gets to the cabin first.

Whoever gets to the cabin first should turn on the heat.

1. I know *something*. (what)
   The thing that needs to be done to solve that problem.

2. They all hope *something*. (that)
   We can finish this project by Friday.

3. Jim understands *something*. (how)
   How that program works.

4. Have you decided *something*? (where)
   The place you want to spend your vacation.

5. We need to tell Dad *something*. (when)
   The time he should pick us up at the airport.

6. You should have *something* by tomorrow morning. (whatever)
   The things you need to finish the new cabinets.

7. *Someone* should move that car. (whoever)
   The person who left it in my driveway.

8. They think *something* is unlikely. (that)
   Jim will arrive in time for the meeting.

9. *Someone* should return my textbook and lecture notes. (whoever)
   The person who picked them up by mistake.

10. I just figured *something* out. (how)
    The way I can print my article in three columns per page.

Lesson 11 *Subordination: Gerund and Infinitive Phrases*

A **phrase** is a group of related words that does *not* contain a subject and a verb in combination. Like the subordinate clause, the phrase is used in a sentence as a single part of speech. Many of the sentences that you have studied so far have contained a prepositional phrase, which consists of a preposition, a noun or a pronoun used as its object, and any modifiers of the object. Most prepositional phrases are used as adjectives or adverbs:

> Most *of my friends* live *in the East.*
> [The first phrase is used as an adjective to modify the pronoun *most;* the second is used as an adverb to modify the verb *live.*]

Much less commonly, a prepositional phrase is used as a noun:

> *Before lunch* is the best time for the meeting.
> [The phrase is the subject of the verb *is.*]

> She waved to us from *inside the phone booth.*
> [The phrase is the object of the preposition *from.*]

Another very important kind of phrase makes use of a verbal. A **verbal** is a word formed from a verb but used as a different part of speech. There are three kinds of verbals: the gerund, the infinitive, and the participle.

Gerunds

A **gerund** is a noun formed by adding *-ing* either to the base of the verb *(studying)* or to an auxiliary *(having studied, being studied, having been studied).* You might think of the gerund phrase as the equivalent of a noun. It can appear in any place in a sentence where a noun might appear: subject, direct object, renaming subjective complement, object of preposition, or (rarely) appositive.

> *Studying* demands most of my time. [Subject]
> I usually enjoy *studying.* [Direct object]
> My main activity is *studying.* [Renaming subjective complement]
> You won't pass the course without *studying.* [Object of preposition]
> Might I suggest to you another activity: *studying*? [Appositive]

These single-word gerund uses are uncomplicated. "He enjoys *studying*" and "He enjoys football" are alike in their structure; the only difference is that in one the direct object is a word formed from a verb and in the other it is a regular noun. Because they are formed from verbs, and are thus "verbal nouns," gerunds can have a direct object or a subjective complement. The following examples will help to clarify this important point.

He enjoys *walking in the snow.*
[The gerund has no complement. Compare "He walks in the snow."]

She enjoys building model airplanes.
[*Airplanes* is the direct object of the gerund *building.* Compare "She builds model airplanes."]

He enjoys *being helpful.* He enjoyed *being elected treasurer.*
[*Helpful* is the subjective complement of the gerund *being; treasurer* is the subjective complement of the passive gerund *being elected.* Compare "He is helpful." and "He was elected treasurer."]

She enjoyed *telling us the good news.*
[*Us* is the indirect object and *news* is the direct object of the gerund *telling.* Compare "She told us the good news."]

He enjoyed *making our vacation pleasant.*
[*Vacation* is the direct object of the gerund *making* and *pleasant* the objective complement of *vacation.* Compare "He made our vacation pleasant."]

Infinitives

An **infinitive** is a verbal consisting of the base of the verb, usually preceded by *to* (*to* is called the sign of the infinitive). The infinitive uses auxiliaries to show tense and voice: *to study, to have studied, to be studying, to have been studying, to be studied, to have been studied.* An **infinitive phrase** consists of an infinitive plus its modifiers and/or complements. Infinitive units are used as nouns, as adjectives, and as adverbs:

To attend the party without an invitation would be tactless.
[The infinitive phrase is used as the subject of the sentence. Within the phrase, *party* is the direct object.]

It would be tactless *to attend the party without an invitation.*
[In this pattern the infinitive phrase is called a delayed subject; hence it serves a noun use. The signal word is *it; although it* stands in subject position, the infinitive phrase is the meaningful subject. Sometimes the *it* is in the direct object slot with the delayed infinitive phrase following an objective complement: I would consider it tactless *to attend the party without an invitation.* Compare a similar noun clause use in Lesson 10.]

I wanted *to give Charles another chance.*
[The infinitive phrase is the direct object of *wanted.* Within the phrase, *Charles* is the indirect object and *chance* the direct object of the infinitive. Compare "I gave Charles another chance."]

My plan is *to become an active precinct worker.*
[The infinitive phrase is used as a noun; it is a subjective complement that renames the subject *plan.* Within the phrase, *worker* is the subjective complement of the infinitive. Compare "I became an active precinct worker."]

The test *to be taken next Friday* is an important one.
[The infinitive phrase is used as an adjective modifying *test.*]

I am happy *to meet you.*
[The infinitive phrase is used as an adverb modifying the adjective *happy.*]

To be sure of a good seat, you should arrive early.
[The infinitive phrase is used as an adverb modifying *should arrive.*]

Infinitive phrases sometimes include their own subjects. Notice that when a pronoun is used as the subject of an infinitive, the pronoun is in the objective case (see Lesson 24).

> We wanted *her to resign.*
> We know *him to be a good referee.*

In a rather common sentence type, the subject of an infinitive is preceded by *for,* which in this case is considered part of the phrase.

> *For us to leave now* would be impolite.
> It's silly *for you to feel neglected.*

The infinitive without *to* may form a phrase that is used as the direct object of such verbs as *let, help, make, see, hear,* and *watch:*

> The teacher let *us leave early.*
> Martha watched *her son score the winning touchdown.*

The infinitive without *to* is also sometimes used as the object of a preposition, such as *except, but,* or *besides:*

> He could do nothing except *resign gracefully.*
> He did everything but *write the paper for me.*

Supplement 1

In Lesson 6 you learned that an interrogative unit in a direct question stands at the beginning of the sentence. Notice how this positioning can affect the internal makeup of a gerund phrase or an infinitive phrase:

> *How many natives* did the missionaries succeed in *converting*?
> [*Converting* is the gerund form of a transitive verb and therefore requires a direct object, in this case *natives.*]

> *Which car* did you finally decide *to buy*?
> [*Car* is the direct object of the infinitive *to buy.*]

Supplement 2

When the gerund is preceded by a pronoun, the pronoun should be in the possessive case.

> The audience *enjoyed Maria's dancing in the first act.*
> [Compare "The audience enjoyed Maria's dance in the first act."]

> We appreciated *your helping the class with that project.*
> [Compare "We appreciated your help with that project."]

SUMMARY OF GERUND PHRASES; INFINITIVE PHRASES

Gerund Phrases

1. Forms: *studying, having studied, being studied, having been studied*
2. Function: as a noun within the larger unit
3. Positions: subject, renaming subjective complement, direct object, object of preposition, and (rarely) appositive

Infinitive Phrases

1. Forms: *to study, to have studied, to be studying, to have been studying, to be studied, to have been studied.* Some infinitive phrases have subjects (We wanted her to run for office) in the objective case.
2. Function: as adjective (Here are the letters *to be mailed today*), as adverb (I am happy *to meet you*), or as noun (*To leave* now would be unwise)
3. Positions: subject (or delayed subject), direct object (or delayed direct object), renaming subjective complement, and (rarely) object of preposition.
4. Special structures:
   a. *For* sometimes introduces an infinitive phrase that has a subject.

      For you to criticize his work would be presumptuous.

   b. A phrase with a subject but without the marker *to* is often used as a direct object following one of these verbs: *let, help, make, see, hear, watch:*

      Mother let *us mix the cookie dough.*
      Ms. Jones heard *the man threaten the cashier.*

   c. The infinitive without *to* is used as object of prepositions *except, but, besides.*

      He could do nothing but *leave quietly.*

NAME _____   SCORE _____

Directions: In the space at the left, copy one of the following abbreviations to identify the use of the italicized gerund phrase:

    S.   [subject]   S.C. [subjective complement]
    D.O. [direct object]   O.P   [object of preposition]

_____ 1. The children surprised us *by washing all of the dishes, pots, and pans.*

_____ 2. *Packing the station wagon* was in itself a half-day's chore.

_____ 3. Why don't you try *using a coarser blade on the slicing machine?*

_____ 4. Many students object strenuously to the school's *increasing the parking fee.*

_____ 5. Betty's worst habit is constantly *interrupting other people's stories.*

_____ 6. *Disciplining the child before strangers* is not recommended.

_____ 7. *By using a better grade of gasoline,* you could eliminate that engine knock.

_____ 8. I always enjoy *showing visitors our beautiful campus.*

_____ 9. "Professor, would you mind *repeating that formula?*" asked Lou.

_____ 10. A favorite student pastime is *criticizing the dormitory food.*

_____ 11. *Collecting old shaving mugs* seems to me a rather peculiar activity.

_____ 12. Within a few years the small country was successful in *raising the literacy level.*

_____ 13. Some of the dissidents even discussed *forming a new political party.*

_____ 14. Nothing annoys me more than *watching these repeated TV commercials.*

_____ 15. The committee finished *tabulating the ballots* and reported the results to the chairman.

_____ 16. *Taking part in election campaigns* is good experience for young people.

_____ 17. For years Ted's hobby has been *making his own trout flies.*

_____ 18. Isn't *keeping studded tires on your car all year* illegal in this state?

_____ 19. "Have you ever considered *wearing a larger size?*" the shoe clerk asked.

_____ 20. Why don't you ride your bike instead of *thumbing a ride to school every day?*

107

Directions: In the space at the left, write one of the following abbreviations to identify the use within the sentence of the italicized infinitive phrase:

    N. [noun (subject, delayed subject,   Adj. [adjective]
        direct object, subjective complement,   Adv. [adverb]
        object of preposition)]

_____ 1. *To select an option from this menu,* press the designated number on the phone.

_____ 2. We will make a great effort *to correct that problem in your account.*

_____ 3. Please help *me find that route on the map.*

_____ 4. *To teach you a few new things in word processing* was the reason Jim came today.

_____ 5. In the morning the staff will make another attempt *to install that program.*

_____ 6. You should try *to avoid that construction zone on I-27 going north.*

_____ 7. I think I'll be prepared *to take that test in the morning.*

_____ 8. All new students need *to check with the counseling staff before Friday.*

_____ 9. Janice will not be able *to go with us tomorrow morning.*

_____ 10. *To improve my typing speed* is the reason I took that class.

_____ 11. Al's idea was *to work late today and finish the project.*

_____ 12. "I've done everything but *type the final copy of the paper,*" said Marta.

_____ 13. We watched *the crane operator lift the steel onto the roof of the building.*

_____ 14. Mark's efforts *to improve his spelling* have produced great results.

_____ 15. "Today's first priority is *to find that lost file on the Matthews case,*" said Art.

_____ 16. My little brother wants *to learn something about gorillas.*

_____ 17. Can you let *us work a little longer on this problem?*

_____ 18. We need a new way *to keep track of our hours on these projects.*

_____ 19. "We can't do anything except *start over in the morning,*" said Cathy.

_____ 20. Would it be possible *to send me another copy of that prospectus?*

NAME _____   SCORE _____

Directions: Each sentence contains one gerund phrase. Underline it. In the space at the left, write one of the following abbreviations to identify the use of the gerund phrase.

    S.   [subject]   S.C.   [subjective complement]
    D.O. [direct object]   O.P.   [object of preposition]

_____ 1. Walking three miles a day might be a good thing for your health.

_____ 2. That neighborhood committee argued against making Church Street a one-way street.

_____ 3. The hardest part of that project was finding the sources of information.

_____ 4. Organizing the final version of the paper was also a difficult task.

_____ 5. We got great satisfaction from handing the paper in on time.

_____ 6. I certainly enjoyed learning about the early history of the town.

_____ 7. Those players should try working out with weights to improve their strength.

_____ 8. Last summer my parents enjoyed driving on the Blue Ridge Parkway.

_____ 9. We can make up that lost time by taking that shortcut over the mountain.

_____ 10. Having coffee on the porch is an enjoyable way to start the day.

_____ 11. An enjoyable way to start the day is having coffee on the porch.

_____ 12. I like to start my day by having coffee on the porch.

_____ 13. Do you enjoy having coffee on the porch?

_____ 14. The new manager encourages arriving on time for work every day.

———— 15. Trying to find that lost file took us almost two hours.

———— 16. The most frustrating part of my job today was finding that lost file.

———— 17. Since beginning my work here at the college, I have improved my GPA.

———— 18. My objective for this semester is improving my GPA.

———— 19. Improving my GPA required a careful selection of courses and some very hard work.

———— 20. The first step in that research project is administering a survey to twenty volunteers.

Directions: Each sentence contains one infinitive phrase (some with subjects). Underline each infinitive phrase. In the space at the left, write one of the following abbreviations to identify the use of the phrase in the sentence:

N. [noun (subject, delayed subject,   Adj. [adjective]   Adv. [adverb]
subjective complement, direct
object, object of preposition)]

_____ 1. The instructor asked us to close our books in preparation for taking the quiz.

_____ 2. It required a great deal of time and effort to locate Jim in Alaska.

_____ 3. Our first idea was to call a tow truck for help with the dead battery.

_____ 4. It was extremely difficult to decide between the convertible and the hardtop.

_____ 5. Lauren recently bought a Zip drive to use as a backup for her computer files.

_____ 6. "I'm not quite ready to leave yet," said Al, opening another file on his computer.

_____ 7. The new computer lets us gain access to the Internet without any delay.

_____ 8. Can't we do anything but watch while the boat sinks?

_____ 9. It is very important for you to be at the meeting tomorrow morning.

_____ 10. The boss wants everyone to be at the meeting tomorrow morning.

_____ 11. To be sure your car is ready, call the service department before you leave the office.

_____ 12. I was delighted to see Mary after all these months.

_____ 13. The work to be done tomorrow is the most important of the week.

_____ 14. We wanted to avoid that band of severe weather moving across the state.

_____ 15. It would be smart to plan our trip around the baseball schedule.

_____ 16. To stay awake during that boring movie was a major accomplishment.

_____ 17. We asked him to get us reservations for dinner.

_____ 18. We all heard him shout as his raft flipped in the rapids.

_____ 19. Where have you decided to go on your vacation?

_____ 20. It would be pointless to try calling Jim at this hour of the morning.

Directions: Combine the two sentences in each item into a single sentence by resolving one sentence into a gerund phrase or an infinitive phrase to replace the italicized word(s) in the other sentence.

1. Mowing the lawn was no longer difficult.
   It was no longer difficult *to do something* once we bought a new riding lawn mower.

   _____

2. Finding that lost book is our first job for today.
   Our first job for today is *to do something*.

   _____

3. You can buy tickets for the game over the Internet.
   It is very convenient *to do something*.

   _____

4. Our only choice at that point was *something*.
   We had to turn around and go back to the house.

   _____

5. If you call tech support, perhaps the people there can help *you do something*.
   They can help you correct that problem with your new computer.

   _____

6. The storm struck without any warning.
   Without *doing something*, the storm struck.

   _____

7. As a young girl, Margaret lived in seven different cities.
   Doing something as a young girl made Margaret quite flexible.

   _____

8. When the Thompsons first moved into town, they needed to find a house.
   Doing something was the Thompson's first job when the moved into town.

   _____

9. Andrew wants to hit .300 in this upcoming baseball season.
   For the upcoming baseball season *doing something* is Andrew's goal.

   _____

10. Barb drives her new BMW every time she has an excuse.
    Barb enjoys *doing something*.

   _____

Lesson 12 — *Subordination: Participial and Absolute Phrases*

A **participle** is an adjective formed from a verb by adding *ing* or *ed* to the base form of the verb (*studying, studied*) or to an auxiliary (*having studied, being studied, having been studied*). (Note that many verbs have irregular past participles. See pages 204–205 for lists of such verbs.) By itself, a participle works exactly as any one-word adjective works:

> The *injured* bird clung to the *swaying* branch.
> [The past participle *injured* modifies the noun *bird;* the present participle *swaying* modifies the noun *branch.*]

Often, however, the participle is combined with other words to form a **participial phrase** that modifies a noun.

> The taxi driver, *being a war veteran,* signed the petition.
> [The participial phrase modifies the noun *taxi driver.* Within the phrase, *veteran* is a subjective complement.]
>
> *Calling the man a hero,* the mayor gave him an award.
> [The participial phrase modifies the noun *mayor.* Within the phrase, *man* is a direct object and *hero* is an objective complement.]

Participial Phrases

The similarity between an adjective clause and a participial phrase is obvious:

1. A man grabbed the microphone. The man [*or* He] was wearing a black mask.
   [Two independent clauses.]

   a. A clown *who was wearing a painted mask* grabbed the microphone.
   [Adjective clause. *Mask* is a direct object of the verb.]
   b. A clown *wearing a painted mask* grabbed the microphone.
   [Participial phrase. *Mask* is a direct object of the participle.]

2. Jo's parents left the concert early. They found the music uncomfortably loud.
   [Two independent clauses.]

   a. Jo's parents, *who found the music uncomfortably loud,* left the concert early.
   [Adjective clause. *Music* is a direct object and *loud* an objective complement.]
   b. Jo's parents, *finding the music uncomfortably loud,* left the concert early.
   [Participial phrase. *Music* is a direct object and *loud* an objective complement.]

These two examples point out another similarity: Like the adjective clause, the participial phrase can be either restrictive or nonrestrictive. The phrase in the first example identifies the clown; it is restrictive and is not set off by commas. The phrase in the second example is not needed to identify parents; it requires commas because it is nonrestrictive.

Like adjective clauses, participial phrases must be very close to the noun they modify. An adjective clause must follow the noun it modifies. A restrictive (identifying) participial phrase normally follows the noun it modifies, as in the example, "A man wearing a black mask. . . ." Unlike a nonrestrictive adjective clause, however, a nonrestrictive participial phrase can move into another position in the sentence. Observe the positions of the participial phrase in the following sentences:

Steve, having passed the test with flying colors, decided to celebrate.
Having passed the test with flying colors, Steve decided to celebrate.

Occasionally, the participial phrase can be moved to the end of the clause:

Steve decided to celebrate, having passed the test with flying colors.

Because a participle is an adjective formed from a verb and thus suggests an action, the participial phrase can be used to relieve the monotony of a series of short, independent clauses:

Pam wanted desperately to hear the rock concert, but she was temporarily short of funds, and she knew that her cousin Alice had an extra ticket, and so she decided to call her. [Four independent clauses]

Wanting desperately to hear the rock concert but being temporarily short of funds, Pam decided to call her cousin Alice, knowing that she had an extra ticket. [One independent clause and three participial phrases]

Jensen stood at home plate. He waggled his bat. He eyed the pitcher coldly. He took a mighty swing at the first pitch. He hit the ball out of the park. [Five independent clauses]

Standing at home plate, waggling his bat, and eyeing the pitcher coldly, Jensen took a mighty swing at the first pitch, hitting the ball out of the park. [One independent clause and four participial phrases]

Absolute Phrases

The **absolute phrase** is a special kind of phrase, different from the standard participial phrase in both form and function. Within the absolute phrase, the participle follows a noun or a pronoun that is part of the phrase. The phrase adds to the meaning of the whole sentence, but it does not directly modify any noun or pronoun in the sentence. The absolute phrase is a versatile structure capable of many variations and widely used in modern writing to point out subtle relationships underlying the ideas within a sentence:

All things being equal, Mary should easily win the race.

The storm having passed, the ball game resumed.

The police recovered eight of the paintings, *three of them badly damaged.*

The mob reached the palace gates, *the leader (being) a burly, red-haired sailor.*
[Occasionally an absolute phrase having a noun and a complement appears with the participle unexpressed.]

A special kind of phrase using *with* to introduce the absolute phrase can add subtle modifying and narrative coloring to a sentence:

With the band playing and the crowd applauding furiously, Jim Kinman was obviously uncomfortable as he stood on the stage.

They held the funeral on the second day, *with the town coming to look at Miss Emily beneath a mass of bought flowers, with the crayon face of her father musing profoundly above the bier. . . .* (William Faulkner)

But we can't possibly have a garden party *with a dead man just outside the front gate.* (Katherine Mansfield)

The face was a curious mixture of sensibility, *with some elements very hard and others very pretty*—perhaps it was in the mouth. (Katherine Anne Porter)

Notice that the *with* in this construction is quite unlike *with* in its common prepositional use:

The acquitted woman left the courtroom *with her* lawyer.
[*with* used as a preposition]

The acquitted woman left the courtroom *with her head held high.*
[*with* used to introduce the absolute phrase]

SUMMARY OF PARTICIPIAL PHRASES; ABSOLUTE PHRASES

Participial Phrases

1. Forms: *studying, studied, having studied, being studied, having been studied, having been studying*
2. Function: to modify a noun or pronoun. Those that identify the noun or pronoun are restrictive and require no punctuation; others are nonrestrictive and are set off by commas.
3. Position: if restrictive, always following the word it modifies. Nonrestrictive phrases may stand after the noun, at the beginning of the sentence, and occasionally at the end of the sentence.

Absolute Phrases

1. Form: a noun or pronoun followed by a participle

   The crops having failed, Grandfather sold the farm.

2. Function: adds to the meaning of the entire sentence but does not modify a word or fill a noun "slot"
3. Position: at the beginning, in the interior, or at the end of the larger unit; usually set off by commas
4. Special structures:
   a. The participle *being* is sometimes unexpressed.

   Its chairman [being] a retired military person, the committee is well disciplined.

   b. The phrase sometimes begins with the word *with.*

   With its supply of ammunition exhausted, the garrison surrendered.

Participial and Absolute Phrases

NAME _____ SCORE _____

Directions: The italicized unit in each sentence is either a participial phrase or an absolute phrase. If the noun is a participial phrase, copy in the space at the left the noun or pronoun that the phrase modifies. If the unit is an absolute phrase, leave the space blank. Be prepared to discuss in class the complements, if any, within the phrases.

NOTE: Review also the other verbal phrases. Of the following sentences, some contain gerund phrases, others infinitive phrases.

_____ 1. *Summoned by the Senate committee*, the company president appeared in the committee room with his lawyer.

_____ 2. The men finally left for the field at noon, *the truck having been repaired*.

_____ 3. The crowd applauded wildly, *clearly delighted by the singer's performance*.

_____ 4. The storm, *having dumped ten inches of rain on the town*, threatened residential neighborhoods.

_____ 5. *The storm having dumped ten inches of rain on the town,* the mayor hastily summoned volunteers for work on the dikes.

_____ 6. The boys, *working furiously in the storm*, tried desperately to shore the dike.

_____ 7. "*My paper finally finished*, I think I'll take the rest of the night off," said Marilyn.

_____ 8. The woman *running the drill press* stopped work and left her machine.

_____ 9. "None of our running plays are working" lamented the coach, *his offense having gained only twenty yards in the first half*.

_____ 10. The team, *clearly overmatched by its opponent*, worked desperately at getting its offense started.

_____ 11. *With its offense in a desperate situation*, the team was forced to rely on the defense to keep the game close.

_____ 12. *The concert having ended early*, Ellis and Marge decided to go for dinner.

_____ 13. *Walking slowly from the room,* the students headed out the door and down the hall.

_____ 14. The students moved across the campus, *there being nothing to do except go home for the day.*

_____ 15. Mark, *still looking for a part-time job,* spent every morning at the school's employment office.

_____ 16. *Packing up her books,* Alicia moved to the back of the room without looking at anyone.

_____ 17. *Finding no seats available at the back,* Alicia walked through the door and out of the classroom.

_____ 18. *With no seats available at the back of the classroom,* Alicia was forced to wait outside until class was over.

_____ 19. "There are no new developments in the Rafferty case," said the announcer, *turning to another news item.*

_____ 20. *"There being no new developments in the Rafferty case,"* said the announcer, "let's turn to the next news item."

_____ 21. "Cars *left in the lot overnight* will be towed," said the sign.

_____ 22. *With the last problem on the test completed,* I handed in my paper and left the room.

_____ 23. My brother, *having locked his keys in his car,* called me for a ride.

_____ 24. Jim left for work early today, *needing to put the finishing touches on his presentation before the meeting started.*

_____ 25. *Taking a ten dollar bill from her wallet,* the woman said, "I'll take two boxes of the oatmeal cookies, please."

_____ 26. Watson, *being the new man on the team,* was often asked to do minor, uninteresting tasks.

_____ 27. *With no one supervising the parking lot,* people seemed to park pretty much at random without regard to the marked spaces.

_____ 28. *Waving their strange signs over their heads,* the fans tried to attract the attention of the camera operator.

_____ 29. *With their strange signs held high overhead,* the fans tried to attract the attention of the camera operator.

_____ 30. The audience left the auditorium, *laughing softly at the speaker's last story.*

Exercise 12 — *Participial and Absolute Phrases*

NAME _____ SCORE _____

Directions: Each of the following sentences contains one participial or one absolute phrase. Under-line the phrase. If it is a participial phrase, copy in the space at the left the noun or pronoun that the phrase modifies. If it is an absolute phrase, leave the space blank.

_____ 1. The first students having arrived, the instructor began to pass out copies of the lecture outline.

_____ 2. The donuts, having just been put on the shelf, were warm and fresh.

_____ 3. Martin rushed into the meeting late, his alarm clock having failed to go off at 6:00 A.M.

_____ 4. Having failed to hear his alarm clock, Martin rushed into the meeting a few minutes late.

_____ 5. Gathering at 2:00 P.M., the members of the selection committee began to debate the qualifications of the candidates for the position.

_____ 6. With Reynolds out for a few weeks with a sprained knee, Gonza-lez has taken over as the everyday shortstop.

_____ 7. The children, enchanted by the fairy tales recited by the actors, sat quietly in their seats for almost an hour.

_____ 8. Looking at all the possibilities, I've decided that taking the job in Centerville is my best strategy.

_____ 9. All the possibilities having been examined closely, I've decided that taking the job in Centerville is my best strategy.

_____ 10. Having just completed an intense workout, Mary Ellen left the gym to look for some lunch.

_____ 11. At 7:30 P.M. the ushers closed the doors, all the seats for the recital having been filled by that time.

_____ 12. Everyone needing to buy the textbook tonight should use our thirty-minute break to go to the bookstore.

_____ 13. The old tools were extremely rusty, the weather having taken its toll on them over the years.

_____ 14. The game ended on a high note, Mike's hit having scored the winning run in the bottom of the ninth.

_____ 15. Having finished baling all the hay, the men brought the truck to the field to haul it away.

_____ 16. The rain having settled in for the day, we tied off the boat and went home.

_____ 17. The collapse of the computer system ended our day's work, giving us time to go to a movie.

_____ 18. "I think, having finished my report, that I will go out for a long, leisurely lunch," said Mary Catherine.

_____ 19. "I think I will go out for a long, leisurely lunch," said Mary Catherine, picking up her purse and walking out of the office.

_____ 20. With Tom arriving to take my place tomorrow, I'll feel good about starting my vacation.

_____ 21. Everyone wanting to register by mail for the conference should mail the application form and the check before March 15th.

_____ 22. Bobby Jo is leaving for Spain next week, her work on that project successfully completed.

_____ 23. The last orders having been shipped, the clerks in the shipping department went home for the day.

_____ 24. The police officer directing traffic around the construction project was forced to stand out in the rain today.

_____ 25. Officer Flaherty, directing traffic around the construction project, was forced to stand out in the rain today.

_____ 26. Many people in the crowd left early, the lopsided score giving them an excuse to beat the traffic out of the parking lot.

_____ 27. Leaving the stadium early, many people in the crowd used the lopsided score as an excuse to beat the traffic.

_____ 28. With the lab reports all completed, the teaching assistants sent us home early.

_____ 29. Those clothes should be discarded, with their colors faded and their elbows and knees covered with patches.

_____ 30. Alexis spent a wonderfully enjoyable afternoon in the concert hall, totally enthralled by the work of the young musicians.

NAME _____ SCORE _____

Directions: In the first space at the left, write one of the following letters to identify the italicized verbal phrase:

    G. [gerund phrase]   I. [infinitive phrase]

    P. [participial phrase]   A. [absolute phrase]

In the second space, write one of the following abbreviations to identify the complement printed in boldfaced type within the phrase:

    S.C. [subjective complement]   I.O. [indirect object]

    D.O. [direct object]   O.C. [objective complement]

_____
_____
1. *Giving* **Maria** *the package,* the mail carrier said, "Please sign on that line at the bottom of the yellow slip."

_____
_____
2. *With the team very* **tired,** the coach ended practice and sent the players home.

_____
_____
3. Our best option at this point is *to hire an outside* **consultant** *and leave the project to her.*

_____
_____
4. Try *being* **alert** *during the next test;* you might improve your grade.

_____
_____
5. *Editing that* **paper** *for today's class* took most of last night.

_____
_____
6. James finally left the shop, *the new set of shelves finally* **finished.**

_____
_____
7. James was very happy *to finish the* **shelves** *two days before the deadline.*

_____
_____
8. *Leaving the shop* **closed** *for the next two days,* James took a brief vacation.

_____
_____
9. *After dropping off your* **clothes** *at the dry cleaner,* come to the gym and pick me up so we can go to supper.

_____
_____
10. *With the work only half* **finished,** we were forced to leave the building when the fire alarm rang.

———— 11. With the project only half finished, we were forced *to leave the **building**
———— *when the fire alarm rang.*

———— 12. During the height of the storm, there was nothing for us to do except *sit **hud-**
———— ***dled** together and wait for calm weather.*

———— 13. *The storm having finally left the **area**,* we were able to start cleaning up the
———— mess.

———— 14. The teacher watched *the students work the **problems** on that difficult test.*
————

———— 15. My grandmother's daily ritual was *to read the entire **newspaper** before she
———— left the house in the morning.*

———— 16. *Paying **attention** to current events* made my grandmother an interesting
———— conversationalist.

———— 17. *Being **alert** to the news,* my grandmother always knew what trends would
———— affect the stock market.

———— 18. Richard spent the whole night working at his computer, *his paper **due** the
———— following morning at 8:00* A.M.

———— 19. The defense attorney walked slowly to her seat, *the witness's last answer
———— having left her **speechless.***

———— 20. With the rain beating down so hard, it's nearly impossible *to see **any** of the
———— channel markers.*

Directions: Combine the two sentences in each item into a single sentence by converting the second sentence into a participial phrase or an absolute phrase.

1. We all sat down to dinner.
   The last guest had arrived.

   _____

2. The newly registered freshmen assembled in the auditorium.
   All were carrying their bright red registration packets.

   _____

3. Jenny sat down and opened the letter.
   A brief frown crossed her face.

   _____

4. The two men ran up the ramp in the stadium.
   They were trying desperately to make the kickoff.

   _____

5. The woman watched as her daughter left for college.
   She wiped away a few tears with her handkerchief.

   _____

6. I looked for days in the reference books.
   I was trying to find facts about my grandmother's family.

   _____

7. Thomas searched eagerly through the classified ads for a good used car.
   His present car had blown an engine.

   _____

8. Christina identified those actors immediately.
   She had watched the movie for the third time just last night.

   _____

9. All the phone lines at the ticket center were busy.
   Tickets for the popular concert had gone on sale at 9:00 A.M.

   _____

10. All the fans stood during the seventh-inning stretch.
    The announcer led them in "Take Me Out to the Ball Game."

    _____

Sentence Building

Lessons, Practice Sheets, and Exercises

Lesson 13 *Completeness*

To be complete, a sentence must

1. Contain a subject and a verb.

2. Be able to stand alone as an independent unit.

A group of words without both a subject and a verb cannot be a complete sentence. A group of words containing both a subject and a verb but opening with a subordinating conjunction cannot be a complete sentence. The subordinating conjunction makes the clause dependent instead of independent.

Sentence Fragments

A group of words that does not have a subject and a verb and cannot stand alone is called an incomplete sentence, or **sentence fragment.** Sometimes a sentence fragment is punctuated as if it were a sentence. This mistake of punctuation is called a **period fault.** Sentence fragments almost always fit one of the following patterns:

1. A subordinate clause standing as a sentence. (But remember that *and, but, or, nor, for, yet,* and *so* do not subordinate. A clause introduced by one of these words may stand as a sentence.)

   Fragments: The clerk finally let us see the contract. *Although she clearly hated to reveal its contents.*

   Bob tried to start the old lawn mower. *Which never seemed to work properly for him.*

2. A verbal phrase punctuated as a sentence:

   Fragments: The delegates agreed on a compromise wage scale. *Realizing that the strike could not go on indefinitely.*

   Nell had ordered her tickets a month ago. *To be sure of getting good seats.*

3. A noun followed by a phrase or a subordinate clause but lacking a main verb:

> **Fragments:**   The committee should include Ms. Jones. *A tireless worker with many constructive ideas.*
>
> The mayor asked Bentley to take the job. *Bentley being the only available person with field experience.*
>
> The coach thinks our prospects are good. *A chance, perhaps, to win back the conference championship.*
>
> Junior will require a special kind of tutor. *Someone who will realize how sensitive the child really is.*

You should learn to avoid using fragments in your writing. Usually a close reading of anything you have written will reveal sentence fragments so that you can correct them. You can improve your skill at identifying fragments by using the following strategy: When you check what you have written, read the sentences in a paragraph in reverse order. Start with your last sentence and work back to your first. This process, which breaks the tie between a fragment and the sentence that it depends on, makes any grammatically incomplete sentence stand out.

Correcting Sentence Fragments

When you have discovered a fragment in your writing, any one of several possible corrections is easy to make.

- You can attach the fragment to the preceding sentence by doing away with the fragment's capital letter and supplying the right punctuation.
- You can change the fragment to a subordinate clause and attach it to the appropriate main clause by means of the right connective.
- You can change the fragment to an independent clause by supplying a subject or a verb or both.
- You can change the fragment to an appositive or some other appropriate phrase.

Consider the following corrected sentences:

> The clerk finally let us see the contract, *although she clearly hated to reveal its contents.*
>
> Bob tried to start the old lawn mower, *which never seemed to work properly for him.*
>
> The delegates agreed on a compromise wage scale *because they realized that the strike could not go on indefinitely.*
>
> *To be sure of getting good seats,* Nell had ordered her tickets a month ago.
>
> The committee should include Ms. Jones, *a tireless worker with many constructive ideas.*
>
> The mayor asked Bentley to take the job, *Bentley being the only available person with field experience.*
>
> The coach thinks our prospects are good; *we have a chance, perhaps, to win back the league championship.*

Junior will require a special kind of tutor. *He or she must be someone who will realize how sensitive the child really is.*

There are a few types of word groups that are not considered fragments. Although they lack a complete subject–verb combination, these types of word groups are accepted as legitimate language patterns. They are

1. **Commands:** in which the subject *you* is understood:

   Please be seated. Put your name on a slip of paper. Pass the papers to the left aisle.
   [See Lesson 21, Supplement.]

2. **Exclamations:**

   What excitement! Only two minutes to go! Good Heavens, not a fumble? How terrible!

3. **Bits of dialogue:**

   "New car?" she asked. "Had it long?"
   "Picked it up last week," he replied.

4. **Occasional transitions between units of thought:**

   On with the story.
   And now to conclude.

You have very likely observed in your reading that experienced writers sometimes use sentence fragments, especially in narrative and descriptive writing. But these writers are skilled workers who know how to use fragments to achieve particular stylistic effects. You should first master the fundamental forms of the sentence. Once you have learned to write clear, correct sentences without faltering, there will be plenty of time for experimenting.

NAME _____ SCORE _____

Directions: Study the following word groups for completeness. In the space at the left, write **S** if the word group is a grammatically complete sentence. Write **F** if the word group is a fragment.

_____ 1. Only a few of the people in the band played at the state title game two years ago.

_____ 2. A good book, some sunscreen, a cooler full of sandwiches and cold drinks— everything anyone would need for a day at the beach.

_____ 3. A surprising, twisted ending to the movie that shocked almost everyone.

_____ 4. No, I had never met Jim Collins before last night.

_____ 5. Yes, that's the answer I was looking for.

_____ 6. At last, after all that walking, a glimpse of the end of the trail.

_____ 7. Closing all the windows and turning off the lights, Kathleen set out for class.

_____ 8. A pitching performance so dreadful that none of us ever wants to see another like it.

_____ 9. Standing at the back of the auditorium, a man holding a fat file folder and asking very pointed questions.

_____ 10. But we were not able to find any solution to the problem posed by Professor Watson.

_____ 11. Walk slowly down the street and look in every store window as you pass.

_____ 12. The cliff appearing much higher than it seemed from a distance.

_____ 13. Will Thomson, a man of great intelligence whose integrity has never been questioned.

_____ 14. After we had called several times and sent a registered letter to the office.

_____ 15. Despite our occasional disagreements, James and I have been friends for many years.

_____ 16. And we thought that you should have checked those statements with the boss before you published them in the company paper.

_____ 17. Although we thought you should have checked those statements with the boss before you published them in the company newspaper.

_____ 18. What do you think will happen now, given the state of the economy?

_____ 19. A strange idea that seems to have come from some sort of fantasy, or perhaps from a movie.

_____ 20. His next job, he decided, would certainly have to pay more and require fewer hours of work.

_____ 21. Exhausted from the day's work and looking forward to a long weekend, the staff closed the office and left for home.

_____ 22. Learning to view current events in the light of the nation's history.

_____ 23. Learning that we need to view current events in the light of the nation's history.

_____ 24. Learning that we need to view current events in the light of the nation's history will improve your perspective.

_____ 25. Please park your car in back of the building in a marked spot.

_____ 26. Ever since we tried to locate a new house out in the country and begin to live in a quiet, rural setting.

_____ 27. Ever since, we tried to locate a new house out in the country and begin to live in a quiet, rural setting.

_____ 28. Soaring high above the clouds in a glider has always been one of Mike's hobbies.

_____ 29. Soaring high above the clouds in a glider and watching the clouds roll by underneath him.

_____ 30. My little sister's room, always neatly arranged with everything in its proper place.

Exercise 13   *Completeness*

NAME _____ SCORE _____

Directions: Each numbered unit consists of a sentence plus a fragment. In the space provided, rewrite enough of the material to show how you would correct the error, either by attaching the fragment to the sentence or recasting the fragment into a complete sentence.

1. Alan volunteered to work at the community center last summer. Tutoring young children who were having difficulty in school.

   _____

2. Returning from a trip to Wyoming last summer. The Jacksons stopped briefly in St. Louis to visit an art museum.

   _____

3. The work crew tried desperately to finish painting the school before the term began. Even though bad weather interrupted the work quite regularly.

   _____

4. The President has appointed Robert Smith as ambassador to France. A man who has great experience in diplomacy and speaks fluent French.

   _____

5. Walking through the mall and going into every shop that was having a sale. Jim and Marcy spent an entire afternoon shopping for her mother.

   _____

6. The strike by the airline workers having ended. Then travel agents were once again able to sell tickets for that company's flights.

   _____

7. A devoted public servant who has worked faithfully to improve county government. Marcia Gonzalez is retiring after twenty-five years as county tax assessor.

   _____

8. Ever since they moved from the east coast to the middle west because Mr. Winston changed jobs. He and his wife have gone on a cruise every year.

   _____

9. Katherine and Mario registered for classes as soon as registration opened. To be sure that they would be able to be in Professor Alexander's class.

   _____

10. The men's basketball team seems unable to win two games in a row. No matter how hard they practice and no matter how hard they play.

_____

11. Rhonda thinks she has a good chance for that job. With a solid resumé and two successful interviews behind her.

_____

12. The water in the river is going to crest far above flood stage. The only hope being that the dike will hold and protect the village.

_____

13. The leaders of the revolution, people who were completely dissatisfied with the operation of the government. Ten people were arrested yesterday.

_____

14. Looking as though they hadn't eaten for two or three days. The three girls walked in off the mountain trail.

_____

15. Jack Farley seems to be the only person qualified for the manager's job. A degree in business and several years of experience as a manager.

_____

16. A man with a degree in business and several years of experience as a manager. Jack Farley seems to be the only person qualified for the manager's job.

_____

17. The clean-up crew worked diligently for several hours. To clean up the trash and get ready for the next game.

_____

18. Last summer Johnson worked on a Forest Service crew out west. Cutting new fire lanes and removing underbrush from existing lanes.

_____

19. That new group project should include Williams and Lopez. People with great experience and almost tireless energy.

_____

20. Dad hired Jennifer Acevedo as a tutor for my little brother. Having great skills in math and incredible patience with reluctant students.

_____

Exercise 13A

Completeness

NAME _____ SCORE _____

Directions: Each numbered unit consists of a sentence plus a fragment. In the space provided, rewrite enough of the material to show how you would correct the error, either by attaching the fragment to the sentence or recasting the fragment into a complete sentence.

1. In the house down the street lives a famous author. A woman who writes clever mystery stories featuring a woman detective.

   _____

2. But I've never enjoyed car chases in movies. Seeming much too life-like and scaring me half to death.

   _____

3. Although they ordered the tickets early, they lost them. Failing to pick them up and pay for them on time.

   _____

4. The two lost boys wandered for hours on the mountain. The trail being hard to follow in the dense woods.

   _____

5. We assigned that proposal to Morgan. Morgan being the only staff member capable of analyzing it.

   _____

6. John doesn't know which job he will accept. Possibly the one in the town closer to his hometown.

   _____

7. The two little boys looked everywhere for their lost books. In the house, out in the garage, and even in both cars.

   _____

8. Maria Alvarez is a great asset to our company. A woman who makes great contributions to every group she joins.

   _____

9. The Block family plans to move out of town. Looking for a small town where they can open a business.

   _____

10. If Alicia raises her GPA this semester, she can apply for an internship with a major company. A great accomplishment if she can manage it.

_____

11. Everyone in the office came in late today. Traffic on all the freeways being an absolute nightmare.

_____

12. My brother wants me to take an accounting course. Hoping that I will keep the books for his business.

_____

13. My father has an interesting definition of good luck. Hard work and careful preparation meeting an opportunity.

_____

14. Running, turning to his right, and leaping high against the wall. The centerfielder made a spectacular catch.

_____

15. We could not use the GPS to locate our position. The trees and the cloud cover keeping it from finding the third satellite.

_____

16. Mary Alice has a very valuable collection of vinyl recordings. Concentrating especially on the early era of rock music.

_____

17. Because Kelly was running a little late. She was flustered and slightly embarrassed when she walked into the meeting.

_____

18. Alex turned down a job in that big city. Wanting rather to work in a small college town.

_____

19. The members of the class went immediately to the library. To work with the librarians to find sources for their papers.

_____

20. To work in some branch of the film industry is Jennifer's secret dream. Studying film courses and working on a screenplay in her spare time.

_____

Lesson 14 *Misplaced Modifiers; Dangling Modifiers*

Proper arrangement of the parts of your sentence will help make your meaning clear. Ordinarily the main parts—the subjects, the verbs, the complements—cause no problems. Modifying words and phrases and subordinate clauses can cause problems if they are not located carefully. Here we shall consider five possible trouble spots in the placing of modifiers.

1. Although we sometimes use a rather loose placement for some common adverbs, such as *only, nearly, almost,* and *hardly,* we can write precise sentences only when such adverbs are placed close to the words they modify:

Loose:	This will *only* take five minutes.
	Jill *nearly* saw ninety movies last year.
Better:	This will take *only* five minutes.
	Jill saw *nearly* ninety movies last year.

2. Words and phrases that attach themselves to the wrong word can confuse the reader:

Loose:	I wish every person in this class could know the man I'm going to talk about *personally.*
Better:	I wish every person in this class could know *personally* the man I'm going to talk about.
Loose:	It was reported that the Italian premier had died *on the eight o'clock newscast.*
Better:	*On the eight o'clock newscast,* it was reported that the Italian premier had died.
Loose:	The police department will be notified of all reported obscene phone calls *by the telephone company.*
Better:	The police department will be notified *by the telephone company* of all reported obscene phone calls.

3. The **squinting modifier** is one that is placed between two units, either of which it could modify:

Loose:	Students who can already type *normally* are put into an advanced class.
Better:	Students who can already type are *normally* put into an advanced class.
Loose:	He said *after the dinner* some color slides would be shown.
Better:	He said some color slides would be shown *after the dinner.*

4. The **split infinitive** results from the placing of an adverbial modifier between the *to* and the verb stem of an infinitive. Although greatly overemphasized by some as an error, the split infinitive, particularly with a modifier consisting of more than one word, is usually avoided by careful writers:

Loose:	Dad likes to *once in a while* plan and cook a dinner.
Better:	*Once in a while,* Dad likes to plan and cook a dinner.

5. The conjunctions *both . . . and, not only . . . but also, either . . . or,* and *neither . . . nor* are used in pairs and are called **correlatives.** Because they point out the equal relationship between units, they should be placed immediately before the parallel units that they connect:

Loose: We sent invitations *both* to Webster *and* Jenkins.
Better: We sent invitations to *both* Webster *and* Jenkins.
            [The parallel words are *Webster* and *Jenkins.*]

Loose: This woman *not only* can get along with young people *but also* with their parents.
Better: This woman can get along *not only* with young people *but also* with their parents.

Loose: You must *either* promise me that you will come *or* send a substitute.
Better: You must promise me that you will *either* come *or* send a substitute.

Dangling Modifiers

There should be a clear relationship between a word being modified and the modifying phrase. Any modifying phrase that does not attach itself clearly to the word it is supposed to modify is called a **dangling modifier.** A dangling modifier can create a confusing sentence. Participial phrases are especially apt to float free in a sentence.

Stepping into the boat, my camera fell into the water.

This sentence contains a participial phrase and a main clause, but the phrase does not actually modify any word in the main clause. The sentence is made up of two thoughts that can be expressed as

I stepped into the boat.
My camera fell into the water.

We can make the two sentences into a compound sentence:

I stepped into the boat, and my camera fell into the water.

Or we can make the first clause an introductory adverbial element:

As I stepped into the boat, my camera fell into the water.

But we cannot convert the first sentence into a participial phrase because the only noun the phrase could modify is *camera,* and the camera did not step into the boat. The sentence, if read literally, becomes nonsense. We could rework the sentence by changing the subject of the second clause in a way that allows the participial phrase to modify the new subject:

Stepping into the boat, I dropped my camera into the water.

Because the person who dropped the camera and the person who is stepping into the boat are the same, *I,* the sentence is now correct.

Gerund Phrases and Infinitive Phrases

Gerund phrases and infinitive phrases can also cause problems when they are randomly inserted into sentences:

> *After studying all morning,* a nap was Mary's only goal for the afternoon.

The intended meaning of the sentence is clear, but the literal meaning is that the nap studied all morning; the phrase attaches itself to the first available noun, in this case, a noun that produces a nonsense statement.

> *To qualify for that job,* good typing skills are a necessity.

Again, the intended meaning is clear, but the literal meaning is nonsense: good typing skills are not qualifying for that job; a person with good typing skills is qualifying for that job. Remember the phrase that contains the verbal must have a word to refer to, and that word must be close enough to the phrase so that the reader does not associate the phrase with the wrong word.

Correcting Danglers

The easiest way to correct a dangler is to supply the word that the phrase should modify and to place the phrase next to that word. Another way is to change the dangling phrase to a subordinate clause with a subject and verb expressed.

1. Participial phrase at the beginning of a sentence

    Dangler: *Burned to a cinder,* I could not eat the toast.
    [The sentence sounds as if I were burned to a cinder. The word that the dangler should modify is *toast,* but this word is too far from the phrase immediately associated with it.]

    Better: Burned to a cinder, the toast could not be eaten.
    I could not eat the toast because it was burned to a cinder.

2. Gerund following a preposition

    Dangler: Before *making a final decision,* other cars should be driven.
    [Are the other cars making a final decision? That is not what is meant, and yet that is what the sentence states.]

    On graduating from high school, my father let me work in his office.
    [The sentence says that your father let you work in his office when he, not you, graduated from high school.]

    Since *breaking my leg,* my neighbors have helped with my farm chores.
    [A logical sentence only if the neighbors broke your leg.]

    Better: Before making a final decision, drive other cars.
    Before you make a final decision, you should drive other cars.

On graduating from high school, I went to work in my father's office.
After I had graduated from high school, my father let me work in his office.

Since breaking my leg, I have been helped with my farm chores by my neighbors.
My neighbors have helped with my farm chores since I broke my leg.

3. Elliptical "time" clause (see Lesson 8), usually introduced by *when* or *while*

Dangler: *When ten years old,* my father sold the farm and moved to Dallas.
While weeding my vegetable garden, a garter snake startled me.
[The understood subject of the adverb clause is different from the subject of the main clause, but the reader assumes that both clauses have the same subject. The result is a ridiculous meaning that the writer never intended.]

Better: When ten years old, I moved to Dallas after my father sold the farm.
When I was ten years old, my father sold the farm and we moved to Dallas.

While weeding my vegetable garden, I was startled by a garter snake.
While I was weeding my vegetable garden, a garter snake startled me.

4. Introductory infinitive phrase naming a specific action

Dangler: *To enter the contest,* a box top must be sent with your slogan.
[*box top* is not entering the contest. To avoid this problem, be sure that the word that the phrase attaches to names the logical doer of that action.]

Better: To enter the contest, you must send a box top with your slogan.
If you want to enter the contest, a box top must be sent with your slogan.
When you enter the contest, send a box top with your slogan.

NAME _____ SCORE _____

Directions: From each of the following pairs of sentences, select the one that is clearer and write its letter in the space at the left. Be prepared to explain your choice.

_____ 1. A. This afternoon there was an account of my accident on Channel 5.
B. On Channel 5 this afternoon there was an account of my accident.

_____ 2. A. I advise you to take a short rest just before the examination.
B. I advise you to just before the examination take a short rest.

_____ 3. A. The class could only find one copy of *Hard Times.*
B. The class could find only one copy of *Hard Times.*

_____ 4. A. Look very carefully at any orders written by the new salesman.
B. Look at any orders written by the new salesman very carefully.

_____ 5. A. By standing on tiptoe we can just barely see the workman behind the wall hauling bricks across the yard.
B. We can just barely see the workman behind the wall hauling bricks across the yard by standing on tiptoe.

_____ 6. A. You either can write a check or pay the amount in cash.
B. You can either write a check or pay the amount in cash.

_____ 7. A. We nearly had to wait until two o'clock before we had anything to eat.
B. We had to wait until nearly two o'clock before we had anything to eat.

_____ 8. A. For the past fifteen years camping out in the mountains has been our favorite vacation.
B. Camping out in the mountains for the past fifteen years has been our favorite vacation.

_____ 9. A. Mr. McCoy, reading the newspaper, almost wrecked his car.
B. Mr. McCoy almost wrecked his car reading the newspaper.

_____ 10. A. The women watched the symphony standing in the balcony as it rehearsed.
B. Standing in the balcony, the women watched the symphony as it rehearsed.

Directions: In the space at the left, write either **A** or **B** to indicate the logical placing of the modifier in the parentheses.

———— 1. *(only)* The club needs **A** to recruit **B** two more members for this year.

———— 2. *(either)* To qualify for the scholarship, one must **A** be able to speak **B** French or Spanish.

———— 3. *(from the top of the ladder)* I watched in frustration **A** as the dog ate my hamburger **B**.

———— 4. *(not only)* I know that Myra **A** is **B** intelligent but also wealthy.

———— 5. *(by telephone)* We were informed yesterday **A** that my uncle is coming to visit us **B**.

———— 6. *(not all)* I'm afraid that **A** the members are **B** here.

———— 7. *(with dismay and disgust)* **A** Local Bearcat fans have been watching the team lose its high conference standing **B**.

———— 8. *(neither)* The women **A** were **B** happier nor healthier after their week at the spa.

———— 9. *(when the occasion demands)* He has trained himself to **A** resort to street language **B**.

———— 10. *(in his largest tank)* **A** He told us that he kept a python measuring eleven feet **B**.

———— 11. *(in his first talk with graduate students)* **A** Dean Shaw discussed plagiarism and shoddy scholarship **B**.

———— 12. *(by the county agricultural agent)* It was reported **A** that the ground-water level has been lowered dangerously **B**.

———— 13. *(on the bulletin board)* The teacher has posted **A** the projects the class will complete this term **B**.

———— 14. *(not only)* Driving this fast on the rain-slick pavement **A** is **B** foolish but dangerous.

———— 15. *(not)* These eager contestants must often be reminded that **A** everyone can **B** be a winner.

Exercise 14   *Misplaced Modifiers*

NAME _____   SCORE _____

Directions: In each of the following sentences, there is a poorly positioned word or phrase. Rewrite each sentence.

1. This morning I saw an enormous flight of ducks on a quiet walk.

   _____

2. I saw a waterspout driving down the shoreline boulevard.

   _____

3. The pear tree nearly was thirty feet tall.

   _____

4. All of my classmates are not interested in the campus election.

   _____

5. While we were walking, John almost told me the same story I heard from Art.

   _____

6. Readers should not accept everything that is written on an editorial page without question.

   _____

7. My grandfather stored all the ship models he made in a closet in the attic.

   _____

8. While the rest of us polished the cars, Max nearly napped for two hours.

   _____

9. My little brother read two detective stories written by Robert Parker because of my father's encouragement.

   _____

10. All the homeowners in the association were asked to complain to the mayor at the meeting yesterday.

    _____

Directions: In the space at the left, write **A** or **B** to indicate the logical placing of the modifier within the parentheses.

_____ 1. *(only)* Hurry, children: you **A** have **B** ten minutes left to finish your test.

_____ 2. *(either)* **A** You **B** pay the tax now or postpone payment and pay a penalty.

_____ 3. *(at least once a month)* **A** The Sunday-school teacher would give his standard lecture on obeying our parents. **B**.

_____ 4. *(not only)* Ms. LaRue **A** is **B** a chemist but has an MBA from Stanford.

_____ 5. *(almost)* Hawkins **A** played in **B** every Tiger game for seven seasons.

_____ 6. *(every ten days)* Junior promised **A** to cut the lawn **B**.

_____ 7. *(once)* A neighbor of mine who had played lacrosse **A** tried **B** to explain the game to me.

_____ 8. *(either)* That broker of yours **A** is **B** very clever or unbelievably lucky.

_____ 9. *(neither)* The embattled prime minister vowed **A** to **B** resign nor to apologize.

_____ 10. *(normally)* Applicants who can use word processors **A** are **B** given preference.

_____ 11. *(in spite of the rain)* We were determined to **A** finish our golf game **B**.

_____ 12. *(in his sermon)* **A** Dr. Thornton discussed the need for harmony **B**.

_____ 13. *(by the visiting nurse)* We were told **A** to raise our hands if we had already been vaccinated **B**.

_____ 14. *(not)* **A** All college professors are **B** vitally interested in conducting research.

_____ 15. *(only)* Jack decided to **A** invest **B** two hundred dollars in the project.

NAME _____ SCORE _____

Directions: One sentence of each pair contains a dangling modifier. Underline the dangler. In the space at the left, write the letter that identifies the correct sentence.

_____ 1. A. Realizing that the streets were very slick from the rains, the car moved slowly down the street.
         B. Realizing that the streets were very slick from the rains, Jim maneuvered the car slowly down the street.

_____ 2. A. Being a very successful young executive, Mary Conners has been selected as the new vice-president.
         B. Being a very successful young executive, the board has selected Mary Conners as the new vice-president.

_____ 3. A. To get the maximum tax benefits, all deductions should be listed.
         B. To get the maximum tax benefits, be sure to list all deductions.

_____ 4. A. Not expecting to see Mary Chase so far from home, my mouth dropped open when she greeted me.
         B. As I was not expecting to see Mary Chase so far from home, my mouth dropped open when she greeted me.

_____ 5. A. Upon receiving the invoice, please pay the bill promptly.
         B. Upon receiving the invoice, the bill must be paid promptly.

_____ 6. A. At eleven years of age, my mother insisted that I take karate lessons.
         B. My mother insisted that I take karate lessons at eleven years of age.

_____ 7. A. Broadcast live from the stadium, the high school championship game was seen by thousands of fans across the state.
         B. Broadcast live from the stadium, thousands of fans across the state saw the high school championship game.

_____ 8. A. When using this powerful detergent, rubber gloves should be worn.
         B. When one is using this powerful detergent, rubber gloves should be worn.

_____ 9. A. Before getting the camera focused, the turtle slipped of the log and disappeared in the water.
         B. Before I could get the camera focused, the turtle slipped off the log and disappeared in the water.

_____ 10. A. Being older and slower, the fat man was left far behind by the leaders in the race.
B. Being older and slower, the leaders in the race left the fat man far behind.

_____ 11. A. Having misunderstood the assignment, I received a low grade on my paper.
B. Having misunderstood the assignment, my paper got a low grade.

_____ 12. A. Exhausted after fourteen hours of driving, the exit to Denver was a welcome sight.
B. Because we were exhausted after fourteen hours of driving, the exit to Denver was a welcome sight.

_____ 13. A. Having stood in the oily marinade for six hours, you are now ready to grill the meat.
B. Having stood in the oily marinade for six hours, the meat is now ready to be grilled.

_____ 14. A. As the spider painstakingly repaired the damaged web, I marveled at its skill and patience.
B. Painstakingly repairing the damaged web, I marveled at the spider's skill and patience.

_____ 15. A. Approaching the Continental Divide, there was a noticeable drop in temperature.
B. Approaching the Continental Divide, we noticed a drop in temperature.

_____ 16. A. The archaeologists could not decipher the inscription covered with the grime of centuries.
B. Covered with the grime of centuries, the archaeologists could not decipher the inscription.

_____ 17. A. To avoid overexposing the picture, use a light meter.
B. To avoid overexposing the picture, a light meter should be used.

_____ 18. A. Meeting Lou after geology class, he suggested a handball game.
B. Meeting Lou after geology class, I suggested a handball game.

_____ 19. A. If unable to attend, please call the reservation clerk.
B. If unable to attend, a call to the reservation clerk would be appreciated.

_____ 20. A. Seen from miles away, the mountain looks like a cloud
B. Seen from miles away, one might think the mountain looks like a cloud.

NAME _____   SCORE _____

Directions: Rewrite each of the following sentences twice. In the first rewrite, change the dangling modifier to a complete clause with a subject and verb. In the second, retain the phrase but begin the clause with a word the phrase can logically modify.

1. After measuring the first board incorrectly, the rest of the work on the cabinet went very badly for Jane.

   a. _____

   b. _____

2. Before making a final selection of a computer, it is a good idea to talk to someone who owns one.

   a. _____

   b. _____

3. Having drilled intensively on those problems, the test seemed was easy for Jackson and the other students.

   a. _____

   b. _____

4. Watching the sunset over the gulf, the cloud formations in the west were extraordinarily beautiful.

   a. _____

   b. _____

5. To find your way safely across the lake to the island, it is a good idea to use a GPS.

   a. _____

   b. _____

6. After working all day pouring concrete, a quick swim in the cool surf was very refreshing for Tom and his friends.

   a. _____

   b. _____

7. To play that video game, a special control box is needed.

   a. _____

   b. _____

8. At the age of sixteen, my father bought me a beautiful Chevelle SS396.

   a. _____

   b. _____

9. Upon entering the room, the lights and the air conditioning should be adjusted for your comfort.

   a. _____

   b. _____

10. Reaching high over my head to the top shelf, a half dozen books toppled off the shelf and hit me on the head.

    a. _____

    b. _____

Lesson 15 *Subordination*

Beginning writers sometimes string together too many short sentences, or they tie clauses together with conjunctions—*and, but, or*—that fail to establish precise relations between the clauses.

Poor: Sally usually attends each concert. She missed this one. She went to the airport to meet her cousin Ellen. Ellen was arriving from Atlanta.

I rode around town for three days, but I couldn't find a place to stay, and then I located this apartment, and so I am comfortable.

If you use the methods of creating and combining sentences that we have studied, you will make your writing more precise, more economical, and more meaningful:

Improved: Although Sally usually attends each concert, she missed this one because she went to the airport to meet her cousin Ellen, who was arriving from Atlanta.

After riding around town for three days without finding a place to stay, I finally located this apartment, where I am comfortable.

Get into the habit of trying different methods of subordinating material. Notice in the following sentences how an idea can be expressed in a variety of ways:

Two Sentences:	The small car was inexpensive to drive. It had only four cylinders.
Compound Verb:	The small car had only four cylinders and was inexpensive to drive.
Compound Sentence:	The small car was inexpensive to drive, for it had only four cylinders.
Adverbial Clause:	Because the small car had only four cylinders, it was inexpensive to drive.
Adjective Clause:	The small car, which had only four cylinders, was inexpensive to drive.
Participial Phrase:	The small car, having only four cylinders, was inexpensive to drive.
	Having only four cylinders, the small car was inexpensive to drive.
	The small car was inexpensive to drive, having only four cylinders.
Absolute Phrase:	The small car having only four cylinders, it was inexpensive to drive.
Prepositional Phrase:	The small car with only four cylinders was inexpensive to drive.
Appositive:	The small car, a four-cylinder model, was inexpensive to drive.
Adjective Modifier:	The small four-cylinder car was inexpensive to drive.

The use of subordination produces more than a pleasing sound in writing. It makes a crucial contribution to meaning by eliminating uncertainty about what is most important in a message. Consider the following string of simple sentences:

The management and union representatives announced an agreement. A strike had been threatened but was averted. The employees of Grantex Company reported for work today. They were relieved.

147

There is no way of knowing from these sentences which fact is most significant: The agreement? The avoidance of a strike? The workers' reporting for work? Their relief? Rewritten with proper subordination, the news reveals what the writer believes is most significant:

> The relieved employees of Grantex Company reported for work today after the management and union representatives announced an agreement that averted a threatened strike.

The only independent clause in the sentence concerns the workers' return to work. That is the important message. A writer more interested in strikes and their effect on the general economy might report the event thus:

> The threatened strike was averted at Grantex Company when the management and union representatives announced an agreement, after which the relieved employees reported for work today.

A Note on Sentence Variety

Preceding lessons have demonstrated how subordinate clauses and phrases, by compressing material, help the writer avoid tiresome strings of independent clauses. You have also seen that certain subordinate units—adverbial clauses and participial phrases in particular—can be put in several places within the sentence, thus helping to prevent monotony in your sentences.

Another unit useful for achieving compression and variety is the appositive. (See Lesson 10.) As noun renamers, appositives closely resemble—they might be called the final reduction of—Pattern 2 clause and phrase modifiers of nouns:

> Ted could explain the trick to us. Ted [or He] is an amateur magician. [Two independent clauses]
> Ted, *who is an amateur magician,* could explain the trick to us. [Adjective clause]
> Ted, *being an amateur magician,* could explain the trick to us. [Participial phrase]
> Ted, *an amateur magician,* could explain the trick to us. [Appositive]

Although the usual position of an appositive is immediately following the noun it renames, many appositives, like many nonrestrictive participial phrases, can precede the main noun (in which case they are called *pre-positional appositives*); sometimes they are effectively placed at the end of the clause:

> Lawyer Somers, *a master of wit and guile,* cajoles and browbeats in the courtroom.
> *A master of wit and guile,* Lawyer Somers cajoles and browbeats in the courtroom.
> Lawyer Somers cajoles and browbeats in the courtroom, *a master of wit and guile.*

As a final example of language tools for renaming and modifying nouns, study this tightly constructed sentence:

> One of the five largest towns in Roman England, home of King Arthur's legendary Round Table, seat of Alfred the Great, whose statue looks down its main street, early capital of England, and victim of Cromwell's destructive forces, Winchester is an enchanting cathedral city in which layer after layer of history is visibly present.
>
> Elisabeth Lambert Ortiz, "Exploring Winchester,"
> *Gourmet,* March 1978, p. 21

This sentence is made up of one independent clause, which includes an adjective clause, and five pre-positional appositives, the third of which contains an adjective clause. The statements underlying this sentence might be charted as follows:

[Winchester was] one of the five largest towns in Roman England.
[Winchester was] the home of King Arthur's legendary Round Table.
[Winchester was] the seat of Alfred the Great.
[Alfred the Great's] statue looks down its main street.
[Winchester was] the early capital of England.
[Winchester was] the victim of Cromwell's destructive forces.
Winchester is an enchanting cathedral city.
[In this city] layer after layer of history is visibly present.

We see here that eight statements—enough to make up a paragraph of clear but unrelieved simple sentences—have been shortened into one complex sentence. The layering of appositives and adjective clauses produces compression, sentence variety, and proper emphasis.

NAME _____ SCORE _____

Directions: In each sentence you will find a subordinate unit in italics. In the space at the left, write
one of the following numbers to identify the italicized subordinate clause:

    1. Adverbial clause   4. Gerund phrase   7. Infinitive phrase
    2. Adjective clause   5. Absolute phrase
    3. Participial phrase   6. Appositive

_____ 1. The pilots returned to work last week, *the new union proposals having been accepted by the company.*

_____ 2. *After Coach Bancroft left,* the college hired Sara Jameson as her replacement.

_____ 3. The college has hired a new coach *to replace Coach Bancroft.*

_____ 4. Sara Jameson, *who graduated from Rutgers University,* has been hired as the new coach.

_____ 5. Yesterday I spent four long hours *searching for a shop to repair the damage to my computer.*

_____ 6. James Carson, *having arrived in town only yesterday,* was at work bright and early this morning.

_____ 7. James Carson, *the new director of Management Information Systems,* was at work bright and early this morning.

_____ 8. The package *that came in this morning's mail* contained some chocolate chip cookies.

_____ 9. In this morning's mail, I received a package *containing some of my grand-mother's chocolate chip cookies.*

_____ 10. *After I opened the package,* all the cookies disappeared within about five minutes.

_____ 11. My brother George, *an incredibly sound sleeper,* slept calmly through last night's terrible thunderstorm.

_____ 12. *With a terrible thunderstorm raging outside,* my brother George slept soundly through the night.

_____ 13. *To serve and protect the citizens* is the motto of our local police department.

_____ 14. *Understanding that short, complicated article* was a more difficult task than I had expected.

_____ 15. *While I was working on that short, complicated article,* all the students in the class had already turned in their essays.

151

Directions: Change the italicized sentence to the structure indicated in the parentheses and write the two sentences as one.

1. Go to the registrar's office early tomorrow morning. *You will have a wide choice of classes for your schedule.* (infinitive phrase)

   _____

2. *I found the last of the puppies under the floorboards of the barn.* I took them all in the house and put them in a box on a blanket. (participial phrase)

   _____

3. At a party last week I met Raymond Larson. *He is the road manager for a popular country and western singer.* (adjective clause)

   _____

4. *Frost is predicted for tonight.* You should cover your plants with some old sheets. (adverbial clause of condition)

   _____

5. *Frost is predicted for tonight.* You should cover your plants with some old sheets. (absolute phrase)

   _____

6. When frost is predicted, you should cover your plants with some old sheets. *The sheets will protect the plants.* (infinitive phrase)

   _____

7. Yesterday, you should have spent several hours in the library. *You should have looked for additional sources for your paper.* (gerund phrase)

   _____

8. The woman sitting on the platform with the president is Allison McGee. *She is the president's executive assistant.* (appositive)

   _____

9. *You were stuck in the traffic jam on the freeway.* The meeting started and ended without you. (adverbial clause of time)

   _____

10. I don't remember meeting Rolando Gomez before today. *He is the new chairman of Jackson's re-election committee.* (adjective clause)

   _____

Exercise 15   *Subordination*

NAME _____   SCORE _____

Directions: Rewrite each sentence by removing the coordinating conjunction and changing the italicized material to the construction indicated in the parentheses.

1. Walking briskly past the store window, we saw two men, and *they were setting up a display in the window.* (adjective clause)

   _____

2. Walking briskly past the store window, we saw two men, and *they were setting up a display in the window.* (participial phrase)

   _____

3. *Buy the new sparkplugs for your car,* and I will install them for you Saturday morning. (adverbial clause)

   _____

4. *My cousin Anna has developed an interest in water skiing,* and she wants to buy a good used ski boat. (adverbial clause)

   _____

5. *The rain stopped,* and we all went to the lake for a swim. (absolute phrase)

   _____

6. *Jim locked his keys in his car,* and he was forced to call home for help. (participial phrase)

   _____

7. "I'd like for you to meet my cousin Mario. *He is fascinated by auto racing,*" said John. (adjective clause)

   _____

8. Andy was working out of town for the entire week, and Rebecca had to finish work on his presentation for the meeting. (absolute phrase)

   _____

9. *Andy was working out of town for the entire week,* and Rebecca had to finish work on his presentation for the meeting. (adverbial clause)

   _____

10. Alongside the road, I saw Jim. *He was repairing a flat tire on his bike.* (participial phrase)

   _____

11. Alongside the road, I saw Jim. *He was repairing a flat tire on his bike.* (adjective clause)

_____

12. *The heavy work of unloading the truck was finished,* and Al and Mike breezed in offering to help. (absolute phrase)

_____

13. *The heavy work of unloading the truck was finished,* and Al and Mike breezed in offering to help. (adverbial clause)

_____

14. Surfing the channels, we found a program about two men. *They had kayaked down several rivers in Alaska.* (adjective clause)

_____

15. Surfing the channels, we found a program about Tim Campbell and Mark Wells. *They had kayaked down several rivers in Alaska.* (adjective clause)

_____

16. *You should leave the building early this afternoon,* or you will get in the way of the painters who are going to start work shortly after 1:00 P.M. (adverbial clause)

_____

17. *The outdoor concert that afternoon was cancelled because of a tornado threat,* and we all went home as soon as possible. (absolute phrase)

_____

18. James Oakes has recently joined our baseball team. *He was a high school All-American last year.* (appositive)

_____

19. *Ask Maria to add some charts and graphs to your report,* and you will increase its effectiveness considerably. (gerund phrase)

_____

20. Ask Maria to add some charts and graphs to your report, and *you will increase its effectiveness considerably.* (infinitive phrase)

_____

Lesson 16 *Parallel Structure; Comparisons*

There are two other situations in which the underlying logic of the sentence requires the writer to select very carefully the structure and position of the sentence units.

Parallel Structure

When two or more parts of a sentence are similar in function, they should be expressed in the same grammatical construction; in other words, they should be **parallel.** The principle of parallelism implies that, in a series, nouns should be balanced with nouns, adjectives with adjectives, prepositional phrases with prepositional phrases, clauses with clauses, and so forth. The following sentence owes much of its clarity and effectiveness to its careful parallel arrangement: Two adjective clauses are joined with *and,* two adverbs with *but,* and three noun direct objects with *and.*

> Anyone who studies world affairs *and* who remembers our last three wars will realize, sadly *but* inevitably, that another conflict will endanger the economic strength of our nation, the complacency of our political institutions, *and* the moral fiber of our people.

Anyone ‖ who studies world affairs *and*
‖ who remembers our last three wars will realize, ‖ sadly *but*
‖ inevitably,
that another conflict will endanger ‖ the economic strength of our nation,
‖ the complacency of our political institutions,
‖ *and* the moral fiber of our people.

Two types of errors, the false series and the *and who* construction, work to destroy parallelism by using coordinate conjunctions to join grammatical units that are not alike.

1. The false or shifted series

Weak: Most people play golf for exercise, pleasure, and so they can meet others.
[The *and* ties an adverb clause to two nouns.]
Better: Most people play golf for exercise, for pleasure, and for social contacts.

Weak: Our new teacher was young, tall, slender, and with red hair.
[The *and* suggests that it will be followed by a fourth adjective, not a prepositional phrase.]
Better: Our new teacher was young, tall, slender, and red-haired.

Weak: Mr. Little's speech was tiresome, inaccurate, and should have been omitted.
Better: Mr. Little's speech was tiresome, inaccurate, and unnecessary.

155

2. The *and who* or *and which* construction

Weak:	Their son is an athlete with great talent *and who* will soon be well known.
Better:	Their son is an athlete who has great talent and who will soon be well known.
	Their son is a greatly talented athlete who will soon be well known.
	[Here the unbalanced modification is avoided.]
Weak:	I am taking Physics 388, a difficult course *and which* demands much time.
Better:	I am taking Physics 388, which is a difficult course and demands much time.
	I am taking Physics 388, which is difficult and demands much time.

Comparisons

When you write sentences that make comparisons or contrasts, you need to observe certain forms if your writing is to be clear and precise.

1. Be sure that you compare only those things that are capable of being compared:

Faulty:	The storage capacity of this computer is much greater than our old one.
	[*One* refers to computer; thus, two unlike things, storage capacity and the computer, are being compared.]
Improved:	The storage capacity of this computer is much greater than *the storage capacity of* our old one.
	The storage capacity of this computer is much greater than *that of* our old one.
Faulty:	The influence of the political leader is more ephemeral than the artist.
	[Here, *influence*, an abstract quality, is being compared to a person, the artist.]
Improved:	The influence of the political leader is more ephemeral than *the influence of* the artist.
	The influence of the political leader is more ephemeral than *that of* the artist.
	The political leader's influence is more ephemeral than *the artist's.*

2. When you use the comparative form of an adjective in a comparison, use *any other* when it is necessary to exclude the subject of the comparison from the group:

Faulty:	Wilson, the first-string center, is heavier than any man on the team.
	[In this version the writer is comparing Wilson to the members of a group that includes Wilson.]
Improved:	Wilson, the first-string center, is heavier than *any other* man on the team.

3. When your sentence contains a double comparison, be sure to include all the words necessary to make the idiom complete:

Faulty:	He is now as tall as his mother, if not taller.
Improved:	He is now as tall *as,* if not taller *than,* his mother.
Faulty:	She is one of the best runners in the club, if not the best.
Improved:	She is one of the best *runners,* if not the best *runner,* in the club.

Double comparisons may create sentences that sound somewhat awkward even though they form the comparison correctly and completely. You may want to recast the sentence to make it read more smoothly.

1. Try forming two sentences:

   He is now as tall as his mother. He may, indeed, be taller than she.
   She is one of the best runners in the club. She may even be the best runner in the club.

2. Try writing two independent clauses:

   He is now as tall as his mother, and he may be even taller than she is.
   She is one of the best runners in the club, and she may be the best runner in the club.

(See Supplement for more details on sentences used to compare and contrast.)

Supplement

In addition to requiring the structural units already mentioned, comparison–contrast sentences place a few constraints on the form of the adjective or adverb.

1. When your comparison is limited to two things, use the comparative degree:

   Both Jane and Laura sing well, but Jane has the *better* voice.
   Which takes *more* time, your studies or your job?

2. Use the superlative for more than two things:

   January is the *worst* month of the year.

You learned in Lesson 2 that there are two ways of forming the comparative and superlative degrees. In general, *er* and *est* are used with short words, and *more* and *most* with longer words.

   When I was *younger,* I was *more apprehensive* about thunder and lightning.
   This encyclopedia is the *newest* and the *most comprehensive.*
   Maria works *faster* than I and also *more accurately.*

Remember that in present-day standard English, *er* or *est* is not combined with *more* or *most* in the same word. We don't say, for example, *more pleasanter, most loveliest,* or *more faster.*

NAME _____   SCORE _____

Directions: In the space at the left, copy the letter of the sentence in each pair that is logically structured.

_____   1. A. At school my job is to check books out of the library and to help at the card catalog.
           B. At school my job is to check books out of the library and helping at the card catalog.

_____   2. A. I want to buy a jacket that is down-filled, with a hood, and closing with a zipper.
           B. I want to buy a jacket that is down-filled, has a hood, and closes with a zipper.

_____   3. A. For this job we need a man acquainted with all phases of the oil industry and who knows his way around the Middle East.
           B. For this job we need a man who is acquainted with all phases of the oil industry and knows his way around the Middle East.

_____   4. A. My grandfather pursues many hobbies: chess, woodworking, and stamp collecting.
           B. My grandfather pursues many hobbies: playing chess, woodworking, and collects stamps.

_____   5. A. The caretaker was cantankerous, set in his ways, and wouldn't let us enter the park.
           B. The caretaker, who was cantankerous and set in his ways, wouldn't let us enter the park.

_____   6. A. The best hiking boots are made of soft leather and have a special lug sole.
           B. The best hiking boots are made of soft leather and having a special lug sole.

_____   7. A. Before that day I had never been on board a boat, much less sailed one.
           B. Before that day I had never been on board a boat, much less sailing one.

_____   8. A. The architecture we observed in Brasilia is original, daring, showing imagination, and sometimes it is almost fantastic.
           B. The architecture we observed in Brasilia is original, daring, imaginative, and sometimes almost fantastic.

_____   9. A. My idea for a great day at the beach is to ride a few waves, sun for a while, and eat hot dogs cooked on a grill.
           B. My idea for a great day at the beach is to ride a few waves, sun for a while, and eating hot dogs cooked on the grill.

_____   10. A. Tony signed up for drama, not only for the acting experience but his girl friend had a role in the play.
            B. Tony signed up for drama, not only because he wanted the acting experience but because his girl friend had a role in the play.

Directions: From each of the pairs of sentences, select the one that states the comparison correctly and copy its letter in the space at the left.

_____ 1. A. It is clear that next year's cars will cost more than this year.
   B. It is clear that next year's cars will cost more than this year's.

_____ 2. A. Jake lost his job to a new trainee who is as young as, if not younger than, his son.
   B. Jake lost his job to a new trainee who is as young, if not younger than his son.

_____ 3. A. The tennis team's record for this season is better than any team in our conference.
   B. The tennis team's record for this season is better than that of any other team in our conference.

_____ 4. A. Jim and Luke are both great pitchers, but of the two Luke throws the best curve ball.
   B. Jim and Luke are both great pitchers, but of the two Luke throws the better curve ball.

_____ 5. A. The holes for these rose bushes must be deeper than the holes for the geraniums.
   B. The holes for these rose bushes must be more deeper than the geraniums.

_____ 6. A. That boy in the last row is taller than any other boy in the class.
   B. That boy in the last row is taller than any boy in the class.

_____ 7. A. Which is farthest east, New York City or Santiago, Chile?
   B. Which is farther east, New York City or Santiago, Chile?

_____ 8. A. Will next year's soccer team be more experienced than this year?
   B. Will next year's soccer team be more experienced than year's?

_____ 9. A. I believe that watching the rocket launch was one of the greatest thrills, if not the greatest thrill, of my life.
   B. I believe that watching the rocket launch was one of the greatest, if not the greatest, thrill of my life.

_____ 10. A. My qualifications for the job are as good, if not better than, Mr. Sherwood.
   B. My qualifications for the job are as good as, if not better than, Mr. Sherwood's.

NAME _____ SCORE _____

Directions: Rewrite each sentence to correct the faulty parallelism.

1. Janie took that class to increase her speaking ability and meeting new people.

   _____

2. Looking very tired and with a heavy growth of beard, Jim returned from his fishing trip today.

   _____

3. Mrs. Dorchester is wise and a skilled advisor and who knows the law school curriculum very well.

   _____

4. I enjoy tennis for the exercise, the competition, and taking my mind off school work.

   _____

5. That new car is fast and corners well, having leather interior and a fine sound system.

   _____

6. That class in desktop publishing gave me new capabilities and earning me a raise and a promotion.

   _____

7. It is a fine school, with an excellent library, new laboratories, and has a fairly small student body.

   _____

8. The weather forecast was long and complicated, and which had far too many technical terms for most people.

   _____

9. From those lessons I learned basic cooking skills and practicing several very tasty recipes.

   _____

10. In that class I decided to write a paper rather than making a speech.

   _____

Directions: Rewrite each sentence to correct the faulty comparison.

1. The weather here is often quite hot, but I like the weather here better than St. Louis, where I lived last year.

   _____

2. Melanie is a faster runner than any girl in her class.

   _____

3. My resumé is as strong as, if not stronger than, the other three applicants.

   _____

4. Playing in that championship game was one the greatest, if not the greatest, thrill of my entire life.

   _____

5. Who has the highest GPA, you or your sister?

   _____

6. The geology department here at Johnson College is stronger than any geology department in the state.

   _____

7. That high school's average SAT score is higher than any school in its district.

   _____

8. Sometimes I believe that Sylvia likes that dog more than her sister.

   _____

9. The safecracker was tall and lanky, and he had slender fingers like a surgeon.

   _____

10. Karen, who is a legal secretary, says her work is more important than the firm's lawyers.

    _____

Punctuation
Lessons, Practice Sheets, and Exercises

Lesson 17   *Commas to Separate*

As your writing grows more precise and more economical, you will need to use commas to separate certain parts of the sentence so that your work cannot be misunderstood. There are five rules that cover the occasions when commas are used to separate parts of a sentence.

The Five Rules for Commas to Separate

1. Use commas before *and, but, for, or, nor, yet,* and *so* when they join the clauses of a compound sentence:

> I placed the typed sheet on his desk, and he read it slowly.
> His face turned red, but he did not say a word.
> I knew he was angry, for he rose and stomped out of the room. [Note that no comma is used before the conjunction in a compound predicate.]

At this point you might reread Lesson 7. Remember that a semicolon rather than a comma is usually required in a compound sentence when no coordinating conjunction is present.

2. Use a comma between the items of a series.

> The land looked brown, parched, lifeless, and ominous. [Four adjectives]
> Volunteers may be students, office workers, housewives, or retirees. [Four nouns]
> The dog charged through the door, down the steps, and into the garage. [Three phrases]
> He understands what he must do, when he must do it, and why it must be done. [Three subordinate clauses]
> Larry brought the wood, Mark built the fire, and I got the steaks ready. [Three independent clauses]

A series is composed of three or more words, phrases, or clauses of equal grammatical rank. A series usually takes the form of *a, b,* ***and*** *c;* sometimes it may be *a, b,* ***or*** *c*. Although commas may be used to separate a series of short clauses, the punctuation must change if the clauses have commas within them.

163

Larry, who has a pickup truck, brought the wood, Mark, who was once a Boy Scout, built the fire, and I got the steaks ready.

Obviously commas do not effectively separate the independent clauses in this sentence, so we need to use a mark with greater strength, in this case the semicolon.

Larry, who has a pickup truck, brought the wood; Mark, who was once a Boy Scout, made the fire; and I got the steaks ready.

In journalism, writers often omit the comma before the final conjunction. It is easier to remember the rule if you develop a consistent pattern of using the comma before the final conjunction.

3. Use a comma between coordinate adjectives preceding a noun.

the harsh, cold wind

When applied to adjectives, the word **coordinate** indicates that two adjectives modify a single noun with equal force. We usually separate coordinate adjectives with a comma. Sometimes it is difficult to know whether or not two adjectives are equal. Consider the following:

the harsh cold wind
the difficult final exam

Two tests will help you to decide if the adjectives are equal.

First, if you can use the word *and* instead of a comma between the two words and still produce a correct statement, the adjectives are equal, and a comma should be used to separate them. *The harsh and cold wind* makes perfect sense in English, demonstrating that the adjectives are equal in force and need a comma. But you would never say *the difficult and final exam;* thus the adjectives are not coordinate, and the comma is not needed.

Second, if the adjectives sound natural in reversed position, they are equal and can be separated by a comma if the word *and* is not used. The phrase *the cold, harsh wind* is just as readable as *the harsh, cold wind,* again demonstrating that the adjectives are equal.

When you use more than two adjectives before a noun, you should use the *and* test, checking the adjectives by pairs, the first with the second, the second with the third, and so on to determine the need for commas. It may help you to know that we usually do not use commas before adjectives denoting size or age. And remember that you never use a comma between the last adjective and the noun.

Observe how use of these tests determines punctuation like the following:

a neat, courteous little boy
a hot, steamy summer day

Because we don't say, "a neat and courteous and little boy," we would place a comma between neat and courteous, but not between courteous and little. We could say *a hot, steamy summer day* or *a steamy, hot summer day,* but not *a hot and steamy and summer day.*

4. Use a comma after most introductory modifiers. The following specific applications of this rule will help you to use it correctly.

a. Put commas after introductory adverbial clauses:

Unless the flood water recedes soon, we're in trouble.

If we can prove that the signature was forged, we will win the case.

Before sophomores will be admitted to courses numbered 300 or above, they must have official permission.

Before I answer you, I want to ask another question.

When he arrived, he seemed distraught.

b. Put commas after introductory verbal-phrase modifiers:

Having climbed the steep trail up Cougar Mountain, Bob decided to take some pictures.
To get the best view of the valley, he walked to the edge of the cliff.
After opening his backpack, he searched for his new telephoto lens.

c. Put a comma after an introductory absolute element, such as a phrase, an adverb modifying the whole sentence, a mild exclamation, and *yes* and *no.*

In fact, there was no way to keep the front door closed.
Certainly, I'll be glad to help you.
Well, what are we to do now?
No, we are not in danger.

d. Ordinarily, do not put a comma after a single prepositional phrase at the beginning of a sentence. If the opening element contains two or more phrases, use a comma to separate the phrases from the main clause. A long introductory prepositional phrase is not followed by a comma when the subject and verb are reversed.

After a heavy dinner we usually went for a short walk.

In early summer many birds nested there.

In spite of the very heavy wind and the pelting hailstones, the third race was completed.

In the name of justice, please help these people.

After school, or during the evening, teachers were expected to find time for grading papers and preparing lessons.

Between the dusty night table and the unmade bed were all the magazines that I wanted to read.

5. Use a comma between any two words that might be mistakenly read together:

Before, he had been industrious and sober. [Not *before he had been*]
Once inside, the dog scampered all over the furniture. [Not *inside the dog*]
While we were eating, the table collapsed. [Not *eating the table*]
After we had washed, Mother prepared breakfast. [Not *washed Mother*]
Ever since, he has been afraid of deep water. [Not *ever since he has been*]
Shortly after ten, thirty new recruits appeared. [Not *shortly after ten thirty*]

FOR, AND, NOR, BUT, OR, YET, SO
FAN BOYS

NAME _____   SCORE _____

Directions: Each of the following sentences has two commas missing. Add the commas where they are necessary. In the spaces at the left, write the numbers of the rules that apply to the commas you have added:

1. Before a coordinating conjunction in a compound sentence
2. Items in a series
3. Between coordinate adjectives
4. After an introductory modifier
5. To prevent misreading

___4___
___1___
1. After she finished her paper, Claudia printed two copies, and then she left for class, taking one copy with her and leaving the other at home.

___2___
___3___
2. We waxed our skis, rode the lift to the top of the run, and made the fastest, most exciting descent in our short experience as skiers.

___4___
___1___
3. Shortly after, the rain began to fall, and we had to hurry to get back to the house before we got totally drenched.

___4___
___3___
4. Shortly after, the rain began to fall, we put on our raincoats and made the long, dismal walk, to the library.

___1___
___3___
5. The only copy of that book is due today, and I will try to check it out because I need to find a short, catchy quote to use in the introduction of my paper.

___4___
___2___
6. Having looked everywhere in the house, I went to the garage and finally located my fishing rod, my tackle box, and my lucky hat.

___4___
___1___
7. After leaving, the people in the class went to lunch, and then they all called their friends on their cell phones.

___4___
___3___
8. Rick had once flown to a small cabin in Alaska; after that, adventure in far-away places become an overwhelming, expensive hobby.

___4___
___2___
9. Leaving for work early in the morning, Kelly drove downtown parked her car, and stopped in a small diner for breakfast.

___3___
___4___
10. Because Anna was able to find a competent, efficient assistant, her work as manager, is now much more enjoyable.

___3___
___4___
11. Taking off his patched, dirty raincoat, the detective moved quickly to the phone, and began to talk with his informants.

_____ 12. Elizabeth wants to study photography, but she must first take courses in
_____   colors, composition, and perspective.

_____ 13. After he had worked for an hour, Charles had to go to class, so he printed off
_____   the notes he'd been working on and walked out to his car.

_____ 14. Andres called Spencer Alex, and Ryan, but none of them knew tomorrow's
_____   assignment, so he had to call someone else.

_____ 15. After Maria and Patty finished painting, the walls looked like new, and the
_____   women decided to work on the floors next.

_____ 16. After three days without air conditioning in their apartment, Fred, Jorge, and
_____   Oscar were delighted when the repairman finished fixing their unit.

_____ 17. The beautiful, expensive painting arrived at the office, and the entire staff
_____   gathered around to admire it.

_____ 18. Accepting the challenge of the two boys, the two older gentlemen actually
_____   defeated them in a long, grueling, basketball game by a score of 48 to 46.

_____ 19. We had bacon and eggs, toast, and coffee for breakfast, but we worked
_____   through lunch and didn't get anything to eat until late afternoon.

_____ 20. When Joe stood, the chair fell over backwards, and everyone in the room
_____   laughed at him.

NAME _____ *Test* _____ SCORE _____

Directions: Each of the following sentences has two commas missing. Add the commas where they are necessary. In the spaces at the left, write the numbers of the rules that apply to the commas you have added:

1. Before a coordinating conjunction in a compound sentence
2. Items in a series
3. Between coordinate adjectives
4. After an introductory modifier
5. To prevent misreading

___4___
___3___
1. Because there was very little time, the men hurried to the stage and began to dismantle the huge, complicated sound system. 3

___4___
___1___
2. After, the boy ran, the machine ground to a halt, and the crew went to work trying to clean up the mess. 1

___4___
___2___
3. Trying desperately to find the lost colt, the boys looked in the pasture, searched along the creek, and then began to look in the woods. 2

___3___
___1___
4. The tall, slender woman, walked quietly into the room, but hardly anyone noticed her presence.

___4___
___2___
5. As the rain began to fall, the people at the picnic packed up their food, put on their jackets, and began to move toward their cars. 2

___1___
___3___
6. Jim called Al Marcus, and Tony, but they had all left earlier for the ballgame and could not help him with his math. 3

___1___
___2___
7. That difficult, last problem puzzled the entire class, but Mary Ellen found the solution and dazzled everyone with her clear, understandable explanation.

___4___
___3___
8. Listening carefully to the last track on the CD, Will recognized an old song and began to hum the soft, haunting, melody. 3

___4___
___2___
9. When the load in the truck shifted, the bottom box split open and scattered nails, screws and other fasteners all over the floor of the truck. 2

___4___
___2___
10. At the end of that long, difficult morning, we still had to make 1000 sandwiches, 2100 cookies, and two dozen chocolate cakes for the governor's reception. 2

169

Directions: Under each rule write two sentences of your own composition to illustrate the punctuation to be used. Bring your work to class for discussion. The purpose of this exercise is to help you recognize punctuation situations in your own writing.

1. Comma used before a coordinating conjunction in a compound sentence.

    a. *Joe ran fast, but Frank walked.*

    b.

2. Commas used in a series (one series of single words and one series of phrases).

    a. *I was equipted with a nine inch a knife, a rifle, and a side arm.*

    b.

3. Comma used after an introductory modifier (one adverbial clause and one verbal phrase).

    a. *although I read the sentence over and over, I did not understand it.*

    b.

4. Comma used between coordinate adjectives.

    a. *His answers were true, Blue and to the point.*

    b.

5. Comma used to prevent misreading.

    a.

    b.

Exercise 17A

Commas and Semicolons to Separate

NAME _____ SCORE _____

Directions: The following sentences contain numbered spots where punctuation might be needed. In the correspondingly numbered spaces at the left, write C if a comma is needed, S if a semicolon is needed, or 0 if no punctuation is needed.

1. __C & S__ (1) "When you have nothing to say, don't say anything, and you won't get

2. __C__ yourself into trouble," said my wise old grandmother.

3. __C__ (2) Racing swiftly to the fence, Garnett turned, leaped high and snared the ball

4. __C__ in the webbing of her glove.

5. __C__ (3) Because he had a few spare minutes before lunch, Jim checked the library

6. __S__ shelves he was delighted to find a book he had been trying to locate.

7. __C__ (4) Inside, the room was lit by a single small bulb I was barely able to make my

8. __S__ way through the tangle of furniture to the phone.

9. __0__ (5) My father grinned broadly and hugged the small, tired girl but she

10. __C__ continued to sob softly into her handkerchief.

11. __0__ (6) She has a fine collection of beautiful antique cars, a 1937 Cord and a 1955

12. __S__ Chevy Nomad station wagon are the showpieces of the entire group.

13. __C__ (7) While the flustered young man was trying to answer, an expensively

14. __0__ dressed older woman interrupted with another question.

15. __0__ (8) "Senator, we need to know why you voted against that bill," said an irate

16. __S__ citizen, "it would have provided the city with badly needed jobs."

17. __0 C__ (9) Three beautiful, well-dressed children sat quietly in the airport lounge and

18. __0__ read magazines while waiting for their flight.

19. __C__ (10) Down below, the boat had a large stateroom complete with sauna and

20. __S__ television; the owner, however, always slept in a hammock on the foredeck.

171

21. ___S___ (11) The reputation of the new bank president is excellent^S people say he is
                                                                        21
22. ___C___   intelligent, hard-working,and scrupulously honest.
                                          22
23. ___C___ (12) A few minutes later^C the three girls left the campus^O and began their trip to
                                    23   24
24. ___D___   New York.

25. ___C___ (13) If our money lasts^C the living room and sun porch will be enlarged^A and
                                   25   26
26. ___O___   completely redecorated in bright cheerful pastel colors.

27. ___C___ (14) Although I studied French grammar and French conversation in middle
28. ___C___   school, high school^C and college^C my accent is atrocious.
                                    27   28
29. ___C___ (15) Joan tried to comfort the lost puppy^C and Jim soon found its dis-
                                                     29
30. ___O___   traught^O weeping owner.
                        30
31. ___O___ (16) A graceful^O gray and white sea gull soared past us, banked suddenly^O and
                           31   32
32. ___O___   floated off on the wind.

33. ___S___ (17) Looking down from the mountain for the first time^S I knew I wanted to
                                                                  33
34. ___C___   buy the property^C for the view was magnificent.
                                 34
35. ___S___ (18) We'll not need the forklift today^S the three of us can turn the rock^C roll it
                                                  35   36
36. ___C___   down the hill, and set it in place.

37. ___O___ (19) Shortly before midnight, a cranky, old^O neighborhood grouch called me^O and
                                                      37   38
38. ___O___   complained about my barking dogs.

39. ___C___ (20) Standing in front of the house^C painters and carpenters argued over the use
                                              39
40. ___C___   of the ladders^C and the other workmen laughed out loud at their childishness.
                              40

Lesson 18   *Commas to Enclose*

Just as there are times when you need to use commas to separate items, there are times when you need to use commas to enclose items. Use commas to enclose **interrupters**—those words, phrases, or clauses that interrupt the normal word order of a sentence.

Common Interrupters

The most common types of interrupters are discussed below.

1. Nonrestrictive adjective clauses and phrases

   The coach's Awards Banquet speech, *which was one of her best,* should be published. [Nonrestrictive adjective clause]
   Jan's mother, *holding a winning ticket,* went to the desk. [Nonrestrictive participial phrase]
   Professor Angela Cheney, *at the far end of the head table,* summoned a waiter. [Nonrestrictive prepositional phrase]

Clauses and phrases not essential to identify a noun are set off by commas. (See Lesson 9 to review restrictive and nonrestrictive clauses and phrases.) Note that, in some cases, the meaning of the sentence depends on whether a clause is taken as restrictive or nonrestrictive.

   My brother-in-law *who lives in Akron* is a chemist.
   [The writer has more than one brother-in-law. The restrictive clause is needed to distinguish this brother-in-law from other brothers-in-law.]
   My brother-in-law, *who lives in Akron,* is a chemist.
   [The writer is telling us that he or she has only one brother-in-law. Identification is not explicit.]

2. Most appositives

   One comedian, *the one with the the lisp,* was booed.
   The major, *a veteran of three wars,* accepted the award.
   Mr. Tate, *our head counselor,* will speak.
   Our head counselor, *Mr. Tate,* will speak.

As you learned in Lesson 10, the most common type of appositive immediately follows the noun or pronoun that it renames. Appositives like these are called loose or nonrestrictive appositives and are set off. Sometimes, however, an appositive functions in the same way that a restrictive adjective clause functions: It identifies a preceding noun that, without the appositive, could refer to any member of a class. An appositive of this sort is not set off:

   my brother Jack
   the poet Keats

173

the apostle Paul
the preposition *to*

3. Absolute phrases

Today being a holiday, I plan to loaf and relax.
Her replacement having arrived early, Bea had time to shop.
He sat there in silence, *his left cheek twitching as usual.*
He stood in the doorway, *his wet cloak dripping water on the rug,* and waited for some sign of recognition.

An absolute phrase, which consists of a noun or a pronoun and a verbal (see Lesson 12), modifies the sentence as a whole, not any special part of it. Because the phrase is not restricted to any special part of the sentence, the phrase should be set off.

4. Parenthetical expressions

The text, *moreover,* had not been carefully proofread.
You will find, *for example,* that the format is not attractive.
The meal, *to tell the truth,* was quite unappetizing.
His appearance, *I must admit,* would startle anyone.

These are words, phrases, or clauses that break into the sentence to explain, to emphasize, to qualify, or to point the direction of the thought and should be set off.

5. Words used in direct address

"Remember, *Jimmy,* that we like your work," he said.
"*Henry,*" said the teacher, "you made an A on your paper."
"I believe, *sir,* that you have been misinformed," she replied.
"And now, *dear friends and neighbors,* let's eat," said Father Jamison.

6. Expressions designating the speaker in direct quotations

"With your permission," *Tom replied,* "I'll go home for the day."
"That will have to do," *said Mrs. Garcia,* "until we think of something better."

Other punctuation marks may be used instead of the comma if the sentence justifies their use.

"How shall I tell him?" asked Mary timidly. [Question mark after question]

"Silence!" he shouted. "Get to work at once!" [Exclamation point]

"Two of the buildings are firetraps," replied the inspector; "moreover, the library needs a new roof." [Semicolon required to avoid a comma fault between independent clauses]

7. Negative insertions used for emphasis, units out of their position, and tag questions (short interrogative clauses combined with statements)

Our plane was an old propeller model, *not the 747 we had expected.*
Tired and footsore, the hikers finally reached camp.
The hikers finally reached camp, *tired and footsore.*
Her answer was a good one, *don't you think?*
You remember, *don't you,* Dr. Wade's eloquent eulogy?

8. Degrees, titles, and the like when they follow names

Helen Lyle, *Ph.D.,* gave the opening address.
The new ambassador is Peter Jones, *Esq.*

9. In dates and addresses

On July 14, *1904,* in a little cottage at 316 High Street, *Mayville, Illinois,* the wedding took place.

When a year follows a month, rather than a day of the month, the year is usually not set off. No comma is needed before a ZIP code number:

As of March 1985 his mailing address was 1675 East Union Street, Seattle, Washington 98122.

Practice
Sheet 18   *Commas to Enclose*

NAME _____   SCORE _____

Directions: Insert commas where they are necessary in the following sentences. Then before each sentence write one of the following numbers to indicate the rule that governs the punctuation:

1. A nonrestrictive clause or phrase
2. An appositive
3. An absolute phrase
4. A parenthetical element
5. A noun in direct address
6. The speaker in dialogue

_____ 1. Your cousin, the captain of the chess team, wants you to join the team.

_____ 2. Only a few spiders, you must remember, are dangerously poisonous.

_____ 3. The shop foreman, who is also a skilled mechanic, demands careful work.

_____ 4. And now, sports fans, we will see whether the team can remain undefeated.

_____ 5. The cowboy, his gun still smoking, pointed excitedly at the dead snake.

_____ 6. "I wish that I had known the truth earlier," sobbed the old woman.

_____ 7. The horse, stung by the whip, raced around the track.

_____ 8. Sam, we have reason to believe, has been embezzling the bank's funds.

_____ 9. Mr. Jones, who is always very solemn, broke into gales of laughter.

_____ 10. Most coaches are happy with only one outcome, victory.

_____ 11. I loaned her my car, a broken-down Plymouth.

_____ 12. "Do you know," the policeman asked, "where she was at noon yesterday?"

_____ 13. My arm, being in a cast, I could not mow the lawn.

_____ 14. Move over, George, and let me sit here with you.

_____ 15. Those trees belong to my sister Joan, who is an avid gardener.

Directions: Each of the following sentences contains an adjective clause or a participial phrase in italics. Insert commas where they are needed. In the space at the left of each sentence write: R. if the clause or phrase is restrictive, N. if it is nonrestrictive

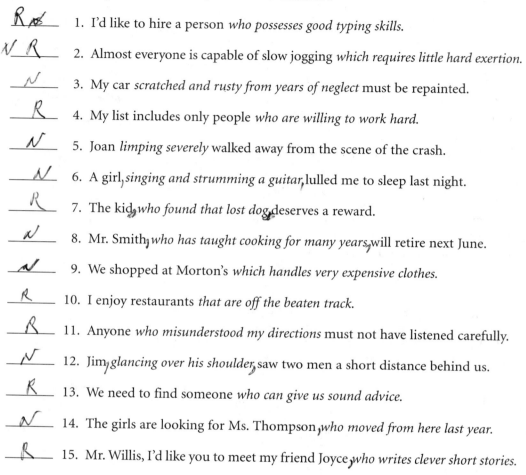

R ~~N~~   1. I'd like to hire a person *who possesses good typing skills.*

N R   2. Almost everyone is capable of slow jogging *which requires little hard exertion.*

N   3. My car *scratched and rusty from years of neglect* must be repainted.

R   4. My list includes only people *who are willing to work hard.*

N   5. Joan *limping severely* walked away from the scene of the crash.

N   6. A girl, *singing and strumming a guitar,* lulled me to sleep last night.

R   7. The kid, *who found that lost dog,* deserves a reward.

N   8. Mr. Smith, *who has taught cooking for many years,* will retire next June.

N   9. We shopped at Morton's *which handles very expensive clothes.*

R   10. I enjoy restaurants *that are off the beaten track.*

R   11. Anyone *who misunderstood my directions* must not have listened carefully.

N   12. Jim, *glancing over his shoulder,* saw two men a short distance behind us.

R   13. We need to find someone *who can give us sound advice.*

N   14. The girls are looking for Ms. Thompson, *who moved from here last year.*

R   15. Mr. Willis, I'd like you to meet my friend Joyce, *who writes clever short stories.*

NAME _____ SCORE _____

Directions: Recognizing typical punctuation situations in your own writing is a very important skill. In the spaces provided write two sentences to illustrate each of the rules indicated. Be sure to include all necessary punctuation.

1. Two sentences with nonrestrictive adjective clauses.

a.

b.

2. Two sentences with nonrestrictive participial phrases.

a.

b.

3. Two sentences with appositives.

a.

b.

4. Two sentences with nouns used in direct address.

a.

b.

5. Two sentences with parenthetical elements.

a.

b.

6. Two sentences with absolute phrases.

a.

b.

Directions: Each of the following sentences contains an adjective clause or a participial phrase. Insert commas where they are needed. In the space at the left of each sentence, write **R** if the clause or phrase is restrictive, **N** if the clause or phrase is nonrestrictive.

_____R_____ 1. In her fiftieth year she wrote a book that made her famous.

_____N R_____ 2. Her latest novel, which critics praised highly, has sold thousands of copies.

_____N_____ 3. My aunt Emma, having a consuming wanderlust and unlimited funds, rarely stays at home.

_____R_____ 4. Children having few aunts, uncles, and cousins are often quite independent.

_____R_____ 5. Spend your vacation in Canyon City where the Old West is re-created for you.

_____R_____ 6. We live in a town where people become acquainted easily.

_____N_____ 7. The man, of whom I speak, is none other than Judge Bolton.

_____R_____ 8. Here is a picture of my maternal grandmother, for whom our oldest daughter is named.

_____N_____ 9. My uncle, being slightly hard of hearing, wanted to sit near the front of the auditorium.

_____N_____ 10. The children, watching the performing animals, were delighted by the comic antics of the chimpanzees.

_____R_____ 11. I can remember a time when you disapproved of such kinds of popular music.

_____R_____ 12. On New Year's Day of 1891 when my grandfather arrived at Ellis Island he was penniless.

_____N_____ 13. No employee except the president's personal secretary, who is at present on leave of absence, has seen the memorandum.

_____R_____ 14. The story had been given to a reporter by a former employee, who maintained that he had been fired unfairly.

_____N_____ 15. I'm looking for some secluded spot where I can study, without interruption.

_____N_____ 16. I often spend my afternoons, in the periodical room of the college library, where I can study without interruption.

_____R_____ 17. A man sitting in the row behind us annoyed us by cracking peanuts during the movie.

_____N_____ 18. Losing the government contract was a blow to the Acme Drilling Company, already suffering financially, because of foreign competition.

_____N_____ 19. The shield in front of the reactor, is made of lead, which is impervious to the radiation.

_____R_____ 20. The committee recommended that the government stockpile certain strategic metals that are in short supply.

NAME _____ SCORE _____

Directions: The following sentences contain numbered spots where punctuation might be needed. In the correspondingly numbered spaces at the left, write **C** if a comma is needed, **S** if a semicolon is needed or **0** if no punctuation is needed.

1._____ (1) Schooled in the arts of witchcraft and black magic the island natives
                                                    1

2._____   terrified the explorers and kept them away from their homes for years.
                 2

3._____ (2) Come now, my friend you cannot hope to make me believe that you have
                             3   4

4._____   invented a perpetual-motion machine.

5._____ (3) It is possible in our opinion, to construct an engine that will run equally
                             5   6

6._____   well on gasoline, kerosene, or diesel fuel.

7._____ (4) He seemed to be a cheerful carefree kid who would never stoop to cheating
                                          7   8

8._____   to improve his status in the class.

9._____ (5) My friends tell me, John, that the advice you gave them on our last visit caused
                                          9   10

10._____   them to lose $10,000.

11._____ (6) "When you wish upon a star it makes no difference who you are because
                                    11   12

12._____   the stars don't grant wishes to anyone," chuckled the cynical comedian.

13._____ (7) After he had examined the rare beautiful books we took a leisurely tour of
                                    13   14

14._____   the art museum.

15._____ (8) The two men took their time going home the roads were covered by a
                                              15

16._____   thin hazy oil slick.
                      16

17._____ (9) Some believe that the election, although won by a wide margin, is not
                                    17

18._____   indicative of the desires of the people and should be disregarded.
                                              18

19._____ (10) After I left the dog and cat fought wildly for two hours and almost
                          19   20

20._____   destroyed the house.

21._____ (11) Those clouds, you understand hid the sun for only a few minutes the rest

22._____ of the day was quite clear.

23._____ (12) No one else who read the book seemed to enjoy the satire which was

24._____ often very subtle.

25._____ (13) And so, boys and girls the gypsy girl and the prince were married that

26._____ very night and lived forever in the magic kingdom beyond the sea.

27._____ (14) We washed the dishes, collected all the books and dusted them then we

28._____ left for the picnic.

29._____ (15) You do remember, Mr. Kent that I explained the operation of the copy

30._____ machine to you including the procedures for recording the number of

copies you have made.

31._____ (16) The man you saw yesterday is Joe Boyd he was once a championship

32._____ squash player.

33._____ (17) Mrs. Simmons you know, is the only living relative of Josiah Matthews a

34._____ local hero in the Spanish-American War.

35._____ (18) Before next Tuesday we will call you otherwise you can assume that we

36._____ we do intend to accept your offer.

37._____ (19) "Now then, team," said the coach "I want you to get out there and fight and

38._____ to avoid embarrassing me the way you did in the first half."

39._____ (20) Instead of seventy seven hundred people were invited to the party the

40._____ room, you can believe was a trifle crowded.

This lesson covers a number of tricky punctuation marks.

Apostrophe

The apostrophe (') has three uses:

1. To form the possessive of nouns and indefinite pronouns
2. To mark the omitted material in contractions
3. To form certain plurals, such as those of letters and abbreviations

Forming Possessives

Any noun, whether singular or plural, that does not end in *s* shows ownership by adding an apostrophe and *s:*

a boy*'s* hat [the hat belongs to the boy], the horse*'s* tail, Carol*'s* car, men*'s* shoes, children*'s* toys

Plural nouns that end in *s* form possessives by adding an apostrophe after the *s:*

boys' hats, horses' tails, the Smiths' home, ladies' dresses

Singular nouns ending in *s* or *z* form the possessive by adding *'s.*

the countess's castle   Frances's reply   Mr. Gomez's report

On rare occassions, if the pronunciation of the word with the additional s-sound would be awkward, it is permissible to form the possessive with an apostrophe alone.

for goodness' sake

For the sake of uniformity, the exercises on possessives will ask that you use the *'s* after singular nouns ending in *s.*

The indefinite pronouns, but not the personal pronouns, form the possessive with the aid of the apostrophe:

somebody*'s* sweater, anyone*'s* opinion, anybody*'s* game [But note the possessive forms of pronouns: *his, hers, its, theirs, ours, yours, whose.*]

Compound words and word groups form the possessive by adding an apostrophe and *s* to the last word of the group:

My sister-in-law*'s* last visit was in December.
Did you get anyone else*'s* opinion of your paper?

Note that establishing ownership of two or more items requires careful attention. For individual ownership, add an apostrophe and *s* at the end of both owners.

Oliver Stones's and Alfred Hitchcock's movies [indicating that each owned certain movies]

For joint ownership of two or more items, add an apostrophe and *s* at the end of the second owner's name:

Rogers and Hammerstein's musicals [indicating that they wrote musicals as joint projects]

Omitted Material

The apostrophe is also used to stand for the omitted material in contractions:

doesn't [does not], won't [will not], she's [she is, she has], o'clock [of the clock], rock 'n' roll [rock and roll]

You must learn to distinguish carefully between the following pairs of contractions and possessives:

Contraction	*Possessive*
it's [it is, it has]	its
there's [there is, there has]	theirs
they're [they are]	their
who's [who is, who has]	whose
you're [you are]	your

Unusual Plurals

Use an apostrophe to form the plural of letters and words that are treated as words.

the three *R*'s; mostly *A*'s and *B*'s; too many *and*'s; no *if*'s, *and*'s, or *but*'s about it.

Although usage is divided, many authorities no longer require the formation of the plurals of numbers and symbols with an apostrophe.

Btus, CPAs, 1980s, scores in the 80s and 90s

Many writers need to be reminded regularly of an important related fact: An apostrophe is never used in forming the plural of either a common or a proper noun.

There are two Kathys in the class. Two grandmas attended.

Colon

The colon (:) is a formal mark announcing an explanation, a list, or a quotation to follow.

My fellow Americans: My speech tonight will examine. . . .
All hikers must bring the following: a flashlight, a small ax, and a waterproof tarp.
Mr. Rankin stood and addressed the group: "I don't intend to take much of your time today."

The colon is used in formal papers to begin a quotation of four or more lines. The text of the quotation is indented from both margins and is set off by quotation marks.

In cases where the colon sets off a quotation, the identifying tag should appear in the independent clause.

Colons are also used as a mark of separation in certain special constructions:

Hours, minutes, and seconds
　　1:14:10 P.M.
Biblical chapters and verses
　　I Kings 2:1
Titles and Subtitles
　　Conversations: Famous Women Speak Out

Note that after a colon it is permissible to have an initial capital letter if the text following the colon is a complete sentence. Do not use a colon to separate a verb from its complement or a preposition from its object.

Faulty:　All hikers must bring: a flashlight, a small ax, and a waterproof tarpaulin.
Faulty:　The things a hiker must bring are: a flashlight, a small ax, and a waterproof tarpaulin.
Faulty:　The hiker's equipment should consist of: a flashlight, a small ax, and a waterproof tarpaulin.

Dash

The dash (—) is used to show an abrupt change in thought in the sentence. It must be used sparingly and never as a substitute for other marks.

Superior students—notice that I said *superior*—will not have to take the test.
New surroundings, new friends, a challenging new job—all these helped Eugene overcome his grief.

Hyphen

The hyphen (-) is used to divide a word at the end of a line and to join words to form various types of compounds. Divide a word only between syllables. With words having a prefix or a suffix, divide the word after the prefix and before the suffix. Avoid dividing a word so that a single letter ends or begins a line. (Consult your dictionary for problems of syllabic division.)

mathe-matics *not* mathem-atics
inter-collegiate *not* intercol-legiate
govern-ess *not* gov-erness
enough *not* e-nough
many *not* man-y

Use hyphens to join the parts of compound modifiers preceding nouns.

Observe his well-kept lawn. His lawn is well kept.
We deplore your devil-may-care attitude.

This use of a hyphen sometimes determines an exact meaning:

a roll of twenty-dollar bills; a roll of twenty dollar bills
all-American boys; all American boys

Use hyphens with compound numbers from twenty-one to ninety-nine and with fractions:

Twenty-two people claimed the one-third share of the reward money but received only one-eighth.

Use hyphens, particularly with prefixes and suffixes, to avoid awkward combinations of letters or to distinguish between two meanings of a word:

anti-intellectual
pre-Aztec
her doll-like face
re-cover a couch [not recover the money]

Quotation Marks

Quotation marks should be used to enclose quoted material and words you may use in some special way. Use double quotation marks (" ") to enclose the exact words of a quoted speech. Quotation marks always come in pairs. The marks show the beginning and the end of a speech, whether it is part of a sentence, one sentence, or several sentences. If a speech is interrupted by material showing who said it, quotation marks set off the quoted material from the explanatory material. Use quotation marks where the directly quoted material begins and where it ends or is interrupted. Indirect quotations are *not* set off by quotation marks:

"I admit," said Ralph, "that I was mistaken."
[Note that the explanatory material is set off from the direct quotation.]
Peg answered, "I didn't attend. I wasn't in town." [More than one sentence.]
Peg answered that she hadn't attended because she hadn't been in town.
[This is an indirect quotation. Words not directly quoted do not need quotation marks.]

Use double quotation marks to set off the subdivisions of books, names of songs, and titles of units of less than book length, such as short stories, short poems, essays, and articles:

The second chapter of *Moby Dick* is entitled "The Carpet-Bag."

Eva Peron sings "Don't Cry for Me, Argentina" in the musical *Evita*.

Our anthology includes "Threes," a poem from Sandburg's *Smoke and Steel*.

The first article I read for my research paper was William Calvin's "The Great Climate Flip-flop" in the *Atlantic Monthly*.

Titles of books, magazines, long poems, newspapers, motion pictures, and radio and television series are not set in double quotation marks. In printed material, these items are set in italic type (*type like this*). Other special uses of italics are for foreign words and phrases and for names of ships, planes, and spacecraft. In handwritten or typewritten papers, underlining (<u>typescript like this</u>) is the equivalent of italics in printed material. Word-processors can produce effects such as bold (**bold**) and italic, which gives students a capability previously not available except through typesetting.

Double quotation marks are also used to set off slang words used in serious writing. Sometimes double quotation marks are used to set off words when they are referred to as words:

> The witness had only recently been released from the "slammer."
> Words like "seize" and "siege" are often misspelled.

Usage is divided on these uses of quotation marks. The two words in the second example would almost certainly appear in italics in printed material. Student writers of handwritten or typed material should either underline such words or set them off by quotation marks, the first method being the more common practice.

Double Quotation Marks with Other Punctuation

Follow this usage in the placing of quotation marks in relation to other marks:

1. Commas and periods always go inside quotation marks.
2. Semicolons and colons always go outside quotation marks.
3. Question marks and exclamation points go inside if they belong to the quoted part, outside if they do not.

> "Come in," said my uncle, "and take off your coats." [Comma and period]
>
> Mr. Lowe said, "I heartily endorse this candidate"; unfortunately most of the audience thought he said *hardly* instead of *heartily*. [Semicolon outside]
>
> "Heavens!" he exclaimed. "Is this the best you can do?" [Exclamation point and question mark]
>
> Mother asked, "Where were you last night?" [No double punctuation]
>
> Did she say, "I came home early"?
> [Question mark belongs to the whole sentence, not to the quoted part]
>
> Did Mother ask, "Where were you last night?"
> [Note that there is only one question mark after a double question like this]

Single Quotation Marks

Use single quotation marks to enclose a speech within a speech:

> "I wonder what he meant," said Betty, "when he said, 'There are wheels within wheels.' "

You may not write many sentences like this one, but just the same, you should note that when you have quotes within quotes, the period comes inside both the single and double quotation marks.

NAME _____ SCORE _____

Directions: In the spaces at the left, write **C** if the punctuation is correct and **W** if it is wrong. Within the incorrect sentences, correct the faulty punctuation by adding, removing, or changing marks.

_____ 1. Some of the coaches' drills—especially the short sprints—are very difficult and often leave the players exhausted.

_____ 2. "Morris' Movers" is the name of that amateur cross-country team; the members don't win any prizes, but they do have lot's of fun.

_____ 3. The list of prizes is impressive; five beautiful guitars, several collections of sheet music, and a biography of Carlos Santana.

_____ 4. A lawyers work must be typed perfectly, with all the *t's* crossed and all the *i's* dotted.

_____ 5. We need someone elses opinion in your case because its difficult to interpret the law in cases such as yours.

_____ 6. Wallace Brothers' Store is offering some real bargains in: women's apparel, mens' work clothes, and childrens' shoes.

_____ 7. "Tomorrow's agenda," said the speaker, "is filled with interesting and fascinating—but I see by your yawns that you've lost interest already.

_____ 8. Its not likely that anyone can replace you, with your lovely smile and great ability to allay peoples fears.

_____ 9. "Someone's coming down the walk," whispered Mary. "I don't recognize him; the footsteps are Jim's, but the whistle's Marvin's.

_____ 10. We're trying to improve our class's image; our reputation suffers because of everyones lack of motivation.

_____ 11. "Lets not panic," said the scoutmaster, "for calm action always lets us conquer trying circumstances."

_____ 12. If it's true that the dog hurt its leg, we'll surely need to find its owner before it's too late to help.

_____ 13. The new cars interior comes equipped with: leather seats, padded dashboard, and a special set of mirrors.

_____ 14. For the past few year's our teams lacked depth and experience, but this years' ought to be much more successful.

_____ 15. At nine oclock you'll need to check the cakes progress and adjust the temperature of the oven.

Directions: Sentences 1–5 are indirect quotations. In the space provided, rewrite each sentence as a direct quotation. Sentences 6–10 are direct quotations. Rewrite each as an indirect quotation. You will have to alter some verb forms and some pronoun forms as well as the punctuation.

1. My brother said that he had lost his wallet.

   _____

2. The sales manager observed that he would need to hire two new division managers.

   _____

3. My teachers often tell me that I am too talkative in class.

   _____

4. The policeman asked if we needed directions to the next town.

   _____

5. Did she tell you that the elevator is being repaired?

   _____

6. The teller said to me, "It will take only a minute to compute your interest."

   _____

7. My father said, "I certainly appreciate all your hard work."

   _____

8. His sister answered, "I don't want to go sailing in this rainy weather."

   _____

9. The salesman asked, "Why did you select the convertible?"

   _____

10. Didn't she say, "You should take the right-hand fork after the covered bridge"?

    _____

NAME _____ SCORE _____

Directions: In the space at the left, write **C** if the punctuation is correct or **W** if it is incorrect. Within the incorrect sentences, correct the faulty punctuation by adding, removing, or changing marks.

_____ 1. What's new about Jim's proposal is it's focus on the prospects open to us in the bond market, isn't it?

_____ 2. You've selected the location of all the game's, haven't you?

_____ 3. "Thats not right," said the captain. "I'm sure I told you to get everyones comments on that incident."

_____ 4. He closed his comments with one final but very important statement: "Remember, friends, there's great hope that we can win, if we use the strength thats our's.

_____ 5. Todays work list includes repairs for: the men's sauna, the womens locker room, and the childrens' play area.

_____ 6. "Your assignment for Monday," said the professor, "is to read all section's on—but we don't have class on Monday, do we?"

_____ 7. The equipment list for tomorrow's climb should include the following items: boots, ropes, pitons, gloves, a helmet, and a good, hearty lunch.

_____ 8. "Its funny," mused Janet, "but these letters aren't addressed to me." "Perhaps they belong to the people next door."

_____ 9. You'll find that todays agenda is filled with: committee meetings, general session's, subcommittee meetings, and several caucuses.

_____ 10. You're probably familiar with Parkinson's Law: In any job, the work expands to fill the available time.

_____ 11. "Everyone's chances in the contest are equal," said Tom. "We'll simply put all the entries into a hat and draw out the name of the winner.

_____ 12. Sam's excuse for quitting football was that the X's and O's used in the coaches' diagrams were too confusing for him to understand.

_____ 13. When I opened the lunch my sister had packed for me, I found: a slice of bread with it's crusts cut off, two days worth of old lunch wrappings, and a note that said, "Now we are even."

_____ 14. Ms. Jones decision to stand for reelection is based on a misinterpretation of the voters' opinions of her past performances.

_____ 15. Just a few day's ago—I can't remember exactly when—Joan ordered a whole years supply of pens' and pencils' for the office.

Directions: Sentences 1-5 are indirect quotations. In the space provided, rewrite each sentence as a direct quotation. Sentence 6-10 are direct quotations. Rewrite each as an indirect quotation. You will have to alter some verb forms and pronoun forms as well as the punctuation.

1. Mr. Raymond reported that he saw an unidentified flying object over his house last night.

   _____

2. Kathleen responded that the last train for the city leaves every evening at 6:30 P.M.

   _____

3. The reporter asked when the murder victim had last been seen alive.

   _____

4. Did she say that there are no rooms left in the hotel for this weekend?

   _____

5. The manager announced that all the part-time employees would receive a ten-percent raise.

   _____

6. "You must answer every question if your application is to be considered," said the receptionist to me.

   _____

7. The secretary looked up slowly from her work and said, "I wonder what the next big crisis will be."

   _____

8. The delighted child said, "This is the best party anyone ever had."

   _____

9. The announcer turned to the woman and asked, "Would you like to tell our audience exactly how you feel about winning the lottery?"

   _____

10. On the boss's wall there is a sign that asks, "Why is there always enough time to do something over and never enough time to do it right?"

    _____

This lesson discusses end marks and summarizes all the punctuation rules presented in this book.

Period

The **period** is used after a complete declarative sentence and after ordinary abbreviations. Its use as end punctuation after sentences needs no examples. Its use after abbreviations is a little more complicated.

Personal Titles

A period is used in the following abbreviations: *Mr., Mrs., Ms., Messrs., Mmes.,* and *Dr.* These abbreviations appear before the name. Periods are also used for *Jr., Sr., Esq., D.D., Ph.D.,* and so forth, which are used after names. Miss does not require a period. *Ms.,* used instead of *Miss* or *Mrs.* when marital status is not indicated, is usually considered an abbreviation and uses a period, although some modern dictionaries have entries for it either with or without a period.

Latin-Based Terms

The following initials and abbreviations, used only in documentation pages and tabulations but not in ordinary writing, require periods: *e.g. (for example), etc. (and so forth), i.e. (that is), p., pp. (page, pages),* and *vol. (volume).* A.D., B.C., A.M., and P.M. (usually set in small caps in printed material) are used only with figures and where necessary for clearness. Note: A.D. should precede the year (A.D. 37); B.C., however, should follow the year (31 B.C.).

Addresses

The following abbreviations require periods and are acceptable in addresses but should be spelled out in ordinary writing: *St. (Street), Ave. (Avenue), Blvd. (Boulevard), Dr. (Drive), Rd. (Road), Co. (Company),* and *Inc. (Incorporated).* Conventionally, periods have been used with abbreviations of the states *(Mass., Minn., Tex., W. Va.).* However, the two-letter capitalized symbols authorized by the U.S. Postal Service *(MA, MN, TX, WV)* do not require periods.

Poor:	Last Mon. P.M. I visited my two older bros., who live in N.Y. Chas. works for a mfg. co. there. Thos. attends NYU, preparing himself for a gov't. job. He's coming home for Xmas.
Right:	Last Monday afternoon I visited my two older brothers, who live in New York. Charles works for a manufacturing company there. Thomas attends New York University, preparing himself for a government job. He's coming home for Christmas.

Acronyms and Measurements

In modern usage, the "alphabet" name forms, or acronyms, of various governmental or intergovernmental agencies, social or professional organizations, and units of measurement used in scientific contexts are usually not followed by periods: *ACLU, CARE, CBS, CIA, NAACP, NCAA, NATO, PTA, SEC, UNESCO, Btu* (British thermal unit), *mpg, mph, rpm*. New acronyms and abbreviated forms spring into existence nowadays with regularity. The following examples contain some that have gained common acceptance fairly recently: *AIDS* (acquired immune deficiency syndrome), *CAT scan* (computerized axial tomography), *CATV* (community antenna television), *CD* (certificate of deposit), *CEO* (chief executive officer), *COLA* (cost-of-living adjustment), *CPR* (cardiopulmonary resuscitation), *DWI* (driving while intoxicated), *IRA* (individual retirement account), *MIA* (missing in action), *MRI* (magnetic resonance imaging), *OPEC* (Organization of Petroleum Exporting Countries), *PC* (personal computer), *STOL* (short takeoff and landing), *VCR* (videocassette recorder). Refer to your dictionary when in doubt about the meaning of an abbreviated form or the possibility of using periods. Be prepared to find apparent inconsistencies and divided usage.

Question Mark

The **question mark** is used after a *direct question,* which is an utterance that calls for an answer. (See Lesson 6.) A question mark is not used after an *indirect question,* which is a statement giving the substance of a question but not the words that would be used in a direct question.

Direct: Who goes there? Is that you? When do we eat? How much do I owe you? "Who goes there?" he demanded. [In dialogue]

Indirect: She asked me how old I was. I wondered why she would ask such a question. [Note that these are statements, not direct questions.]

Refer to page 187 to review the use of question marks with quotation marks.

Exclamation Point

The **exclamation point** is used sparingly in modern writing and should be reserved for statements of strong feeling. Mild exclamations, such as *oh, goodness, well, yes,* and *no,* are followed by commas, not exclamation points. Be sure to place the exclamation mark after the exclamation itself.

"Help! I'm slipping!" he shouted. [Note the period after *shouted.*]
"Stop that!" she screamed. [Do not put the exclamation point after *screamed.*]
"Well, it was exciting, wasn't it?" "Oh, I had a pleasant time."

SUMMARY OF PUNCTUATION RULES

This summary provides the indispensable punctuation rules for anything you write. Colons, commas, periods, and even question marks and exclamation points do have other uses for special occasions or effects, but these occasional applications rarely cause problems for most writers.

Commas to Separate: Five Rules

1. Compound sentences
2. Items in a series
3. Coordinate adjectives
4. Introductory modifiers
5. Words that may be misread together

Colon: Two Rules

1. Use a colon to announce a list, an explanation, or a long quotation.
   a. If the text following a colon is a complete sentence, use an initial capital letter.
   b. Do not use a colon to separate a verb from its complement or a preposition from its object.
2. Use a colon to separate hours, minutes, and seconds; Biblical chapters and verses; titles and subtitles.

Apostrophe: Two Rules

1. With possessives
2. With contractions

Period: Two Rules

1. After declarative sentences
2. After most abbreviations

Commas to Enclose: Eight Rules

1. Nonrestrictive clauses and phrases
2. Appositives
3. Absolute phrases
4. Parenthetical expressions
5. Words in direct address
6. The speaker in dialogue
7. Negative insertions
8. Dates, addresses, degrees, and titles

Semicolon: Two Rules

1. In compound sentences without a conjunction joining the independent clauses
2. To separate items in a series when commas occur within items

Quotation Marks: Three Rules

1. Enclose direct quotations
2. Set off titles
3. Set off words used in some special way

Question Mark: One Rule

1. After direct questions

Practice Sheet 20

Review of Punctuation

NAME _____ SCORE _____

Directions: In the space at the left, write **C** if the punctuation is correct and **W** if it is wrong. Within the incorrect sentences, correct the faulty punctuation by adding, removing, or changing marks.

_____C_____ 1. My new address is 646 Senecca Ave., Rolling Hills, MI 20202.

_____C_____ 2. I have an appointment with Mr. Billings and Miss Williams at 3:30 P.M. today.

_____C_____ 3. Alexander the Great conquered the known world in the fourth century B.C.

_____C_____ 4. "Coming about! Watch the boom!" shouted the helmsman.

_____W_____ 5. The teacher asked if the date I meant was 27 B.C. or A.D.?

_____C_____ 6. Mr. Krashow has gone to the office of the IRS to pay a tax penalty.

_____W_____ 7. I found those pictures on pp 13-17 of vol 3.

_____W_____ 8. "Dr Kane," asked Jim, "just what do you mean by 'punitive grading'?"

_____W_____ 9. Some of the later plays, e.g. *The Tempest,* show this trend.

_____W_____ 10. John asked when I had arrived and where I planned to stay?

_____W_____ 11. Who was it that told me, "Trust everyone, but count your change?"

_____W_____ 12. The chairman asked, "Who said, 'It's unbearably hot in here'?"

_____W_____ 13. We lost shoes, jackets, money, etc, in our haste to escape the fire.

_____W_____ 14. Can you tell me what Dr Newton's subject for tonight's lecture will be.

_____W_____ 15. "Run," she shouted! "It's too late to save the secret files."

Directions: In the following sentences correct every error in punctuation. Then, in the column at the left, circle every number that represents an error in that sentence.

1. Comma omitted
2. Apostrophe omitted or misused
3. Comma misused for semicolon
4. Semicolon misused for comma

1 2 3 4   (1) The storekeeper nodded his head and replied, "It was ten below zero at six oclock this morning; most unusual weather for this time of the year."

1 2 3 4   (2) The basic requirements are a pole, a line, a hook and some bait, if you have these and few spare hours, youre ready to go fishing.

1 2 3 4   (3) "I dont agree with you entirely but I admit that you might have a good case," said Mr. Wiley, my father's partner.

1 2 3 4   (4) Notice this vase with the fragile delicate figures on it, my art teacher tells me that its a valuable and authentic piece.

1 2 3 4   (5) "Since the old battle-ax in the attendance office rejected my excuse; she probably won't even listen to your's," said Jerry.

1 2 3 4   (6) The tramp said, "I swear ma'am, I haven't smelled such cooking aromas since I left Charleston, I thought you looked like a Southern lady.

1 2 3 4   (7) This being a holiday with no garages open; Id better call Lafe Loftus who might come over and help me work on my car.

1 2 3 4   (8) Mother and Susan will probably get home late, they went downtown to the Bon Marche Store which is having a sale on childrens' clothing.

1 2 3 4   (9) Our firm's long-range planning included retiring the bank loans for now; provided, of course, that the present volume of business continues.

1 2 3 4   (10) The receptionist approached Jane and me and said "I wonder if you'd move to a smaller booth, theres a party of eight waiting to be seated."

NAME _____ SCORE _____

Directions: The following sentences contain 40 numbered spots between words or beneath words. (The number is beneath a word when the punctuation problem involves the use of an apostrophe in that word.) In the correspondingly numbered spaces at the left, write C if the punctuation is correct or W if it is incorrect.

1. _W_   (1) The Smiths left yesterday on their vacation, they will return shortly after

      1

2. _W_   our's begins.

      2

3. _____   (2) "I ought to try to wash the car tomorrow," said Charlie, "the dirt has almost

      3

4. _____   obscured it's windshield."

      4

5. _____   (3) "Whenever it rains, my basement floods," groaned Harry, my father's best

      5

6. _____   friend, whose problems seem to be endless.

      6

7. _W_   (4) "I wonder when we will be able to use the new boat? complained Wanda,

      7   8

8. _W_   I've never seen people work so slowly."

9. _W_   (5) Although our distant relatives, the Clark's, have five beautiful intelligent

      9

10. _W_   daughters; they secretly long for a son.

      10

11. _W_   (6) Jeb hurried to keep a nine-oclock appointment, but the traffic jam delayed

      11   12

12. _C_   him until almost noon.

13. _W_   (7) Mr. Jones walked into the office this morning, and said, "Im sure you will

      13   14

14. _14_   be happy to learn that we are all getting a raise."

15. _W_   (8) The landlady replied, "I have just the kind of place you are looking for; a

      15

16. _W_   clean spacious room with a view of the park

      16

17. _W_   (9) "Everyones going to be at the party," complained Martha, "but I have to

      17   18

18. _C_   work the entire evening shift."

19. _W_   (10) Underneath the house had almost completely rotted out, we had to replace

      19   20

20. _W_   all the joists before we could move in.

21. __W__ (11) "Thats just wonderful," gushed Aunt Agnes, "we'll be delighted to come to
                                                      21   22

22. __W__   dinner Tuesday evening."

23. __N__ (12) Moving slowly down the street, the two small boys examined each trash
                                                   23

24. __W__   pile carefully, and took with them any treasures they found.
                      24

25. _____ (13) Pointing to one of the old pictures in the album, Sue said, "I'm fascinated

26. __ˇ__   by the womens' hairstyles, some of them are really modern.
                        25 W   26

27. __C__ (14) "Their advice is no better than your's," laughed Jane; "none of you guys
                                       27   28

28. __e__   knows anything about cooking."

29. __e__ (15) I hope the company refuses my request for a transfer; I've decided, that the
                                         29   30

30. __W__   winters in Calgary will be far too cold for me.

31. __C__ (16) My requirements for a job are quite uncomplicated: short hours, high salary,
                                             31

32. __C__   and simple, interesting work.
                     32

33. _____ (17) My tax assessment having doubled last year and this year; I called the
                                                   33

34. _____   mayor, who's an old friend of mine, to complain.
                     34

35. _____ (18) Looking out at us over the top of his reading glasses the librarian smiled
                                                 35

36. _____   and said, "Put up the cards, boys; the game's over."
                     36

37. __C__ (19) Someone—certainly not one of you nice people—tracked muddy foot-
                                             37

38. __C__   prints through the school's hallways.
                     38

39. __W__ (20) Somehow I seem to have lost or misplaced: my baseball glove, my new
                                             39

40. __C__   socks and a year's supply of bubble gum.
                     40

NAME _____ SCORE _____

Directions: The following sentences contain forty numbered spots between words or beneath words. (The number is beneath a word when the punctuation problem involves the use of an apostrophe in that word.) In the correspondingly numbered spaces at the left, write **C** if the punctuation is correct or **W** if it is incorrect.

1. _W_ (1) "On a bright sunny day like this we should get some really good pictures,
1

2. _W_   don't you think," Laura asked.
2

3. _W_ (2) My cousin studied, at Oxford, where he became acquainted with Judge
           3

4. _C_   Coleman's only grandson, Herman Coleman.
           4

5. _W_ (3) The chairman began his report as follows; "Fellow stockholders, today I
           5   6

6. _RC_   must give you both good news and bad news."

7. _W_ (4) "Yes Ms. Lambert," explained Dr. Davis, "your term paper showed much
           7

8. _W_   careful reading, but it's organization is weak."
           8

9. _C_ (5) Jane interrupted me by saying, "Wasn't it Theodore Roosevelt, not Franklin
           9

10. _C_   Roosevelt , who said, 'Speak softly and carry a big stick'?"
                                                                  10

11. _W_ (6) On these hot, humid, August days I think of the Colorado mountains and
                                  11

12. _W_   wonder why I ever came to Arizona?
                                       12

13. _W_ (7) Her application having been acted upon favorably; Laura drove to
                                                            13

14. _W_   Washington, D.C. where she received her final orders.
                  14

15. _W_ (8) I was surprised to hear, that Andy has already paid his income tax, he
                                    15   16

16. _W_   usually waits until the very last minute.

17. _W_ (9) "Is this what you men consider a neat tidy room," growled the drill
                                         17   18

18. _W_   instructor.

19. _W_ (10) The wall decorations in the tiny room consisted of: a last year's calendar
                                                                19

20. _C_   and someone's graduation picture.
                  20

21. _C_   (11) Dr. Stephens has written many lengthy articles on child psychology but
22. _W_   his own children can't be trusted in a group.

23. _W_   (12) Although I left Norfolk nearly thirty years ago I still correspond with a
24. _C_   few friends who still live there.

25. _W_   (13) You'll find this hard to believe, I'm sure but for breakfast Tom and his friend
26. _C_   ordered pancakes, sausages, and chocolate milkshakes.

27. _C_   (14) One student asked, "Since we say 'myself' rather than 'meself' why don't we
28. _W_   say 'hisself' rather than 'himself'"?

29. _C_   (15) Let me conclude, ladies and gentlemen, by reminding you that water
30. _C_   pollution is a problem that cannot be solved in a short time.

31. _W_   (16) Ron is an exceedingly handsome healthy lad who's mind is never going to
32. _W_   lead him into disturbing quandaries.

33. _W_   (17) "I wonder," said Ms. Berg, "if you can recommend someone, who can tutor
34. _____   me in algebra."

35. _W_   (18) In spite of everything the dean said that my absences would be excused, that
36. _____   I could reenter the class, and that I could graduate in June.

37. _____   (19) The program was planned by Miss Lockhart, the drama instructor and
38. _____   Mr. Coburn, department chair.

39. _W_   (20) Although the auditorium seats nearly two thousand three hundred people
40. _W_   weren't able to get tickets for the concert.

5

Usage

Lessons, Practice Sheets, and Exercises

Lesson 21 *Using Verbs Correctly: Principal Parts; Tense*

In Lesson 2 you learned that some verbs are regular and others are irregular. Regular verbs add an *ed* ending in the past tense (earn, earned), but irregular verbs change their form (grow, grew). Since verb forms change to indicate changes in tense and voice, it is necessary to pay close attention to the forms of all verbs. We shall now review certain places where incorrect forms sometimes appear because of confusion in the use of the principal parts (the base, past tense, and past participle) of verbs. (See Supplement.)

Verb Forms

To gain assurance in your use of verbs, you must remember how the past tense and the past participle are used. The **past tense** is always a single-word verb; it is never used with an auxiliary:

I *ate* my lunch. [Not: I *have ate* my lunch.]

The **past participle**, when it is used as a verb, is *never* a single word; it is used with the auxiliary *have* (in the correct tense) to form the perfect tenses or the auxiliary *be* (in the correct tense) to form the passive voice:

I *have done* the work. [Not: I *done* the work.]
The work *was done*. [Not: I the work *was did*.]

(The past participle is, of course, used as a single word when it is a modifier of a noun: the *broken* toy, the *worried* parents, some *known* criminals.)

There are four groups of verbs that often cause confusion. Each group contains verbs that have similar trouble spots. The basic solution for the problem in each group is to master the principal parts of the verbs. The principal parts are listed in this lesson in the customary order: base form, past tense, and past participle (P.P.).

Past Tense versus Past Participle

Sometimes errors occur because the past tense of a verb is confused with the past participle of the verb.

Verb	Past tense	P.P.

(handwritten: Simple, Past Participle)

Later they *became* [not *become*] more friendly.	become	became	become
They *began* [not *begun*] to laugh at us.	begin	began	begun
He had never *broken* [not *broke*] the law.	break	broke	broken
I should have *chosen* [not *chose*] a larger car.	choose	chose	chosen
Yesterday the child *came* [not *come*] home.	come	came	come
I *did* [not *done*] what she told me to do.	do	did	done
He *drank* [not *drunk*] some water.	drink	drank	drunk
I had *driven* [not *drove*] all day.	drive	drove	driven
The lamp had *fallen* [not *fell*] over.	fall	fell	fallen
The bird has *flown* [not *flew*] away.	fly	flew	flown
Small puddles have *frozen* [not *froze*] on the sidewalks.	freeze	froze	frozen
Dad has *given* [not *gave*] me a car.	give	gave	given
Theresa has *gone* [not *went*] to school.	go	went	gone
I've never *ridden* [not *rode*] a horse.	ride	rode	ridden
We ran out when the fire alarm *rang* [not *rung*].	ring	rang	rung
Lenny has *run* [not *ran*] in two marathons.	run	ran	run
I *saw* [not *seen*] your nephew yesterday.	see	saw	seen
It must have *sunk* [not *sank*] in deep water.	sink	sank	sunk
She should have *spoken* [not *spoke*] louder.	speak	spoke	spoken
The car had been *stolen* [not *stole*].	steal	stole	stolen
The witness was *sworn* [not *swore*] in.	swear	swore	sworn
John has *swum* [not *swam*] across the lake.	swim	swam	swum
Someone had *torn* [not *tore*] the dollar bill.	tear	tore	torn
You should have *worn* [not *wore*] a hat.	wear	wore	worn
I have already *written* [not *wrote*] my essay.	write	wrote	written

Regular versus Irregular

Sometimes errors occur because an irregular verb is thought to be regular.

Verb	Past tense	P.P.
The wind *blew* [not *blowed*] steadily all day.	blow	blew	blown
John *brought* [not *bringed*] Mary some flowers.	bring	brought	brought
This house was *built* [not *builded*] in 1795.	build	built	built
Barbara *caught* [not *catched*] two trout.	catch	caught	caught
Slowly they *crept* [not *creeped*] up the stairs.	creep	crept	crept
He *dealt* [not *dealed*] me a good hand.	deal	dealt	dealt
The men quickly *dug* [not *digged*] a pit.	dig	dug	dug
She *drew* [not *drawed*] a caricature of me.	draw	drew	drawn
All the men *grew* [not *growed*] long beards.	grow	grew	grown
Ben *hung* [not *hanged*] his cap on the hook.	hang	hung	hung
I *knew* [not *knowed*] him at college.	know	knew	known
I have never *lent* [not *lended*] him money.	lend	lent	lent
We *sought* [not *seeked*] shelter from the rain.	seek	sought	sought
The sun *shone* [not *shined*] all day yesterday.	shine	shone	shone
The prince *slew* [not *slayed*] the fierce dragon.	slay	slew	slain
I soon *spent* [not *spended*] the money.	spend	spent	spent
Ms. Andrews *taught* [not *teached*] us algebra.	teach	taught	taught

Lou *threw* [not *throwed*] the receipt away.

The old man *wept* [not *weeped*] piteously.

	Verb	Past Tense	P.P.
	throw	threw	thrown
	weep	wept	wept

Obsolete or Dialectal Forms

A third type of error results from the use of an obsolete or dialectal form of the verb, a form not considered standard now:

I *am* [not *be*] working regularly.

I *have been* [not *been*] working regularly.

The child *burst* [not *bursted*] out crying.

I've *bought* [not *boughten*] a car.

I *climbed* [not *clumb*] a tree for a better view.

The women *clung* [not *clang*] to the raft.

The dog *dragged* [not *drug*] the old shoe home.

The boy was nearly *drowned* [not *drownded*].

At the picnic I *ate* [not *et*] too many hot dogs.

Betty *flung* [not *flang*] the stick away.

You *paid* [not *payed*] too much for it.

It had been *shaken* [not *shooken*] to pieces.

He had never *skinned* [not *skun*] an animal.

A bee *stung* [not *stang*] me as I stood there.

The girl *swung* [not *swang*] at the ball.

I wonder who could have *taken* [not *tooken*] it.

Verb	Past Tense	P.P.
be*	was, were	been
burst	burst	burst
buy	bought	bought
climb	climbed	climbed
cling	clung	clung
drag	dragged	dragged
drown	drowned	drowned
eat	ate	eaten
fling	flung	flung
pay	paid	paid
shake	shook	shaken
skin	skinned	skinned
sting	stung	stung
swing	swung	swung
take	took	taken

Confusing Verb Forms

A fourth type of verb error results from a confusion of forms of certain verbs that look or sound almost alike but are actually quite different in meaning, such as *lie, lay; sit, set;* and *rise, raise*. Note that three of these troublesome verbs—*lay, set,* and *raise*—in their ordinary uses take an object. The other three—*lie, sit, rise*—do not take an object.

Please *lay* your books [D.O.] on the table.

Mary *laid* several logs [D.O.] on the fire.

The men have *laid* some boards [D.O.] over the puddle.

Our cat often *lies* [not *lays*] on the couch.

Yesterday our cat *lay* [not *laid*] on the couch.

Our cat has *lain* [not *laid*] on the couch all morning.

She *sets* the plate [D.O.] in front of me.

An hour ago Tom *set* out some food [D.O.] for the birds.

I had *set* the camera [D.O.] at a full second.

Verb	Past Tense	P.P.
lay	laid	laid
lie	lay	lain
set	set	set

*As you learned in Lesson 2, the irregular verb *be* has three forms (*am, are, is*) in the present tense, and two forms (*was, were*) in the past tense.

I usually *sit* in that chair.
Yesterday he *sat* in my chair.
I have *sat* at my desk all morning.

sit　　　sat　　　sat

At her command they *raise* the flag [D.O.].
The boy quickly *raised* his hand [D.O.].
He had *raised* the price [D.O.] of his old car.

raise　　raised　　raised

He *rises* when we enter the room.
Everyone *rose* as the speaker entered the room.
The water has *risen* a foot since midnight.

rise　　　rose　　　risen

Exceptions

The rules and illustrations given here will serve as a guide in most situations. They show the importance of knowing the principal parts of these verbs. Note, however, that there are a few exceptions, such as the intransitive uses of *set:*

A *setting* [not *sitting*] hen *sets*. [Of course, a hen, like a rooster, may be said to *sit* when that is what is meant.]

The sun *sets* in the west.

Cement or dye *sets*.

A jacket *sets (fits)* well.

With a few verbs, special meanings demand different principal parts. For example, the past tense and the past participle of *shine*, when the verb is used as a transitive verb, are *shined:*

This morning I *shined* [not *shone*] my shoes.

The verb *hang* with the meaning "to execute by suspending by the neck until dead" uses *hanged*, not *hung*, for the past tense and the past participle. When in doubt, always refer to your dictionary.

Sequence of Tenses

In Lesson 2 you studied a partial conjugation showing the forms of three sample verbs as they occur in six tenses. In Lesson 5 you were told the basic uses of the six tenses. Although most student writers usually have little difficulty in establishing and maintaining logical time relationships in their sentences, there are a few situations that sometimes cause confusion.

Subordinate Clauses

The tense in a subordinate clause is normally the same as that in the main clause unless a different time for the subordinate statement is clearly indicated.

We think that Mary studies hard all the time.
We think that Mary studied hard for the last test.
We think that Mary will study hard for the next test.
We think that Mary has studied hard for all her tests.
We think that Mary had studied hard before last week's test.

We thought that Mary studied hard all the time.
We thought that Mary studied hard in the past.
We thought that Mary would study hard for the next test.
We thought that Mary <u>has</u> studied hard all year.
We thought that Mary had studied hard last semester.

Universally True Statements

The present tense is used for a statement that is universally true.

The dietitian reminded us that whipped cream *is* (not *was*) fattening.
I wonder who first discovered that oysters *are* (not *were*) edible.

Shifting Tenses

In narrative writing a shift from past tense to present tense, a device sometimes used effectively by skilled writers, should be used cautiously.

The library *was* silent except for an occasional whisper, when suddenly a side door *opened* [not *opens*] and a disheveled young man *dashed* [not *dashes*] in and *started* [not *starts*] yelling "Man the lifeboats!" After the librarians *had managed* to restore order . . .

Present Perfect Tense

The perfect form of an infinitive should not be used when the controlling verb is in the present perfect tense.

Correct: I would have liked to see that performance.
Incorrect: I would have liked to have seen that performance.

In the indicative mood, there is rarely any confusion over the correct form of the infinitive.

Correct: I have wanted to run that marathon for years.

Supplement

When a sentence makes a statement or asks a question, the verb is said to be in the **indicative mood** or **mode** (see Lesson 2). Two other moods indicate a different purpose in the sentence.

Imperative Mood

When a sentence gives a direction or command, the verb is in the **imperative mood.** The imperative of all regular verbs simply uses the base form of the verb without a subject.

Please *give* me the ball.
Take out your pen and paper.

Even the verb *to be*, irregular in most formations, uses the base to form the imperative.

Be careful; the steps are slippery.
Please *be* on time; the bus will depart promptly.

Subjunctive Mood

The present subjunctive uses the base form of the verb, regardless of the subject.

> The catalogue recommends that she *study* accounting in the first semester.

The past subjunctive takes the same form as the past tense of the verb. (The auxiliary *be* is always *were* regardless of the number or person of the subject.)

> I wish I *were* at home today.

The past perfect subjunctive has the same form as the past perfect.

> I wish I *had gone* home earlier.

We also use the subjunctive in these special ways:

1. In clauses beginning with *that* when they follow words such as *ask, suggest, require, recommend,* and *demand.*

   > The policy requires that we *submit* our requests in writing.
   > The manager insisted that we *be* present for the ceremony.

2. In clauses beginning with *if* when the clause makes a statement that is clearly and unmistakably contrary to fact.

   > If I *were* able to sing, I would try out for the Met.
   > If he were young again, he would live life differently.

NAME _____ SCORE _____

Directions: In the space at the left, write the correct form of the verb shown in parentheses. Do not use *–ing* forms.

~~Sink~~ Sunk
brought
1. Although my average in the class had (sink) lately, I (bring) it up with a good grade on the last test.

Ran
Driven
2. Fred (run) into the living room and told us that someone had just (drive) a car over our front lawn.

flew
Frozen
3. Yesterday we (fly) over two lakes that have (freeze) solid in early November.

LAIN
LAID
4. The dog has (lie) outside all morning next to the logs that Charlie (lay) there last night.

Took
CAUGHT
5. Yesterday Bob (take) his fishing rod down to the creek and (catch) three fine trout.

BEGUN
EATEN
6. Before we had (begin) to serve ourselves, those girls had (eat) all the sandwiches.

SPOKEN
CLIMBED
7. The three girls have often (speak) of the exciting time they had when they (climb) Mount Fuji.

SAT
TAKEN
8. The guests have already (sit) down, but the host and hostess have not yet (take) their places.

DID
PAID
9. You (do) the wise thing when you followed my advice and (pay) the fine under protest.

WRITTEN
CAME
10. I have not (write) you because I have been very busy since I (come) home from my trip to England.

BECAME
STOLEN
11. Before long, the old man (become) convinced that his nephew had (steal) the copy of the will.

ROSE
BEGAN
12. Immediately after the sun (rise), the rain (begin) to fall in a slow, steady drizzle.

FLOWN
CHOSEN
13. Although she had never (fly) a light plane before, Roberta was (choose) "Miss Private Aviation."

WORN
HUNG   14. I had (wear) a hat and coat to the party, but I (hang) them up shortly after I arrived.

GIVEN
BROKEN   15. "This car has (give) me nothing but trouble," he complained. "In the past month it has (break) down three times."

KNOWN
RIDDEN   16. You should have (know) better than to get on a horse that had never been (ride) before.

SHINED
LAID   17. Before breakfast this morning the boy (shine) his shoes and then (lay) them on the table.

RISSEN
DROWNED   18. The lake has (rise) two feet since morning; it has (drown) the flowers I planted on the shore.

GROWN
SAW   19. "You must have (grow) two inches since I (see) you last year," said my old uncle.

SPENT
LENT   20. Sam has already (spend) all the money my father (lend) him for his college expenses.

Directions: Each sentence contains two italicized verb forms. If the verb form is the form proper in serious writing, write **C** in the corresponding space at the left. If the verb is incorrect, write the correct form in the space.

<u>*Saw*</u>
<u>*C*</u>
1. Joan *seen* them when they entered the room but had *paid* little attention because she was busy.

<u>*C*</u>
<u>*taken*</u>
2. The dogs have *lain* in the yard all day; I'm sure they have not *took* more than two steps all morning.

<u>*Sworn*</u>
<u>*Torn*</u>
3. "I could have *swore* that this sleeve was not *tore* when I put the jacket on this morning," said Ginny.

<u>*SPOKEN*</u>
<u>*C*</u>
4. The speaker had *spoke* with great enthusiasm, but his message had *fallen* on deaf ears.

<u>*C*</u>
<u>*began*</u>
5. The referee had not *given* the signal, but the game *begun* anyway.

<u>*C*</u>
<u>*CLIMBED*</u>
6. The wind had *blown* in the wrong direction all day, and most of the boats *lay* at anchor till evening.

<u>*C*</u>
<u>*LENT·LOANED*</u>
7. After Keli said that she had never *climbed* a mountain before, a friend *lended* her all the necessary equipment.

<u>*SAW*</u>
<u>*had C·HIDDEN*</u>
8. "I *seen* my hammer around here somewhere," said Samantha, "but someone must have *hid* it from me since then."

<u>*RISEN*</u>
<u>*RISEN*</u>
<u>*C*</u>
9. The water has *rose* nearly ten feet since the workmen *broke* the small dam upstream.

<u>*LIE*</u>
<u>*C*</u>
10. "*Lay* down, you dumb old dog," ordered the small boy; "I have *thrown* your ball till my arm is nearly falling off."

<u>*DONE*</u>
<u>*KNOW*</u>
11. The boys haven't *did* any of their homework because they didn't *knew* you wanted to leave early for the game.

<u>*SAT*</u>
<u>*C*</u>
12. Marilyn *set* down in the extra chair that I had *drawn* up to the table.

<u>*C*</u>
<u>*RUN*</u>
13. The yellow jackets *stung* me about a thousand times before I could *ran* away from them.

_____*C*_____
_____*WORN*_____ 14. After I had *written* the last page of my paper, I was completely *wore* out.

_____*THREW*_____
_____*LAID*_____ 15. The exhausted man *throwed* his hat and coat on the floor and *lied* down on the couch for a nap.

_____*DRAGGED*_____
_____*SANK*_____ 16. "I *drug* that old boat half way across the state behind my car, and now you tell me it *sunk* last night," said Marge.

_____*DROWNED*_____
_____*CAME*_____ 17. "No one actually *drownded* in that heavy rain during the race, but some people thought they *come* awfully close.

_____*CREPT*_____
_____*CAUGHT*_____ 18. The detective *creeped* quietly down the hall and *catched* the burglar as he slipped out of the room.

_____*FROZEN*_____
_____*C*_____ 19. The lake had finally *froze* solid, and we *went* skating almost every afternoon.

_____*LEFT*_____
_____*BEGAN*_____ 20. I had just *leaved* my room when the fire alarm *begun* to ring.

NAME _____ SCORE _____

Directions: In the space at the left, write the correct form of the verb shown in the parentheses. Do not use *–ing* forms.

BURST
BROKEN
1. Upon hearing the news, Jane (burst) into laughter and said, "That jerk has (break) my heart for the last time."

RUN
SUNK
2. The morning news announced that the storm had (run) its course and had only (sink) two small boats along the coast.

FELL
DROWNED
3. The heavy rains (fall) for two days and had (drown) out two baseball games and the company picnic.

LAID
SHOOK
4. When I entered the room, the handsome older man (lay) aside his newspaper and (shake) my hand enthusiastically.

SPOKEN
GIVEN
5. Before the caller had (speak) a dozen words, I interrupted and said, "My family has already (give) to that cause this year."

RIDDEN
SEEN
6. Although in the past Jack had often (ride) his motorcycle on the beach, he had never before (see) the warnings about high tides.

HUNG
DRAWN
7. After her grandchildren left, Mrs. Riley (hang) on the kitchen wall all the pictures they had (draw) for her that day.

SPENT
WORN
8. Although Aunt Jenny probably (spend) a great deal of money on that sweater, I have never (wear) it.

DRUNK
BECAME
9. When Jackie told me that she had (drink) only a small glass of water before the race, I was not surprised when she (become) dehydrated.

KNOWN
RIDDEN
10. "Had I (know) that your car was in the shop, you could have (ride) with me today," said Matt.

FLOWN
TAUGHT
11. Alicia had never (fly) a plane solo before today, but her instructor had (teach) her well and she was quite confident in her abilities.

LIE
SLID
12. Saturday morning I (lie) in the hammock in the back yard and watched the clouds as they (slide) up over the horizon.

THREW
CAUGHT

13. When a friendly farmer stopped his old truck beside us, we (throw) our backpacks in the back of the truck and (catch) a ride to town.

LAIN
STRUCK

14. Tom had just (lie) down for a nap when lightning (strike) nearby and set off all the car alarms in the neighborhood.

GONE
CHOSE

15. We could have (go) into town to watch the game, but we (choose) to stay home and watch it on TV.

DEALT
SPENT

16. "I have not (deal) with this woman before, but I know that in the past she has (spend) a great deal of money on cars," said Alice.

FELL
FLEW

17. As the tree (fall), all the birds in the nearby trees (fly) away in a panic.

SWAM
SWUM

18. At the beginning of the workout, the team (swim) fifty laps; by the end of the workout each member of the team had (swim) well over a mile.

BECOME
BECOME
DRIVEN

19. By the end of the week, I had (become) convinced that I had never before (drive) myself to work so hard in preparation for a test.

BROUGHT
PAID

20. "It has been (bring) to my attention," said the clerk, "that you have not (pay) your taxes on that property for this year."

Directions: Each sentence has two italicized verb units. If the verb form is correct, write **C** in the corresponding space at the left. If the verb form is incorrect, write the correct form in the corresponding space.

_____ 1. Yesterday my neighbor *brought* over his new leaf blower to help
_____ me clean up all the leaves that had *blowed* into my yard.

_____ 2. The frightened girl *climbed* up out of the river and said, "For a
_____ minute there, I thought I was *drownding*."

_____ 3. Shortly after noon, Jerry *come* inside and reported that he had
_____ *tore* his jacket while climbing over the fence.

_____ 4. Because the baby was *laying* in the crib asleep, we *crept* out of the
_____ room as quietly as possible.

_____ 5. We *sat* the water outside in the cold, and in less than an hour it
_____ had *froze* solid.

_____ 6. As we left camp, we *throwed* water on the fire and *hanged* the food
_____ sacks high up in a tree away from the bears and raccoons.

_____ 7. When I *seen* the first two questions on the test, I *grew* panicky and
_____ walked out of the room.

_____ 8. The boys have never *went* near that old hollow tree again; they
_____ have already been *stinged* enough by those bees.

_____ 9. The water has *rose* and covered the entire yard; in fact, the rising
_____ waters *catched* us all by surprise.

_____ 10. "Hurry," said Alexis, "the game has already *beginned* and we
_____ haven't even *left* the stadium's parking lot yet."

_____ 11. The swing over the river *breaked* and Jan *clang* to the rope for a
_____ moment before she dropped into the water.

_____ 12. By the time we had *dug* the last posthole, the sun had *set* and we
_____ were late for supper.

_____ 13. I would have *swore* that this package was not *setting* here when I
_____ went into the house earlier this afternoon.

_____ 14. Joyce *eated* breakfast very early this morning, so by noon she felt
_____ as if she had not *ate* for a whole day.

_____ 15. "I am *wore* out," said Charlene; "I have *lain* tile all day and my
_____   back is about to break."

_____ 16. A yellow rat snake was *laying* on the back porch where the cat
_____   had *leaved* it earlier this afternoon.

_____ 17. Haven't I *telled* you a hundred times or more that you shouldn't
_____   *lay* down on my new couch while you're wearing your sweaty
                     gym clothes?

_____ 18. We *rised* the flag over the stadium and *sang* The Star Spangled
_____   Banner.

_____ 19. Two centuries ago in this country, a man could be *hung* if he had
_____   *stole* even one horse.

_____ 20. Were you *taught* in that astronomy class that the diameter of the
_____   planet Mars *is* 4,200 miles?

Examine the following conjugation. Note that in the present tense, the third-person singular *(he, she, it)* verb form differs from the third-person plural *(they)* verb form.

I earn	We earn
You earn	You earn
He, She, It *earns*	They *earn*

We refer to this change as a change in number. As noted in Lesson 2, **singular number** refers to only one thing; **plural number** refers to more than one thing. Notice how verbs and nouns differ in this respect: The *s* ending on nouns is a plural marker, but on verbs it designates the singular form.

The following examples show how the number of the subject (one or more than one) affects the form of the verb. (See Supplement.) The verbs *have, do,* and *be* are important because they have auxiliary uses as well as main-verb uses. *Be* is an exceptional verb; it changes form in the past tense as well as in the present tense.

Singular S+VERB	*Plural*
She *walks* slowly.	They *walk* slowly.
Mother *seems* pleased.	My parents *seem* pleased.
Mary *has* a new dress.	All of the girls *have* new dresses.
He *has traveled* widely.	They *have traveled* widely.
She *does* her work easily.	They *do* their work easily.
Does he *have* enough time?	*Do* they *have* enough time?
He *is* a friend of mine.	They *are* friends of mine.
My brother *is coming* home.	My brothers *are coming* home.
His camera *was taken* from him.	Their cameras *were taken* from them.

Verb Agrees in Number

The relation of verb form to subject follows an important principle of usage: **The verb always agrees in number with its subject.** Although the principle is simple, some of the situations in which it applies are not. You will avoid some common writing errors if you keep in mind the following seven extensions of the principle. The first is probably the most important.

1. The number of the verb is not affected by material that comes between the verb and the subject.

   Immediate *settlement* of these problems *is* [not *are*] vital. [The subject is *settlement*. *Problems,* being here the object of the preposition *of,* cannot be a subject.]

   The *cost* of replacing the asbestos shingles with cedar shakes *was* [not *were*] considerable.

   Tact, as well as patience, *is* [not *are*] required.

   Mr. Sheldon, together with several other division heads, *has* [not *have*] left.

Each of the plans *has* [not *have*] its good points.
Is [not *Are*] *either* of the contestants ready?

Determine the *real* subject of the verb; watch out for intervening words that might mislead you. The number of the verb is not altered when other nouns are attached to the subject by means of prepositions such as *in addition to, together with, as well as, with,* and *along with.* Remember that indefinite pronoun subjects like *either, neither, each, one, everyone, no one,* and *somebody* take singular verbs. *None* may take either a singular or a plural verb, depending on whether the writer wishes to emphasize "not one" or "no members" of the group.

None of us *is* [or *are*] perfect.

2. A verb agrees with its subject even when the subject follows the verb.

On the wall *hangs* a *portrait* of his father. [*portrait hangs*]
On the wall *hang portraits* of his parents. [*portraits hang*]
He handed us a piece of paper on which *was scribbled* a *warning.* [*warning was scribbled*]
There *was* barely enough *time* remaining.
There *were* only ten *minutes* remaining.
There *seems* to be one *problem* remaining.
There *seem* to be a few *problems* remaining.
Here *is* a free *ticket* to the game.
Here *are* some free *tickets* to the game.

Be especially careful to find the real subject in sentences starting with *there* or *here.*

3. Compound subjects joined by *and* take a plural verb.

A little *boy* and his *dog were* playing in the yard.
On the platform *were* a *table* and four *chairs.*

But the verb should be singular if the subjects joined by *and* are thought of as a single thing, or if the subjects are considered separately, as when they are modified by *every* or *each:*

Plain *vinegar* and *oil is* all the dressing my salad needs. [one thing]
Every *man* and every *woman is* asked to help. [considered separately]

4. Singular subjects joined by *or* or *nor* take singular verbs.

Either a *check* or a money *order is* required.
Neither the *manager* nor his *assistant has* arrived yet.
Was Mr. *Phelps* or his *son* put on the committee?

In some sentences of this pattern, especially in questions like the last example, a plural verb is sometimes used, both in casual conversation and in writing. In serious and formal writing, the singular verb is considered appropriate. If the subjects joined by *or* or *nor* differ in number, the verb agrees with the subject nearer to it:

Neither the *mother* nor the two *boys were* able to identify him.
Either the *players* or the *coach is* responsible for the defeat.

5. Plural nouns of amount, distance, and so on, when they are used as singular units of measurement, take singular verbs.

> A hundred *dollars was* once paid for a single tulip bulb.
> Thirty *miles seems* like a long walk to me.
> Seven *years* in prison *was* the penalty that he had to pay.

6. A collective noun is considered singular when the group is regarded as a unit; it is plural when the individuals of the group are referred to.

> The *audience is* very enthusiastic tonight.
> The *audience are* returning to their seats. [Notice pronoun *their.*]
> The *band is* playing a rousing march.
> Now the *band are* putting away their instruments. [Again note *their.*]
> *Most* of the book *is* blatant propaganda.
> *Most* of her novels *are* now out of print.
> The *rest* of the fortune *was* soon gone.
> The *rest* of his debts *were* left unpaid.
> The *number* of bank failures *is* increasing.
> A *number* of these bank failures *are* being investigated.

Words like *number, all, rest, part, some, more, most, half* are singular or plural, depending on the meaning intended. A word of this type is often accompanied by a modifier or referred to by a pronoun, either of which gives a clue to the number intended. When the word *number* is a subject, it is considered singular if it is preceded by *the* and plural if it is preceded by *a*.

7. When the subject is a relative pronoun, the antecedent of the pronoun determines the number (and person) of the verb. (See Lesson 23, page 225.)

> He told a joke *that was* pointless. [*joke was*]
> He told several jokes *that were* pointless. [*jokes were*]
> I paid the expenses of the trip, *which were* minimal. [*expenses were*]
> Jack is one of those boys *who enjoy* fierce competition. [*boys enjoy*]

The last example, sometimes called the "one of those . . . who" sentence, is particularly troublesome. Often a singular verb is used. If we recast the sentence to read "Of those boys who enjoy fierce competition, Jack is one," however, it becomes clear that the logical antecedent of *who* is the plural noun *boys*. However, usage is divided. And notice that a singular verb must be used when the pattern is altered slightly:

> Jack is the only one of my friends *who enjoys* fierce competition.

Because a relative pronoun subject nearly always has an antecedent that is third-person singular or third-person plural, we are accustomed to pronoun–verb combinations like these:

> A boy *who is* . . .
> Boys *who are* . . .

A woman *who knows* . . .
Women *who know* . . .

But in those occasional sentences in which a relative pronoun subject has an antecedent that is in the first or second person, meticulously correct usage calls for subject–verb combinations like the following:

I, *who am* in charge here, should pay the bill. [*I* . . . *am*]
They should ask me, *who know* all the answers. [*I* . . . *know*]

You, *who are* in charge here, should pay the bill. [*You* . . . *are*]
They should ask you, *who know* all the answers. [*you* . . . *know*]

Supplement

One particular error of subject–verb agreement warrants special attention. The third-person singular present tense form of the verb *do* is *does*. The plural form is *do*. The misuse of the negative contraction *don't* (instead of *doesn't*) with a third-person singular subject is quite often encountered in spoken English. Many people, justly or unjustly, look on the "it-don't" misuse as an important marker of grossly substandard English. Such forms as the following should be avoided in all spoken and written English:

Faulty: My father *don't* like broccoli.
Faulty: It really *don't* matter.
Faulty: Jack Johnson *don't* live here now.
Faulty: One of her teachers *don't* like her.
Faulty: This fudge tastes good, *don't* it?
Faulty: The fact that the bill is overdue *don't* bother him.

SUMMARY OF CORRECT VERB USE

1. The principal parts of a verb are the present, the past, and the past participle. Avoid confusing the principal parts of irregular verbs (*run, ran, run; eat, ate, eaten; fly, flew, flown*) with those of regular verbs (*study, studied, studied*). Be especially careful with the often confused principal parts of *lie* and *lay, sit* and *set*.
2. Singular verbs are used with singular subjects; plural verbs are used with plural subjects.
   a. Nouns intervening between the subject and the verb do not determine the number of the verb. (Resistance to the actions of these government agencies *is* [not *are*] growing.)
   b. Singular subjects joined by *and* normally take plural verbs. Singular subjects joined by *or* or *nor* normally take singular verbs.
   c. Some nouns and pronouns (collective nouns, and words like *number, all, half,* etc.) are singular in some meanings, plural in others.

NAME _____ SCORE _____

Directions: These sentences are examples of structures that often lead to errors in subject-verb agreement. In the space at the left, copy the correct verb in the parenthesis. In each sentence, the subject of the verb is printed in bold type.

makes   1. Dr. McKay's scholarly **approach** to social problems (makes, make) this lecture series worthwhile.

WERE   2. No one was in the warehouse at the time of the fire, and there (was, were) no **injuries**.

IS   3. In difficult times like these, the budgetary **item** that suffers most (is, are) teachers' salaries.

IS   4. **General Bliss**, together with his staff, (is, are) due to arrive at the airport within the hour.

HAS   5. Neither **Ann** nor **I** (has, have) any musical ability.

HAVE   6. Neither **Ann** nor her two **brothers** (has, have) any musical ability.

QUALIFIES   7. Ms. Wood maintains that her 3.5 grade point **average**, in addition to her placement test scores, (qualifies, qualify) her for the job.

SEEM   8. "There (seems, seem) to be only two **items** left on our agenda," said Ms. Trimble.

IS   9. **Twenty dollars** a month (is, are) all I can afford for recreation.

IS   10. **Nobody** except last-quarter seniors (is, are) are admitted to the course.

WAS   11. Seated directly behind us (was, were) a **woman** with three children who chattered during the performance.

HAS   12. It seems to me that there (has, have) never been a more urgent **need** for increased state funds.

TAKES   13. The final **one** of the best-two-out-of-three qualifying games (takes, take) place tomorrow afternoon

WAS   14. **None** of my answers on the first two pages of the test (was, were) correct.

IS   15. The **need** for rather drastic fiscal reforms (is, are) becoming apparent to the leaders of the school board.

221

Directions: If you find an error in subject-verb agreement, underline the incorrect verb and write the correct form in the space at the left. Circle the subject of every verb you change. If the sentence is correct, write **C** in the space.

LESSENS 1. Your critic's obvious bias against Cooper and other theatrically oriented performers lessen his credibility with young readers.

SHOW 2. Latest census figures representing national life expectancy shows that teachers live longer than other members of the general public.

HAS 3. Every one of your reading, writing, and speaking experiences have *HAS* been preparing you for these final tests.

C SEEMS 4. There seems to be a better than fifty-fifty chance of higher annuity payments next year.

HAS 5. Because of the added expense of unexpected road repairs, a deficit of over forty thousand dollars have resulted.

IS C 6. A sense of civic responsibility, rather than considerations of personal gain, is expected of our public servants.

INCREASE 7. Uncle Jerry's huge collection of theater programs and reviews increase in value with each passing year.

HAS 8. Not one of our three dozen overworked staff members have had *HAS* a day off since last July.

C 9. Nine thousand dollars, the mayor reported, was required to repair city streets damaged in last winter's freeze.

C 10. Neither Mrs. Thornton's tiara nor her husband's diamond stickpin was ever recovered.

SEEMS 11. The architectural plan of the building, as well as the statuary on the grounds, seem like a symbolic break with the past.

DECIDE 12. In any case, I suspect that time and the accidents of fortune decides what a man or woman ultimately becomes.

FACES 13. The possibility of a serious shortage of teachers for the elementary and intermediate grades now face the Glenwood district.

C 14. Vital to the solution of the serious problems is, of course, the education of our voters.

EXCEEDS 15. The amount of money spent on cosmetics, according to some authorities, exceed that spent on public education.

Exercise 22 — *Using Verbs Correctly: Subject–Verb Agreement*

NAME _____   SCORE _____

Directions: If you find an error in subject-verb agreement, underline the incorrect verb and write the correct form in the space at the left. Circle the subject of every verb you change. If the sentence is correct, write **C** in the space.

believes   1. My brother, in addition to the two investigators, believe that the boss's secretary took the money.

is   2. The last of the three men in the line is the tallest, but the youngest of the three are in the middle

are   3. There are still a few players yet to arrive, but the biggest star of all has been here for three days.

are, needs   4. Death and taxes are supposed to be the only sure things in our country, but I believe that the scarcity of good television programs need to be dealt with.

is   5. Lack of available mortgage funds are driving housing costs sky high, but few of the experts know of a solution to the problem.

is   6. One of the judges has failed to arrive; I hope that one of the spectators are qualified to take her place.

HAVE BEEN   7. Two elements in our continuing string of successes in the high-risk game of investing in over-the-counter stocks has been constant attention to detail and a vast amount of luck.

is   8. Here are two secondhand lawn mowers, either of which are light enough for your daughter to operate.

has.   9. Every single one of our scouts have filed glowing reports on Stockbridge, the goalie at Southwestern Tech.

C — are   10. The exciting possibilities open to anyone who is willing to take some risk are almost too numerous to explain.

have been   11. There's been no fundamentally important developments in personal transportation since the invention of the mountain bike.

   12. All of us know that his wife's inheritance, not his ventures into the world of high finance, account for his present happy situation.

has   13. "Have every one of the garden tools been cleaned and put away properly?" asked Mr. Swensen.

correct   14. A knowledge of physics and metallurgy is a necessity for anyone entering automotive engineering.

does   15. How much do the cost of operating taxicabs vary from state to state?

223

Seems ~~to~~ _____ 16. Not one ~~of the applicants who have~~ responded to our advertisements seem qualified to do the job.

has _____ 17. Fortunately, the new bracing system for ~~the engine mounts on the older cars~~ have proved quite strong enough for the task.

is _____ 18. One or the other ~~of the two~~ candidates are sure to call for ~~a new tax or a new tax increase.~~

C _____ 19. The manager, ~~along with a full crew of assistants,~~ is departing this morning for Montreal.

C *have* _____ 20. The early arrival of the people who are going to attend the homecoming game and related activities has placed an undue burden on our housing facilities.

are _____ 21. A number of ~~stereo units from the last shipment~~ is defective and will have to be returned ~~to the factory~~.

C _____ 22. The impression that there are too many people involved in our efforts to aid the migrant workers is totally erroneous.

is _____ 23. One thing you forgot to mention in your letter applying for the coach's job are your five victories in major track meets last year.

are _____ 24. Either my sister or my brothers is coming to help us with the moving.

~~have~~ *C* _____ 25. Relegating those veteran players to ~~substitute status~~ has caused great dissension on the team.

is _____ 26. The moderator asked, "Are there any new business we need to take up before we adjourn tonight?"

has _____ 27. Only one of ~~the last ten~~ shots I made with that pistol have come close to the bull's eye.

does _____ 28. Two hours do seem a sufficiently long time for ~~you~~ to complete your work on that short experiment.

has _____ 29. The presence of the ~~two past~~ presidents and the current chairman of the board of directors have not prevented a great deal of wrangling in the stockholders' meeting.

is C _____ 30. Either my brothers or my sister is coming to help us with the moving.

Lesson 23 *Using Pronouns Correctly: Reference; Agreement*

As you learned in Lesson 1, a pronoun is a word that substitutes for a noun or another pronoun. The word for which a pronoun stands is called the pronoun's **antecedent:**

> I called *Harry,* but *he* didn't answer. [*He* substitutes for *Harry. Harry* is the antecedent of *he.*]
>
> My *cap and scarf* were where I had left *them.* [The antecedent of *them* is the plural unit *cap and scarf.*]
>
> *I* will wash *my* car tomorrow.
>
> *One* of my friends is painting *his* house.
>
> *Three* of my friends are painting *their* houses.

To use pronouns effectively and without confusing your reader, you must follow two basic principles:

1. Establish a clear, easily identified relationship between a pronoun and its antecedent.
2. Make the pronoun and its antecedent agree in person, number, and gender.

Let us examine these requirements more fully.

Role of Antecedents

Personal pronouns should have definite antecedents and should be placed as near their antecedents as possible. Your readers should know exactly what a pronoun stands for. They should not be made to look through several sentences for a pronoun's antecedent, nor should they be asked to manufacture an antecedent for a pronoun. When you discover in your writing a pronoun with no clear and unmistakable antecedent, your revision, as many of the following examples demonstrate, will often require rewriting to remove the faulty pronoun from your sentence.

Faulty: A strange car followed us closely, and *he* kept blinking his lights at us.
Improved: A strange car followed us closely, and the driver kept blinking his lights at us.

Faulty: Although Jenny was a real sports fan, her brother never became interested in *them.*
Improved: Although Jenny really liked sports, her brother never became interested in them.

Faulty: Mike is an excellent typist, although he never took a course in *it.*
Improved: Mike is an excellent typist, although he never took a course in typing.

The indefinite *you* or *they* is quite common in speech and in chatty, informal writing, but one should avoid using either in serious writing:

Faulty: In Alaska *they* catch huge king crabs.
Improved: In Alaska huge king crabs are caught. [Often the best way to correct an indefinite *they* or *you* sentence is to use a passive verb.]

225

Faulty:	Before the reform measures were passed, *you* had few rights.
Improved:	Before the reform measures were passed, people had few rights.
	Before the reform measures were passed, one had few rights.

Faulty:	At the employment office *they* gave me an application form.
Improved:	A clerk at the employment office gave me an application form.
	At the employment office I was given an application form.

A pronoun should not appear to refer equally well to either of two antecedents:

Faulty:	Frank told Bill that *he* needed a haircut. [Which one needed a haircut?]
Improved:	"You need a haircut," said Frank to Bill. [In sentences of this type, the direct quotation is sometimes the only possible correction.]

Avoid the Indefinite It

The "it says" or "it said" introduction to statements, although common in informal language, is objectionable in serious writing because the "it" has no antecedent. (See Supplement.)

Faulty:	*Run* *It says* in the directions that the powder will dissolve in hot water.
Improved:	The directions say that the powder will dissolve in hot water.

Faulty:	*It* said on the morning news program that a bad storm is coming.
Improved:	According to the morning news program, a bad storm is coming.

Avoid Unclear References

Avoid vague or ambiguous reference of relative and demonstrative pronouns.

Faulty:	Only twenty people attended the lecture, *which* was due to poor publicity.
Improved:	Because of poor publicity, only twenty people attended the lecture.

Faulty:	Good writers usually have large vocabularies, and *this* is why I get poor grades on my papers.
Improved:	I get poor grades on my papers because my vocabulary is inadequate; good writers usually have large vocabularies.

Special Cases: Which, This, That

Sometimes the antecedent of the pronouns *which, this,* and *that* is an idea rather than the expressed noun. In a sentence such as "The children giggled, *which* annoyed the teacher" or "The children giggled, and *this* annoyed the teacher," what annoyed the teacher is not the *children* but "the giggling of the children" or "the fact that the children giggled." This kind of reference to a preceding idea rather than to an expressed noun is unobjectionable provided that the meaning is instantly and unmistakably clear. But you should avoid sentences like those shown below. In the first example readers would be hard pressed to discover exactly what the *which* means, and in the second they must decide whether the antecedent is the preceding idea or the noun immediately preceding the *which*:

Faulty:	Hathaway's application was rejected because he spells poorly, *which* is very important in an application letter.
Improved:	Hathaway's application was rejected because he spells poorly; correct spelling is very important in an application letter.

Faulty: The defense attorney did not object to the judge's concluding remark, *which* surprised me.

Improved: I was surprised that the defense attorney did not object to the judge's concluding remark.

Pronoun Agreement

Pronouns should agree with their antecedents in person, number, and gender. The following chart classifies for you the three forms of each personal pronoun on the basis of person, number, and gender:

	Singular	*Plural*
1st Person	*I, my, me*	*we, our, us*
2nd Person	*you, your, you*	*you, your, you*
3rd Person	*he, his, him*	
	she, her, her	*they, their, them*
	it, its, it	

A singular antecedent is referred to by a singular pronoun; a plural antecedent is referred to by a plural pronoun.

> Dad says that *he* is sure that *his* new friend will visit *him* soon.
> Dad and Mother say that *they* are sure that *their* new friend will visit *them* soon.

This principle of logical pronoun agreement is not as simple as these two examples might suggest. Recent language practices have given rise to two situations for which it is impossible to make rules that apply in every instance. Student writers must, first, be aware of certain changing ideas about pronoun usage; they must then prepare themselves to make decisions among the choices available.

Indefinite Pronouns

The first of these two troublesome situations relates to some of the indefinite pronouns: *one, everyone, someone, no one, anyone, anybody, everybody, somebody, nobody, each, either,* and *neither.* These words have generally been felt to be singular; hence, pronouns referring to them have customarily been singular and, unless the antecedent specifies otherwise, masculine. Singular pronouns have also been used in formal writing and speaking to refer to noun antecedents modified by singular qualifiers such as *each* and *every.* The four following examples illustrate the traditional, formal practice:

> Everybody has *his* faults and *his* virtues.
> Each of the sons is doing what *he* thinks is best.
> England expects every man to do *his* duty.
> No one succeeds in this firm if Dobbins doesn't like *him.*

The principal difficulty with this usage is that these indefinites, although regarded by strict grammarians as singular in form, carry with them a group or plural sense, with the result that people are often unsure whether pronouns referring to them should be singular or plural. Despite traditional pronouncements, every day we hear sentences of the "Everyone-will-do-*their*-best" type. Beginning writers, however, would do well to follow the established practice until they feel relatively secure about recognizing the occasional sentence in which a singular pronoun referring to an indefinite produces a strained or unnatural effect even though it agrees in form with its antecedent.

Gender Issues

Closely related to this troublesome matter of pronoun agreement is the second problem, gender. What reference words should be used to refer to such a word as *student*? Obviously there are female students, and there are male students. With plural nouns there is no problem; *they, their,* and *them* refer to both masculine and feminine. For singular nouns there is *she, hers, her* and *he, his, him,* but there is not a pronoun to refer to third-person singular words that contain both male and female members.

Here again, as with the reference to third-person singular indefinites, the traditional practice has been to use masculine singular pronouns. Eighty or so years ago Henry James wrote the following sentence: "We must grant the artist his subject, his idea, his *donné;* our criticism is applied only to what he makes of it." In James's day that sentence was undoubtedly looked upon as unexceptionable; the pronouns followed what was then standard practice. But attitudes have changed. In the 1990s, if that sentence got past the eyes of an editor and appeared on the printed page, its implication that artists are exclusively male would make the sentence unacceptably discriminatory to many readers.

Reliance on the *he or she* pronoun forms is an increasingly popular solution to some of these worrisome problems of pronoun reference. The *he or she* forms agree in number with the third-person singular indefinites. And the use of these forms obviates any possible charge of gender preference. However, excessive use of *he or she, his or her,* and *him or her* is undesirable. (Notice the cumbersome result, for instance, if a *he or she* form is substituted for all four of the third-person singular masculine pronouns in the Henry James sentence.)

Here is a very important point for you to remember: When you are worried about a third-person singular masculine pronoun you have written, either because its reference to an indefinite antecedent does not sound quite right to you or because it shows an undesirable gender preference, you can remove the awkwardness, in nearly every instance that arises, by changing the antecedent to a **plural** noun, to which you then refer by using *they, their,* and *them.*

By way of summary, study these four versions of a sentence as they relate to the two problems just discussed:

> Every member of the graduating class, if *he* wishes, may have *his* diploma mailed to *him* after August 15. [This usage reflects traditional practice that is still quite widely followed. The objection to it is that the reference words are exclusively masculine.]

> Every member of the graduating class, if *he or she* wishes, may have *his or her* diploma mailed to *him or her* after August 15. [The singular reference is satisfactory, but the avoidance of masculine reference has resulted in clumsy wordiness.]

> Every member of the graduating class, if *they* wish, may have *their* diplomas mailed to *them* after August 15. [This version, particularly if used in spoken English, would probably not offend many people, but the lack of proper number agreement between the pronouns and the antecedent would rule out its appearance in edited material.]

Members of the graduating class, if *they* wish, may have *their* diplomas mailed to *them* after August 15. [In this version the pronouns are logical and correct in both number and gender.]

A few other matters of pronoun reference, mercifully quite uncomplicated, should be called to your attention. If a pronoun refers to a compound unit or to a noun that may be either singular or plural, the pronoun agrees in number with the antecedent. (See Lesson 22, Rule 6.)

Wilson and his wife arrived in *their* new car.
Neither Jill nor Martha has finished *her* term paper.
The rest of the lecture had somehow lost *its* point.
The rest of the workers will receive *their* money soon.
The eight-o'clock class has *its* test tomorrow.
The ten-o'clock class finished writing *their* themes.

Beware of "You"

An antecedent in the third person should not be referred to by the second person *you*. This misuse develops when writers, forgetting that they have established the third person in the sentence, shift the structure and begin to talk directly to the reader:

Faulty: In a large university a *freshman* can feel lost if *you* have grown up in a small town.
Improved: In a large university a freshman can feel lost if he or she has grown up in a small town.

Faulty: If a *person* really wants to become an expert golfer, *you* must practice everyday.
Improved: If a person really wants to become an expert golfer, she or he must practice every day.

Supplement

At this point you should be reminded that *it* without an antecedent has some uses that are completely acceptable in both formal and informal English. One of these is in the delayed subject or object pattern. (See Lesson 10.) Another is its use as a kind of filler word in expressions having to do with weather, time, distance, and so forth.

It is fortunate that you had a spare tire.
I find *it* difficult to believe Ted's story.
It is cold today; *it* snowed last night.
It is twelve o'clock; *it* is almost time for lunch.
How far is *it* to Phoenix?

NAME _____ SCORE _____

Directions: One sentence in each of the following pairs is correct, and the other contains at least one reference word that is poorly used. In the space at the left, write the letter that identifies the correct sentence. In the other sentence, circle the pronoun or pronouns that have vague or incorrect reference.

_____ 1. A. Since my older brother was a football player, I worshiped them as a little kid and wanted very much to play it when I got to college.
B. Since my older brother was a football player, I worshiped many players as a little kid and wanted very much to play football when I got to college.

_____ 2. A. We decided to stay on the eastern side of the bay because the weather bureau reported the possibility of thunderstorms on the western side.
B. We decided to stay on the eastern side of the bay because it said in the weather report that they might have thunderstorms on the western side.

_____ 3. A. On that silly TV program, they answer trivial questions and jump around and scream whenever they get the answers right.
B. On that silly TV program, the contestants answer trivial questions and jump around and scream whenever they get the answers right.

_____ 4. A. It was a strange company: they expected you to work long hours for low pay and smile all the time you were on duty.
_____ B. It was a strange company: employees were expected to work long hours for low pay and smile all the time they were on duty.

_____ 5. A. If anyone stops by my desk, tell them to leave a telephone number and I'll give them a call later today.
_____ B. If anyone stops by my desk, tell her or him to leave a telephone number and I'll call later today.

__B___ 6. A. In my campaign I tried to identify anyone who might be helpful to me and ask them personally if they would work on my team.
B. In my campaign I tried to identify anyone who might be helpful to me and ask each one personally if he or she would work on my team.

__?___ 7. A. The letter from the opinion-polling company asked a number of personal questions, and they closed by telling me they would pay ten dollars for filling out their form and returning it by May fifteenth.
B. The letter from the opinion-polling company asked a number of personal questions, and it closed by telling me the company would pay ten dollars for filling out its form and returning it by May fifteenth.

_____ B 8. A. Just this past week Jerry's new article received an award, and they said it was one of the best ever submitted in its category.
   B. Just this past week Jerry's new article received an award, and the judges said the article was one of the best ever submitted in its category.

_____ B 9. A. Anyone who takes the trip up Thunder River will be delighted with the view when they get up close to the falls.
   B. Anyone who takes the trip up Thunder River will be delighted with the view when he or she gets up close to the falls.

_____ B 10. A. The elevator in my apartment building is broken; if anyone wants to visit me, they have to climb five flight of stairs.
   B. The elevator in my apartment building is broken; anyone who wants to visit me has to climb five flights of stairs.

_____ A 11. A. An announcement in last night's paper said that the main exit from the North-South Expressway will be closed this week; commuters will need to find a new route to their jobs.
   B. In last night's paper it said that the main exit from the North-South Expressway will be closed this week; everyone will need to find a new route to their jobs.

_____ B 12. A. When I asked in the library about back copies of that magazine, they told me that they had all disappeared weeks ago, and they didn't know how to replace them.
   B. When I asked the librarians about back copies of that magazine, they told me that the copies had all disappeared weeks ago, and they didn't know how to replace the missing copies.

_____ B 13. A. Jane told Mary that she didn't know when she would be able to leave work because she had a great deal of work to do before she could leave.
   B. Jane told Mary, "I don't know when you will be able to leave work because you have a great deal of work to do before you can leave."

_____ B 14. A. Student waiters at the College Bowl are paid a minimum wage, which is why they allow you to keep your own tips.
   B. Because they are paid a minimum wage, student waiters at the College Bowl are allowed to keep their own tips.

_____ B 15. A. In the paper this morning I read two articles, neither one of which made their point very clearly or told their story very well.
   B. In the paper this morning I read two articles, neither one of which made its point very clearly or told its story very well.

NAME _____   SCORE _____

Directions: In the space at the left, copy the correct pronoun, or pronoun-verb combination, given in parentheses. Circle the antecedent of the pronoun.

_____ 1. Every young woman in this room believes that (she, you, they) will find a special place in the world.

_____ 2. "In the good old days," said Grandmother, "if (one) expected a day's pay, (he, you, they) gave a day's work."

_____ 3. I can't understand how (anyone) in (his or her, their) right mind would drive a car without any insurance.

_____ 4. The Homestead Marching and Chowder (Society) will hold (it's, its, their) annual parade and clambake next Monday afternoon.

_____ 5. Very few upper-echelon (executives) can remember what life was like when (he was, they were) starting out and struggling to get ahead in business.

_____ 6. My father's insurance (agency) will be moving into (its, it's, their) new offices about the first of next month.

_____ 7. When I remember that several important elections have been decided by only a few votes, I realize how vital it is that every (voter) cast (his, her, their) vote.

_____ 8. A (homeowner) who wants to maintain the value of (his or her, your, their) property must be sure to take good care of the home.

_____ 9. "Somehow," said Jim, "I never seem to get credit for my good ideas; my boss always claims (it, them) as his own and gets the credit."

_____ 10. Not a single person out of the hundred or so we surveyed said that (he or she, they) remembered our product's advertisements.

_____ 11. At Camp Woodbridge the (girl) learned how to paddle (her, their) own canoe and how to survive a boating accident.

_____ 12. (Everyone) likes to believe that (he or she has, you have, they have) succeeded through intelligence and skill rather than by luck.

_____ 13. The Letterman's (Club) sends (its, it's, their) members out regularly to help underprivileged children develop athletic skills.

_____ 14. "In the business world, " said the cynical old professor, "it's every (man,)er, every (person) for (himself, himself or herself, themselves)."

_____ 15. (The members) of the homeowners' association will meet next Tuesday to decide how (it wants, they want) to vote in the next election.

233

Directions: Each sentence contains at least one reference word that is poorly used. In the space at the left copy the pronoun or pronouns that have vague or incorrect reference. In the space below each sentence, rewrite enough of the sentence to make the meaning clear.

_____ 1. Mary explained to her sister that she needed to work harder on her physical conditioning if she intends to play volleyball.

Her sister needed to work harder on her phys. condit., Her sister expl

_____ 2. It says on the money-back guarantee that anyone who is not satisfied with a piece of merchandise can return it and get their money back.

According to the money-g. Back

_____ 3. Anyone interested in becoming a doctor should know that there is a long road ahead of them, and you have to be tough and dedicated to reach your goal.

_____ 4. On television last night they said that they were expecting a sellout at today's game and you couldn't get a ticket anymore.

_____ 5. Bobbie always insisted that she wanted to go into horse racing even though you have a hard time finding steady work and they don't pay much money to beginners.

_____ 6. Anyone driving through Locust Grove on the state highway should know that they enforce the speed limits quite strictly and you will surely get a ticket if they catch you speeding.

_____ 7. The city has been in a sort of recession for two years, but they seem to be coming out of it now.

_____ 8. In our tennis club every player, regardless of their skill level, can find an opponent who is just about at their level.

_____ 9. People who hike the trails in the state park can be certain that they will rescue you if you get lost in the forest.

_____ 10. My father used to tell his brother that he should use his time and money wisely so that he could be successful and wealthy in his old age.

Lesson 24 *Using Pronouns Correctly: Case*

In Lesson 23 the chart on page 227 classifies the personal pronouns on the basis of person, number, and gender. The three forms that are listed there for each person—first, second, and third, singular and plural—illustrate the three cases nouns and pronouns fall into: nominative, possessive, and objective. *I* and *they* are nominative, *my* and *their* are possessive, and *me* and *them* are objective, for example.

The way you use these pronouns in everyday language, in sentences such as "Two of *my* books have disappeared; *they* cost *me* twenty dollars, and *I* must find *them*," demonstrates that the case form you choose depends on how the word is used within the sentence. In this lesson we shall examine instances where the wrong choice of pronoun form is possible.

The only words in modern English that retain distinctions between nominative and objective case forms are the first- and third-person personal pronouns and the relative pronouns *who* and *whoever*. In nouns the nominative and objective forms are identical, and the correct use of the one distinctive form, the possessive, requires essentially only a knowledge of how the apostrophe is used. (See Lesson 19.)

Here are the pronouns arranged according to their case forms. The first eight are the personal pronouns; notice that the only distinctive form of *you* and *it* is the possessive. The last three pronouns, which we shall examine separately from the personal pronouns, are used only in questions and in subordinate clauses. (See Supplement for a discussion of *which* in the possessive case.)

Nominative	Possessive	Objective
I	my, mine	me
you	your, yours	you
he	his, his	him
she	her, hers	her
it	its, its	it
we	our, ours	us
you	your, yours	you
they	their, theirs	them
which	———	which
who	whose	whom
whoever	whosever	whomever

Personal Pronouns in the Possessive Case

The **possessive case** is used to show possession. Review carefully the following three possible trouble spots.

Modifiers and Nominals

The preceding chart shows two possessive forms for the personal pronouns. The first form for each pronoun is used as a *modifier* of a noun. The second form is used as a nominal;

235

in other words, it fills a noun slot, such as the subject, the complement, or the object of a preposition:

This is *your* seat; *mine* is in the next row.
Jane preferred *my* cookies; some of *hers* were burned.
Their product is good, but the public prefers *ours*.

Indefinite Pronouns

The indefinite pronouns use an apostrophe to form the possessive case: *everybody's* duty, *one's* lifetime, *everyone's* hopes, someone *else's* car. But the personal pronouns do not:

These seats are *ours* [not *our's*]. *Yours* [not *Your's*] are in the next row.

Learn to distinguish carefully between the following possessives and contractions that are pronounced alike; *its* (possessive), *it's* (it is, it has); *theirs* (possessive), *there's* (there is, there has); *their* (possessive), *they're* (they are); *whose* (possessive), *who's* (who is, who has); *your* (possessive), *you're* (you are):

It's obvious that the car has outworn *its* usefulness.
There's new evidence that *they're* changing *their* tactics.

Possessive Pronouns with Gerunds

Formal usage prefers the possessive form of pronouns (occasionally of nouns also) preceding gerunds in constructions like the following:

He was unhappy about *my* [not *me*] voting for the bill.
Her report led to *our* [not *us*] buying additional stock.
Chad boasted about his *son's* [not *son*] having won the scholarship.

Personal Pronouns in the Nominative and Objective Cases

The rules governing the uses of the other two cases are very simple. A pronoun is in the **nominative case** when it is used

1. As a subject: *They* suspected that *he* was lying.
2. As a subjective complement: This is *she* speaking.
3. As an appositive of a nominative noun: *We* editors help young writers.

A pronoun is in the **objective case** when it is used

1. As an object of a verb or verbal: Ted told *her* the news. We enjoyed meeting *them*.
2. As an object of a preposition: Everyone except *me* had left the room.
3. As the subject of an infinitive: The police officer ordered *me* to halt.
4. As an appositive of an objective noun: Three of *us* truck drivers stopped to help.

We need not examine in detail every one of these applications. As people become more adept at using the English language, they learn that such usages as "*Them* arrived late" and

"I spoke to *she*" do not conform to the system of the language. Instead, we should examine the trouble spots where confusion may arise.

When you use the nominative and objective personal pronouns, exercise care in the following situations.

A Pronoun as Part of a Compound Unit

When the pronoun follows *and* (sometimes *or*) as part of a compound unit, determine its use in the sentence and choose the appropriate case form. The temptation here is usually to use the nominative, although the last example in the following list shows a trouble spot where the objective case is sometimes misused. If you test these troublesome constructions by using the pronoun by itself, you will often discover which form is the correct one:

The man gave Sue and *me* some candy. [Not: Sue and *I*. Both words are indirect objects. Apply the test. Notice how strange "The man gave . . . *I* some candy" sounds.]

Send your check to either my lawyer or *me*. [Not: to . . . *I*.]

Have you seen Bob or *her* lately? [Direct objects require the objective case.]

Just between you and *me*, the lecture was a bore. [Never say "between you and I." Both pronouns are objects of the preposition *between*. If this set phrase is a problem for you, find the correct form by reversing the pronouns: You would never say "between I and you."]

Ms. Estes took *him* and *me* to school.
[Not *he* and *I* or *him* and *I*. Both pronouns are direct objects.]

Will my sister and *I* be invited? [Not *me*. The subject is *sister* and *I*.]

Comparisons after As and Than

In comparisons after *as* and *than*, when the pronoun is the subject of an understood verb, use the nominative form:

He is taller than *I* [*am*]. I am older than *he* [*is*].
Can you talk as fast as *she* [*can talk*]?
No one knew more about art than *he* [*did*].

Sentences like these nearly always call for nominative case subjects. Occasionally the meaning of a sentence may demand an objective pronoun. Both of the following sentences are correct; notice the difference in meaning:

You trust Mr. Alton more than *I*. [Meaning ". . . more than I (trust Mr. Alton")."]
You trust Mr. Alton more than *me*. [Meaning ". . . more than (you trust) me."]

"It is" Expressions

Ordinarily, use the nominative form for the subjective complement. The specific problem here concerns such expressions as *It's me, It is I, It was they,* or *It was them.* Many people say *It's me,* but they would hesitate to say *It was her, It was him,* or *It was them,* instead of *It was she, It was he,* or *It was they.* However, this is a problem that does not arise often in the writing of students. The following are examples of correct formal usage:

> It is *I.*
> It could have been *he.*
> Was it *she?*
> Was it *they* who called?

"We" versus "Us" and "I" versus "Me"

An appositive should be in the same case as the word that it refers to. Notice particularly the first three examples that follow. This usage employing *we* and *us* as an appositive modifier preceding a noun is a real trouble spot:

> *We* boys were hired. [The unit *We boys* is the subject and requires the nominative.]
> Two of *us* boys were hired. [The object of a preposition requires the objective case.]
> Mr. Elder hired *us* boys. [Not *we boys* for a direct object.]
> Two boys—you and *I*—will be hired. [In apposition with the subject.]
> Mr. Elder will hire two boys—you and *me.* [In apposition with the object.]

Problems with Who and Whom

The only other pronouns in standard modern English that have distinctive nominative, possessive, and objective forms are *who/whose/whom* and *whoever/whosever/whomever.* (See Supplement.) The rules that apply to the personal pronouns apply to these words as well: In the subject position *who/whoever* should be used, in the direct object position *whom/whomever* should be used; and so forth. (These pronouns, it should be noted, are never used as appositives.)

The special problem in the application of the case rules to these words comes from their use as interrogatives and as subordinating words. As you learned in Lessons 6, 9, and 10, these words, because they serve as signal words, always stand at the beginning of their clauses. To locate the grammatical function of the pronoun within its clause, you must examine the clause to determine the normal subject–verb–complement positioning.

Direct Object or Object of a Preposition

In formal usage, *whom* is required when it is a direct object or the object of a preposition, even though it stands ahead of its subject and verb:

> *Whom* did Mr. Long hire?
> [If you are troubled by this sort of construction, try substituting a personal pronoun and placing it after the verb, where it normally comes: "Did Mr. Long hire *him?*" You would never say "Did Mr. Long hire *he?*" The transitive verb *hire* requires a direct object pronoun in the objective case.]
>
> He is a boy *whom* everyone can like. [*Whom* is the object of *can like.*]
>
> Wilson was the man *whom* everybody trusted. [Everybody trusted *whom.*]
>
> She is the girl *whom* Mother wants me to marry. [Object of the verbal *to marry.*]
>
> *Whom* was she speaking to just then? [To *whom* was she speaking?]

Beginning a Subordinate Clause

When *who(m)* or *who(m)ever* begins a subordinate clause that follows a verb or a preposition, the use of the pronoun *within its own clause* determines its case form:

> We do not know *who* broke the window.
> [*Who* is the subject of *broke,* not the direct object of *do know.*]

> No one knows *who* the intruder was.
> [*Who* is the subjective complement in the noun clause.]

> We do not know *whom* the police have arrested.
> [The objective form *whom* is used because it is the direct object of *have arrested.* The direct object of *do know* is the whole noun clause.]

> I will sell the car to *whoever* offers the best price.
> [The whole clause, *whoever offers the best price,* is the object of the preposition *to. Whoever* is the subject of *offers.* The subject of a verb must be in the nominative case.]

After a Parenthetical Insertion

When the pronoun subject is followed by a parenthetical insertion like *do you think, I suspect, everyone believes,* or *we know,* the nominative case form must be used:

> *Who* do you think *has* the best chance of winning?
> [*Who* is the subject of *has.* The *do you think* is a parenthetical insertion.]

> Jenkins is the one *who* I suspect *will make* the best impression.
> [Determine the verb that goes with the pronoun. If you are puzzled by this type of sentence, try reading it this way: "Jenkins is the one *who will make* the best impression—I suspect."]

But if the pronoun is not the subject of the verb, the objective form should be used:

> He is an achiever *whom* I suspect you will eventually envy.
> [*Whom* is the direct object of *will envy.*]

Supplement

The chart on page 235 shows that the pronoun *which* has no possessive case form, a situation that brings about a minor problem of word choice. As you learned when you studied the adjective clause, *who(m)* normally refers to persons, and *which* to things. But *whose* may be used in an adjective clause as the possessive form of *which* to refer to a nonhuman antecedent:

> It is a disease *whose* long-term effects are minor.

If *whose* is not used in such a sentence, the "of-which" form must be used, producing a perfectly correct but cumbersome sentence:

> It is a disease the long-term effects *of which* are minor.

SUMMARY OF CORRECT PRONOUN USE

1. A pronoun should have a clearly identified antecedent, with which it agrees in person, number, and gender.
2. Be aware of the special problem of pronoun reference to third-person singular antecedents that include both masculine and feminine members—pronouns like *everybody* and *someone* and nouns like *person, student, employee,* and so on.
   NOTE: Using a plural rather than a singular antecedent is one obvious way of avoiding this problem.
3. Use nominative forms of pronouns for subjects, subjective complements, and appositives that rename nominative nouns. Use objective forms of pronouns for objects of verbs or prepositions, subjects of infinitives, and appositives that rename objective nouns.
4. Be aware of a particular pronoun problem when a personal pronoun is tied to a noun or another pronoun by *and* or *or:*

   Mickey and I [not *Mickey and me*] were sent to the principal's office.
   Mr. Case sent *Mickey and me* [not *Mickey and I*] to the principal's office.
   And so, neighbors, please vote for *Ms. Stone and me* [not *Ms. Stone and I*].

5. Remember that the case of *who* is determined by its use in its own clause. It may be a direct object that precedes the subject [*Whom* has your wife invited?] or a subject immediately following a verb or a preposition [We wonder *who* will win. Our dog is friendly with *whoever* pets it.]

NAME _____   SCORE _____

Directions: Each italicized pronoun in the sentences is correctly used. In the space at the left, write one of the following numbers to identify the use of the pronoun:

    1. Subject   4. Direct or indirect object
    2. Subjective complement   5. Object of a preposition
    3. Appositive modifier of a   6. Appositive modifier of an
        nominative noun   objective noun

_____ 1. *Whoever* gave you that news was badly misinformed

_____ 2. I wish Mother wouldn't worry so much about my sister and *me* when we are hang-gliding.

_____ 3. Betty deserves the promotion: no one else in the office works harder than *she.*

_____ 4. No one admires Coach Hall more than *we* substitute players.

_____ 5. For all of *us* soccer players, the budget cuts were a great disappointment.

_____ 6. The newscaster did not tell his listeners *who* had given him the incriminating documents.

_____ 7. *Who* do you think will replace the injured quarterback?

_____ 8. *Whom* do you think the coach will use instead of the injured quarterback?

_____ 9. No one else in the class except Fred and *me* flunked the test.

_____ 10. The survey asked us *who* our favorite rock stars are.

_____ 11. In Rome I looked up a fellow *whom* I had known in high school.

_____ 12. Marilyn showed Lou and *me* some of the pictures she had taken in Crete.

_____ 13. One attraction at the carnival was a boxer who would fight against *whoever* challenged him.

_____ 14. The carnival boxer never fights against whomever he can't defeat.

_____ 15. The guard warned *us* kids about skating on the thin ice.

_____ 16. He's one politician *whom* I get pleasure from voting against

_____ 17. The honored guests at the banquet will be *we* six graduating football players.

_____ 18. That's our state treasurer on the podium; it was *she* who completely reorganized the office.

_____ 19. People like you and *me* can hardly afford such luxuries.

_____ 20. I wonder why the superintendent wants to see you and *me.*

Directions: In the space at the left, copy the correct pronoun from within the parenthesis.

_____ 1. Older men like you and (I, me) ought to curtail our intake of fatty foods.

_____ 2. It was (I, me) who first suggested that you begin to collect pottery.

_____ 3. Joan asked John and (I, me) where we had seen the bear.

_____ 4. (Who, Whom) did you see when you were downtown?

_____ 5. Several of the other players are much stronger than (I, me).

_____ 6. If you were (he, him), would you have responded in the same way?

_____ 7. Tomorrow we shall find out (who, whom) passed the exam.

_____ 8. Please keep this information just between you and (I, me).

_____ 9. No one tried harder than (her, she).

_____ 10. (Who, Whom) will be assigned to that project with Marsha and me?

_____ 11. (Who, Whom) do you think will win the gold medal?

_____ 12. It was (he, him) who said that the weather has been wonderful this spring.

_____ 13. The winner, (whoever, whomever) he or she may be, will receive a new car and a trophy.

_____ 14. The committee has granted you and (her, she) another chance to practice.

_____ 15. My father asked me (who, whom) I was thinking about when I mentioned another possible candidate.

_____ 16. At that point we would have hired (whoever, whomever) could make the repair.

_____ 17. I got a letter from my brother Sam, (who, whom) you met in Germany.

_____ 18. Anyone as beautiful as (her, she) will certainly attract attention.

_____ 19. She expressed no desire to know (who, whom) the last qualifiers were.

_____ 20. Everyone in the room except Marshall and (I, me) had heard the shots.

NAME _____   SCORE _____

Directions: If you find an incorrectly used pronoun, underline it and write the correct form in the space at the left. If a sentence is correct, leave the space blank.

_____   1. The police do not know yet whom it was that started the fight
_____   that caused the injuries to you and he.

_____   2. It was John from who Jack and me bought our first car, an old
_____   Ford.

_____   3. Many of we students do not believe that the new scheduling sys-
_____   tem works very well.

_____   4. Mr. Wilson told Robert and I that the job can be done by who-
_____   ever we select.

_____   5. My parents don't agree with my sister and me that those friends
_____   of their's are impossibly boring.

_____   6. Its not possible that people like you and me can be so ignorant
_____   of basic business principles.

_____   7. It told my brother that its likely that anyone as short as him will
_____   have difficulty making the basketball team.

_____   8. Paul and me intend to keep that information a secret between
_____   him and I.

_____   9. Joan gave Mildred and I presents from she and Sally.

_____ 10. "It is everyone's hope that the platform committee can complete
_____   its deliberations by tomorrow evening," said the chairman.

_____ 11. The first letter addressed to we girls had one of its pages missing.

_____ 12. It's anyone's guess who he will choose as his running mate in the
_____   next election now that Jones has retired to Brazil.

243

_____ 13. If I were him, I wouldn't think of going to that expensive restau-
_____ rant in sneakers and a coat and tie.

_____ 14. The announcer said, "The president is now walking up the stairs;
_____ that is he wearing the blue checked jacket.

_____ 15. My little brother is nice, but only to people who he thinks can
_____ beat him up.

_____ 16. The receptionist said, "It's okay to go in now. May I say who you
_____ represent?"

_____ 17. Whom do you think could have invented such an amazingly
_____ complex machine?

_____ 18. Did you find out whom that distinguished-looking woman was,
_____ the one helping the waitresses with the sandwiches?

_____ 19. The only students you can count on for answers are Jim, Joan,
_____ and me.

_____ 20. My car is faster than your's, but you should realize that mine gets
_____ far fewer miles per gallon than any other car around.

_____ 21. John, please hand this package to whomever answers the door
_____ when you ring the bell.

_____ 22. The changes in the class schedule benefit everyone but we new-
_____ comers to the company.

_____ 23. Who will the new manager assign to the branch office opening
_____ next month in Akron?

_____ 24. Martha is camping in Alaska this month; it could not have been
_____ she that you saw in the mall on Saturday.

_____ 25. I told Joan that, if I were she, I would take my required courses
_____ before I began to take electives.

NAME _____   SCORE _____

Directions: Whenever you find an incorrectly used pronoun, copy it in the space at the left. Then in the space below the sentence, write enough of the sentence to show how you would make it clear and correct. No sentence contains more than two poorly used pronouns; some sentences may be correct.

_____   1. The director told we students that they've decided not to use any students as extras in the movie.

_____   2. Ask Jenny if that book on the back seat of my car is hers; it's not mine or yours.

_____   3. The clerk told Ed that you have to have your registration form signed by someone in the dean's office.

_____   4. Give this note to whoever you can find downstairs and tell them to take it to the coach's office, please.

_____   5 Mary asked Sue if her sister had brought back her clean laundry when she came for the weekend.

_____   6. It says in the handbook that March first is the last day you can withdraw from a course.

_____   7. "You can select whoever you wish for a partner; its your choice," said the teacher.

_____   8. The boss called earlier; she wants to know who we've hired and how we located them.

_____   9. Uncle Walt, who is a scuba diver, says he can teach us to dive if we are interested in it.

245

_____ 10. Each student should have their own computer and they should give each one individual instructions.

_____ 11. Jane Roberts, whom most of us think should be the next manager, has better credentials for it than anyone else.

_____ 12. I lost yesterday's lecture notes, but John and Anne, who sit next to me, will lend me their's.

_____ 13. On the television last night they announced that people who use well water should boil it before drinking it.

_____ 14. Every entering freshman must attend orientation before they can sign up for their courses.

_____ 15. My parents, who both attended a local college, allowed my sister and I to choose an out-of-state school.

_____ 16. The guides gave each hiker a picnic lunch, but they had eaten everything well before noon.

_____ 17. "The climax of that movie was so frightening it made you forget how funny you thought the opening was," said Tom.

_____ 18. I wonder if our leaving the party early angered anyone who was there.

_____ 19. Everyone who my father employed last summer has returned to college to pursue their degree.

_____ 20. Please send copies of the schedule to all we freshmen so we can pick out our classes early.

In Lesson 2 you learned that an adjective is a word that describes or limits a noun or a pronoun. You also learned that an adverb modifies a verb, an adjective, or another adverb. Many adverbs end in *ly,* such as *happily, beautifully,* and *extremely.* But some adjectives—*lovely, likely, deadly, neighborly,* and *homely,* for instance—also end in *ly.* Some adverbs do not end in *ly,* and these happen to be among the most frequently used words in speech and writing: *after, always, before, far, forever, here, not, now, often, quite, rather, soon, then, there, too, very.* Some words can be used either as adjectives or as adverbs, as the following examples show:

Adverbs	*Adjectives*
He came *close.*	That was a *close* call.
She talks too *fast.*	She's a *fast* thinker.
Hit it *hard.*	That was a *hard* blow.
She usually arrives *late.*	She arrived at a *late* hour.
He went *straight* to bed.	I can't draw a *straight* line.

Some adverbs have two forms, one without and one with the *ly: cheap, cheaply; close, closely; deep, deeply; hard, hardly; high, highly; late, lately; loud, loudly; quick, quickly; right, rightly; slow, slowly.* In some of these pairs the words are interchangeable; in most they are not. The idiomatic use of adverbs is a rather complex matter; no rules can be made that govern every situation. We can, however, make a few generalizations that reflect present-day practice.

1. The shorter form of a few of these—*late, hard,* and *near,* for example—fills most adverbial functions because the corresponding *ly* forms have acquired special meanings:

We must not stay *late.*	I have not seen him *lately* [recently].
I studied *hard* last night.	I *hardly* [scarcely] know him.
Winter is drawing *near.*	I *nearly* [almost] missed the last flight.

2. The *ly* form tends toward the formal, with the short form lending itself to more casual, informal speech and writing:

Informal	*Formal*
It fell *close* to the target.	You must watch him *closely.*
They ate *high* off the hog.	She was *highly* respected.
Drive *slow*!	Please drive more *slowly.*
Must you sing so *loud*?	He *loudly* denied the charges.
We searched far and *wide.*	She is *widely* known as an artist.

3. Because the short form seems more direct and forceful, it is often used in imperative sentences:

   Hold *firm* to this railing.
   "Come *quick*," yelled the officer.

4. The short form is often the one used when combined with an adjective to make a compound modifier preceding a noun:

a *wide*-ranging species   The species ranges *widely.*
a *slow*-moving truck   The truck moved *slowly.*

Typical Adverb/Adjective Trouble Spots

For the sake of simplifying the problem of the right use of adverbs and adjectives, we may say that there are three main trouble spots.

Misusing an Adjective for an Adverb

A word is an adverb if it modifies a verb, an adjective, or another adverb. The words that usually cause trouble here are *good, bad, well; sure, surely; real, really; most, almost; awful, awfully;* and *some, somewhat:*

Chip played *well* [not *good*] in the last game. [Modifies the verb *played.*]
This paint adheres *well* [not *good*] to concrete. [Modifies the verb *adheres.*]
Almost [not *Most*] every student has a job. [Modifies the adjective *every.*]
Today my shoulder is *really* [or *very*—not *real*] sore. [Modifies the adjective *sore.*]
He was driving *really* [or *very*—not *real*] fast. [Modifies the adverb *fast.*]
This rain has been falling *steadily* [not *steady*] for a week.
The champion should win his first match *easily* [not *easy*].
You'll improve if you practice *regularly* [not *regular*].
She wants that prize very *badly* [not *bad*].

Misusing Adverbs for Adjectives as Subjective Complements

The most common verb to take the subjective complement is *be;* fortunately, mistakes with this verb are nearly impossible. A few other verbs—like *seem, become, appear, prove, grow, go, turn, stay,* and *remain,* when they are used in a sense very close to that of *be*—take subjective complements. This complement must be an adjective, not an adverb.

The house *seems empty.* [House *is* empty.]
Their plans *became apparent.* [Plans *were* apparent.]
The work *proved* very *hard.* [Work *was* hard.]

The adjective subjective complement is also used with another group of verbs, the so-called verbs of the senses. These are *feel, look, smell, sound,* and *taste:*

You shouldn't feel *bad* about this. [Not *badly.*]
His cough sounds *bad* this morning. [Not *badly.*]
At first our prospects looked *bad.* [Not *badly.*]
Doesn't the air smell *sweet* today? [Not *sweetly.*]

The verb *feel* is involved in two special problems. In the first place, it is often used with both *good* and *well.* These two words have different meanings; one is not a substitute for the other. When used with the verb *feel, well* is an adjective meaning "in good health."

The adjective *good*, when used with *feel*, means "filled with a sense of vigor and excitement." Of course, both *well* and *good* have other meanings when used with other verbs. In the second place, the expression "I feel badly" has been used so widely, especially in spoken English, that it can hardly be considered an error in usage. Many careful writers, however, prefer the adjective here, with the result that "feel bad" is usually found in written English.

Misusing a Comparative or a Superlative Form of a Modifier

Most adverbs are compared in the same way as adjectives. (For a discussion of the comparison of adjectives, see Lesson 2.) Some common adverbs cannot be compared, such as *here, now, then, when,* and *before*. As you learned in Lesson 16, we use the comparative degree *(taller, better, more intelligent, more rapidly)* in a comparison limited to two things. We use the superlative degree *(tallest, best, most intelligent, most rapidly)* for more than two things.

Two other problems, both of minor importance, are involved in comparisons. First, we do not combine the two forms *(more + er, most + est)* in forming the comparative and superlative degrees:

Later the landlord became *friendlier* [not *more friendlier*].
Please drive *slower* [not *more slower*].
Please drive *more slowly* [not *more slower*].

Second, some purists object to the comparison of the so-called absolute qualities, such as *unique* ("being the only one"), *perfect, round, exact,* and so forth. They argue that, instead of such uses as *most perfect, straighter, more unique,* the intended meaning is *most nearly perfect, more nearly straight, more nearly unique*. General usage, however, has pretty well established both forms.

Problems with Prepositions

Three reminders should be made about the use of prepositions. One problem is the selection of the exact preposition for the meaning intended.

Idioms Using Prepositions

Many words, especially verbs and adjectives, give their full meaning only when modified by a prepositional phrase. In most cases the meaning of the preposition dictates a logical idiom: to sit *on* a couch, to walk *with* a friend, to lean *against* a fence, and so on. For some more abstract concepts, however, the acceptable preposition may seem to have been selected arbitrarily. Here are a few examples of different meanings of different prepositions:

agree *to* a proposal, *with* a person, *on* a price, *in* principle
argue *about* a matter, *with* a person, *for* or *against* a proposition
compare *to* to show likenesses, *with* to show differences [sometimes similarities]
correspond *to* a thing, *with* a person
differ *from* an unlike thing, *with* a person
live *at* an address, *in* a house or city, *on* a street, *with* other people

Note: Any good modern dictionary will provide information about and examples of the correct usage of prepositions.

Unnecessary Prepositions

Although at colloquial levels of language we sometimes find unnecessary prepositions used, examples like the following are improved in serious contexts if written without the words in brackets:

> I met [up with] your uncle yesterday.
> We keep our dog inside [of] the house.
> Our cat, however, sleeps outside [of] the house.
> The package fell off [of] the speeding truck.

Avoid especially the needless preposition at the end of a sentence or the repeated preposition in adjective clauses and in direct or indirect questions:

> Where is your older brother *at*?
>
> He is one of the few people *to* whom I usually feel superior *to*.
> To what do you attribute your luck at poker *to*?
> [Use one *to* or the other, but not both.]

Repeated Prepositions in Compound Units

When two words of a compound unit require the same preposition to be idiomatically correct, the preposition need not be stated with the first unit:

Correct: We were both *repelled* and *fascinated by* the snake charmer's act.

But when the two units require different prepositions, both must be expressed:

Incomplete: The child shows an *interest* and a *talent for* music. [interest . . . *for* (?)]
Correct: The child shows an *interest in* and a *talent for* music.

Incomplete: I am sure that Ms. Lewis would both *contribute* and *gain from* a summer workshop. [contribute . . . *from* (?)]
Correct: I am sure that Ms. Lewis would both *contribute to* and *gain from* a summer workshop.

NAME _____   SCORE _____

Directions: In the first space at the left, write the word (or words) that the italicized word modifies. In the second space write **Adj.** if the italicized word is an adjective or **Adv.** if it is an adverb.

_____   1. The old district manager was *highly* respected by all the workers.
_____

_____   2. I saw two falcons soaring *high* above the mountain top.
_____

_____   3. Despite the recession, we opened our new business with *high* hopes.
_____

_____   4. We were pleasantly surprised by the *gentlemanly* behavior of the boys at the dance.
_____

_____   5. We try to sympathize with Joan, although some of her problems are *real* and some are imaginary.
_____

_____   6. The doctor's prognosis on Anderson's knee injury was not *really* optimistic.
_____

_____   7. Sand the wood *well* before you apply the first coat of lacquer.
_____

_____   8. Last week my father was ill, but this week he is *well* again.
_____

_____   9. The spring weather, warm and breezy, made me feel *good* again.
_____

_____   10. The floors of the kitchen must be *spotless* before the inspector arrives.
_____

_____   11. That car would look *better* if you gave it a new coat of paint.
_____

_____   12. The engine will run *better* after a tune-up.
_____

_____   13. *Most* football players are fairly good students.
_____

_____ 14. Hurricane Alma was our *most* destructive storm in the last five
_____ years.

_____ 15. The suburbs are growing *rapidly.*
_____

_____ 16. The boy has grown quite *independent* in both thought and
_____ action.

_____ 17. The man walked *straight* down the hall and out the door.
_____

_____ 18. It is important to keep your pattern *straight* when you cut the
_____ fabric for that shirt.

_____ 19. Rather than face the storm-whipped waves, we remained *will-
_____ ingly* at the dock.

_____ 20. This pool is *stagnant* because the tide does not reach it.
_____

Directions: In the space at the left, copy the correct form given in parentheses.

_____ 1. George did not sound at all (happy, happily) when he heard the news from the main office.

_____ 2. The amount of rainfall in the valley has increased (considerable, considerably) over last year's.

_____ 3. The track team performed (good, well) at the state meet.

_____ 4. If we leave by ten o'clock, we should (easy, easily) make it to St. Louis by dinner time.

_____ 5. You punctuated nearly a dozen sentences in your paper (incorrect, incorrectly).

_____ 6. This money should be divided (equal, equally) among the four partners.

_____ 7. Jose wants very (bad, badly) to learn to play football.

_____ 8. Although I have taken some lessons, I still dance (awkward, awkwardly).

_____ 9. In spite of my lessons, I still felt (awkward, awkwardly) on the floor.

_____ 10. It rained (steady, steadily) for two weeks this summer.

_____ 11. When Paul had been missing for three days, we became (real, really) worried about him.

_____ 12. The butter-cream icing on the chocolate cake tasted very (sweet, sweetly).

_____ 13. The storm came up so (sudden, suddenly) that we did not have time to get the people off the island.

_____ 14. Frozen orange juice tastes (different, differently) from fresh juice.

_____ 15. This special glue bonds (good, well) on all most any surface.

_____ 16. We (sure, surely) hope that your brother will recover soon from his injury.

_____ 17. The musicians played so (bad, badly) that we could not recognize the tune.

_____ 18. He is quite short, but he can become a good basketball player if he will practice (regular, regularly).

_____ 19. The blouse will look (good, well) with your new mauve slacks.

_____ 20. After a cold shower Maria felt (some, somewhat) more cheerful.

Exercise 25   *Using Modifiers and Prepositions Correctly*

NAME _____   SCORE _____

Directions: Study these sentences for misused adjectives, adverbs, and prepositions. If you find a misused modifier, underline it and write the correct form in the space at the left. If you find a superfluous preposition, circle it and write **omit** in the space at the left. If you find a spot that requires a preposition, write the preposition in the space at the left and use a caret (^) to show where it should be inserted in the sentence. Some sentences are correct as they stand; in these cases leave the spaces blank.

_____ 1. "It was real kind of you to speak well of my daughter's piano playing," Mrs. Hartwell told the teacher.

_____ 2. After the stern warning from the vice principal, the conduct of the class improved noticeable.

_____ 3. "The people here seem much more friendlier than those in Oakdale," said the new renter.

_____ 4. "Our quarterback was injured seriously," said Coach Saunders, "and we had to cut down on our offense and play more conservative."

_____ 5. The accused man testified that he had neither knowledge nor access to any secret Swiss bank accounts.

_____ 6. When I saw how weary the two old men looked, I admit that I felt somewhat guilty.

_____ 7. Mr. Evans confidently assured us that he could control the boat easy in any kind of weather.

_____ 8. Our chances for a successful season were hurt badly when Locke, the fastest of our two fullbacks, was declared ineligible.

_____ 9. Where at do you think I might be able to buy two hubcaps for my 1977 Mustang?

_____ 10. Your front yard certainly looks differently now that you have removed those two scraggly junipers.

_____ 11. Cynthia surely talks differently now that the braces have been removed from her teeth.

———————— 12. At the state meet last year, McCray failed to place in the high jump but did real good in the hundred-yard dash.

———————— 13. August Denby is a total incompetent local politician for whom I will never in my life cast a vote for.

———————— 14. At the recital Cathy's violin solo sounded good, and her accompanist played really well.

———————— 15. Brandowski's devotion and fascination with modern art led to the writing of his first critical essays.

———————— 16. If you use thinner as needed and clean your brushes regularly, you'll find that the painting job will move ahead more faster.

———————— 17. Although the scoutmaster set a rather leisurely pace, some of the boys were awful tired at the end of the hike.

———————— 18. Wally reluctantly admitted that, although his black eye looked ugly, it didn't hurt him real bad.

———————— 19. Dad and Fran worked hard and fast in the kitchen, and the excellent meal was ready for us promptly at six o'clock.

———————— 20. My uncle has always been interested in, in fact fascinated by, steam locomotives.

———————— 21. I am really sorry, Mrs. Frame, to have to report that your son has been behaving quite bad in class.

———————— 22. Mrs. Martin, the chairperson, made me promise solemnly that I would tell none of the children where I had hidden the Easter eggs at.

———————— 23. I'm sorry that Larry felt really bad when he confessed that he had not done very well on the final examination.

———————— 24. The author shows both a deep understanding and sympathy for the men who risk their lives fighting fires.

———————— 25. We had worried needlessly, for the young people behaved unusually well at the wedding reception.

The forms suggested in many of the entries in this glossary are those usually preferred in standard formal English—the English appropriate to your term papers, theses, term reports, examination papers in all your courses, and most of the serious papers written for your English classes. Many of the words or expressions in brackets are appropriate enough in informal conversation and in some informal papers.

Some of the entries are labeled *colloquial,* a term you should not think of as referring to slang, to forms used only in certain localities, or to "bad" English. The term applies to usages that are appropriate to informal and casual *spoken* English rather than to formal written English. However, expressions marked *substandard* should be avoided at all times.

A, an. Use *a* when the word immediately following it is sounded as a consonant; use *an* when the next sound is a vowel sound: *a, e, i, o,* or *u* (*a* friend, *an* enemy). Remember that it is the consonantal or vowel *sound,* not the actual letter, that determines the choice of the correct form of the indefinite article: *a* sharp curve, *an* S-curve; *a* eulogy, *an* empty house; *a* hospital, *an* honest person; *a* united people, *an* uneven contest.

Ad. Clipped forms of many words are used informally, such as *ad* (advertisement), *doc* (doctor), *exam* (examination), *gent* (gentleman), *gym* (gymnasium), *lab* (laboratory), *math* (mathematics), and *prof* (professor). Formal usage prefers the long forms.

Aggravate. In standard formal English the word means "make more severe," "make worse." Colloquially it means "annoy," "irritate," "exasperate."

Walking on your sprained ankle will aggravate the hurt. [*Informal:* All criticism aggravates him.]

Ain't. Substandard for *am not, are not, is not, have not.*

Am I not [not *Ain't I*] a good citizen?

The command hasn't [not *hain't* or *ain't*] been given yet.

They are not [not *ain't*] going either.

All the farther, all the faster, and the like. Generally regarded as colloquial equivalents of *as far as, as fast as,* and the like.

This is as far as [not *all the farther*] I care to go.

That was as fast as [not *all the faster*] he could run.

A lot. Always use as two words. See also *lots of, a lot of.*

A lot of. See *Lots of.*

Alright. This spelling, like *allright* or *allright,* although often used in advertising, is generally regarded as very informal usage. The preferred form is *all right.* In strictly formal usage, *satisfactory* or *very well* is preferred to *all right.*

Very well [not *Alright*], you may ride in our car.

The members agreed that the allocation of funds was satisfactory [not *all right*].

Among, between. *Among* is used with three or more persons or things, as in "Galileo was among the most talented people of

257

his age," or "The estate was divided among his three sons." *Between* usually refers to two things, as in "between you and me," "between two points," "between dawn and sunset."

Amount, number. Use *number*, not *amount*, in reference to units that can actually be counted:

the *amount* of indebtedness, the *number* of debts.

And etc. Because *etc. (et cetera)* means "and so forth," *and etc.* would mean "and and so forth." You should not use *etc.* to replace some exact, specific word, but if you do use it, be sure not to spell it *ect.* And remember that *etc.* requires a period after it.

Anywheres. Colloquial for *anywhere.* Similar colloquial forms are *anyways* for *anyway* or *anyhow*, *everywheres* for *everywhere*, *nowheres* for *nowhere*, *somewheres* for *somewhere.*

I looked for my books everywhere.
They must be hidden somewhere.

Apt to, liable to, likely to. *Apt to* implies a natural tendency. *Liable to* implies a negative outcome or result. *Likely to* suggests a strong possibility.

That car is apt to increase in value.

We are liable to have a bad leak unless we fix the roof.

The new vaccine is likely to cause a disappearance of chicken pox.

As, like. See *Like.*

As to whether. *Whether* is usually enough.

Awful, awfully. Like *aggravate*, these words have two distinct uses. In formal contexts, they mean "awe-inspiring" or "terrifying." Often in conversation and sometimes in writing of a serious nature, *awful* and *awfully* are mild intensifiers, meaning "very."

Because. See *Reason is because.*

Because of. See *Due to.*

Being that, being as how. Substandard for *because, as,* or *since.*

Beside, besides. These two prepositions are clearly distinguished by their meanings. *Beside* means "at the side of" and *besides* means "in addition to."

Lucy sits *beside* me in class.
Did anyone *besides* you see the accident?

Between. See *Among.*

Bring, take. *Bring* means to convey from a farther to a nearer place. *Take* means to convey from nearer to farther.

Bring home a loaf of bread from the store.
Take that book back to the library.

But what, but that. Colloquial for *that.*

Both sides had no doubt *that* [not *but what*] their cause was just.

Calculate, figure, reckon. These are colloquial for *imagine, consider, expect, think,* and similar words.

He must have *expected* [not calculated] that she might not be pleased to see him after he did not return her calls.

Can, may. *Can* suggests ability to do something. *May* is the preferred form when permission is involved.

Little Junior *can* already count to ten.
May [not Can] I borrow your pencil?

Can't hardly, couldn't hardly, can't scarcely, couldn't scarcely. Substandard for *can hardly, could hardly, can scarcely, could scarcely.* These are sometimes referred to as double negatives.

I *can hardly* [not *can't hardly*] believe that story.

We *could scarcely* [not *couldn't scarcely*] hear the foghorn.

Caused by. See *Due to.*

Consensus means an agreement of the majority; thus *consensus of opinion* is redundant. Say simply, "The consensus was . . . ," not, "The consensus of opinion was. . . ."

Continual, continuous. A fine distinction in meaning can be made if you remember that *continual* means "repeated regularly and frequently" and that *continuous* means "occurring without interruption," "unbroken."

Could(n't) care less. This worn-out set phrase indicating total indifference is a colloquialism. A continuing marvel of language behavior is the large number of people who insist on saying "I could care less" when they obviously mean the opposite.

Could of, would of, might of, ought to of, and so on. Substandard for *could have, would have,* and so on.

Couple, couple of. These expressions are fine for informal conversation, but not precise enough for more formal occasions. In writing, be specific. Say "three points," for example, of "four issues," rather than "a couple of points/issues."

Criteria. The singular noun is *criterion;* the plural is *criteria* or *criterions.* Such combinations as "*a criteria,*" "*one criteria*" and "*these criterias*" are incorrect.

Data. Originally the plural form of the rarely used Latin singular *datum, data* has taken on a collective meaning so that it is often treated as a singular noun. "This data has been published" and "These data have been published" are both correct, the latter being the use customarily found in scientific or technical writing.

Different from, different than. *Different from* is generally correct. Many people object to *different than,* but others use it, especially when a clause follows, as in "Life in the Marines was different than he had expected it to be."

Their customs are *different from* [not *different than*] ours.

Life in the Marines was *different from* what he had expected it to be.

Different to, a form sometimes used by British speakers and writers, is rarely used in the United States.

Disinterested, uninterested. Many users of precise English deplore the tendency to treat these words as loose synonyms, keeping a helpful distinction between *disinterested* ("impartial," "free from bias or self-interest") and *uninterested* ("lacking in interest," "unconcerned"). Thus we would hope that a referee would be disinterested but not uninterested.

Due to, caused by, because of, owing to. *Due to* and *caused by* are used correctly after the verb *to be:*

His illness was *caused by* a virus.

The flood was *due to* the heavy spring rains.

Many people object to the use of *due to* and *caused by* adverbially at the beginning of a sentence, as in "Due to the heavy rains, the streams flooded," and "Caused by the storm, the roads were damaged." It is better to use *because of* or *owing to* in similar situations. *Due to* and *owing to* are also used correctly as an adjective modifier immediately following a noun:

Accidents *due to* excessive speed are increasing in number.

Note in the examples what variations are possible:

The streams flooded *because of* the heavy rains.

The flooding of the streams was *due to* the heavy rains.

The floods were *caused by* the rapid melting of the snow.

Emigrate, immigrate. To *emigrate* is to *leave* one region to settle in another; to *immigrate* is to *enter* a region from another one.

Enthuse. Colloquial or substandard (depending on the degree of a person's aversion to this word) for *be enthusiastic, show enthusiasm.*

The director *was enthusiastic* [not *enthused*] about her new program.

Everyday, every day. *Everyday* is an adjective meaning "ordinary." *Every day* is an adjective and noun combination.

Just wear your everyday clothes; don't dress up.

I wore those shoes almost every day last week.

Everywheres. See *Anywheres.*

Explicit, implicit. *Explicit* means "stated directly." *Implicit* means "implied," "suggested directly."

She explicitly told us to bring two pencils and ten pages of notebook paper.

The idea implicit in her statement was that we should come prepared to take the test.

Farther, further. Careful writers observe a distinction between these two words, reserving *farther* for distances that can actually be measured.

Tony can hit a golf ball *farther* than I can.

We must pursue this matter *further.*

Fewer, less. *Fewer* refers to numbers, *less* to quantity, extent, or degree.

Fewer [not *Less*] students are taking courses in literature this year.

Food costs *less,* but we have less money to spend.

Figure. See *Calculate.*

Fine. Colloquial, very widely used, for *well, very well.*

The boys played *well* [not *just fine*].

Graffiti. The singular form is *graffito.* In serious writing *graffiti* takes a plural verb. Avoid combinations such as "a graffiti," "this graffiti," etc.

Had(n't) ought. *Ought* does not take an auxiliary.

You *ought* [not *had ought*] to apply for a scholarship.

You *ought not* [not *hadn't ought*] to miss the lecture.

Hardly. See *Can't hardly.*

Healthy, healthful. *Healthy* means "having health," and *healthful* means "giving health." Thus a person or an animal is healthy; a climate, a food, or an activity is healthful.

Immigrate. See *Emigrate.*

Implicit. See *Explicit.*

Imply, infer. Despite the increasing tendency to use these words more or less interchangeably, it is good to preserve the distinction: *Imply* means "to say something indirectly," "to hint or suggest," and *infer* means "to draw a conclusion," "to deduce." Thus you *imply* something in what you say and *infer* something from what you hear.

Incredible, incredulous. An unbelievable *thing* is incredible; a disbelieving *person* is incredulous.

In regards to. The correct forms are *in regard to* or *as regards.*

Inside of. *Inside* or *within* is preferred in formal writing.

We stayed *inside* [not *inside of*] the barn during the storm.

The plane should arrive *within* [not *inside of*] an hour.

Irregardless. Substandard or humorous for *regardless.*

The planes bombed the area *regardless* [not *irregardless*] of consequences.

Is when, is where. The *is-when, is-where* pattern in definitions is clumsy and should be avoided. Write, for example, "An embolism is an obstruction, such as a blood clot, in the bloodstream," instead of "An embolism is where an obstruction forms in the bloodstream."

Kind, sort. These words are singular and therefore should be modified by singular modifiers. Do not write *these kind, these sort, those kind, those sort.*

Those kinds [not *those kind*] of videos sell very well.

Who could believe *that sort* [not *those sort*] of arguments?

Kinda, sorta, kind of a, sort of a. Undesirable forms.

Kind of, sort of. Colloquial for *somewhat, in some degree, almost, rather.*

They felt *somewhat* [not *sort of*] depressed.

Learn, teach. *Learn* means "to acquire knowledge"; *teach* means "to give or impart knowledge."

Ms. Brown taught [not *learned*] me Spanish.

Leave. Not to be used for *let.*

Let [not *Leave*] me carry your books for you.

Less. See *Fewer.*

Let. See *Leave.*

Let's us. The *us* is superfluous because *let's* means "let us."

Liable to, likely to. See *Apt to.*

Like, as, as if. The use of *like* as a conjunction (in other words, to introduce a clause) is colloquial. It should be avoided in serious writing.

As [not *Like*] you were told earlier, there is a small entry fee.

She acts *as if* [not *like*] she distrusts us.

Do *as* [not *like*] I tell you.

Line. Often vague and redundant, as in "What do you read *in the line* of books?" "Don't you enjoy fishing and other sports *along that line*?" It is better to say, more directly,

What kind of books do you read?

Don't you enjoy fishing and sports like that?

Lots of, a lot of. Used informally to mean a large extent, amount, or number, a usage that is enjoying increased acceptance. This usage should be avoided in formal writing.

A great many [not *Lots of*] families vacation here every summer.

The storms caused a great deal [not *lots of*] damage.

All of us owe you a great deal [not *a lot*].

As one word, **alot** is still unacceptable spelling.

Mad. Colloquially *mad* is often used to mean "angry." In formal English, it means "insane."

Marge was *angry* [not *mad*] because I was late.

May. See *Can.*

Media. A plural noun referring to all mass communicative agencies. The singular is *medium.* Careful writers and speakers avoid the use of *media* as a singular noun, as in "Television is an influential media." Even more objectionable is the use of *medias* as a plural.

Might of. See *Could of.*

Most. This word is the superlative form of *much* and *many* (*much, more, most; many, more, most*). Its use as a clipped form of *almost* is colloquial.

Almost [not *Most*] all of my friends work during the summer.

Nauseated, nauseous. Despite the increasingly wide use of these words as synonyms, there are still speakers and writers of precise English who insist that *nauseated* should be used to mean "suffering from or experiencing nausea" and that *nauseous* should be used only to mean "causing nausea."

Nohow. This emphatic negative is substandard.

Not all that. A basically meaningless substitute for *not very* or *not really*; it can easily become a habit.

The movie was *not very* [not *not all that*] amusing.

Nowheres. See *Anywheres.*
Number. See *Amount.*
Of. See *Could of.*
Off of. Dialectal or colloquial for *off.*

> She asked me to get *off* [not *off of*] my high horse.

OK. This form calls attention to itself in serious writing. It is appropriate only to business communications and casual speech or writing. Modern dictionaries offer several permissible forms: *OK, O.K.,* and *okay* for the singular noun; *OKs, O.K.s,* and *okays* for the plural noun; and *OK'd, OK'ing, O.K.'d, O.K.'ing, okayed,* and *okaying* for verb forms.

Ought. See *Had(n't) ought.*
Ought to of. See *Could of.*
Owing to. See *Due to.*
Party. Colloquial for *individual* in the sense of *man, woman, person.*

> A man [not *a party*] called while you were out.

Percent, percentage. Use *percent* when referring to a specific number.

> Ten percent of the class made an A.

Use *percentage* when referring to no specific number.

> A small percentage of the class made an A.

Phenomenon, phenomena. A *phenomenon* is a single observable fact or event. *Phenomena* is a plural noun. When using either, be sure to make adjectives such as *this* and *these* and all verbs agree in number.

Plenty is a noun meaning "an abundance" and is used with the preposition *of.*

> There are *plenty* of jobs available.

Do not use the word as an adverb meaning "very" or "quite."

> It was very [not *plenty*] scary in that movie.

Pretty is an informal modifier. In writing, use *quite,* or *very.*

> The flood waters were very [not *pretty*] deep.

Quote, unquote. Although these words may be needed in the oral presentation of quoted material, they have no use in written material, in which quotation marks or indentation sets off the quoted material from the text proper.

Real, really. The use of *real,* which is an adjective, to modify another adjective or an adverb is colloquial. In formal contexts *really* or *very* should be used.

> We had a *really* [not *real*] enjoyable visit.

> The motorcycle rounded the corner *very* [not *real*] fast.

Reason is because, reason is due to, reason is on account of. In serious writing, a *reason is* clause is usually completed with *that,* not with *because, due to,* or *on account of.*

> The reason they surrendered *is that* [not *because*] they were starving.

> The reason for my low grades *is that I have poor eyesight* [not *is on account of my poor eyesight*].

Reckon. See *Calculate.*
Same. The use of *same* as a pronoun, often found in legal or business writing, is inappropriate in most other types of writing.

> I received your report and look forward to reading *it* [not *the same*].

So, such. These words, when used as exclamatory intensifiers, are not appropriate in a formal context. Sentences like the following belong in informal talk: "I am *so* tired," "She is *so* pretty," or "They are having *such* a good time."

Some. Colloquial for *somewhat, a little.*

> The situation at the border is said to be *somewhat* [not *some*] improved today.

Somewheres. See *Anywheres.*
Sort. See *Kind.*
Such. See *So.*
Suppose to, use to. Although these incorrect forms are difficult to detect in spoken

English, remember that the correct written forms are *supposed to, used to.*

Sure. *Sure* is correctly used as an adjective:

We are not *sure* about her plans.
He made several *sure* investments.

Sure is colloquial when used as an adverbial substitute for *surely, extremely, certainly, indeed, very, very much.*

The examination was *surely* [not *sure*] difficult.

The lawyer's plea *certainly* [not *sure*] impressed the jury.

Sure and. See *Try and.*

Suspicion. *Suspicion* is a noun; it is not to be used as a verb in place of *suspect.*

No one *suspected* [not *suspicioned*] the victim's widow.

Swell. Not to be used as a general term of approval meaning *good, excellent, attractive, desirable,* and so on.

Take. See *Bring.*

Teach. See *Learn.*

That there, this here, those there, these here. Substandard for *that, this, those, these.*

Them. Substandard when used as an adjective.

How can you eat *those* [not *them*] parsnips?

Try and, sure and. *Try to, sure to* are the preferred forms in serious writing.

We shall *try to* [not *try and*] make your visit a pleasant one.

Be *sure to* [not *sure and*] arrive on time.

Type. Colloquial when used as a modifier of a noun. Use *type of* or *kind of.*

I usually don't enjoy that *type of* [not *type*] movie.

Uninterested. See *Disinterested.*

Unique. In its original meaning, the word meant either "the only example" or "without a like or equal." In modern use, it has also acquired an additional meaning: "unusual." In the first sense, it cannot be modified by an adjective.

As a politician, he is unique.

She gave him a unique [*very special*] pen as a present.

Many object to the use of a modifier with unique; in formal writing, it is best to choose some other adjective to convey the meaning "special" or "unusual."

Use to. See *Suppose to.*

Want in, want off, want out. Colloquial and dialectical forms for *want to come in, want to get off, want to go out.* Inappropriate in serious writing.

Ways. Colloquial for *way,* in such expressions as

It is just a short *distance* [not *ways*] up the canyon.

We do not have a long *way* [not *ways*] to go.

What. Substandard when used for *who, which,* or *that* as a relative pronoun in an adjective clause.

His raucous laugh is the thing *that* [not *what*] annoys me most.

When, where clauses. See *Is when.*

Where . . . at. The *at* is unnecessary. Undesirable in both speech and writing.

Where [not *Where at*] will you be at noon?

Where is your car? [Not *Where is your car at?*]

-wise. The legitimate function of this suffix to form adverbs like *clockwise* does not carry with it the license to concoct such jargon as "Entertainmentwise this town is a dud" or "This investment is very attractive long-term-capital-gainswise."

Without. Not to be used as a conjunction instead of *unless.*

He won't lend me his car *unless* [not *without filling*] I fill the gas tank.

Would of. See *Could of.*

NAME _____   SCORE _____

Directions: In the space at the left, write the word or phrase given in parentheses that you consider the more appropriate form to use in serious writing.

_____ 1. Did you (imply, infer) from Jim's comment that you were (sup-
_____   pose, supposed) to attend that dinner?

_____ 2. "If we had another hour," said the foreman, "we could (try and,
_____   try to) extend that ditch a little (farther, further)."

_____ 3. (Can, May) we ask some (disinterested, uninterested) party to
_____   settle the dispute between the two unions?

_____ 4. Morris (sure, surely) (could have, could of) found a better invest-
_____   ment than that old rental property.

_____ 5. "(Beside, Besides) me, there isn't anyone in the company who
_____   knows (lots of, many) people in the county government."

_____ 6. "(Let's, Let's us) leave early today; we haven't gone (anywhere,
_____   anywheres) out of town recently."

_____ 7. There is no doubt (but what, that) (among, between) the four of
_____   us we can figure out the puzzle.

_____ 8. The (amount, number) of people standing in line is (fewer, less)
_____   today than it was yesterday.

_____ 9. "I'm not (real, very) (enthused, enthusiastic) about that difficult
_____   exercise class," said Marta.

_____ 10. The reason I failed that test is (because, that) I lost (almost, most)
_____   all my notes when I moved.

_____ 11. The hotel was such a long (way, ways) from the restaurant that
_____   we were (plenty, very) tired by the time we walked there.

_____ 12. "This is (all the farther, as far as) I can go because my backpack
_____   is getting (awfully, very) heavy," said Marge.

_____ 13. (Being that, Because) winter is just around the corner, we (should
_____   have, should of) stocked up on firewood.

265

_____ 14. The (continual, continuous) dripping of that faucet severely (aggravated, irritated) my mother.

_____ 15. The graduate school has established one (real, very) rigid (criterion, criteria) for admission to the program.

_____ 16. (Due to, Because of) the high winds, (a couple, three) people withdrew from the bicycle race.

_____ 17. What do you (figure, think) Marcia will do now that she has won that (incredible, incredulous) prize in the lottery?

_____ 18. (That, Those) kind of question makes a test (kind of, rather) difficult, don't you think?

_____ 19. (Lots of, Many) students were extremely (angry, mad) because Professor Howard postponed the test.

_____ 20. "Men, we (had ought, ought) to (learn, teach) those kids to play baseball the proper way," said Mr. Ames.

Directions: Each sentence contains two italicized words or expressions. If you think that the word or expression is inappropriate in serious writing, write an acceptable form in the space at the left. If the expression is correct, write **C** in the space.

1. *Due to* the heavy rains, we will have to find *somewhere's else* for soccer practice.

2. *Those criteria* we *use to* employ for selecting new managers were far too loosely worded.

3. *Those kind* of admissions policies *aggravated* an already bad relationship with the local high schools.

4. *Lots of* students *inferred* from your absences that you intend to drop the course.

5. *Being that* her GPA has fallen a long *ways* from its original high point, Sally has started to study again.

6. "Jim was *suppose* to sit *beside* me at the game," said Helen, "but he had to work."

7. *Let's* ask for some help; this report is *awfully* complex.

8. *Can* you find out *where* Jim bought that painting *at*?

9. "*Hadn't you ought* to divide that work *between* those three workers?" asked Melvin.

10. If they investigate that matter *further*, I *have* no *doubt* that they will discover a political scandal.

11. "*In regards to* the campaign, the candidate has *nothing in the line of* comments at this time," said the article.

12. In *a couple of* major details, the mayor's platform is *different from* his opponent's.

13. Marilyn does not *suspicion* that she will get *less* money next year than she received this year.

14. *These data* suggest that, *irregardless* of a person's age, a low-fat diet is beneficial.

_____ 15. A set of *them* new snowshoes would *sure* be nice for this winter.
_____

_____ 16. Alice says she *wants in on* that project because there is *plenty of*
_____   money to be made in overtime.

_____ 17. The reason I called to change my reservation is *because* I must go
_____   home early *due to* a family emergency.

_____ 18. The new model of that tractor pulls *really* well, and we are *enthu-*
_____   *siastic* about buying several for the farm.

_____ 19. Jill asked to be taken *off of* that committee because *almost* all of
_____   the members skip the meetings.

_____ 20. I *should of* guessed that Rachel would act *like* she hated all the
_____   other guests.

Exercise 26   *Appropriate Use*

NAME _____   SCORE _____

Directions: In the space at the left, write the word or phrase given in parentheses that you consider more appropriate in serious writing.

_____*Let's*_____
_____*Further*_____ 1. (Let's us, Let's) move that chair a bit (farther, further) toward the front so that we can see the speaker.

_____*used to*_____ 2. Before we did those drills, we all (use to, used to) make a far greater (amount, number) of errors on our essays.

_____ 3. (Irregardless, Regardless) of my past failures, I think I can pass (almost, most) all of the remaining tests.

_____ 4. "Well," said Mary, "you acted (as if, like) you were (real, really) angered by the boss' decision."

_____ 5. (Because, Being that) I lost my books, I had (fewer, less) notes for writing my paper.

_____ 6. William said, "I (can hardly, can't hardly) believe that people still sell (that kind, those kind) of inefficient engine.

_____ 7. The president (suspects, suspicions) that there is an industrial spy (somewhere, somewheres) in our company.

_____ 8. We all (inferred, implied) from that speech that we (hadn't ought, ought not) to expect any bonuses.

_____ 9. (Because of, Due to) rising costs, there have been (lots of, many) lay-offs in the plant.

_____ 10. The (party, person) who wrote that anonymous memo couldn't be anyone (beside, besides) Raymond.

_____ 11. "We (should have, should of) called Mary when we didn't get an (invite, invitation) to that dinner party," said Ralph.

_____ 12. This message is (suppose, supposed) to go to the coach as soon as she walks in (that, that there) door this morning.

_____ 13. Helen's plan for replanting the garden is different (from, than)
_____ yours in (a couple, two) important ways.

_____ 14. The reason Bob left the party so early is (because, that) his
_____ daughter fell (off, off of) a swing and hurt herself.

_____ 15. My watch is (kinda, almost) ruined; I'd like to know (where,
_____ where . . .) I can buy a new one (at).

_____ 16. (Can, May) you find copies of (them, those) contracts so that I
_____ can review them?

_____ 17. (In regard, In regards) to my payment, I'll (try and, try to) mail
_____ it tomorrow.

_____ 18. "An (incredible, incredulous) thing just happened," said Ron;
_____ "my sister repaid (almost, most) all the money she owed me.

_____ 19. We ate a (healthful, healthy) lunch, but I'm already (real, really)
_____ hungry.

_____ 20. Her work is (alright, adequate), but she needs to make (a signif-
_____ icant, some kind of an) improvement to earn a raise.

Directions: Each sentence contains two italicized words or expressions. If you think that the word or expression is inappropriate in serious writing, write an acceptable form in the space at the left. If you think the expression is correct, write **C** in the space.

_____
_____   1. Do you know *whether* or not *this data* have been verified by the research office?

_____
_____   2. Mr. James *can't hardly* understand why he can't find a *couple of* strong young men to mow his yard.

_____
_____   3. If you turn *off of* Highway 270 at the second light, you'll be just a short *way* from our house.

_____
_____   4. Jerry's work in that situation was *plenty* effective, but he is still not *real* popular with his colleagues.

_____
_____   5. In the late 19th century, my grandfather *immigrated* from England and moved to *somewheres* near Little Rock.

_____
_____   6. "*Leave* me *try and* find a replacement for that book you lost," said Mary helpfully.

_____
_____   7. My teacher said I made *less* errors on this last test *due to* your excellent tutoring.

_____
_____   8. The reason we were unable to accept your *invite* to the dance is *because* we don't own tuxedos.

_____
_____   9. Please find enclosed a memo *in regard to* changes in personnel policy and read *same* before Tuesday's meeting.

_____
_____   10. The trainer says that we are *supposed* to run three miles this morning and then take a *healthy* nap.

_____
_____   11. I thought her note *implied* that she *would of* come to the meeting if she had not had a previous commitment.

_____
_____   12. *This kind of* long, boring lecture *had ought* to be banned from the campus.

_____
_____   13. In the next announcements, be sure *to tell* people *where* they can pick up their exams *at*.

_____
_____   14. Maureen won the essay contest because she worked *really* hard and made *a lot of* good points.

_____ 15. That novel is *like* a healthful meal; it's good for you, but it's *not*
_____   *all that* exciting.

_____ 16. If a *couple more* people had signed up, we *could of* made that trip
_____   with no problems.

_____ 17. Jane was *incredible* when she learned that she had walked *further*
_____   than any other contestant.

_____ 18. Roberta suggested, "*Let's* ask for a different evaluator, someone
_____   who is totally *uninterested*."

_____ 19. "If I *may*, I'd like to suggest that the *amount* of time for that pro-
_____   ject be limited to no more than two hours."

_____ 20. Your solution worked *just fine*, but there is no doubt *but what* it
_____   was a very unusual approach to that problem.

6 Spelling and Capitalization
Lessons, Practice Sheets, and Exercises

Lesson 27 *Spelling Rules; Words Similar in Sound*

This lesson presents spelling rules that will help you improve your written work.

Rule 1: A word ending in silent *e* generally drops the *e* before a suffix beginning with a vowel and retains the *e* before a suffix beginning with a consonant.

After *c* or *g*, if the suffix begins with *a* or *o*, the *e* is retained to preserve the soft sound of the *c* or *g*.

Drop E *before a Vowel*

become	+ ing	—becoming	hope	+ ing	—hoping
bride	+ al	—bridal	imagine	+ ary	—imaginary
conceive	+ able	—conceivable	noise	+ y	—noisy
desire	+ able	—desirable	remove	+ able	—removable
fame	+ ous	—famous	white	+ ish	—whitish
force	+ ible	—forcible	write	+ ing	—writing

Retain E *before a Consonant*

excite	+ ment	—excitement	life	+ like	—lifelike
force	+ ful	—forceful	pale	+ ness	—paleness
hope	+ less	—hopeless	sincere	+ ly	—sincerely

Retain E *after* C *or* G *if the Suffix Begins with* A *or* O

advantage	+ ous	—advantageous	notice	+ able	—noticeable
change	+ able	—changeable	outrage	+ ous	—outrageous
manage	+ able	—manageable	service	+ able	—serviceable

(See Supplement.)

Rule 2: In words with *ie* or *ei* when the sound is long *ee*, use *i* before *e* except after *c*.

Use I before E

apiece	frontier	priest
belief	grieve	reprieve
fiend	niece	shriek
fierce	pierce	thievery

Except after C

ceiling	conceive	perceive
conceited	deceit	receipt

The common exceptions to this rule may be easily remembered if you memorize the following sentence: Neither financier seized either species of weird leisure.

Rule 3: In words of one syllable and words accented on the last syllable, ending in a single consonant preceded by a single vowel, double the final consonant before a suffix beginning with a vowel.

Words of One Syllable—Suffix Begins with a Vowel

ban	—banned	hit	—hitting	rid	—riddance
bid	—biddable	hop	—hopping	Scot	—Scottish
dig	—digger	quit	—quitter	stop	—stoppage
drag	—dragged	["qu"-consonant]		wet	—wettest

Accented on Last Syllable—Suffix Begins with a Vowel

abhor	—abhorrence	equip	—equipping
acquit	—acquitted	occur	—occurrence
allot	—allotted	omit	—omitted
begin	—beginner	prefer	—preferring
commit	—committing	regret	—regrettable
control	—controlled	repel	—repellent

Not Accented on Last Syllable—Suffix Begins with a Vowel

differ	—different	open	—opener
happen	—happening	prefer	—preference
hasten	—hastened	sharpen	—sharpened

Suffix Begins with a Consonant

allot	—allotment	mother	—motherhood
color	—colorless	sad	—sadness
equip	—equipment	sin	—sinful

(See Supplement.)

An apparent exception to this rule affects a few words formed by the addition of *ing*, *ed*, or *y* to a word ending in *c*. To preserve the hard sound of the *c*, a *k* is added before the vowel of the suffix, resulting in such spellings as *frolicking, mimicked, panicked, panicky, picnicked,* and *trafficking.*

Another irregularity applies to such spellings as *quitting* and *equipped.* One might think that the consonant should not be doubled, reasoning that the final consonant is preceded by two vowels, not by a single vowel. But because *qu* is phonetically the equivalent of *kw*, the *u* is a consonant when it follows *q.* Therefore, because the final consonant is actually preceded by a single vowel, the consonant is doubled before the suffix.

Rule 4: Words ending in *y* preceded by a vowel retain the *y* before a suffix; most words ending in *y* preceded by a consonant change the *y* to *i* before a suffix.

Ending in Y Preceded by a Vowel

boy	—boyish	coy	—coyness	enjoy	—enjoying
buy	—buys	donkey	—donkeys	stay	—staying

Ending in Y Preceded by a Consonant

ally	—allies	easy	—easiest	pity	—pitiable
busy	—busily	icy	—icier	study	—studies
cloudy	—cloudiness	mercy	—merciless	try	—tried

The Y Is Unchanged in Words Like the Following:

baby	—babyish	lady	—ladylike
carry	—carrying	study	—studying

Words Similar in Sound

Accept. I should like to accept your first offer.

Except. He took everything except the rugs.

Advice. Free advice [noun] is usually not worth much.

Advise. Ms. Hull said she would advise [verb] me this term. (Similarly, devi*c*e [noun] and devi*s*e [verb], prophe*c*y [noun] and prophe*s*y [verb].

Affect. His forced jokes affect [verb] me unfavorably.

Effect. His humor has a bad effect [noun]. Let us try to effect [verb] a lasting peace.

All ready. They were all ready to go home.

Already. They had already left when we telephoned the house.

All together. Now that we are all together, let us talk it over.

Altogether. They were not altogether pleased with the results.

Altar. In this temple was an altar to the Unknown God.

Alter. One should not try to alter or escape history.

Ascent. The ascent to the top of the mountain was quite steep.

Assent. The judge did not give assent to our request.

Bare. The bare and leafless limbs of the trees were a dark gray.

Bear. He could not bear to look at the accident.

Breath. His breath came in short gasps at the end of the race.

Breathe. The problem is solved; you can breathe easily now.

Canvas. We used a piece of canvas to shelter us from the wind.

Canvass. The candidate wanted to canvass every person in her precinct.

Capital. A capital letter; capital gains; capital punishment; state capital.

Capitol. Workers are painting the dome of the Capitol.

Cite. He cited three good examples.

Site. The site of the new school has not been decided on.

Sight. They were awed by the sight of so much splendor.

Climactic. The climactic moment in that movie was extremely exciting.

Climatic. According to NOAA, climatic conditions in North America have not changed much over the past 100 years.

Coarse. The coarse sand blew in my face.

Course. We discussed the course to take. Of course he may come with us.

Complement. Your intelligence is a complement to your beauty.

Compliment. It is easier to pay a compliment than a bill.

Consul. Be sure to look up the American consul in Rome.

Council. He was appointed to the executive council.

Counsel. I sought counsel from my friends. They counseled moderation. He employed counsel to defend him.

Decent. The workers demanded a decent wage scale.

Descent. The descent from the mountain was uneventful.

Dissent. The voices of dissent were louder than those of approval.

Desert. Out in the lonely desert [noun—desert], he tried to desert [verb—desert] from his regiment.

Dessert. We had apple pie for dessert.

Device. The device that controls the alarm system has malfunctioned.

Devise. We should devise a new system to cope with that problem.

Die. Old habits certainly die hard.

Dye. That dye produced a strange color in that new fabric.

Dining. We eat dinner in our dining room. Dining at home is pleasant.

Dinning. Stop dinning that song into my ears!

Fair. The decision of the umpire seemed very fair.

Fare. By plane, the fare from here to Toledo is $115.67.

Formerly. He was formerly a student at Beloit College.

Formally. You must address the presiding judge formally and respectfully.

Forth. Several witnesses came forth to testify.

Fourth. We planned a picnic for the Fourth of July.

Gorilla. The zoo has built a new habitat for the gorillas.

Guerrilla. The guerrilla forces are operating in the mountains beyond the city.

Heard. I had not heard that news.

Herd. The herd of cows moved slowly toward the barn.

Hole. The hole in my sock is growing bigger every minute.

Whole. The whole office is filled with a strange odor.

Incidence. Better sanitation lowered the incidence of communicable diseases.

Incidents. Smugglers were involved in several incidents along the border.

Instance. For instance, she was always late to class.

Instants. As the car turned, those brief instants seemed like hours.

Its. Your plan has much in its favor. [Possessive of *it.*]

It's. It's too late now for excuses. [Contraction of *it is, it has.*]

Later. It is later than you think.

Latter. Of the two novels, I prefer the latter.

Lead. Can you lead [lēd—verb] us out of this jungle? Lead [lĕd—noun] is a heavy, soft, malleable metallic element.

Led. A local guide led us to the salmon fishing hole.

Loose. He has a loose tongue. The dog is loose again.

Lose. Don't lose your temper.

Meat. We did not have any meat at lunch.

Meet. We intend to meet you after lunch.

Mete. The judge will mete out the punishment tomorrow.

Passed. She smiled as she passed me. She passed the test.

Past. It is futile to try to relive the past.

Patience. The teacher has little patience for lame excuses.

Patients. Twelve patients will be discharged from the hospital today.

Personal. Write him a personal letter.

Personnel. The morale of our company's personnel is high.

Pore. For hours they pored over the mysterious note.

Pour. Ms. Cook poured hot water into the teapot.

Precede. The Secret Service agents always precede the President when he enters a building.

Proceed. They all left the building and proceeded immediately to the parking lot.

Precedence. Tax reform takes precedence over all other legislative matters.

Precedents. The judge quoted three precedents to justify his ruling.

Presence. We are honored by your presence.

Presents. The child received dozens of Christmas presents.

Principal. The principal of a school; the principal [chief] industry; the principal and the interest.

Principle. He is a man of high principles.

Quiet. You must keep quiet.

Quite. The weather was quite good all week.

Rain. A soaking rain would help our crops greatly.

Reign. Samuel Pepys was briefly imprisoned during the reign of William III.

Rein. Keep a tight rein when you ride this spirited horse.

Right. Take a right turn on Oak Street.

Rite. Taking that course is a rite of passage for many students.

Write. Please write me a letter when you arrive.

Scene. The last scene in that movie was exceptionally touching.

Seen. I had not seen Frank for two weeks.

Sense. That statement makes a great deal of sense to me.

Since. Ten more people have arrived since we got here this morning.

Scents. The scents of those flowers are not easy to distinguish.

Sent. We sent a copy of the report to you yesterday.
Cent. We won't pay another cent.

Shone. The cat's eyes shone in the dark.
Shown. He hasn't shown us his best work.

Stationary. The benches were stationary and could not be moved.
Stationery. She wrote a letter on hotel stationery.

Statue. It was a statue of a pioneer.
Stature. Athos was a man of gigantic stature.
Statute. The law may be found in the 1917 book of statutes.

Than. She sings better than I.
Then. He screamed; then he fainted.

Their. It wasn't their fault. [Possessive pronoun.]
There. You won't find any gold there. [Adverb of place.]
They're. They're sure to be disappointed. [Contraction of *they are.*]

Thorough. We must first give the old cabin a thorough [adjective] cleaning.

Threw. The catcher threw the ball back to the pitcher.
Through. The thief had entered through [preposition] a hole in the roof.

To. Be sure to speak to her. [Preposition.]
Too. He is far too old for you. [Adverb.]
Two. The membership fee is only two dollars. [Adjective.]

Waist. She wore a beautiful silver belt around her waist.
Waste. Save every scrap; don't let anything go to waste.

Weather. The weather last week was very cold.
Whether. Do you know whether Jim has arrived?

Whose. Whose book is this? [Possessive pronoun.]
Who's. I wonder who's with her now. [Contraction of *who is.*]

Your. I like your new car. [Possessive pronoun.]
You're. You're not nervous, are you? [Contraction of *you are.*]

Supplement

Rule 1: A few common adjectives with the suffix *able* have two correct spellings:

likable/likeable, lovable/loveable, movable/moveable, sizable/sizeable, usable/useable.

Rule 3: Dictionaries show two spellings for the *ed* and *ing* forms (and a few other derived forms) of dozens of verbs ending in single consonants preceded by single vowels. In general, the single-consonant spelling is usually found in American printing; some of the dictionaries label the double-consonant spelling a British preference.

biased/biassed, canceling/cancelling, counselor/counsellor, diagraming/diagramming, equaled/equalled, marvelous/marvellous, modeled/modelled, totaling/totalling, traveler/traveller

NAME _____   SCORE _____

Directions: Each of the following sentences contains three italicized words, one of which is incorrect. Underline each incorrect word and write the correct form in the space at the left.

_____ 1. Two *different pieces* of *equiptment* are needed to complete that part of the paint job.

_____ 2. *Accept* for Audrey, everyone in the club had a *preference* for that new *colorless* cola drink.

_____ 3. The sailmaker will *alter* that piece of *canvass* to make it run *past* the end of the cockpit.

_____ 4. The *opening* of that *writting* lesson was *altogether* too difficult for most people in the class.

_____ 5. "Is it *conceivable* that Tom can do a *thorough* job in the time *alloted*?" asked Andrea.

_____ 6. Two of the men are *too* short to play the *role* opposite Ms. France, who is *extremly* tall.

_____ 7. A *removable* cover would be a *desireable* feature for a billiards table, if it is not *excessively* expensive.

_____ 8. The architects will *advice* the board about selecting a *site* for the stable for the *donkeys*.

_____ 9. It is *regretable* that we do not have the *capital* needed to fund the construction of a new *dining* hall.

_____ 10. Jan's *references* made her the *preffered* candidate; therefore, the *personnel* office offered her the job.

_____ 11. Any change in our *hireing policies* seems *unlikely* at this time.

_____ 12. One of Raymond's favorite *activities* is a *leisurely* walk along the lakeshore among *it's* beautiful trees.

_____ 13. After the two *incidence*, the *duties* of the *cashiers* were simplified considerably.

_____ 14. "*Your* not likely to find better *opportunities* for *studying* migratory birds," said the guide.

_____ 15. *There fourth* attempt to climb the mountain failed at the *iciest* part of the trail.

_____ 16. New cars are *fitted* with very *servicable batteries*.

_____ 17. She was an *adorable* baby, but she seemed to *loose* all her charming *qualities* as she grew older.

_____ 18. The firefighters made the difficult *dissent* from the top floor by *rappelling* down the exterior *past* the fire zone.

_____ 19. Anne has *committed* herself to taking an *extremely* technical *coarse* in mechanical engineering.

_____ 20. One of the *presence* Marty *received* for his birthday contained large *quantities* of various chocolate candies.

_____ 21. Winning that tournament against such *fierce* competitors was *quiet* an *achievement*.

_____ 22. The *principle* reason Arline is *quitting* that job is that she finds it very *boring*.

_____ 23. The people *living* on Shorewood Road hope that the city *counsel* will provide funds for *repaving* its surface.

_____ 24. All the team members had a different reaction to the *weird, unforgetable occurrences* at the season's end.

_____ 25. The students who took that course have *shone* a *noticeable improvement* in their math scores.

_____ 26. *Latter* that day the three *buddies* gathered at the *desert* campsite for a steak dinner.

_____ 27. In his *journeys* around the West, Martin collected large *quantities* of *fascinateing* relics.

_____ 28. "Those were the *noisiest*, most *irritable* children we've ever had *picnicing* with us," said the guide.

_____ 29. The race leaders were *adversely effected* by the *changeable* winds and the high waves.

_____ 30. In all *likelihood* this year's team will *lose* more games *then* last year's.

NAME _____   SCORE _____

Directions: Each of the following sentences contains three italicized words, one of which is incorrect. Underline each incorrect word and write the correct form in the space at the left.

_____ 1. Intensive *studies* of that problem by *you're committee* have provided no solution up to this point.

_____ 2. *Unmanageable* salary demands by that *fameous* player did not cause the owner to *alter* her position.

_____ 3. I do not know *whose* book that is *lying forgoten* on our living room table.

_____ 4. The *changable* weather did not have any great *effect* on the size of the crowd *coming* to see the game.

_____ 5. *Writting* reports is fast *becoming* the only way people use *their* computers.

_____ 6. "Wally, for *instance*, is only the *forth* person today to ask for the *allotted* travel money," said Al.

_____ 7. *Happyness* and joy *reigned* in the office after Mr. Alcott explained the *desirable* terms of the contract.

_____ 8. Those *presence* at the birthday party produced a *noisy* kind of *excitement* among the children.

_____ 9. A *lifelike statue* of the three boyish heroes of the *dessert* war was unveiled today.

_____ 10. *Dinning* in our ears through the entire morning was the *altogether* horrible sound of the *begining* trumpet class.

_____ 11. Any *descent* effort of her part probably would have earned a *different* response from the *hopeful* crowd.

_____ 12. We *poured* over our notes for hours, but we found nothing *notably* important about work *stoppages*.

_____ 13. Does new federal law take *precedents* over *personnel* policies *formerly* in effect in our company?

281

_____ 14. Denice seemed *knowledgeable* about computers, but she has *shown* no ability at *compilling* reports.

_____ 15. After the *festivities* my *neice* took my wife and me out for a *quiet* meal at a local restaurant.

_____ 16. The new *management counsel* has met several times but has *expressed* no opinion on quality control.

_____ 17. The *studious priest* went to the *capital* building to testify in the hearings.

_____ 18. "Jim *denies* that his view of the incident is *biased* by his *earlyer* experiences," said Yolanda.

_____ 19. The *attorneys councilled* us to move rapidly to correct that *regrettable* mistake.

_____ 20. Everyone *complimented* the women in the *brideal* party for the beauty of their *dresses*.

_____ 21. We replaced the office *stationary* because our new printer is not *equipped* to handle odd-sized *envelopes*.

_____ 22. The crew is *all ready removing* the tarpaulin although the rain has not yet completely *stopped*.

_____ 23. We were *lead* to *believe* that we had not used up our *allotment* of funds for studying the election results.

_____ 24. If Jim is forced to choose between his *studies* and a nap, he *usualy* chooses the *latter*.

_____ 25. As a beginning golfer, Julie *preferred coarses* that had the *easiest* finishing holes.

_____ 26. The *exciteable* crowd responded *immediately* to the *imaginative* story told by the lecturer.

_____ 27. The staff has made every *conceivable* effort to find a more *servicable copier* for the office.

_____ 28. Isn't that *they're equipment gathering* dust on that shelf in the back room?

_____ 29. No one is *happier then* Joan about the *arrival* of the new office manager.

_____ 30. A person of your *statute* in the community could *easily* obtain *complimentary* tickets to that playoff game.

Lesson 28 *Plurals and Capitals*

This lesson covers the formation of plurals and the conventions for using capitals.

Plurals

Plurals of most nouns are regularly formed by the addition of *s*. But if the singular noun ends in an *s* sound *(s, sh, ch, x, z)*, *es* is added to form a new syllable in pronunciation:

crab, crabs	foe, foes	kiss, kisses	tax, taxes
lamp, lamps	box, boxes	church, churches	lass, lasses

Nouns ending in *y* form plurals according to Rule 4. (See Lesson 27.)

toy, toys	army, armies	fly, flies	attorney, attorneys
key, keys	lady, ladies	sky, skies	monkey, monkeys

Some words ending in *o* (including all musical terms and all words having a vowel preceding the *o*) form their plurals with *s*. But many others take *es:*

alto, altos	folio, folios	tomato, tomatoes
piano, pianos	hero, heroes	potato, potatoes

For several nouns ending in *o*, most modern dictionaries give both forms. Here are some examples, printed in the order they are found in most dictionaries. The first spelling is the more common one:

banjos, banjoes	frescoes, frescos	lassos, lassoes	volcanoes, volcanos
buffaloes, buffalos	grottoes, grottos	mottoes, mottos	zeros, zeroes
cargoes, cargos	halos, haloes	tornadoes, tornados	

Some nouns ending in *f* or *fe* merely add *s;* some change *f* or *fe* to *ves* in the plural; and a few *(hoofs/hooves, scarfs/scarves, wharves/wharfs)* use either form. Use your dictionary to make sure:

leaf, leaves	life, lives	half, halves	wolf, wolves
roof, roofs	safe, safes	gulf, gulfs	elf, elves

A few nouns have the same form for singular and plural. A few have irregular plurals:

deer, deer	ox, oxen	child, children	goose, geese
sheep, sheep	man, men	foot, feet	mouse, mice

Many words of foreign origin use two plurals; some do not. Always check in your dictionary:

alumna, alumnae	bon mot, bons mots
alumnus, alumni	crisis, crises
analysis, analyses	criterion, criteria
appendix, appendixes, appendices	datum, data
basis, bases	thesis, theses
beau, beaus, beaux	focus, focuses, foci
curriculum, curriculums, curricula	fungus, funguses, fungi
memorandum, memorandums, memoranda	index, indexes, indices
tableau, tableaus, tableaux	

Note: Do *not* use an apostrophe to form the plural of either a common or a proper noun.

Wrong: Our neighbor's, the Allen's and the Murray's, recently bought new Honda's.
Right: Our neighbors, the Allens and the Murrays, recently bought new Hondas.

Capitals

A capital letter is used for the first letter of the first word of any sentence, for the first letter of a proper noun, and often for the first letter of an adjective derived from a proper noun. Following are some reminders about situations that cause confusion for some writers.

1. Capitalize the first word of every sentence, every quoted sentence or fragment, and every transitional fragment. (See Lesson 14.)

   The building needs repairs. How much will it cost? Please answer me.
   Mr. James said, "We'll expect your answer soon." She replied, "Of course."
   And now to conclude.

2. Capitalize proper nouns and most adjectives derived from them. A proper noun designates by name an individual person, place, or thing that is a member of a group or class. Do not capitalize common nouns, which are words naming a group or class:

   Doris Powers, woman; France, country; Tuesday, day; January, month; Christmas Eve, holiday; Shorewood High School, high school; Carleton College, college; *Mauretania*, ship; Fifth Avenue, boulevard; White House, residence

   Elizabethan drama, Restoration poetry, Chinese peasants, Indian reservation, Red Cross assistance

3. Do not capitalize nouns and derived forms that, although originally proper nouns, have acquired special meanings. When in doubt, consult your dictionary:

   a set of china; a bohemian existence; plaster of paris; pasteurized milk; a mecca for golfers; set in roman type, not italics

4. Capitalize names of religions, references to deities, and most words having religious significance:

   Bible, Baptist, Old Testament, Holy Writ, Jewish, Catholic, Sermon on the Mount, Koran, Talmud

5. Capitalize titles of persons when used with the person's name. When the title is used alone, capitalize it only when it stands for a specific person of high rank:

I spoke briefly to Professor Jones. He is a professor of history.
We visited the late President Johnson's ranch in Texas.
Jerry is president of our art club.
Tonight the President will appear on national television.

6. Capitalize names denoting family relationship but not when they are preceded by a possessive. This rule is equivalent to saying that you capitalize when the word serves as a proper noun:

At that moment Mother, Father, and Aunt Lucy entered the room.
My mother, father, and aunt are very strict about some things.

7. Capitalize points of the compass when they refer to actual regions but not when they refer to directions:

Before we moved to the West, we lived in the South for a time.
You drive three miles west and then turn north on the Pacific Highway.

Do not capitalize adjectives of direction modifying countries or states:

From central Finland the group had emigrated to northern Michigan.

8. Capitalize names of academic subjects as they would appear in college catalog listings, but in ordinary writing capitalize only names of languages:

I intend to register for History 322 and Sociology 188.
Last year I took courses in history, sociology, German, and Latin.

9. In titles of books, short stories, plays, essays, and poems, capitalize the first word and all other words except the articles *(a, an, the)* and short prepositions and conjunctions. (See Lesson 19 for the use of italics and quotation marks with titles.)

Last semester I wrote reports on the following: Shaw's *The Intelligent Woman's Guide to Socialism and Capitalism,* Joyce's *A Portrait of the Artist as a Young Man,* Pirandello's *Six Characters in Search of an Author,* Poe's "The Fall of the House of Usher," Yeats's "An Irish Airman Foresees His Death," Frost's "Stopping by Woods on a Snowy Evening," and Muriel Rukeyser's "The Soul and Body of John Brown."

Note: Traditionally, a capital letter begins every line of poetry. This convention, however, is not always followed by modern poets; when you quote poetry, be sure to copy exactly the capitalization used by the author.

NAME _____   SCORE _____

Directions: Write the plural form or forms for each of the following words. When in doubt as to the correct form, consult your dictionary. If you find two plural forms for a word, write both of them.

1. basis _____   _____

2. biopsy _____   _____

3. bistro _____   _____

4. craftsman _____   _____

5. curriculum _____   _____

6. datum _____   _____

7. fleece _____   _____

8. flunky _____   _____

9. fox _____   _____

10. Jones _____   _____

11. journey _____   _____

12. memorandum _____   _____

13. moose _____   _____

14. ox _____   _____

15. ploy _____   _____

16. portfolio _____   _____

17. proof _____   _____

18. ratio _____   _____

19. reindeer _____   _____

20. son-in-law _____   _____

21. spy _____   _____

22. volley _____   _____

23. wharf _____   _____

24. wife _____   _____

25. zero _____   _____

Directions: The following selection contains fifty numbered words. If you think the word is correct as it stands, write **C** in the space at the left with the corresponding number. If you think the word is incorrect, write **W** in the space.

1	2	3
4	5	6
7	8	9
10	11	12
13	14	15
16	17	18
19	20	21
22	23	24
25	26	27
28	29	30
31	32	33
34	35	36
37	38	39
40	41	42
43	44	45
46	47	48
49	50	

(1) Every Woman on the City Council, including Dolores James and mary McGraff, Voted against charging families for using the City's Parks.

(2) In our American history Class professor York read Thomas Catton's *The Red And The Black.*

(3) and now We must go on to our study of Western authors, Writers who used their knowledge of the West and their understanding of history to weave exciting tales from the Frontier.

(4) "sometimes," said Mr. Dolan, "It is quite important to be precise in our statements about our Opponents. and Yesterday's News Conference was certainly one of those times."

(5) Although I enjoyed *All the President's men,* I think it left many issues about watergate unresolved.

(6) All Sophomores are required to take History 201 and a Math class; it does not matter whether they think they enjoy history and mathematics or not.

(7) The Encyclopedia says that Central America and central Europe have remarkably different Climates. It is hotter in Tropical jungles than it is in Northern forests.

(8) Try to imagine reading *War And Peace* and *Gone with the wind* in the same Summer.

NAME _____   SCORE _____

Directions: Write the plural form or forms for each of the following words. When in doubt as to the correct form, consult your dictionary. If you find two plural forms for a word, write both of them.

1. autopsy   _____   _____

2. banjo   _____   _____

3. belief   _____   _____

4. berry   _____   _____

5. boss   _____   _____

6. crisis   _____   _____

7. editor in chief _____   _____

8. elephant   _____   _____

9. gulf   _____   _____

10. helmsman   _____   _____

11. key   _____   _____

12. kitty   _____   _____

13. Morris   _____   _____

14. mouse   _____   _____

15. nickel   _____   _____

16. nucleus   _____   _____

17. oboe   _____   _____

18. précis   _____   _____

19. pry   _____   _____

20. rock   _____   _____

21. safety   _____   _____

22. silo   _____   _____

23. sleeve   _____   _____

24. stand-in   _____   _____

25. thief   _____   _____

Directions: The following selection contains fifty numbered words. If you think the word is correct as it stands, write **C** in the space at the left with the corresponding number. If you think the word is incorrect, write **W** in the space.

1	2	3
4	5	6
7	8	9
10	11	12
13	14	15
16	17	18
19	20	21
22	23	24
25	26	27
28	29	30
31	32	33
34	35	36
37	38	39
40	41	42
43	44	45
46	47	48
49	50	

On a recent visit to New York city[1], my uncle[2] Ted and his Friends[3]

Joan and David Hammersmith toured the statue[4] Of[5] Liberty and

rode the Staten island[6] ferry. Then they watched a baseball[7] game at

Yankee Stadium[8]. At the game they spoke with captain[9] Morris

about his uncle[10] who is Superintendent[11] at the U.S. Naval academy[12]

at Annapolis. After they left the City[13], they went to Washington,

d.C.[14] and visited the Smithsonian institute[15] and the capitol[16]. They

had lunch with Ted's sister[17] who is an agent with the federal Bureau[18]

of Investigation[19]. Ted's sister wants to be transferred to phoenix[20],

Arizona, because she likes the weather there, and as she said, "the[21]

west[22] and western[23] life look like fun." Then Uncle Ted went to Cave

Of[24] The[25] Winds State Park and another Park[26] nearby. The assistant[27]

Director[28] of the park has a ph.d[29] in Geology[30] from an Eastern[31]

University[32]. The park is a Mecca[33] for Anthropologists[34] and students

of Prehistoric[35] animals. Often students from West[36] Virginia State

College and other nearby Colleges[37] study the caves. Uncle[38] Ted[39] then

climbed Teepee[40] Mountain, the highest Mountain[41] in that County[42].

Ted is a Teacher[43] at Forest High School, a rural School[44] where he[45]

teaches Psychology[46] and English[47] Literature[48] courses. He is an expert

on elizabethan[49] drama and Shakespearean Sonnets[50].

Lesson 29 *Spelling List*

This list includes words frequently misspelled by high-school and college students. Each word is repeated to show its syllabic division. Whether this list is used for individual study and review or in some kind of organized class activity, your method of studying should be the following: (1) Learn to pronounce the word syllable by syllable. Some of your trouble in spelling may come from incorrect pronunciation. (2) Copy the word carefully, forming each letter as plainly as you can. Some of your trouble may come from bad handwriting. (3) Pronounce the word carefully again. (4) On a separate sheet of paper, write the word from memory, check your spelling with the correct spelling before you, and, if you have misspelled the word, repeat the learning process.

abbreviate	ab-bre-vi-ate	audience	au-di-ence
absence	ab-sence	auxiliary	aux-il-ia-ry
accidentally	ac-ci-den-tal-ly	awkward	awk-ward
accommodate	ac-com-mo-date	barbarous	bar-ba-rous
accompanying	ac-com-pa-ny-ing	basically	ba-si-cal-ly
accomplish	ac-com-plish	beneficial	ben-e-fi-cial
accumulate	ac-cu-mu-late	boundaries	bound-a-ries
acknowledge	ac-knowl-edge	Britain	Brit-ain
acquaintance	ac-quaint-ance	bureaucracy	bu-reauc-ra-cy
acquire	ac-quire	business	busi-ness
across	a-cross	calendar	cal-en-dar
additive	ad-di-tive	candidate	can-di-date
admissible	ad-mis-si-ble	cassette	cas-sette
aggravate	ag-gra-vate	category	cat-e-go-ry
always	al-ways	cemetery	cem-e-ter-y
amateur	am-a-teur	certain	cer-tain
among	a-mong	chosen	cho-sen
analysis	a-nal-y-sis	commission	com-mis-sion
analytical	an-a-lyt-i-cal	committee	com-mit-tee
apartheid	a-part-heid	communicate	com-mu-ni-cate
apparatus	ap-pa-ra-tus	communism	com-mu-nism
apparently	ap-par-ent-ly	comparative	com-par-a-tive
appearance	ap-pear-ance	competent	com-pe-tent
appreciate	ap-pre-ci-ate	competition	com-pe-ti-tion
appropriate	ap-pro-pri-ate	completely	com-plete-ly
approximately	ap-prox-i-mate-ly	compulsory	com-pul-so-ry
arctic	arc-tic	computer	com-put-er
argument	ar-gu-ment	concede	con-cede
arithmetic	a-rith-me-tic	condominium	con-do-min-i-um
association	as-so-ci-a-tion	conference	con-fer-ence
astronaut	as-tro-naut	confidentially	con-fi-den-tial-ly
athletics	ath-let-ics	conscience	con-science
attendance	at-tend-ance	conscientious	con-sci-en-tious

conscious	con-scious	foreign	for-eign
consistent	con-sist-ent	forty	for-ty
continuous	con-tin-u-ous	frantically	fran-ti-cal-ly
controversial	con-tro-ver-sial	fundamentally	fun-da-men-tal-ly
convenient	con-ven-ient	generally	gen-er-al-ly
counterfeit	coun-ter-feit	ghetto	ghet-to
criticism	crit-i-cism	government	gov-ern-ment
criticize	crit-i-cize	graffiti	graf-fi-ti
curiosity	cu-ri-os-i-ty	grammar	gram-mar
curriculum	cur-ric-u-lum	grievous	griev-ous
decision	de-ci-sion	guarantee	guar-an-tee
definitely	def-i-nite-ly	guerrilla	guer-ril-la
describe	de-scribe	harass	ha-rass
description	de-scrip-tion	height	height
desperate	des-per-ate	hindrance	hin-drance
dictionary	dic-tion-ar-y	humorous	hu-mor-ous
difference	dif-fer-ence	hurriedly	hur-ried-ly
dilapidated	di-lap-i-dat-ed	hypocrisy	hy-poc-ri-sy
dinosaur	di-no-saur	imagination	im-ag-i-na-tion
disappear	dis-ap-pear	immediately	im-me-di-ate-ly
disappoint	dis-ap-point	impromptu	im-promp-tu
disastrous	dis-as-trous	incidentally	in-ci-den-tal-ly
discipline	dis-ci-pline	incredible	in-cred-i-ble
dissatisfied	dis-sat-is-fied	independence	in-de-pend-ence
dissident	dis-si-dent	indispensable	in-dis-pen-sa-ble
dissipate	dis-si-pate	inevitable	in-ev-i-ta-ble
doesn't	does-n't	influential	in-flu-en-tial
dormitory	dor-mi-to-ry	initiative	in-i-ti-a-tive
during	dur-ing	intelligence	in-tel-li-gence
efficient	ef-fi-cient	intentionally	in-ten-tion-al-ly
eligible	el-i-gi-ble	intercede	in-ter-cede
eliminate	e-lim-i-nate	interesting	in-ter-est-ing
embarrass	em-bar-rass	interpretation	in-ter-pre-ta-tion
eminent	em-i-nent	interrupt	in-ter-rupt
emphasize	em-pha-size	irrelevant	ir-rel-e-vant
enthusiastic	en-thu-si-as-tic	irresistible	ir-re-sist-i-ble
entrepreneur	en-tre-pre-neur	irritation	ir-ri-ta-tion
environment	en-vi-ron-ment	knowledge	knowl-edge
equipment	e-quip-ment	laboratory	lab-o-ra-to-ry
equivalent	e-quiv-a-lent	laser	la-ser
especially	es-pe-cial-ly	legitimate	le-git-i-mate
exaggerated	ex-ag-ger-at-ed	library	li-brar-y
exceed	ex-ceed	lightning	light-ning
excellent	ex-cel-lent	literature	lit-er-a-ture
exceptionally	ex-cep-tion-al-ly	livelihood	live-li-hood
exhaust	ex-haust	loneliness	lone-li-ness
existence	ex-ist-ence	maintenance	main-te-nance
exorbitant	ex-or-bi-tant	marriage	mar-riage
experience	ex-pe-ri-ence	mathematics	math-e-mat-ics
explanation	ex-pla-na-tion	memento	me-men-to
extraordinary	ex-traor-di-nar-y	miniature	min-i-a-ture
extremely	ex-treme-ly	miscellaneous	mis-cel-la-ne-ous
familiar	fa-mil-iar	mischievous	mis-chie-vous
fascinate	fas-ci-nate	misspelled	mis-spelled
February	Feb-ru-ar-y	mortgage	mort-gage

mysterious   mys-te-ri-ous   remembrance   re-mem-brance
naturally   nat-u-ral-ly   repetition   rep-e-ti-tion
necessary   nec-es-sar-y   representative   rep-re-sent-a-tive
ninety   nine-ty   respectfully   re-spect-ful-ly
ninth   ninth   respectively   re-spec-tive-ly
nowadays   now-a-days   restaurant   res-tau-rant
nuclear   nu-cle-ar   rhetoric   rhet-o-ric
obedience   o-be-di-ence   rhythm   rhythm
oblige   o-blige   ridiculous   ri-dic-u-lous
obstacle   ob-sta-cle   robot   ro-bot
occasionally   oc-ca-sion-al-ly   sacrilegious   sac-ri-le-gious
occurrence   oc-cur-rence   sandwich   sand-wich
omission   o-mis-sion   satellite   sat-el-lite
opportunity   op-por-tu-ni-ty   satisfactorily   sat-is-fac-to-ri-ly
optimistic   op-ti-mis-tic   schedule   sched-ule
original   o-rig-i-nal   scientific   sci-en-tif-ic
pamphlet   pam-phlet   secretary   sec-re-tar-y
parallel   par-al-lel   separately   sep-a-rate-ly
parliament   par-lia-ment   sergeant   ser-geant
particularly   par-tic-u-lar-ly   significant   sig-nif-i-cant
partner   part-ner   similar   sim-i-lar
pastime   pas-time   sophomore   soph-o-more
performance   per-form-ance   spaghetti   spa-ghet-ti
permissible   per-mis-si-ble   specifically   spe-cif-i-cal-ly
perseverance   per-se-ver-ance   specimen   spec-i-men
perspiration   per-spi-ra-tion   speech   speech
persuade   per-suade   strictly   strict-ly
politics   pol-i-tics   successful   suc-cess-ful
possession   pos-ses-sion   superintendent   su-per-in-tend-ent
practically   prac-ti-cal-ly   supersede   su-per-sede
preceding   pre-ced-ing   surprise   sur-prise
prejudice   prej-u-dice   suspicious   sus-pi-cious
preparation   prep-a-ra-tion   syllable   syl-la-ble
prevalent   prev-a-lent   synonymous   syn-on-y-mous
privilege   priv-i-lege   synthetic   syn-thet-ic
probably   prob-a-bly   technology   tech-nol-o-gy
procedure   pro-ce-dure   temperament   tem-per-a-ment
proceed   pro-ceed   temperature   tem-per-a-ture
processor   pro-ces-sor   together   to-geth-er
professional   pro-fes-sion-al   tragedy   trag-e-dy
professor   pro-fes-sor   truly   tru-ly
pronunciation   pro-nun-ci-a-tion   twelfth   twelfth
propaganda   prop-a-gan-da   unanimous   u-nan-i-mous
psychiatrist   psy-chi-a-trist   undoubtedly   un-doubt-ed-ly
psychological   psy-cho-log-i-cal   unnecessarily   un-nec-es-sar-i-ly
pursue   pur-sue   until   un-til
quantity   quan-ti-ty   usually   usu-al-ly
questionnaire   ques-tion-naire   various   var-i-ous
quizzes   quiz-zes   vegetable   veg-e-ta-ble
realize   re-al-ize   video   vid-e-o
really   re-al-ly   village   vil-lage
recognize   rec-og-nize   villain   vil-lain
recommend   rec-om-mend   Wednesday   Wednes-day
regard   re-gard   whether   wheth-er
religious   re-li-gious   wholly   whol-ly

NAME _____   SCORE _____

Directions: Each sentence contains two words from the first half of the spelling list. In each of these words at least one letter is missing. Write the words, correctly spelled, in the spaces at the left.

_____
_____
1. John seems to have only a nodding aqu__int__nce with the members of the new site selection com__it__ee.

_____
_____
2. I felt an almost irresist__ble urge to laugh out loud as I watched the awkw__rd gestures of the speaker.

_____
_____
3. Mr. Willis was fas__nated by the display of digital photographic equip__nt at the trade show.

_____
_____
4. The ex__rbit__nt costs of cleaning up the envir__ment in the case of a toxic waste spill should make us all more careful.

_____
_____
5. F__ty people called the radio station to ask for an int__rpr__tation of last night's editorial.

_____
_____
6. Our plan for the political campaign was fund__ment__lly sound, but the staff was not sufficiently compet__nt to execute it.

_____
_____
7. Serving as an auxil__ry power unit, that small generator can assure us of a contin__us supply of electricity.

_____
_____
8. Cont__versial campaign tactics are charact__r__stic of our local elections.

_____
_____
9. Softball is one of the most popular sports in all of amat__r ath__tics.

_____
_____
10. It once was thought good sport to ha__ss and embar__ss fraternity and sorority pledges.

_____
_____
11. "Int__rupt me if you think my comments are irr__l__vant to the situation as you understand it," said the mayor.

_____
_____
12. Approx__mately half of the third graders in my class have substandard skills in arith__tic.

_____ 13. Your extre__ly cons__ient__ous work on the dormitory council
_____   has earned you a promotion to dorm supervisor.

_____ 14. Janet and Maria packed hurr__dly for the trip last week and for-
_____   got two indisp__ns__ble items of the sound system.

_____ 15. The storm dis__pated as it moved ac__oss the large island.
_____

_____ 16. App__r__ntly our carefully phrased arg__ents changed the boss's
_____   mind about the holiday schedule.

_____ 17. The ex__llent response to our call for volunteers el__m__nated
_____   the need for any further advertising.

_____ 18. "The h__ght of those waves is simply incr__d__ble," cried Carla
_____   as she rested on the beach.

_____ 19. Our improm__tu confer__nce in the hallway broke up when
_____   members of the other delegations joined our conversation.

_____ 20. The Pinecrest Homeowners' Asso__ation considered several
_____   items of new bus__ness at its last meeting.

_____ 21. The constant pounding of the waves on the seawall d__ing the
_____   storm aggr__vated the cracked condition of its foundation.

_____ 22. There is no effic__nt way to operate the bure__cracy now exist-
_____   ing in our village government.

_____ 23. Astr__nauts and test pilots are in a cat__gory all by themselves
_____   when it comes to risky occupations.

_____ 24. In my abs__nce Tom and Joan became the acknowled__d experts
_____   on rose growing in our neighborhood.

_____ 25. Any ar__ic expedition is extr__rdinarily dangerous because the
_____   severe cold can cause hypothermia in only a few minutes.

Exercise 29   *Spelling*

NAME _____   SCORE _____

Directions: Each sentence contains three italicized words from the first half of the spelling list. One of the three words is misspelled. Write the misspelled word correctly in the space at the left.

_____ 1. The *dictionary* acknowledges the *existance* of two and sometimes three *pronunciations* for some words.

_____ 2. *Foriegn* films do not *generally* get an *enthusiastic* response in the small town where I live.

_____ 3. Most Americans *conceed* that physical *appearance* is an important qualification in political *candidates.*

_____ 4. A careful *analysis* of *attendence* patterns for our baseball games revealed *unusually* low attendance on week nights.

_____ 5. In my high school the *curriculum* in the fine arts was *extremly* strong and *always* well supported by the parents.

_____ 6. The *calender* established for the *commission's* activities did not *successfully* schedule all the necessary events.

_____ 7. *Dissident* members of the *geurrilla* force worked to establish *detente* between the parties vying for power in the country.

_____ 8. *Humorous* skits about *dormitory* life focused on *familair* problems occurring among the residents.

_____ 9. In *February* we *exceded* our budget for fuel and almost *exhausted* our entire budget for utilities.

_____ 10. I can offer no *explanation* for my *exceptionaly* strong performance before the opening night's *audience.*

_____ 11. We can *accommodate* two additional *elegible* players, but any others will have to stay *across* the river in Rexfort.

_____ 12. The *dilapidated* cabin simply *dissappeared* under the impact of that *disastrous* storm last week.

297

_____ 13. The ponderous size of the *government bureaucracy* almost *gaurantees* inefficiency in every kind of operation.

_____ 14. Her *desparate* efforts to hide her *disappointment immediately* aroused everyone's sympathy.

_____ 15. Your *decision* to leave camp *definately* caused a storm of *criticism* in the local press.

_____ 16. The staff worked *frantically* to make the *disatisfied* but extremely *influential* customer happy.

_____ 17. Since we see so much *counterfiet* money, we must *emphasize consistent*, careful checking to our sales people.

_____ 18. It may be *convenient* to *abbreviate* some words in your writing, but such shortcuts are not *admissable* in formal writing.

_____ 19. Janet's *curiosity* leads her to explore different *disciplines;* she learns more *accidently* than in organized study.

_____ 20. My Dad *appreciates* the *comperitive* quiet of the North Woods; he goes there *immediately* whenever he gets the chance.

_____ 21. Don't *critisize* Martha's *description* of that event; she is providing an *exaggerated* version for our amusement.

_____ 22. Our professional group *originally* began selling *computers* because they are *benificiul* to our image as engineers.

_____ 23. Archeologists work in ancient *cemeteries* trying to *acquire* more information from the *accummilated* relics.

_____ 24. The report *accompaning* the *conference* minutes seems too *analytical* for easy reading.

_____ 25. *Finally* we have a test to measure both *intellegence* and *initiative* in one short session.

NAME _____　　SCORE _____

Directions: Each sentence contains two words from the second half of the spelling list. In each of these words at least one letter is missing. Write the words, correctly spelled, in the spaces at the left.

_____　1. A legit__ate political candidate would not need to employ such
_____　　cheap prop__g__nda in her campaign.

_____　2. On Wed__sday we will have the twel__h class meeting of the new
_____　　semester.

_____　3. The by-laws of the union require a unan__mous vote of the
_____　　repres__nt__tives in order to call a strike.

_____　4. All the mi__pelled words in our company's questionn__ire will
_____　　need to be corrected before we mail it to the clients.

_____　5. It was not a s__prise that the Founding Fathers chose not to
_____　　establish a parl__ment for the newly formed United States.

_____　6. The club's pam__let on entertainment and dining listed two
_____　　excellent san__ich shops in the vicinity of the college.

_____　7. Let's proce__ with our efforts to develop a s__h__dule for pur-
_____　　chasing raw materials for that project.

_____　8. The s__entific community does not agree on methods for the
_____　　disposal of nuc__ar waste.

_____　9. The department secr__tary will assist in the prep__r__tion of the
_____　　final report.

_____　10. The team's perform__nce has not been who__y satisfactory since
_____　　the ninth game of the season.

_____　11. The instructor at the gym recom__nds ten rep__t__tions for
_____　　each exercise in the beginner's workout.

_____　12. Janie didn't rec__nize any of the members of the soph__more
_____　　class because she left school after six weeks.

_____　13. Pers__erance is required if you wish to be suc__es__ful in any
_____　　business venture.

299

_____ 14. The maint__n__nce pro__dures on my new car are much sim-
_____   pler and cheaper than I had anticipated.

_____ 15. Margaret could not complete even a low-level math__m__tics
_____   course satisfacto__ly.

_____ 16. In the computer business, new tech__logy super__des the old
_____   with frightening regularity.

_____ 17. Rid__cul__us stories and questions seem to purs__ those who
_____   enter political races in this country.

_____ 18. All the laboratory spec__m__ns are arranged sep__r__tely on
_____   shelves along each wall.

_____ 19. Practi__lly speaking, it is almost impossible to prevent
_____   misch__vous children from disturbing our assemblies.

_____ 20. I feel obl__ged to install that new temper__at__re gauge before
_____   the engine develops any problems.

_____ 21. "It is my privil__e to introduce our new superint__nd__nt of
_____   schools," said the chairman of the school board.

_____ 22. Most sat__lites are quite simi__r in appearance, but they have
_____   many different uses when they are in orbit.

_____ 23. Her most prec__us memento of her high school years is a
_____   bracelet adorned with several min__ture charms.

_____ 24. When the light__ng struck at the end of the field, we r__lized it
_____   was time to call off the ballgame.

_____ 25. If you lose any lib__ry books, you will be l__ble to pay the cost
_____   of the book and a fine.

Exercise 29A

Spelling

NAME _____ SCORE _____

Directions: Each sentence contains three italicized words from the second half of the spelling list. One of the three words is misspelled. Underline the misspelled word and write it, correctly spelled, in the space at the left.

_____ 1. After my *ninth* day at work in the *librery,* I had found enough sources for my paper on *synthetic* fabrics.

_____ 2. In *obedience* school, my dog learned to run the *obsticle* course, and he improved his *temperament* a great deal.

_____ 3. For the past *ninety* days the *temperiture* has been *significantly* higher than normal for this time of year.

_____ 4. The stir-fried *vegatables* at that small *restaurant* are all *particularly* good at this time of year.

_____ 5. The collection of *literature* on *relegious* subjects in our library is far smaller than *necessary* for writing good papers.

_____ 6. A person who can combine a *livelihood* with a *passtime* is *probably* quite fortunate; not many people can.

_____ 7. Sort the two thousand *miscellaneous* hardware items in the back room *specifically* according to our standard *proceedures.*

_____ 8. *Nowadays lazer* beams perform *various* commonplace functions in both business and industry.

_____ 9. In many folk tales a hardhearted *villian* was *liable* to take control of the *village* at any time.

_____ 10. *Loneliness* overcame the movie's heroine as she sat for *ninetey* minutes in the office of her *psychiatrist.*

_____ 11. *Occassionally* you will have an *opportunity* to improve your *performance* drastically; seize every one that comes your way.

_____ 12. *Lightning* is a common *occurance* in our area; you should be careful in order to avoid a *tragedy.*

301

————————————— 13. The drill *seargeant* exerted subtle *psychological* pressure on his troops to follow his original instructions quite *strictly*.

————————————— 14. I was *surprized* to find that I had added one *syllable* to the word nuclear when I used it in my *speech* to the class.

————————————— 15. Your *omision* of her name is *truly* a serious mistake, and it will be taken as a sign of *prejudice* against brilliant women.

————————————— 16. The vast *quantity* of *synonymous* words you have strung together makes your speech lose all its *rythm* and pace.

————————————— 17. Since Majorie misses class *unnecessarily,* she will *undoubtedly* perform poorly on tests and *quizes*.

————————————— 18. A *professional marriage* counsellor is often helpful to restore an *optomistic* and joyful tone to a relationship.

————————————— 19. *Paralel* structure is a device used in *rhetoric* to emphasize a point and *persuade* listeners.

————————————— 20. *Really,* it's not *necessary* to go contrary to practices *prevelent* in the industry in order to become successful.

————————————— 21. He said that it's always *permissable* for a *partner* in a company to share in its property and other *possessions*.

————————————— 22. When they are all *together,* my friends usually talk *politics* and argue about *practicly* anything that interests them.

————————————— 23. Scientific study and *technology* are not *synonymous* since the latter applies the principles developed in the *labratory*.

————————————— 24. "I'm certain I have the *perseverence necessary* to follow the program *recommended* for a professional degree," said Tom.

————————————— 25. The *questionnaire* from the *Maintenence* Department asked especially about *mysterious* noises from the cars' engines.

NAME _____   SCORE _____

Directions: A sentence may have no misspelled words, one misspelled word, or two misspelled words. Write the misspelled words correctly, in the spaces at the left.

_____ 1. Your proposal seems fundamentally sound, but we are obliged to
_____   show it to the committee before we procede.

_____ 2. The county has purchased some kind of new fire-fighting appa-
_____   ratus designed to rescue people from skyscrapers.

_____ 3. My sister's allottment of Girl Scout cookies filled up our utility
_____   room and several shelfs in the garage.

_____ 4. Janie pleaded, "All I want is a good, servicable car, one that all
_____   ready has a few dents and scratches on it."

_____ 5. If you wish to start a business succesfully, you need capital, talant,
_____   and perspiration.

_____ 6. Athletics recieves entirely to much emphasis in some schools, but
_____   certainly not in ours.

_____ 7. Sometimes we have dificulty recognizing propaganda because it
_____   is cleverly perpared and extremely subtle.

_____ 8. "Pronunciation" and "pronouncement" are derived from the
_____   same root words in ancient languages.

_____ 9. The parrot mimiced my grandfather's words, saying each word
_____   presicely as my grandfather said it.

_____ 10. The donkeys are staying in the barn this mourning because the
_____   weather is all together too icy for them to be outside.

_____ 11. The casheir's nimble fingers flew over the keys of the cash regis-
_____   ter, never missing a number or making a mistake.

_____ 12. The company needs new stationary; the old letterhead has sev-
_____   eral names mispelled.

_____ 13. "Your presents here in court is a great assistence to my case," said
_____ the indicted city commissioner.

_____ 14. The Coast Guard Auxilary assists in porviding help to stranded
_____ boaters.

_____ 15. Be conscientous about attendance; you never know when you
_____ will learn something important in class.

_____ 16. The dinning hall had vegatables, roast beef, and strawberry
_____ shortcake on the menu last night.

_____ 17. It will be necessary for ninety people to sign up for the trip before
_____ we can set up the schedule and make reservations.

_____ 18. Morris appeered embarrassed to be scene in his new lime green
_____ sportcoat and yellow slacks.

_____ 19. Interpertation of that coded massage was necessary before the
_____ general could commit any troops.

_____ 20. To become an entrepenure and gain great wealth is a dream held
_____ by many and acheived by few.

Writing Paragraphs and Essays

Although it may come as a surprise to you, you will be called on to do a great deal of writing in college and in your career. Lecture notes, essays, research papers, and tests are the very stuff of which college courses are made. Memorandums, letters, e-mail correspondence, reports, and proposals are basic tools in almost any career you can name. And all this writing, whether in or out of college, is in great measure a key to your progress and success. In fact, in many large organizations, people are known to those in other areas more through their written work than through personal contact. Often progress and promotion ride as much on the quality of written work as on any other factor. Writing skills, then, will be a major factor in your success.

Writing is also an effective tool for learning. Writing about a subject leads to greater understanding and control of the material itself and new connections to other facts and concepts. Writing out lecture notes and textbook materials in your own words, for example, will give you better control of those materials and will help you to connect the new materials with facts and concepts you learned earlier.

In the previous sections of this book, you examined the operating principles of the language and applied those principles to writing correct, effective sentences. Now you need to learn to combine those sentences into paragraphs and the paragraphs into papers that will fulfill your college writing assignments.

The assignments you receive in college may range from a single paragraph narrating an event in your life to a complex research paper. Look briefly at a list of these possible assignments:

1. *Personal Essays*
   - Recount an event in your life, explaining its importance.
   - Discuss your position on the approaching presidential election.

2. *Essay Tests*
   - Answer two of the following three questions, using well-developed paragraphs and complete sentences in your answer.

3. *Essays and Discussions*
   - Explain the causes of structural unemployment in our country today.
   - Discuss the ramifications of using gene therapy to treat diseases.

305

4. *Critical Papers*
   - Evaluate the enclosed proposal for the construction of a new dam.
   - Assess the legacy of industry irresponsibility toward the environment in the United States.

5. *Persuasive or Argumentative Papers*
   - Argue for or against the use of government spending to retrain displaced workers.
   - Discuss the arguments against universal military training in the United States.

6. *Documented Papers*
   - After thorough research into the subject, write a paper discussing the use of nuclear power in this country. Be sure to discuss the history, the current situation, and the arguments for and against continued use and further development.

Although this list may seem extremely diverse and the types of writing quite varied, you can take comfort in the fact that underneath this diversity and complexity lies a fairly straightforward process that can be applied to all types of writing. You need only to learn one set of steps, the basic writing process, in order to deal effectively with any writing project you might face.

The Writing Process

Writing is a process, a set of steps, not a project that is started and finished in a single session. Often people believe that successful writers have happened onto a secret method of production that allows them, almost by magic, to sit down and write out a nearly perfect draft on the first try. This happens only rarely and always to writers with long experience; most people can assume that good writing rises out of slow, painstaking, step-by-step work.

The steps in the writing process group themselves naturally into two phases, and each phase requires an approach, a mind-set, that is quite different from the other. In the first phase, composing, you should be very free and creative. Think of this phase as a search, an adventure, an opportunity to try out many possibilities for ideas, content, and strategies. In the second phase, editing, you must be very critical of the materials you have composed. This is the time when you must evaluate, rewrite, reject, and correct the materials you developed while composing.

You must be careful not to mix the modes of operation. Don't edit when you should be composing. Don't delete materials, or decide not to pursue an idea, or ponder the correctness of a mark of punctuation. Such distractions will almost certainly stop your flow of ideas. But don't allow yourself to be free and creative when you are working as an editor. Keeping a word that is not quite right or failing to cut out a section that does not fit will produce papers that lack focus and are full of distractions. Remember that each phase in the process is separate and distinct. Each one requires separate and distinct attitudes toward the work at hand.

The following brief explanation provides a general introduction to the steps that make up the writing process. In later sections you will see these steps applied to different types of writing; those applications will illustrate minor changes to suit specific types of writing.

Composing

Step 1. Select or identify the subject.

Basic Question: What should I write about? Or (if the assignment is very specific): What does the assignment require me to write about?

Strategy: Select the subject on the basis of these questions:
• Are you and your reader interested in it?
• Do you have enough knowledge to write on it? If not, can you locate enough?
• Can you treat the subject completely within the length allotted for the assignment?

Step 2. Gather information about the subject.

Basic Question: What do I know about the subject? More importantly, what do I need to know to write about this subject fully and effectively?

Strategy: Record what you know, whether the information comes from recollection or research. Seek more information where necessary. ("A Few Words Before Starting," pages 311–315, will give you some helpful hints about this process.) Continue research and writing until you arrive at Step 3.

Step 3. Establish a controlling statement, or thesis, for the paper.

Basic Question: Exactly what can I say about this subject on the basis of the information and ideas I developed in Step 2?

Strategy: Continue to gather information and write about the subject until a specific idea develops. Write out that idea in a single sentence.

Step 4. Select specific items of support to include in the paper.

Basic Question: What ideas, facts, and illustrations can I use to make the thesis completely clear to the reader?

Strategy: Review the stockpile of materials gathered in Step 2. Select from these materials only those ideas, facts, and illustrations that will develop and support the thesis.

Step 5. Establish an order for presenting the materials you have selected.

Basic Question: What is the most effective order for presenting the materials I have selected?

Strategy: Choose an order of presentation that offers your reader a logical progression for the development of your idea. The orders used in paragraph development are sometimes useful in developing an order for an essay. (See pages 330–340.) Write the draft in any order you choose, starting with the easiest section. Assemble the draft in the order you have selected.

Step 6. Select a technique.

Basic Question: What is the most effective technique for presenting the materials I have selected?

Strategy: Explore different writing techniques to determine which one best complements your thesis and supporting materials.

Step 7. Write the first draft.

Basic Question: What will the materials look like when presented in the order I have chosen?

Strategy: Write out a complete version of the paper, following the plan developed in the first five steps.

Revising

Before you begin to revise the first completed draft of the paper, be sure that you shift from the role of composer/writer to the role of critic or editor. You have before you a completed product, not a perfect product. You must examine that product with a critical eye, testing and weighing each part to be sure that it is as good as it can be.

Step 8. Assess the thesis of the draft.

Basic Question: Is the thesis a proper expression of your knowledge on the subject?

Strategy: Read each supporting paragraph or section of the essay individually and create a sentence outline by writing a topic statement for each one. From the topic statements produce a thesis statement for the draft. Compare it to the original thesis. If there are differences between the two, create a new, better thesis.

Step 9. Assess the content.

Basic Question: Does each paragraph or section offer genuine support for the thesis?

Strategy: Check the topic statement for each paragraph or section to be sure each one supports the new thesis. Remove and replace any paragraph or section that does not support the thesis.

Step 10. Assess the order of presentation.

Basic Question: Does the order of presentation provide the reader with a logical progression or pathway through the essay?

Strategy: Try different orders of presentation, shifting sections around to see if you can find a better order than the one you used for the first finished draft.

Step 11. Assess the paragraphs.

Basic Question: Is each paragraph unified and complete? Is each paragraph developed following the best possible method of development?

Strategy: Using the sentence outline created above, check the content of each paragraph to be sure it develops one idea and only one idea. Check the content to be sure that the paragraph contains enough specific, concrete details to make the topic statement clear to the reader.

Step 12. Assess the technique.

Basic Question: Does this technique present my thesis and supporting materials in the best way possible?

Strategy: Consider whether other techniques might better complement your thesis.

Step 13. Correct the mistakes in the draft.

Basic Question: What errors in grammar and mechanics do I need to correct?

Strategy: Read each sentence as an independent unit, starting at the end of the paper and working to the beginning. Reading "backward" in this fashion assures that you will not make mental corrections or assumptions as you read.

Step 14. Write the final draft.

Basic Question: What form shall I use for the final copy of the paper?

Strategy: Follow the guidelines for manuscript preparation specified by your teacher, printing or typing the final copy on plain white paper. Be sure to read the final copy carefully for errors.

The Process in Action

These steps can be followed with only minor changes for any writing assignment. Study the steps carefully as we apply them to various types of assignments. Make the steps second nature to you, a set of habits followed anytime you write. The more you practice, the greater will be your facility in writing.

Before we begin to examine the writing process as it applies to specific projects in college writing, take a few moments to study the results that a professional writer can achieve using these steps—or similar ones—in writing an article about a personal experience.

The setting for the experience and the article is Australia; the writer is an editor of *Car and Driver,* a magazine for auto enthusiasts. The occasion is a trip across the Outback, a sparsely settled region in the interior of Australia. The author and a passenger are driving on a 1,500-mile trip to survey Australian methods of improving auto safety. They have been driving in desolate country almost all day when, late in the afternoon, they meet disaster.

A Drive in the Outback, with Second Chances

DAVID ABRAHAMSON

It took less than two seconds. The stab of oncoming headlights, a blur of looming sheet-metal in the center of the windshield, a jabbing reaction at the steering wheel and then that awful, indelible noise. And then an unearthly silence, as if nature itself knew that something irrevocable had happened and that a moment—maybe much more—was needed for the reality to be dealt with.

I had been driving fast most of the afternoon. Not really at the car's limit, but well above the posted speed. I enjoy fast driving for its own sake, and this new and isolated environment seemed to urge me on. After all, Australia's wide open spaces are exactly that, and we'd encountered less than one car an hour in either direction of the towns. And besides, Baker, my passenger, didn't seem to mind. We were in the middle of a long, sweeping right-hander when suddenly the windshield was filled with another set of headlights. Coming at us, in the middle of the road, was a monstrous truck. The left front corner of the truck cab buried itself in the left front door of our car. The sound was absolutely deafening. Bits of metal and glass were everywhere. The impact ripped the watch off my wrist and the lenses out of my glasses. But I was lucky. Because it was a righthand-drive car, as the driver I was at least three feet away from the point of impact. Passenger Baker, however, was not.

The true violence of the crash took place almost in his lap. Part of his seat was torn up and out of its mount. The door and a section of the roof were battered in toward his head and left shoulder. We were both wearing lap-and-shoulder seat belts at the time. Mine saved my life. Baker's did too, but in the process broke his collarbone and badly bruised a few essential internal organs. A grisly tradeoff.

How and why had the accident happened? What exactly had been my mistake? Long after I'd returned to the United States, long after Baker had recovered from his injuries, I was still asking myself those questions. Now, almost a year later, the answers are clear. And they go far beyond any chance encounter on a strange road in a strange land, even beyond the crushing sense of remorse I felt at the time. And they tell me something about who I was and what I might be. I enjoyed driving, and a big part of that enjoyment came from taking a number of risks. Risks I thought were calculated, but in truth were not. Rather they were part of a glorious game, imbued with notions of independence, willful mobility and a heavy dose of virility. I'd had more than my share of near misses, but they merely served to prove the range of my skills at the wheel—my ability to judge relative speed and distance, the speed of my reflexes, the correctness of my kinesthetic instincts. In my car at speed, there was never any hint of my own mortality. Or of anyone else's. So the accident had to happen. Maybe not with that truck on that blind curve on the far side of the Earth, but somewhere. It has less to do with the law of averages than the laws of physics. Roads are a decidedly hostile environment, peopled with an unknown number of other drivers who are certain to do the wrong thing at the wrong time. And no amount of skill, real or imagined, can save you. Sweet reason is the only defense. Prudence, moderation and caution are not the stuff of grand illusions, unbridled exuberance and youthful panache. But they're great for survival.

And that, in the end, is what my experience boils down to. I now see, as I did not before, that my survival (and that of others who choose to ride with me) is at stake. I've never seen myself as a particularly courageous person, but I've always enjoyed sports containing an element of risk: parachuting, scuba-diving, alpine skiing and the like. Strange that something as mundane as an auto accident should, at age 30, give me my first glimpse of my own mortality. Thinking back to that evening south of Bombala, I am certain that I never want to hear that awful sound again. But I also never want to forget it.

Following the writing process as we have outlined it, the writer would have asked himself these questions in the first phase:

1. What should I write about?

   My Australian trip, or some part of it. The most memorable and important part of the trip was the terrible accident near Bombala, in which my passenger Bill Baker was injured.

2. What do I know or remember about the trip and, more specifically, about the accident?

   Beginning with the plane ride from San Francisco, I can record as background material all the things we did on the flight, in Sydney, and on the trip itself. I will record in greatest detail the auto trip, focusing as closely as possible on the moments before and after the crash. I'll continue to write until I reach a statement or conclusion about that accident and its meaning to me now.

3. Exactly what can I say about this subject, the accident? What impression has it made on me?

   The accident changed my view of my driving skills and the importance of those skills in preserving my safety while I drive. I never want to hear the awful sound of the crash again, but I never want to forget it, either.

4. What details, facts, illustrations, and observations can I use to make that thesis clear to my reader?

   I will use visual details and facts surrounding the crash itself. I'll include the aftermath of the crash, the time while we wait to take Baker to the hospital. Finally, I'll record my thoughts on and impressions of the importance and meaning of the accident.

5. What order will most effectively present these supporting materials?

   Because this piece is basically a narrative, a story about my Australian trip, I'll follow chronological order, but I'll use a few details of the actual crash to catch my readers' interest in the introduction.

6. What will the materials look like when I actually write out a first completed version of the article? [You have read the final version of the essay. The rough draft contained much more material.]

   I will cut out distracting material that weakens my statement.

A Few Words Before Starting

Getting started is often the most difficult part of writing. We all have a tendency to avoid the blank page and the work involved in filling it meaningfully. Writing will always be hard work, but three preliminary exercises will help make getting started a little easier.

Strengthen Your Muscles So That You Can Write with Ease

You would not go mountain climbing or run a marathon without getting in shape; you should not expect writing to be enjoyable unless you are in shape for it. Do the following exercises:

- Sit in a place where you can watch people passing by. Writing as rapidly as possible, jot down a description of all that occurs, noting sizes, shapes, descriptions, and other visual details.
- Writing continuously, sign your name or copy other words down as many times as you can in two minutes.
- Without stopping, write everything that comes into your head when you read the following words:

submarine

photosynthesis

chocolate milkshake

You should do these exercises on a regular basis, changing the words in the third exercise to any others that come to mind from your daily life or current events in the news.

   The goal of these exercises is to make you comfortable as a writer, to develop the ability and the patience to write for extended periods without fatigue or frustration. You should work on these exercises until you can write for fifteen minutes without a break or an hour with two short breaks.

Free Your Mind to Write Without Constraints

In the first phase of the writing process, composing, you need to write freely without editing what you write. "Free writing," or "stream-of-consciousness writing" is a way of learning about your subject, a way of making new connections within it. It allows you to record at random all the ideas that come to mind on your subject. In fact, you will probably bring to mind ideas that are technically off the subject of your paper. Don't be afraid to record these stray ideas, as they will often lead back to the subject from a direction that you had not imagined before.

Free writing is especially valuable when you are writing a paper based on personal experience because it allows you to make something important out of that experience. It is also valuable in writing papers of opinion or papers stating a personal position on a controversial subject. Only through extensive writing can you define your opinion or position clearly and firmly. A would-be comic once said, "I don't know what I think until I see what I've written." He may have intended the statement as a joke, but it is, in fact, the truth. Writing about your opinions and ideas helps you to form those opinions and ideas. Be sure to write extensively, randomly, freely, on all such writing assignments before you formulate your final thesis.

Free writing also has an important place in writing more objective papers, papers based on research and written notes. After you have completed your research and put your note cards in reasonably good order, you should read through them two or three times to get a sense of the content. After reading the notes, set them aside and begin to write freely about the subject.

At least two good things should come out of this free writing. First, it will help you to formulate a position on the subject that is your own and not the opinion of the writers you covered in your research. You learn about your subject when you write about it.

Second, free writing will allow you to write about your subject in your own voice rather than in the voices of the writers you read during your research. Without free writing, your writing will sound like every other research paper ever written because we tend to take on the tone and style of the writers we have recently read. Through free writing you can move away from the voices of those other writers and into your own voice. The paper you produce will be uniquely "you," rather than a generic, sounds-like-all-the-other-papers-ever-written sort of production.

Explore Your Topic Extensively

There are various specialized techniques that will help you gather information and formulate your ideas on your writing projects.

Brainstorming. One technique closely allied to free writing is called **brainstorming** or **clustering**. Brainstorming is a *nonlinear, free association* drill. In this drill, the writer sits quietly with pen and pencil, or at a computer, and records words and phrases on a particular subject as they come to mind. To understand how brainstorming works, suppose for a moment that you are taking a United States history or political science course. Your assignment says "Write a paper on American politics." Write the name of the subject on a sheet of paper

American Politics

and then record the words and ideas that come to mind—without editing or limiting the list.

American Politics

Democrat	Republican	liberal	conservative	neo-liberal
	Constitution	Bill of Rights	John F. Kennedy	
	radicalism	William F. Buckley	The Boston Tea Party	
	The Sixties	The Civil Rights Movement		

Note that brainstorming will not work in a vacuum. If you have never studied, or even thought about, American politics, you will not have any associations to make. If you have the background to make constructive associations, however, brainstorming can help you in two ways.

First, brainstorming can help to isolate a manageable topic within a subject area. An assignment that simply says: "Write a paper on American politics" requires a good deal of probing and restriction before a workable topic for a paper emerges. Clearly, you can't write a paper fully exploring American politics in ten pages, or even in a whole semester. To write a successful paper, you will need to restrict and focus your thinking to a single aspect of the subject area.

Thus you might move from John F. Kennedy to the idea that he became president in 1960 to the idea that the Civil Rights Movement began in the late fifties and early sixties to the idea that there must have been some relationship between his administration and the Civil Rights Movement.

At that point you might suspect that you have hit on a workable topic and move off to the library to do some preliminary work on a bibliography and some background reading.

Second, brainstorming can help you to make connections between ideas within a subject area. Writing about one concept can lead to a second concept. Writing about the second concept can lead to a third and then a fourth.

So you might begin to think on a general subject—grades—

and then about grades in high school

and then about your greater motivation in college

and then about your lack of real effort in high school

and then about your much better grades in college

and then about the marked improvement in your grades . . .

At this point, you might make a connection between better grades and greater motivation. From there you might move to a comparison between low motivation in high school and higher motivation in college, and then, **by brainstorming again on that concept,** you might develop several reasons why low motivation existed in high school and higher motivation existed in college.

At that point, you can choose a direction for the paper, depending on the focus required in the assignment. If the assignment asks for a personal paper—observations on your grades and experiences in high school and college—then you must continue into additional brainstorming and then into free writing and other techniques to gather information on the topic.

If, on the other hand, you can move into an objective examination of motivation and grades in high school and college, you can go to the library for bibliography work and preliminary reading.

To develop a paper on personal experience, you can employ the five questions used by journalists to develop articles:

1. **WHO** is involved?
2. **WHAT** happens?
3. **WHEN** does it happen?
4. **WHERE** does the event occur?
5. **WHY** does it happen?

Don't limit yourself to one-word or brief answers. Employ free writing techniques when you answer the questions. Don't answer the question "Who?" by saying, "John and Mr. Smith." Write about John and Mr. Smith. Explore the answers to each question extensively in a free writing mode.

Next, explore your topic by asking questions that focus on parts and relationships that exist in and around your topic. Suppose your assignment asks you to explore some aspect of business in modern Japan. After examining the general subject, you discover that Japanese business executives use a special style of management that has sparked considerable interest among managers in the United States. You might begin your exploration by looking at the topic in three ways.

1. Examine the discrete parts of the topic itself:

   What are the *distinctive features* of Japanese management style?

2. Examine the topic as a whole.

   How do these features *work together as a system?*

3. Examine the place of the topic within the general subject matter.

   How does Japanese management style *fit into the overall subject* we call management?

Or, phrased in a different way, you might ask yourself:

- How do I identify this subject?
- How do I differentiate it from others in the same general area?
- What are the important parts or aspects of this subject?
- What is the physical appearance of these parts?
- What examples of this subject occur in real life?
- How does this subject compare and/or contrast with others of the same general type?

Analogies and Metaphors. Some writers find it useful to construct *analogies* and *metaphors* on a subject. When you make an analogy, you examine ways in which one concept is like another concept.

> My brother, who plays Little League baseball, is a ballplayer out of the Rickey Henderson mold: he is quick on his feet, aggressive, a singles hitter most of the time, and, above all, he loves the game more than anything else in his life.

The writer's brother is unlike Rickey Henderson in a thousand ways, including age, size, and success in the game. But the writer, by recognizing the similarities between the two people, can begin to explore his brother's personality in greater depth. Analogies help both you and a reader learn a little bit more about an idea.

In the same way, on personal topics, it is possible to construct metaphors and similes, figures of speech that establish comparisons.

> Red Grange was *like a will-o'-the-wisp,* dancing and dodging his way through opposing teams to become the greatest running back in the early history of football.

> The invading army *was a tornado,* moving where it wished and destroying everything in its path.

Sometimes even metaphors that seem ridiculous can be productive.

> If your father were an automobile, what make and model would he be?

> He might be a 1938 Cadillac, very classy, but a trifle old-fashioned in some ways.

Images such as these can provide insight that can lead to new information and new insights, if you follow them up with additional reading and writing on the subject.

Using the Senses. Certain subjects can be explored through the senses. Recording visual aspects (shapes, sizes, and colors, for example) or recording words that describe sounds, smells, and textures might offer insights into the subject.

All these methods of exploring a subject and refining a subject into manageable parts simply open areas for reading and writing on a subject. They help you with Step 2 of the writing process, gathering materials. The resulting notes and written materials must not be confused with a first, complete draft or the final draft of a paper. They constitute the raw material of a paper, material that must be evaluated, accepted, rejected, placed in order in the draft, and written out for revision. They are not the finished product; they are background to help with production of that finished product.

So don't wait for inspiration or good beginnings. Write what you can write as well as you can write it. If you can't think of a good way to start, start any way you can. If you can't think of exactly the right word, use a close approximation. Time and condition and the freedom to write without editing will improve your ideas; careful attention to revision and correction will improve the quality of your written expression. Practice and more practice will lead to success.

In the next section you will closely examine a very important type of college writing, the essay test.

Writing Exercises for an Overview of College Writing

1. Each day for the first two weeks of your experience in using the writing sections of this book, follow the instructions on pages 310–311 for getting in shape to write.

2. Follow the steps in the writing process illustrated with "A Drive in the Outback, with Second Chances," and write about an experience in your own life.

3. Find an example of personal writing about an experience or an attitude. Read it to locate the controlling statement, or thesis, (Step 3 in composing). Then outline the supporting details to show how they develop (or fail to develop) that idea.

Essay tests provide an excellent opportunity to apply your writing skills. An answer to an essay test question requires you to work within a very narrow subject area to produce a concise, complete written statement in a short period of time. These tight limitations of time and space force you to be precise in the formulation of a statement about an idea or concept and to distinguish carefully between materials essential to your answer and those that are only related to it. Finally, essay tests often require that you present your answer in a single well-developed paragraph. Working on test taking, then, is very practical; success on tests will improve your grades. Beyond that, and perhaps more important, practice in writing essay test answers will develop your ability to write successful paragraphs.

Getting Ready

The best preparation for taking any test is consistent, effective study throughout the term. In addition, however, the use of special strategies for the last few days before the test will improve your chances of success. Begin your final preparations for the test a few days in advance so that you will have ample time to study and assimilate the material. Follow these suggestions as you study:

Step 1. Make an overview or survey of the materials you have covered for the test. Look for periods, trends, theories, and general conclusions. Try to pinpoint important concepts and basic ideas in the materials. You may find it useful to consult a general encyclopedia for an overview or a summary of the subject areas to be covered by the test. If the subject is technical or complex or is part of an advanced course, consult an appropriate specialized encyclopedia or reference work in that field.

Step 2. Write a series of questions encompassing the major items that you have located. Cover broad areas of material. Use the seven types of direction or command words listed on pages 320–322 to devise a list of questions covering the material you identified in Step 1. Try each type of command word to determine if questions of that type apply to the material. Are there, for example, lists, or comparisons, or definitions, or discussions that seem to rise naturally from the materials? Formulate questions that cover the materials. In six to ten broad-scope questions of your own, you should be able to cover all the possible questions that the teacher may ask. If you have covered all the material in your own questions, you will not be surprised by any questions on the exam.

Step 3. Read your outline, notes, and other materials, looking for answers to the questions you have composed. As you read and review, outline the answers, commit the outlines to memory, and use them as guides during the test. Write out answers to any questions that are difficult for you.

Step 4. Review the outlines, the materials, and the answers to your questions the afternoon before the test. Then put the whole thing aside and get a good night's rest.

317

Step 5. Just before going in to take the test:

- Eat a high-energy snack; fruit is a good choice. Coffee, orange juice, or tea will also help. Do some calisthenics or whatever else is necessary to make you alert.
- Get your equipment ready: pens, pencils, erasers, paper or examination booklets, and scratch paper. Take what you will need so that you will not worry about supplies once you enter the room.
- Arrive a few minutes early for the test. Get yourself and your equipment arranged. Relax for a few seconds before the work begins.

Taking the Test

No student—or at least not very many students—can earn a high grade on a test without proper preparation. But good preparation alone will not guarantee success. You need a strategy for taking tests, a strategy that will help you to decide which questions to answer, what order to use in answering the selected questions, and what organization to use for each question.

When you have made the best possible preparations for taking the test and are in the classroom with the test in your hands, do two things before you write:

1. **Read the test from start to finish,** beginning with the directions. Decide which questions you know the most about. Determine the point value of each question. Answer first the questions you know the most about. Answering them first will ease you into the test, develop your confidence, and keep you from wasting time on questions you can't answer well anyway. Use any remaining time to do the best you can on the rest of the questions.

   Always follow the directions. If options allow you to choose certain questions from a group, be sure you understand the options and make your choices based on your knowledge and on the point value of the questions. Don't waste time on a question of low point value when you could be answering a question with a high point value. Invest your time wisely.

2. **Make careful preparations before you write.** Adapt the first four steps in the writing process to guide you in writing the answers.

   Step 1. Identify the subject. On a test, the teacher has selected the subject for each question. Your job is to identify that subject correctly. A question that asks for a discussion of the causes of the Great Depression is not properly answered by a discussion of the characteristics of the Roaring Twenties. Make sure you answer the question that is asked.

   Step 2. Review what you know about the question. Recall your outlines and notes. Bring to mind the practice answers you wrote in your review exercises. Make notes of these on a sheet of paper. Try to remember as much material as you can. List any special or technical words related to the subject.

   Step 3. Decide exactly what the question asks for and what overall statement you are able to make and support in response to the question. Before you write, construct a specific statement of the idea or concept that you intend to develop in writing your answer. This point, or main idea, will come out of the materials you reviewed in Step 2.

Step 4. Carefully select supporting materials, examples, explanations, and other data that will serve to establish and clarify the main idea. You will have pulled together a considerable amount of material in your quick review. Not all of it will fit exactly the statement you are making; not all of it will be especially effective in your answer. Select materials that will establish and reinforce your point as effectively as possible within the constraints of time and space.

Preparing Your Answer

Let's assume that you have read the test carefully, have selected your questions, and have decided to answer this problem first:

> Select one of the seven species of sea turtles and discuss its physical appearance, its habitat and geographic distribution, and its status in both present numbers and population trends.

Step 1. Step 1 requires careful identification of the subject matter covered in the question. The problem refers to sea turtles, not to all kinds of turtles. In fact, it asks for a discussion of just one of the seven species of sea turtles. It also asks for only three rather simple pieces of information about that species:

1. What is the physical appearance of that species?
2. In what type of habitats is the species found, and where are these habitats located?
3. How many individuals of this species are estimated to be alive, and is that number increasing or decreasing?

Only the last point is at all tricky. *Status* in this question refers to the species' survival potential based on what the estimated living population is and on whether it is increasing or decreasing worldwide.

Step 2. Step 2 is to collect material, to recall what you know about a single species of sea turtle. Remembering the textbook material, your lecture notes, and the brief outside reading assignment you reviewed, you jot down the following notes:

Actually 7 species—only three much covered in class. One stood out because commercial importance (food & other products)—green turtle.

Large: 3 to 6 feet from front to back over curve of upper shell (carapace; lower shell, plastron).

Weighs 200–300 lb. average but reaches 850 lb. some specimens. Color from green-brown to near black.

Scutes (bony plates) clearly marked. Head small compared to body.

Occurs almost worldwide in warmer waters shallow enough to allow growth of sea grass turtles eat.

Present status questionable. Not endangered because lrg. pops. in remote areas—under pressure and declining in pop. areas. Needs protection. First protective law in Caribbean, passed 1620. Used extensively for food by early sailors, who killed mainly females coming on shore to lay eggs. Now used for cosmetics and jewelry.

Large green turtles make good zoo exhibits. W. Indian natives make soup of them.

Nesting habits: Female beaches and lays approx. 100 eggs in shaped hole. First hatchlings on top of nest push out sand covering them and leave. Those on bottom crawl out using sand first hatchlings displaced and crushed shells of vacated eggs as platform. 100 eggs right number—fewer places top of nest too low in hole, more requires nest too deep for last hatchling to escape. Recent increase in ecological pressure because women use more cosmetics based on turtle oil.

These notes, jotted down hastily (perhaps more sketchily on an actual test than in the example), produce enough information to allow you to move to Step 3.

Step 3. In Step 3 you must determine what you can say in response to the question. Before you can make that determination, you must know exactly what the question directs you to do. These directions are usually given at the beginning of the question, and, although their exact wording may vary, they generally fall into one of the following categories:

- **List, name, identify**
  These words require short-answer responses that can be written in one or two complete sentences. Do exactly what the question asks; don't try to expand the scope of the question.

  Example: Name the presidents who served in the military prior to becoming president.

  The word *identify* suggests that you ought to mention the two or three most important facts about a person or a subject area, not just any facts that come to mind. You would thus identify Eisenhower as a military commander and U.S. president, not as a West Point graduate who played golf.

- **Summarize, trace, delineate**
  An instruction to *summarize* asks that you give an overview or a capsule version of the subject.

  Example: Summarize Senator Smith's position on tax reform.

  An answer to this question would provide a three- or four-sentence statement of the main points of Smith's position. The words *trace* and *delineate* usually ask that you describe the steps or process that brought some event to pass.

  Example: Trace the life cycle of the monarch butterfly.

  The answer requires a listing of the steps in the development of the butterfly from egg to adulthood.

- **Define**
  The instruction *define* usually asks that you establish the term within a class and then differentiate it from the other members of the class. "A parrot is a bird" establishes the word *parrot* in a class, and "found in the tropics and capable of reproducing human speech" is an attempt at differentiation. You should be careful to add enough elements

of differentiation to eliminate other members of the class. For instance, as the myna is also a tropical bird capable of reproducing speech, you must complete your definition of *parrot* by specifying such items as size, color, and habitat.

- **Analyze, classify, outline**
  These command words imply a discussion of the relationship that exists between a whole and its parts. *Analyze* asks that you break an idea, a concept, or a class down into its integral parts.

  Example: Analyze the various political persuasions that exist within the Republican party.

  This question asks that you look at the Republican party and identify the various categories of political belief ranging from right to left. *Classify* asks that you position parts in relation to a whole.

  Example: Classify the following parts of an automobile as to location in engine, steering, or drive shaft:
  1. Ball joint
  2. Piston ring
  3. Pinion gear

  Outline requires that you break down an idea or a concept into its parts and show how the parts support and reinforce each other. Whether you arrange your sentences in the form of a whole paragraph or in a listing of main headings and subheadings, your outline must show how the idea or concept is made up of smaller parts and how these parts relate to the idea and to each other.

  Example: Outline Senator Random's position on emission controls for automobiles.

  This question requires that you state Senator Random's position and its supporting points.

- **Discuss, explain, illustrate**
  This type of command word is probably the most general of all the possible directions for essay tests. The request here is that you expose, in detail, the idea, concept, or process in question. Single simple sentences will not suffice to answer such instructions. You must provide all pertinent information and write enough so that your readers have no questions, no gaps left in their information, when they've finished reading. Often such questions can be answered by making a statement of the idea or process and providing examples to illustrate your statements. In fact, if the instruction is *illustrate*, examples are required.

  Example: Discuss the effect of depriving a child of physical affection in the first three years of its life.

  The answer could be given by making a statement or statements of the effects and giving examples of each.

- **Compare, contrast**
  A question that asks you to compare, or to compare and contrast, is simply asking that you discuss the similarities and differences between two or more subjects.

  Examples: Compare the military abilities of Grant and Sherman.
  Make a comparison between Smith's plan and Jones's plan for shoring up the value of the dollar overseas.
  What are the similarities and differences between racquetball and squash?

  All these example questions ask you to establish categories—for example, skill in tactics, ability to motivate, and so on, as they relate to Grant and Sherman—and to explain how the subjects are alike or different in the areas you establish.

- **Evaluate, criticize**
  This type of question is probably the most difficult because it requires that you know what is correct or best or ideal and that you assess the assigned topic against that ideal.

  Example: Evaluate Eisenhower as a leader in foreign affairs.

  The question is, "What are the characteristics of a leader in foreign affairs and how does Eisenhower measure up in each of these categories?" To answer this question, you must know the subject *and* the ideal equally well.

Now let's examine the sample problem again:

> Select one of the seven species of sea turtles and discuss its physical appearance, its habitat and geographic distribution, and its status in both present numbers and population trends.

The subject area is clear: any one of the seven species of sea turtles. The direction, the instruction word, is *discuss* which means make a statement and support it. The direction is clear: discuss the physical appearance, the habitat and general distribution, and the current status of any one of the seven species of sea turtles.

Your opening statement should be simple and direct. It need not state all the facts and details; indeed, it should not try to. It is designed to serve only as a guide for the development of your answer. For this problem, your statement might read:

> The green turtle is a large green-to-black sea turtle residing in warm, shallow waters all over the world; it is numerous but is declining in populated areas.

Step 4. Step 4 requires that you select from the collected materials those items that will develop your statement. Select specific details to explain each area within the statement. For the first section, physical appearance, your notes contain the following concrete details:

1. Size—three to six feet from front to back over the shell; average weight—200–300 pounds, record is 850 pounds.

2. Coloration—greenish brown is lightest color, almost black when splotches are close together.
3. Shape of flippers, head, tail. [Note that these items are not in the original list. New materials often come to mind during preparations.]

You can fill in the other sections by selecting other information from your collection of materials. Do not include any materials that do not specifically develop or illustrate the statement that controls the answer. Provide ample development, but do not pad. For example, in your collection of supporting materials, the long discussion of the nesting habits and the number of eggs laid by the green turtle does not fit into the answer. The material is interesting, it concerns the green turtle, but it does *not* fit any of the three categories in the question. Don't use materials simply because they relate to the general subject. Use only materials that support the answer to the specific question.

Writing the Answer

At this point you have before you on scratch paper:

1. A basic idea.
2. Supporting materials for that basic idea.

These will be useful in writing the answer, but they are not the answer. They are the *content* for the answer. Now you must gather this content into grammatically correct, complete sentences that present the material in a logical, relevant order.

The best way to provide order for your answer is to modify your statement to suggest the order that you intend to follow. This modification will help your reader to follow your answer. A sentence combining elements of the question with a suggestion of your answer's focus offers a good beginning and adequate control:

> Of the seven species of sea turtles, the green turtle is the largest and the most widely distributed, but it is nearing endangered status because it has commercial value.

Note that the sentence establishes your topic, the green turtle, and defines the aspects that you will discuss by using key words from each of those areas:

1. *Largest* leads to a physical description.
2. *Most widely distributed* leads naturally to a discussion of habitat and distribution.
3. *Nearing endangered status* opens the discussion of population size and trends.

The sentence relates your answer to the question and will keep you from wandering into irrelevancy. Try to make your first sentence as specific as possible, but be sure that you can expand on it. A statement that the green turtle is "an interesting species" is little help in controlling the answer because it does not focus on the question. You are not concerned with how interesting the species is; you are concerned with its appearance, its habitat and distribution, and its status. The entire answer to this sample question might read as follows:

Of the seven species of sea turtles, the green turtle is the largest and the most widely distributed, but it is nearing endangered status because it has commercial value. It is a large turtle, measuring between 3 and 6 feet in length over the top of the shell and weighing on the average 200–300 pounds. The largest specimens are over 5 feet in length and weigh 800–1000 pounds. The upper shell (carapace) is light to dark brown, shaded or mottled with darker colors ranging to an almost black-green. The lower shell (plastron) is white to light yellow. The scales on the upper surface of the head are dark, and the spaces between them are yellow; on the sides of the head, the scales are brown but have a yellow margin, giving a yellow cast to the sides of the head. The shell is broad, low, and more or less heart-shaped. The green turtle inhabits most of the warm, shallow waters of the world's seas and oceans, preferring areas 10–20 feet deep where it can find good sea grass pastures for browsing. The turtles prefer areas that have many potholes, because they sleep in the holes for security. In numbers and population trends, the status of the green turtle is in doubt. It is under great pressure in highly populated areas such as the Caribbean Sea, where it is avidly hunted for food and for use in making jewelry and cosmetics. However, because it occurs in large numbers in remote areas, it is not technically an endangered species at this time. It needs better protection in populated areas so that its numbers will not decline any further.

Assignments and Exercises

The suggestions offered in this section will not improve your ability to take tests unless you practice applying them in your own work. Here are some suggested exercises to apply the principles:

1. Analyze your performance on a recent essay test and discuss the ways in which following the suggestions in this chapter might have improved your performance.

2. Assume that you are enrolled in a course in American history and must take an essay test on the Revolutionary War. The materials covered include the textbook, your lecture notes, your outside readings, and two films. Write a paragraph describing your preparations for the test.

3. As a practice test, write answers to the following questions on the chapter you have just read on taking essay tests.

   - Discuss the preparations for taking a test up to the point where you enter the test room.

   - Describe the process by which you would decide which questions to answer (if given options) and in which order you would answer them.

   - Name and define four of the seven instruction-word categories often found in test questions, discussing the kinds of materials that each word requires in its answer.

   - Describe the final form the answers should take. Include a discussion of opening statements and development.

Section 3   *Writing Effective Paragraphs*

A paragraph is a group of sentences (or sometimes just one sentence) related to a single idea. The paragraph originated as a punctuation device to separate ideas on paper and to assist readers in keeping lines separate as they read. Thus, each paragraph begins on a new line, and its first word is indented a few spaces from the left margin.

The Effective Paragraph

The function of a paragraph is to state and develop a single idea, usually called a **topic.** The topic is actually the subject of the paragraph, what the paragraph is about. Everything in the paragraph after the statement of the topic ought to **develop the topic,** to explain and define, to discuss, to illustrate and exemplify the topic. From the reader's point of view, the content of the paragraph should provide enough information and explanation to make clear the topic of the paragraph and the function of the paragraph in the essay or the chapter.

The Topic Sentence

The first rule of effective paragraph writing is as follows:

Usually, declare the topic of the paragraph early in a single sentence (called the *topic sentence*).

Look back to the sample answer to an essay test question on page 324. Note how the first sentence paraphrases a significant part of the question and provides direction for the answer by telling briefly what the answer will contain. It is, in other words, a topic sentence. Every paragraph you write should contain a sentence that names what the paragraph is about and indicates how the paragraph will proceed. It may do so in considerable detail:

> Although the green turtle—a large, greenish-brown sea turtle inhabiting warm, shallow seas over most of the world—is not yet generally endangered, it is subject to extreme pressure in populated areas.

or rather broadly:

> The green turtle is one of the most important of the seven species of sea turtles.

Both of these statements name a specific topic, the green turtle, but neither sentence stops with the name. A sentence that reads "This paragraph will be about green turtles" is not a complete topic sentence because it does not suggest the direction that the rest of the paragraph will take. Unlike the incomplete topic sentence, both good examples are phrased so that a certain type of development must follow. The first example anticipates a discussion that will mention size, color, habitat, and distribution but will focus on the green turtle's chances for survival. The second example anticipates a discussion that will develop the assertion that the species is one of the most important of the sea turtles. Note that neither example tries to embrace the whole idea of the paragraph. The topic sentence should lay the foundation for the paragraph, not say everything there is to be said.

Sometimes a paragraph has no topic sentence; occasionally the topic sentence occurs at the end of the paragraph. These exceptions are permissible, but the early topic sentence is more popular with both writers and readers because it helps in three ways to produce an effective message:

1. It defines your job as a writer and states a manageable objective—a single topic.
2. It establishes a guide for your development of the basic idea. You must supply evidence of or support for any assertion in the topic sentence. The topic sentence is only a beginning, but it predicts a conclusion that the paragraph must reach.
3. It tells your reader what the paragraph is going to contain.

Notice how the italicized topic sentence in the following paragraph controls the paragraph and provides clear direction for the reader:

> Of all the inventions of the last one hundred years, *the automobile assembly line has had the most profound effect on American life.* The assembly line provided a method for building and selling automobiles at a price many could afford, thus changing the auto from a luxury item owned by the wealthy few to an everyday appliance used by almost every adult in America. Universal ownership and the use of the automobile opened new occupations, new dimensions of mobility, and new areas of recreation to everyone. In addition, the automobile assembly line provided a model for the mass production of television sets, washing machines, bottled drinks, and even sailboats. All these products would have been far too expensive for purchase by the average person without the introduction of assembly-line methods to lower manufacturing costs. With the advent of Henry Ford's system, all Americans could hope to possess goods once reserved for a select class, and the hope changed their lives forever.

The italicized sentence states the topic and the purpose of the paragraph: The paragraph is going to argue that the assembly line, more than any other invention, changed America's way of life. The writer is controlled by this sentence because everything in the paragraph should serve to support this argument. Readers are assisted by the sentence, for they know that they can expect examples supporting the position stated in the sentence.

Complete Development

Writing a good topic sentence is only the first step in writing an effective paragraph, for an effective paragraph provides complete development of the topic; that is, it tells the readers all they need to know about the topic for the purposes at hand. This is the second basic rule of effective paragraph writing: **Always provide complete development in each paragraph.**

Complete development tells readers all that they need to understand about the paragraph itself and the way the paragraph fits into the rest of the essay or chapter. Complete development does not necessarily provide all the information the reader *wants* to know; rather, the reader receives what is *needed* for understanding the topic and its development (the internal working of the paragraph) and the relationship between the paragraph and the paper as a whole (the external connection). As an illustration of that rather abstract statement, read the following paragraph, which gives a set of instructions for a familiar process:

> Another skill required of a self-sufficient car owner is the ability to jump-start a car with a dead battery, a process that entails some important do's and don't's. First, make certain that the charged battery to be used is a properly grounded battery of the same voltage as the dead one. Put out all smoking material. Connect the first jumper cable to the positive terminal of each battery. Connect one end of the second cable to the negative terminal of the live battery, and then clamp the other end to some part of the engine in the car with the dead battery. DO *NOT* LINK POSITIVE AND NEGATIVE TERMINALS. DO *NOT* ATTACH THE NEGATIVE CABLE DIRECTLY TO THE NEGATIVE TERMINAL OF THE DEAD BATTERY. A direct connection is dangerous. Choose a spot at least 18 inches from the dead battery. Put the car with the live battery in neutral, rev the engine, and hold it at moderate rpm while starting the other car. Once the engine is running, hold it at moderate rpm for a few seconds and disconnect the NEGATIVE cable. Then disconnect the positive cable. It is wise to take the car to a service station as soon as possible to have the battery checked and serviced if necessary.

While the instructions in this paragraph are clear and will enable anyone to start a car with a dead battery, the reader may have certain questions in mind after reading the paragraph:

1. What is a properly grounded battery?
2. Why is it necessary to extinguish smoking materials?
3. To what parts of the engine may one attach the negative cable?
   (After all, attaching it to the fan will have exciting results.)
4. What is the danger of making a direct connection?

Also, there are at least two important steps left out of the process:

Before connecting the two batteries,
1. Remove the caps to the cells of both batteries.
2. Check the fluid levels in the cells of both batteries.

Without these steps in the process, the car with the dead battery will start, but there is a chance of explosion. A paragraph that lacks material, that is not fully developed, probably won't explode. But it probably won't succeed, either. Questions raised in the mind of the reader will almost always weaken the effect of the paragraph. Sometimes the omissions are so important that the reader will miss the point or give up altogether in frustration.

Most of the time, you can write a well-developed paragraph by following three very simple steps:

1. Make the topic statement one clear, rather brief sentence.
2. Clarify and define the statement as needed.
3. Illustrate or exemplify the topic statement concretely where possible.

As an example of the use of this three-step process, follow the development of a paragraph written to answer the question, "What is the most important quality that you are seeking in an occupation?" The student's answer, found after much preliminary writing and a good bit of discussion, led to the following topic sentence and rough paragraph:

> Above all other qualities, *I want to have variety in the tasks I perform and in the locations where I work.*
>
> I know I must do the general line of work for which I'm trained, but I want to do different tasks in that work every day if possible. Repeating the same tasks day after day must be a mind-numbing experience. Our neighborhood mechanic does one tune-up after another, five days a week. A doctor friend tells me that 90 percent of her practice involves treating people ill with a virus, for which she prescribes an antibiotic against secondary infection. I want no part of that sort of humdrum work. Variety means doing a different part of a job every day, perhaps working on the beginning of one project today and the completion of another tomorrow, or working on broad concepts one day and details the next. I'd also like to work at a different job site as often as possible. The field of architecture is one area that might suit me. I could work in drafting, and then switch to field supervision, and move from that task to developing the overall concepts of a large project. By doing this, I could vary my assignments and the locations of my work.

Following the three simple steps given above, you might revise this paragraph to read as follows:

Topic Sentence { Some people want salary and others want big challenges, *but in my career I want variety, in both assignment and work location,* more than

Clarification and Definition { any other single quality. As much as possible, I want to do a different part of a job every day. Perhaps I could work on the beginning of one project and shift to the completion of another, or work on details for a while and then shift to broad concepts involved in planning. For this reason architecture looks like a promising field for me. I could work in

Concrete Example { drafting and detailing, move next to on-site supervision, and then shift to developing the design concepts of a major project. I know that doing the same task in the same place would be a mind-numbing experience for me. Our family doctor says that 90 percent of her practice consists of treating patients who have a routine virus infection, for which she routinely prescribes an antibiotic against secondary infection. Our neighborhood mechanic spends all his time doing tune-ups. I want none of that humdrum sort of work. Variety is the spice of life; it is also the ingredient that makes work palatable for me.

Unity

Effective paragraphs have two other characteristics: unity and coherence. It would seem to be easy to maintain unity in a paragraph. After all, by definition, a paragraph should deal with only one idea that is completely developed. Second and subsequent ideas should be handled in separate paragraphs. Sometimes, however, ideas can trick you if you don't pay close attention to your topic sentence. A student wrote this paragraph on strawberries some years ago:

> Strawberries are my favorite dessert. Over ice cream or dipped in powdered sugar, they are so good they bring tears to my eyes. My uncle used to grow strawberries on his farm in New Jersey. Once, I spent the whole summer there and my cousins and I went to the carnival. . . .

Things went pretty far afield from strawberries as the paragraph continued, and you can see how one idea, "used to grow strawberries on his farm," led to a recollection of a delightful summer on that farm and opened the door to a whole new idea and a change in form from discussion to narration. "Strawberries" and "that summer on the farm" are both legitimate, interesting, and perfectly workable topics for a paragraph. But they are probably not proper for inclusion in the same paragraph. Unity demands that each topic be treated in a separate paragraph. One paragraph handling one idea equals unity.

Coherence

In paragraph writing, the term *coherence* is used to describe a smooth flow between sentences within the paragraph. In other words, the sentences follow one another without abrupt changes. An effective paragraph reads smoothly, flowing from start to finish without choppiness to distract the reader.

The first step in establishing coherence occurs when you decide how you are going to develop the paragraph. (We shall discuss the various ways in which a paragraph can be developed in the next section.) The way in which you decide to develop the paragraph will help to establish coherence because it will produce a flow and a movement in the paragraph and because it will serve as a frame for providing details of development. There are, however, other writing strategies that contribute to coherence. Three of these strategies are discussed next.

Repetition of Nouns and Use of Reference Words.

My father asked me to dig some postholes. After I finished that, he told me the truck needed washing. It is Father's pride and joy, but I'm the one who has to do such jobs.

These three short sentences show a fairly clear pattern of development that in itself establishes coherence. Events occur one after another, establishing a chronological order for the development of the entire paragraph. But note how strongly the repeated nouns and reference words knit the sentences together within the paragraph:

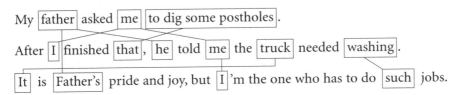

Use of Temporal Words: Conjunctions and Adverbs. Although a series of short, abrupt sentences may create chronological coherence, the paragraph may not read smoothly:

I drove to the corner. I stopped for a light. A car smashed into the back of mine. I got out rubbing my neck. The driver of the other car sat behind the wheel and wept. I realized that the other driver was an elderly, gray-haired man.

A writer, sensing that something is lacking from the paragraph, might revise it this way:

I drove to the corner. *While* I was stopped for a light, a car smashed into the back of mine. *As* I got out, rubbing my neck, the driver of the other car sat behind the wheel and wept. Only *then* did I realize that the other driver was an elderly, gray-haired man.

Two features of the revision have improved on the original draft. The first and most obvious is the addition of the words *while, as,* and *then* to connect the sentences by declaring the chronological sequence. Second, *while* and *as* convert short sentences into dependent clauses, thus replacing four choppy sentences with two longer ones and eliminating the jog-trot rhythm that gave the reader hiccups.

Transitional Words and Phrases At or Near the Beginning of Sentences. Coordinating conjunctions*; adverbs like *however, moreover, therefore, consequently, similarly,* and *thus;* and expressions like *on the other hand, in addition,* and *for example* can produce subtle transitional effects rather like that of reference words. They force the reader to recollect the preceding material, thus making a tie between the thoughts they introduce and what has already been stated. When you read *But* at the beginning of a sentence, the author is declaring to you in loud tones, "You are to interpret the forthcoming statement as being in opposition or in contrast to what you have just read." *Moreover,* in the same place, suggests that what is coming is an addition to the last remarks; *consequently* means "as a result of what I have just stated."

The ploy of cementing the parts of a paragraph together with these words and phrases is used by nearly every writer. It is a perfectly good device, but unfortunately it is also a seductively easy one. The unwary writer larding sentences with *however*'s and *therefore*'s in search of elegance and poise may get into trouble with logic. "Sam drank too much on our dinner date. Consequently he threw up," may leave one wondering whether the nausea stemmed from the liquor or the date.

Patterns for Paragraphs

Now that you know the characteristics of an effective paragraph—topic sentence, complete development, unity, and coherence—you can examine the different ways in which a paragraph can be developed with these characteristics. Over the years writers have created several recognizable development patterns for paragraphs. These patterns are useful for presenting certain types of information for specialized purposes within an essay. You should recognize and practice these development patterns so that you can use them in your own writing.

Comparison/Contrast

The identification of like and unlike qualities is the aim of comparison/contrast. When you compare, contrast, or compare and contrast two or more people, ideas, attitudes, or

---

*Disregard the myth that there is something wrong with starting a sentence with *and, but, for, or, nor, yet,* or *so.* Do realize, however, that these words at the opening of a sentence provide a special effect and call attention to themselves and to what follows them. Don't overuse them, and be sure of your purpose when you do launch a statement with one.

objects, you examine items that fall within the same general group or class and, after this examination, point out ways in which the items are similar and dissimilar. Common test questions or paper assignments that require this type of paragraph pattern read as follows:

Compare the attitudes of General Patton and Bertrand Russell toward war and the maintenance of a standing army.

Compare the effects of heroin and marijuana on the human body.

Compare orange juice and lemon juice in respect to taste, vitamin C content, and usefulness in cooking.

Note that in each statement there is a large class that includes the subjects of the comparison:

Patton and Russell were both famous people who held carefully developed attitudes toward war. [If one had no attitude on war, the comparison couldn't be made.]

Heroin and marijuana are both drugs that act on the human body.

Orange juice and lemon juice are both citrus products.

One of the most useful ways to employ comparison/contrast in any paragraph is to create an understanding of an unfamiliar concept by showing how that concept is like or unlike a more familiar concept.

If you know the stereotype of the Texan—loud, boisterous, bragging about his state and his own possessions—you could appreciate my friend Jack because he is the exact antithesis of that stereotype. He is quiet. . . .

In a business or investment course you might want to compare stocks and bonds as investment instruments. Begin by listing the qualities of a common stock and the qualities of a bond side by side.

A bond is	A stock is
1. an instrument used by investors.	1. an instrument used by investors.

Note how this first point in each list establishes that the two objects of comparison are members of the same large class and can therefore be compared and contrasted.

2. a certificate of indebtedness.	2. a representation of ownership of a fraction of a company.
3. a promise to repay a specific number of dollars.	3. worth the selling price on any day, whether more or less than the purchase price.
4. payable on a specified date.	4. sold anytime, but not ever payable as is a bond.
5. sold at a specific rate of interest.	5. not an interest-drawing instrument; rather, it earns a share of profits.

For a geology course, you might want to compare types of rocks.

Rocks can be divided into three groups:

Igneous	*Sedimentary*	*Metamorphic*
Formed when molten rock material called *magma* cools and solidifies.	Formed from deposits of older rocks or animal or plant life that are deposited on each other and joined by pressure or natural chemicals.	Formed when old rocks change under heat or pressure. They do not divide easily into subgroups.
One type (extrusive) is forced out by pressure from within the earth; for example, a volcano erupts and spews out lava, which, if cooled quickly, becomes glassy or forms small crystals such as obsidian or pumice.	Three types: *Classic*—formed of older rock pieces. *Chemical*—formed of crystallized chemicals. *Organic*—formed of plant and animal remains.	

Here, once you have made your list, you will discover that a detailed comparison of the three basic types of rocks is impossible in a single paragraph because of the enormous complexity of the subject. About all that can be dealt with in a single paragraph is a very broad comparison of the three major groups of rocks.

A comparison of the two muscle groups—skeletal and smooth—for a course on human anatomy can be more detailed because the two groups have a number of things in common. The two groups can be compared on the basis of:

	Skeletal	*Smooth*
1. Location	Attached to skeleton.	Found in blood vessels, digestive system, and internal organs.
2. Function	To move legs, arms, eyes, and so on.	To move food for digestion, contract or expand blood vessels—varies by location.
3. Structure	Long, slender fibers bundled together in parallel, contain many nuclei.	Arranged in sheets or in circular fashion, contain one nucleus.
4. Contraction	Rapid, only when stimulated by nerve; stimulus can be voluntary or involuntary.	Slow, rhythmic; cannot be controlled consciously (voluntarily); stimulated by nerves or by hormones.

It is possible to develop a paragraph of comparison/contrast in two different ways. The first pattern is clearly illustrated in the list of muscle characteristics: The qualities of both muscle groups are listed numerically in the same order. This pattern is useful if you are comparing only a limited number of characteristics. A second pattern, because it focuses the comparison point by point, provides better control of longer or more complicated topics. A paragraph comparing stocks and bonds might read as follows:

Although stocks and bonds are both common investment instruments, they differ in several important aspects and thus appeal to different types of investors. A bond is a certificate of indebtedness; a share of stock represents ownership of a percentage of a company. A bond involves a promise to repay a specified amount of money on a day agreed on in advance. Because it represents ownership, stock must be sold to obtain its value, and it is worth only the selling price on a given day, never a guaranteed amount. A bond earns money in the form of interest at a fixed rate, but stocks share in the profits, partial distributions of which are called *dividends*. Thus the value of a bond, if held to its date of maturity, is fixed, and the periodic interest paid by many bonds is relatively secure. A stock, on the other hand, changes its value on the basis of market conditions and its rate of return on the basis of the profitability of the company. The risk in a bond is the risk that inflation will reduce the value of its fixed number of dollars and its fixed rate of return; stocks risk a possible decline in the general market and a possible reduction of profits that might erode the sale price and the dividends. So bonds are useful where security of investment is a high priority and protection against inflation is not vital. Stocks fit an investment portfolio in which some risk is acceptable and a hedge against inflation is very important.

In the point-by-point pattern, bonds and stocks are compared in respect to the following categories:

1. The nature of the instrument itself
2. The way the value of the instrument is established
3. The method of earning money
4. The relative security of the two instruments
5. The risks inherent in each one
6. The situations in which each might be useful as an investment

As an exercise in comparison/contrast, you might try writing a paragraph on the two groups of muscles using each of the comparison/contrast patterns described earlier.

Definition

We have all read definitions; they are the subject matter of dictionaries. In writing, a paragraph of definition serves to establish meaning for words, concepts, and attitudes. Suppose on a test you found the following instruction:

Define a *boom-vang* and say how it is used in sailing.

The correct response to such an instruction would be a paragraph of definition. Clearly paragraphs of definition ought to follow the same rules of presentation and development that a dictionary does. Let's examine two definitions that follow the pattern used in dictionaries.

Basketball is a game played by two teams of five players on a rectangular court having a raised basket at each end. Points are scored by tossing a large round ball through the opponent's basket.

Football is a game played with an oval-shaped ball by two teams of eleven players defending goals at opposite ends of a rectangular field. Points are scored by carrying or throwing the ball across the opponent's goal or by kicking the ball over the crossbar of the opponent's goalpost.

Notice that both examples begin by identifying their opening words as the names of games. Next, they specify the

- Number of teams in a game
- Number of players on each team
- Type of playing area
- Way in which scoring occurs
- Shape of the ball

This is the classic pattern of definition: First, classify the word within a class or group; second, differentiate the word from other members of its class:

> Football is a game ... [Identify class]
> played by two teams
> of eleven players each
> on a rectangular field.   [Differentiate football from other games.]
>
> Scoring occurs by crossing
> opponent's goal in a special way.

If you are writing a paragraph of definition, however, you ought to offer more than just classification and the basic points of differentiation. You should provide illustrations, examples, and comparisons of the term being defined to terms that might be familiar to your reader. Doing this is often called **extending the definition.** The additional information helps your reader to understand and assimilate the information that you are offering. Examine the following paragraph defining football and note how basic definition and extension are combined to make an effective presentation:

> On any Saturday or Sunday afternoon in the fall, hundreds of thousands of Americans travel to stadiums, and millions more sprawl out in front of television sets to witness the great American spectator sport, football. In simplest form, a definition of football states that it is a game played on a large field by two teams of eleven players and that scoring is accomplished by carrying or throwing an oval ball across the opponent's goal line or by kicking the ball between two uprights called *goalposts.* But such literal definition scarcely does justice to the game or to its impact on Americans. For it is more than a game or a sport; it is a happening, a spectacle, a ritual that is almost a religious experience for its devotees. The game catches them with its color: a beautiful green field surrounded by crowds dressed in a galaxy of hues, teams uniformed in the brightest shades ever to flow from the brush of deranged artists. It holds these fans with its excitement: the long pass, the touchdown run, the closing-minutes' drive to victory. But above all, the game seems to captivate them with its violence, with dangers vicariously experienced, with a slightly veiled aura of mayhem. This element of danger draws casual viewers and converts them into fanatic worshippers of the great American cult-sport, football.

Finally, a word of warning about constructing definitions: A fundamental rule is that a definition must not be circular. A useful definition does not define a term by using a related form of the term itself. To define the word *analgesic* by saying that it causes analgesia means nothing unless the reader knows that *analgesia* means absence or removal of pain. To define *conservatism* as a philosophy that attempts to conserve old values doesn't really add much to a reader's understanding. Thus the rule: **Do not use in the definition a form of the word being defined.**

Analysis

Chemists analyze compounds to isolate and identify their components. Economists analyze the financial data of the nation to determine the factors contributing to recessions. Sports commentators analyze games to explain the strengths leading to a victory.

Analysis is the act of breaking a substance or an entity into its components. It is possible to analyze a football team and to point out the various positions: ends, tackles, guards, and the rest. An army can be broken into infantry, artillery, and engineers. A piano is made up of parts: keys, strings, sounding board, and so on.

A paragraph of analysis provides information derived from this act of breaking into parts, usually by listing, defining, and explaining the parts of the whole in question. As an example, suppose you wanted to analyze that rarest of animals, the good driver. You might begin by listing for yourself the characteristics of the good driver:

The good driver possesses:
- Technical competence
- Physical skills
- Sound judgment
- Emotional stability

A paragraph analyzing the qualities of a good driver might read this way:

> Every American over age fourteen wants to drive, does drive, or just stopped driving because his or her license was revoked. Not every American—in fact, only a very few Americans—can be counted in the ranks of good drivers. Good drivers must possess technical competence in the art of driving. They must know the simple steps of starting, shifting, and braking, and the highly sophisticated techniques of feathering the brakes and the power slide, for example. In addition, they must possess physical skills, such as exceptional eye–hand coordination, fast reflexes, outstanding depth perception, and peripheral vision. They must also possess good judgment. What speed is safe on a rain-slick highway? How far can a person drive without succumbing to fatigue? What are the possible mistakes that the approaching driver can make? And besides the answers to these questions and the technical and physical skills listed above, good drivers possess steel nerves to cope with that potentially lethal emergency that one day will come to everyone who slips behind the wheel of a car. Only with these qualities can a person be called a good driver and be relatively sure of returning home in one piece.

Caution: When you divide or break an entity into its elements, be sure that you establish parallel categories. It is not proper, in analyzing an automobile's major systems, for example, to list

- Frame
- Body
- Drive train
- Engine
- Piston rings

Although the first four items could possibly be called major systems, piston rings are a small part of a large system, the engine, and should not be included in a list of major systems. The rule for analysis is: **Keep categories parallel.**

Process Analysis. A process paragraph is a form of analysis that examines, in the order in which they must occur, the steps involved in an action or a sequence of actions. The most common sort of process analysis is a recipe: To make a rabbit stew, first catch a rabbit, and so forth. Instructions for building stereo receivers or flying kites or cleaning ovens are all process analyses. In addition to instructions, process analysis can be used to trace the steps involved in a historical event. This type of analysis would be required to answer an essay test question that begins with the word *trace* or *delineate*. The following paragraph provides a set of instructions:

> Changing the oil and the filter in your car is a simple process, and "doing it yourself" can save several dollars every time you change the oil. First, go to an auto parts store or a discount store and buy the oil and the oil filter specified for your car. At the same time, buy an oil filter wrench, the only specialized tool necessary for this job. Don't buy these items at your gas station; prices are lower at the other stores. In addition, you will need an adjustable wrench and a pail or bucket low enough to fit under the car to catch the old oil as it drains from the crankcase. Don't lift the car on a bumper jack. Simply crawl under the car and locate the drain plug for the crankcase. From the front of the car the first thing you see underneath will be the radiator—the thing with the large hose running from the bottom. That hose runs to the engine, the next piece of equipment as you work your way back. On the bottom surface of the engine is the drain plug, usually square with a few threads visible where it screws into the oil pan. Place the pail or bucket beneath this plug. Fit the wrench to the plug by adjusting its size. Turn the plug counterclockwise until it falls out of its hole into the pail. Don't try to catch it; the oil may be hot. While the oil drains into the pail, find the oil filter on one side of the engine, usually down low. (It will look exactly like the one you bought.) Reach up (or perhaps down from the top, whichever is easier) and slip the circle of the filter wrench over it. Pull the wrench in a counterclockwise direction and take off the old filter. Put the new filter on in exactly the opposite way, tightening it clockwise by hand until it is snug. Scoop the drain plug out of the cooled oil and put it back in place, tightening it firmly with the adjustable wrench. Now find the oil filler cap on the top of the engine and pour in the new oil. Tighten the filler cap firmly. Dispose of the old oil at a collection station and wipe your hands clean. Finally, record the mileage for this change somewhere so that you will know when the next change is due.

A process paragraph that traces a historical development might seem somewhat more difficult to write than a set of instructions. Essentially, however, tracing the steps in a historical process follows the same form as instructions. Instructions tell a reader to do this, then that, then another thing; a paragraph tracing the steps in a historical process tells a reader first this happened, then that, then another thing. The major difference is that the historical event has already occurred and the paragraph is written in the past tense. Examine the following paragraph, which traces the transformation of the computer from mainframe to microcomputer, and notice how its pattern (this happened, then that, then another thing) follows the pattern of the instructions in the previous example (do this, then that, then the other thing):

> The first computer was made from vacuum tubes about as big as a bread box, and the collection of them filled up a room the size of a classroom. The tubes were inordinately sensitive to changes in temperature and humidity, and the smallest speck of dust caused them to go berserk. They were expensive to build and expensive to maintain; therefore they were operated only by highly trained technicians. Anyone who wished to use the computer was forced to deal with the people in the white lab coats, an inconvenient arrangement at best. The first step in reducing the

size and increasing the reliability of the computer was the invention of transistors, small, inexpensive devices that control the flow of electricity. They are solid and durable, and, most important, they can be made very small. Scientists soon discovered that transistors could also be hooked together into integrated circuits known as *chips*; the chips could contain tremendous amounts of circuitry, an amount comparable to the wiring diagram of an office building, on a piece of silicon no bigger than your thumbnail. Finally, scientists and computer experts developed the microprocessor, the central works of a computer inscribed on a chip. Presto! The way was opened for the development of a microcomputer about the size of a bread box.

Causal Analysis. Causal analysis, as the name implies, is an analysis of the causes leading to a given outcome. On an essay test, you might be asked to explain or discuss the reasons for a lost war, a victory in an election, a depression, or the collapse of a bridge. In your life outside school, you might be called on to explain why you have selected some occupation or particular college or why you wish to drop out of school to hike the Appalachian Trail for four or five months.

Causal analysis differs from process analysis in that it does not necessarily involve a chronological sequence. Instead, it seeks the reasons for an outcome and lists them (with necessary discussion) in either ascending or descending order of importance. A process analysis concerned with the growth of inflation in the last seventy-five years might trace the fall of the dollar's value and the actions and reactions of government and consumers at intervals of ten years. A causal analysis on the same subject would give the reasons why the dollar has declined in value and why the reactions of government and consumers have produced progressively worse conditions. Causal analysis might also be used to explain why a course of action has been taken or ought to be taken.

> It is important that the United States curb inflation over the next few years. Inflation at home is reducing the value of the dollar overseas, making it very difficult for Americans to purchase products from other countries. German automobiles, even those that once were considered low-cost transportation, have increased in price dramatically in the last few years. At home, rapid price increases have made it very difficult for salary increases to keep pace with the cost of living. In spite of large pay increases over the past few years, factory workers have shown little or no gain in buying power; prices have climbed as workers' wages have increased, leaving workers with nothing to show for a larger paycheck. Inflation has been especially hard on retired people who live on a fixed income. They receive only a set number of dollars and do not benefit from pay increases as do wage earners. But while the income of retired people has remained the same, prices have increased; thus they cannot buy the same amounts as they could previously. Unchecked inflation works a hardship on all of us, but it is especially hard on those whose income does not increase to match the increases in prices.

Causal analysis might also be used to explain the reasons why someone holds a particular position or opinion. A student explained her love of sailing as follows:

> A sailboat, a broad bay, and a good breeze form the most satisfying combination in the world of sport. To be sailing before a brisk wind across an open expanse of water allows—no, requires—cooperation with the forces of nature. Working with the wind in moving the boat provides us one of the few times when we are not forced to ignore, or work against, or even overcome the natural rhythms and functions of the universe. Too much of daily life pits us against those forces; finding them on our side, aiding us in a worthwhile project, is indeed a pleasure. The boats used are in themselves very pleasant. They do not bang or clank, nor do they spout

vile fumes or foul the air, suddenly explode, or cease to function altogether. Instead, they offer the soft, sliding sounds of the bow slipping through the sea, the creak of ropes and sails, and the gentle, soothing hum of the standing rigging pulled tight by the pressure of wind on sails. Most important, sailing puts us in close contact, in communion, with that most basic element, the sea. The sea remains constant; winds or storms may stir the surface, but the depths are never moved. The sea always has been and always will be, or so it seems. It offers constancy and permanence in the midst of a world where flux and change are the only constants. Is it any wonder that sailing is such a delight, such a joy?

Exemplification

One of the simplest yet most effective paragraphs states its topic and then uses examples to define and clarify it. The following paragraph explains its topic by using examples:

Youth and beauty are grand attributes, and together they are a wonderful possession. But television commercials and programs extol youth and beauty to such an extreme that those not so young and less than beautiful are made to feel inferior. Cars, beer, clothes, and even lawn mowers are almost always pictured with lithe, beautiful women of tender age or well-muscled young men with luxuriant, well-groomed hair. Cosmetics are always portrayed in use by people who have almost no need of them. Beauty, and especially youthful beauty, sells goods, we surmise, and those who do not become young and beautiful after buying the car or ingesting the iron supplement are obviously unfit to share the planet with the favored ones. And the programs themselves emphasize youthful beauty. There are few homely, few truly decrepit people who play regularly in any series. Any family, and any individual, who cannot compare with those perfect people ought to be exiled from the land of the lovely. We are left to believe that only the beautiful young are acceptable.

Description and Narration

Two important development patterns remain: *description* and *narration*. Each of these patterns involves a direction or a movement. Description requires movement through space: The writer's eye moves through a given space, picking out selected details in order to create an effect. Narration demands movement through time: The writer creates a progression through time, providing details selected to convey a story and its impact. The success of each pattern depends on the careful selection of details of physical qualities or of action and on the vivid presentation of these details.

In *Huckleberry Finn* Mark Twain has Huck give a beautiful description of a sunrise on the Mississippi:

. . . we run nights, and laid up and hid day-times; soon as night was most gone, we stopped navigating and tied up—nearly always in the dead water under a tow-head; and then cut young cottonwoods and willows and hid the raft with them. Then we set out the lines. Next we slid into the river and had a swim, so as to freshen up and cool off; then we set down on the sandy bottom where the water was about knee deep, and watched the daylight come. Not a sound, anywhere—perfectly still—just like the whole world was asleep, only sometimes the bull-frogs a-cluttering, maybe. The first thing to see, looking away over the water, was a kind of dull line—that was the woods on t'other side—you couldn't make nothing else out; then a pale place in the sky; then more paleness, spreading around; then the river softened up, away off, and warn't black any more, but gray; you could see little dark spots drifting along, ever so far away—trading scows, and such things; and long black streaks—rafts; sometimes you could hear a sweep screaking; or jumbled up voices, it was so still, and sound come so far; and by-and-by you could see a streak on the water which you know by the look of the streak that there's a snag there in a swift current which breaks on it and makes that streak look that way; and you see the mist curl up off the water, and the east reddens up, and the river, and you make out a log cabin in the edge of the woods, away on the bank on t'other side of the river, being a wood-yard, likely and piled by them cheats so you can throw a dog through it anywheres; then the nice breeze springs up, and comes fanning you from over there, so cool and fresh, and sweet to smell, on account of the woods and the flowers; but sometimes not that way, because they've left dead fish laying around, gars, and such, and they do get pretty rank; and next you've got the full day, and everything smiling in the sun, and the song-birds just going it!

Two qualities of this description are important for you to note. First, notice the direction or movement of the unfolding picture. Beginning with the dim view of the far bank, the narrator observes traces of paleness in the sky. He then notes that the river has softened up "away off"; notice the logical progression from sky to horizon to river. After he gives details of the changing sights and sounds at river level, the mist curling up from the river focuses his attention again on the sky as the "east reddens up." Then he returns to the river and develops the picture as new details become visible in the light of morning. This movement from mid-picture to background to foreground to background to foreground follows a sensory logic, an order of increasing visibility as the sun rises and the light increases. It is important to select an order of presentation (or, as here, a logic) and to stick with the order, whether it be left-to-right, right-to-left, middle-to-left-to-right, or any other easily followed combination. Second, Twain provides details that appeal to the senses:

Color:	dull line of woods
	pale sky
	river changing from black to gray
	dark spots and black streaks
	east reddening
Sound:	complete absence of sound
	bullfrogs a-cluttering
	sweep screaking
	jumbled up voices
	song birds
Smell:	woods
	flowers
	dead fish
Motion:	dark spots drifting
	snag in swift current
	mist curling up off the water
Touch:	cooling off in water
	sitting on sandy bottom of river
	cool breeze springing up

Supply your reader with sensory appeal. Keep your description lively and colorful.

In another section of *Huckleberry Finn,* Twain provides us with a heart-stopping piece of narration, the killing of the old drunk, Boggs.

So somebody started on a run. I walked down the street a ways, and stopped. In about five or ten minutes, here comes Boggs again—but not on his horse. He was a-reeling across the street towards me, bareheaded, with a friend on both sides of him aholt of his arms and hurrying him along. He was quiet, and looked uneasy; and he warn't hanging back any, but was doing some of the hurrying himself. Somebody sings out—"Boggs!"

I looked over there to see who said it, and it was that Colonel Sherburn. He was standing perfectly still, in the street, and had a pistol raised in his right hand—not aiming it, but holding it out with the barrel tilted up towards the sky. The same second I see a young girl coming on the run, and two men with her. Boggs and the men turned round, to see who called him, and when they see the pistol the men jumped to one side, and the pistol barrel came down slow and steady to a level—both barrels cocked. Boggs throws up both of his hands, and says, "O Lord, don't shoot!" Bang! goes the first shot, and he staggers back clawing at the air—bang goes the second one, and he tumbles backwards onto the ground, heavy and solid, with his arms spread out. That young girl screamed out, and comes rushing, and down she throws herself on her father, crying, and saying, "Oh, he's killed him, he's killed him!" The crowd closed up around them, and shouldered and jammed one another, with their necks stretched, trying to see, and people on the inside trying to shove them back, and shouting, "Back, back! give him air, give him air!"

Colonel Sherburn he tossed his pistol onto the ground, and turned around on his heels and walked off.

Again, two aspects of the narrative are important. The order is simple, straight chronology. But notice the action words. The girl comes on the run, the men jump, Boggs staggers. Few forms of the verb *to be* intrude to slow the action, and no statements of thought or emotion stop the progression. All of the impact and emotion is conveyed through action, and that use of action is the essence of good narrative.

A Final Note

Good paragraphs are not necessarily restricted to a single pattern of development. Sometimes it is necessary to include more than one pattern of development in a paragraph. A narration, for example, may demand a passage of description. And quite often it is useful to combine patterns to produce a desired effect. The following paragraph on spider webs illustrates such a combination of patterns. The predominant device used here is analysis: The larger unit, spider webs, is broken down into three separate types or categories. But the writer uses an additional strategy; he clarifies his analysis by comparison/ contrast, pointing out like and unlike details of the three kinds of spider webs:

Web-spinning spiders construct three kinds of webs. The first type is the tangled web, a shapeless helter-skelter jumble attached to some support such as the corner of a room. These webs are hung in the path of insects and serve to entangle them as they pass. The second type of web is the sheet web. This web is a flat sheet of silk strung between blades of grass or tree branches. Above this sheet is strung a sort of net, which serves to knock insects into the sheet. When an insect hits the sheet, the spider darts out and pulls it through the webbing, trapping the insect. Finally, perhaps the most beautiful of the webs, is the orb. The orb web consists of threads that extend from a center like a wheel's spokes and are connected to limbs or grass blades. All the spokes are connected by repeated circles of sticky silk, forming a kind of screen. Insects are caught in this screen and trapped by the spider.

Don't hesitate to shift methods where a switch is useful. Do so with care, however, and keep in mind that a new method of development might suggest the need for a new paragraph.

Exercises for Patterns for Paragraphs

1. Examine the following facts and observations about two methods for recording and playing music and other sound:

   - Cassette tapes can stretch and lose sound quality.
   - Compact discs are resistant to damage.
   - Compact discs maintain their sound quality.
   - Cassette tapes are less expensive than compact discs.
   - Cassette tapes can be damaged by tangling or unwinding.
   - In general, sound quality on compact discs is higher than sound quality on cassette tapes.

   Write a paragraph of comparison/contrast discussing the merits of these two media.

2. Write a paragraph giving directions for preparing your favorite dessert. Include every step and provide enough detail and information for a beginning cook to be able to make the dessert successfully. Check your work by preparing the dessert following your instructions.

3. Write a description of one of the buildings on your campus. Provide sufficient detail so that a person can identify the building that you are describing. Do not use the name, the location, or any identifying colors in the description.

Once you have mastered the steps in the writing process by creating paragraphs, you will need to make only a few adjustments to follow that same process in writing a longer essay, the sort of essay you might be assigned in a college class in biology, business, or English. After all, whether you are writing essay tests or special paragraph arrangements, or full length essays, the writing process we described on pages 306–309 is the same.

Composing

Let's assume you need to develop a paper for your English class. Because the paper is a class assignment, the first step requires a look at the nature of class assignments and the problems of defining the subject and limiting it to an appropriate, manageable length.

Step 1. Select the Subject

Usually writing assignments fall into one of three categories.

1. **Very General:** Write a two-page paper on something we've covered in this course.
2. **Somewhat Specific:** Write a two-page paper on some aspect of the novel *Huckleberry Finn.*
3. **Very Directive:** Write a two-page paper explaining why Huck Finn's experiences led him to make his final statement: "Aunt Sally's going to adopt me and sivilize me and I can't stand it. I been there before."

The very general assignment grants considerable latitude in the selection of a subject for a paper. Often this latitude will prove more of a problem than a blessing because it is necessary to find something to write about that you *and* the teacher consider interesting and worthwhile. It is of little value to write a fine paper and find that the teacher (the grader) thinks the topic so insignificant that the whole effort can't be worth more than a C. The best approach here is to review the textbook, your lecture notes, and previous tests (if any); to select from these an important content area, concept, or personality; and to use that selection as a starting point for your work. Be sure to choose an area that interests you, an area about which you have some knowledge and some readily accessible sources of information. Once you have made this initial selection, you have converted the assignment from "general" to "somewhat specific." Next, you need to restrict the area you selected or were assigned so that you can develop it fully within the assigned length of the paper. Suppose, for example, the assignment said to write a two-page paper on *Huckleberry Finn*. Several areas are open to you:

1. Autobiographical aspects of the novel
2. Problems of plot and structure
3. Problems of characterization
4. Philosophical aspects of the novel

For the selection or restriction process, choose one of the areas and make a final selection of a topic within that area. The final selection should be fairly small in scope, something manageable within two pages. In the example of *Huckleberry Finn,* the process of restriction might look like this:

Philosophical aspects of the novel

1. The relationship between individuals and society
2. Huck Finn's attitude toward the world as he saw it
3. Why Huck's experiences led him to say that he couldn't stand to be "sivilized"

The final version of the topic (Number 3) is probably limited enough for it to be treated adequately within the assigned length. The topic asks a single question about one person. It should be possible to answer that question and offer examples supporting your answer in two pages.

Note that the way in which your teacher states the assignment dictates the starting point for your work. A general assignment requires that you go through three stages:

1. Selection of a general subject area
2. Selection of a portion or phase of this general area to form a limited subject area
3. Final selection of a specific limited topic within the limited subject area

A somewhat specific assignment completes the first two stages for you by limiting you to a general area. You need deal with only the third stage to complete the restriction process for this assignment. A very directive assignment accomplishes all three stages and leaves you free to begin work on the organization of the paper itself.

Step 2. Gather Information

Once you have established your topic, you need to establish what you know about the topic. Continuing with our *Huckleberry Finn* example, what were Huck's experiences? Why did they make him want to avoid Aunt Sally's attentions? List some of the experiences he had in the "sivilized" world. Here are some possibilities:

1. The confining life at the Widow Douglas's home and Miss Watson's efforts to teach Huck manners and religion
2. The brutal shooting of Boggs by Colonel Sherburn and the mob violence of the attempted lynching that was faced down by Sherburn's single-handed capacity for even greater violence
3. The Grangerford–Shepherdson feud
4. Huck's obvious pleasure at living outside civilization with Jim on Jackson's Island and on the raft

While other experiences may come to mind as you work on the paper, this list leads directly to Step 3.

Step 3. Establish a Controlling Statement

The controlling statement, or **thesis,** serves the longer essay much as the topic sentence serves the paragraph. The topic sentence states the subject of the paragraph and tells what will be said about it. The thesis statement controls the writer before the paper is written by defining the subject and what is to be said about the subject. It keeps the writer from wandering away from the subject; sometimes it is so specific that it establishes the order in which the essay will be arranged. Reviewing your list of Huck's experiences, the thesis statement for your paper is obvious:

> Huck could not stand to be "sivilized" because his experiences in civilization were confining, frightening, or dangerous.

Step 4. Select Specific Items of Support

Keeping the thesis statement in mind, you need to select from the book experiences and observations that will clearly illustrate the conditions in civilization. All the possible pieces of evidence listed above can be used to point out the conditions that Huck wanted to avoid. Even the pleasant experiences with Jim on Jackson's Island serve to make the bad experiences more vivid. As you select the content, you produce an outline, which is a simple list of the points you wish to make in support of your thesis. Each point in the outline then becomes a paragraph of support in your short paper. In a longer paper, more than one paragraph may be required to develop a single point.

Step 5. Establish an Order of Presentation

Several orders are possible, but the easiest one to follow is to take the materials in the order in which they occur in the book.

Step 6. Write the First Draft

Begin by writing an introduction. The introduction might read this way:

> At the close of the novel *Huckleberry Finn,* Huck concludes his story by saying that he intends to "light out for the Territory" because Aunt Sally intends to "sivilize" him, and he feels that he can't stand any more efforts to make him an upstanding, moral, and religious citizen. His attitude is understandable, for his experiences in society as it existed along the Mississippi were confining, unpleasant, or downright terrifying.

We will discuss introductions again in the next section.

Continue now to the **paragraphs of development.** Paragraphs of development are the paragraphs you write to support your thesis. In this example, the paragraphs of development will discuss Huck's experiences with the "sivilized" world.

> Huck's experiences of "home," or at the two places where he lives at the opening of the novel, are decidedly unpleasant. The home of Widow Douglas and Miss Watson tends to oppress and constrict a boy's natural energy and interests. Regular meals eaten with careful manners and polite small talk work against Huck's tendency to roam at will through the woods. Lectures on

morality and religion tend to confuse him. If one can obtain his or her desires through prayer, why are folks poor, or sick, or crippled? If being good makes one blessed, why is Miss Watson so sour and seemingly unhappy? Life with Pap may be more free from the repressions of etiquette, but it also has its frightening side of drunkenness, violence, and delirium tremens. So Huck decides to leave these situations behind to look for something better.

Something better turns out to be life on the river with Jim, the runaway slave. They meet on Jackson's Island and camp there for a time. Their experiences on the island are mostly pleasant: loafing, camping, fishing, and generally hanging out, all of which suit Huck just fine. The idyll is interrupted by a snakebite (from which Jim recovers) and is ended by the threat of a search party coming out to find Jim. Jim is a slave and, by all the measures of that day, less than human, but in reality he is the only truly civilized person Huck meets in his travels. Jim loves Huck and cares for him, in spite of Huck's tendency to play cruel jokes on him. He shelters Huck from the knowledge of Pap's death and doesn't reject Huck after he discovers the hoax of Huck's dream fabrication when they have been separated in a fog. It is ironic that the only civilized person Huck meets is not considered truly human by those who regard themselves as civilized.

The other people Huck meets in his travels do very little to improve his suspicious view of the world. He and Jim happen upon some fairly terrible people as soon as they venture out on the river: slave hunters, the gamblers who are trying to kill their partner, and a nonhuman agent of civilization, a steamboat that runs them down and puts Huck back on shore. There he meets the Grangerfords, gentlemen and ladies all, living in a fine house and enjoying prosperity. The Grangerfords are aristocrats and moral churchgoing people who have only one fault: They are engaged in a murderous, generations-old feud with the Shepherdsons. One Sunday afternoon Huck witnesses an outbreak of this feud that leaves most of the people from both families dead.

Fleeing from the killing, Huck returns to the river and finds Jim. They continue down the river. Later they meet the King and the Duke, two great con artists who dupe the people in a nearby town and are eventually tarred and feathered for their efforts. During the adventures with the King and the Duke, Huck witnesses the shooting of the harmless drunk Boggs and the attempted lynching of Colonel Sherburn, the man who shot him. Taken on balance, most of Huck's experiences on shore are grim and frightening, good reasons for his lack of enthusiasm for civilization.

Even the last episode of the book does little to increase Huck's desire to live in the civilized world. Huck comes by chance on the home of Tom Sawyer's Aunt Sally and adopts Tom's identity. When Tom shows up, he is introduced as Cousin Sid. Jim is also on the plantation, being held as a runaway slave. The two boys, with Tom leading, enter an incredible plot to free Jim, although, as Tom knows but conceals, Jim has already been freed. After a series of cops-and-robbers antics, the plot resolves into what looks like a happy ending. It is revealed that Jim is free, Pap is dead, and Huck's personal fortune, presumed lost, is intact. Aunt Sally offers to adopt Huck and raise him properly so that he can become a successful, civilized adult. At this point Huck reviews his situation. Life in town and his misadventures on shore with the Grangerfords, the King and the Duke, Sherburn, and others suggest only bad experiences to come if he accepts Aunt Sally's offer. His time with Jim, living free and easy on the river, seems wonderfully pleasant, compared to those recollections. Little wonder, then, that he decides to "light out for the Territory."

This completes the writing process through the writing of the rough draft. We shall review these steps and the remaining steps in the process in the second example of this section.

Sample Business Paper Development

With the first stage of the writing process fresh in your mind, follow how you might apply it in writing a paper of six to eight paragraphs for a business course.

Suppose your class has been studying men who have greatly influenced American business, past and present, and the assignment is to write a paper of about 800 words discussing the contributions of one of these men.

1. ***Select the Subject.*** Several names come to mind from the history of American business: F. W. Taylor, Thomas Watson, Douglas McGregor, Alfred Sloan, Frederick Herzberg. But perhaps the most interesting and certainly one of the most important contributors to the theory and practice of business in America is Peter F. Drucker. His contributions are famous and respected in this country and abroad, and they have been cataloged and discussed in two well-respected books. Thus Drucker's contributions meet the criteria for selection as a subject. They are important and interesting, and information on them is readily available.

2. ***Gather Materials.*** What is there to know about Peter Drucker? From your class notes, texts, and outside readings, you might jot down the following notes:

> He has written twenty-seven books and many articles on business. He was born in Vienna, Austria. Father was a college teacher in America. Drucker started his career as a bookkeeper and a writer. He left Germany early in WWII. Went to London and worked in a bank. Then worked for American newspapers as a British correspondent. Worked for the U.S. government during the war, then taught at two colleges, moving in 1950 to New York University, where he taught till 1970.
>
> His first consulting job was a massive study of General Motors Corporation, a study highly critical of its management systems. From this work he wrote *The Concept of the Corporation,* a book that was the beginning of management thought in the modern sense of the word. His latest book, *Management: Tasks—Responsibilities—Practices,* is a very broad study of modern management philosophy and practices.
>
> He continues to consult for major corporations, but he requires that the client come to him in California. He charges $1,500 a day and still manages to stay booked up far in advance.
>
> Drucker is well-known as a teacher. He taught first at NYU in a special program for active business people. He now teaches in the Claremont Graduate School in California, a position he has held since 1971. Drucker loves teaching so much that some believe he would pay to do it if necessary. He especially enjoys teaching those who are currently employed in management positions. He uses a case-study method of his own invention, not following accepted case-study methods from other colleges. His case studies are short and are not loaded with data and statistics. Instead they concentrate on analysis and on finding the right questions to ask in a given situation. Often high-level executives attend his classes for enrichment and pleasure, even though they do not need any further course work or degrees to augment their careers. His associations in the classroom often ripen into rich and enduring friendships.

Much more information could be collected about Drucker, and more probably would be needed to fill an essay of eight hundred words. But this is enough material to allow us to move to the next step.

3. ***Establish a Controlling Statement.*** It is clear from the information gathered about Peter Drucker that he is active in three general areas of business: as a teacher, consultant, and writer. But the key word in the assignment is *contributions,* not *activity.* The fact that Drucker has been active as a writer does not automatically mean that he has made a contribution to the theory and practice of American business in his writings. That remains to be determined; you must return to the information gathered in Step

2 to see what is known about his *contributions*. (**Note:** It is not uncommon to discover that writing the statement for a paper [Step 3] requires a return to the information-gathering stage [Step 2] to find additional information to use in formulating the thesis statement.)

The information already collected provides only a suggestion of Drucker's contributions: he wrote a book that was the "beginning of management thought in the modern sense of the word." Now you must collect information directly related to this.

Further reading in books and articles about Peter Drucker indicates two very important areas of contribution, one theoretical and the other practical, which you summarize as follows:

> In the theory of management, Drucker was the first to identify the corporation as a whole as something that needed management and that could be managed. Prior to his work, discussions of corporation management were rather fragmented, dealing with isolated problems such as accounting and materials handling. Drucker developed a theory for the operation of the entire corporation.
>
> On the practical side, Drucker developed the concept of the manager and his or her role in the corporation, and he has written guides to the day-to-day functions of those in management. He has worked as a consultant for major corporations, and the solutions to their problems have filtered to other companies and influenced institutions such as schools and hospitals. He also did initial work on ideas that later were more fully developed by others: The "hygiene" theory of the effects of wages on motivation and the theories of motivation often labeled X and Y were initially discussed in Drucker's works, at least in concept, and were developed by other writers, Herzberg and McGregor in particular.

The addition of this information to the information previously collected provides a solid basis for working on Step 3, establishing the statement.

The nature of Drucker's contributions is now clear enough for you to try writing a statement about them. Such a statement might read:

> Peter Drucker has made both a theoretical and a practical contribution to American business.

or

> Peter Drucker was the first to develop a theory of the nature and function of the corporation, and he has made practical application of that theory to the day-to-day work of the manager through his writings and his work as a consultant. He also did initial work on concepts fully developed by others.

The second version captures most of what needs to be said, but the order is jumbled and the statement is too wordy. A better version is

> Peter Drucker developed the overall concept of the corporation, its place in society, and its operation; he also began work on specific concepts that were later developed by other men. His practical work as writer and consultant has provided direction to many managers.

Now you are ready to move to Step 4.

4. *Select Specific Items of Support.* You can shape the controlling statement into a general outline for a paper and get an idea of the kinds of materials you will need to support the statement.

Drucker's Contributions

- Developed theory and concept of the corporation.
- Began work on concepts later fully developed by others.
- Provided practical applications of those theories in writings and in consulting work.

To develop the first point in the outline, you will need to discuss the state of management theory when Drucker began his work. Then you will need to explain how he developed his theory, where he first began to publish it, and, in general terms, what that theory of the corporation and its management is. For the second point, you need to identify the concepts that Drucker began to develop, the people who completed that development, and the name or the final form of those concepts. A discussion of his more practical books and some of the guidelines in them can be joined with a brief discussion of his work as a consultant to present the third point in the outline.

5. *Establish an Order of Presentation.* There is an order already built into the outline from the materials collected in Step 2: first, theories and concepts of the corporation as a whole, then specific theories, and then practical applications of those theories. This order also seems to arrange the contributions in descending order of importance, taking the larger, more global contributions first and moving to less important theories and practical matters next. It would be possible to reverse that order and work from least important to most important, from practical to theoretical. But such a progression does not seem to suit the materials as well as the first order, so you should present the materials in the draft in the order suggested by the outline.

6. *Write the First Draft.* It might seem logical to begin writing a draft of a paper with the beginning, the introduction. If a clear, effective introduction comes to mind rather handily, begin with the introduction. But do not wait with pen in hand for the perfect introduction to appear on the page. Make one attempt at an introduction; if nothing comes of that first attempt, begin to write the body of the paper wherever you find the writing easiest, even if you begin with what is actually the last paragraph in the essay. Get the material written and then put the paper in the proper order. Write, don't wait for the inspiration.

There are two elements in Step 6 of your business paper development that need to be discussed in greater detail. These are the introduction to your topic and the conclusion of your paper.

The Introduction

The introduction should serve two important functions. *First,* and more important, the introduction must catch the interest of the reader. *Second,* it must give the reader an idea of the direction the paper will take. This sense of direction may come from a restating of the thesis statement you developed in Step 3 or from a paraphrase of your thesis statement. On the other hand, you may provide a sense of direction by offering a general identifying statement of the topic. For the paper on Peter Drucker a paraphrase of the Step 3 statement might read:

> Peter Drucker developed a philosophy of the corporation, devised specific concepts within that philosophy, and showed managers how to make a practical application of that philosophy.

Identifying the topic and making a general statement of the ideas to be covered might produce:

> Of all those who have helped to develop our ideas of the nature and workings of the corporation, Peter Drucker is among the most important.

With this effort to provide a sense of direction, you must also catch the reader's interest. If you have trouble thinking of methods for developing introductions, you might try one of the following strategies:

- Use a quotation or a paraphrase of a striking statement:

> Peter Drucker is, in the words of C. Northcote Parkinson, "preeminent among management consultants and also among authors of books on management."

- Cite an important fact or statistic:

> Prior to the writing of *The Concept of the Corporation*, the idea of the corporation as an entity that needed management did not exist. Drucker invented the corporate society.

- Recount an anecdote:

> "What *is* your business?" the famous consultant asked the directors of a firm that made bottles. "Everyone knows," responded the chairman, "that we make bottles for soft drinks and other foods." "I disagree," replied the consultant to the astounded board. After a pause to let his words sink in, he continued, "Your business is not the making of bottles; you are in the packaging business." With that one question Peter Drucker, America's foremost business consultant, opened the board's eyes and provided new direction for a foundering company.

- Use a dictionary definition:

> The dictionary defines a corporation as a group of individuals legally united to conduct business. Peter Drucker defines the corporation as the cornerstone of our society.

- Set up a contrast between two ideas:

> The original management consultant was really an efficiency expert, timing workers on an assembly line and suggesting ways of improving their speed and productivity. Peter Drucker's work is as far removed from that practice as the supersonic transport is from the Wright brothers' first plane.

As you become a more experienced writer, you will find less and less need for these strategies. Use them now, but feel free to experiment as your confidence grows.

The Conclusion

Always provide a conclusion for your paper. As a rule, a short sentence of summary or a restatement of the topic will suffice. The function of a conclusion for a short paper is to let the reader know that the paper has been completed, to provide a sense of "finished-ness." Don't leave the reader with the impression that he or she ought to be looking for more material. Don't try to provide an extensive restatement or summary for a short paper. And be very careful that you never use the conclusion to introduce a new point or add additional information. A one-sentence conclusion should be ample for most college essays.

Revising

The first completed draft of the paper on the contributions of Peter Drucker might read this way:

Of the business people, scholars, and writers who have attempted to analyze and influence the business world of the twentieth century, none has made a greater contribution or been more interesting to observe than Peter Drucker. Drucker is a teacher, a consultant, and a writer who has drawn from each role to construct a philosophy or theoretical concept of the corporation and a workable application of the theory to actual business problems and challenges. In theory and in practice, Drucker has been a major influence on American business for the last fifty years.

In the minds of many, Drucker is the person who almost single-handedly invented the idea of the corporation. Prior to Drucker's introduction of the idea in *The Concept of the Corporation,* the study of business management was the study of individual problems such as accounting or materials handling. Drucker changed that view and suggested that the corporation was an entity, a whole, and needed to be managed as a whole, not as a series of isolated services or problems. Much of this book, and the ideas within it, arose from a massive study of General Motors under-taken in 1943. Having examined the operation of that company in great detail, and having reported that he thought it was managed chaotically, he set about developing a unified view of the corporation and its management. He did develop such a view and, in the process, suggested that the key institution and the chief influence on the future of the Western world would be the corporation, complete with assembly lines. This view of the corporation as a whole and his real-ization that the corporation was a major political, social, *and* economic force have made Drucker a major contributor to the present-day theory of business.

Drucker has written extensively in the area of management and has been a leader in the development of important concepts in specific areas of management. He was a leader, or at least an important forerunner, of the management system commonly called *management by objec-tives* (MBO). He first used the term in his book *The Practice of Management* and says he first heard it used by Alfred Sloan in the 1950s. Essentially, MBO tries to focus the attention of man-agers on their objectives. Managers of the old school had always asked themselves, "What do I do?" Drucker turned their attention from the process to the product or objective and said that the proper question is "What do I wish to accomplish?" That principle of management is now so commonplace in business and government that it seems always to have existed. Two concepts in the area of motivation were suggested by Drucker and developed by others. The first is the now famous "hygiene" theory of compensation, which says that wages and certain other condi-tions of employment do not cause high morale and motivation; instead they prevent low morale and allow other positive motivators to have an impact on the workers. These *hygiene factors* do not increase motivation and production, but motivation and the accompanying higher pro-duction cannot occur without them. Drucker also was an early contributor to the theories of motivation commonly called *Theory X* and *Theory Y,* which are widely discussed by writers such as Douglas McGregor. Theory X says that people are motivated best by threat and fear, by neg-ative or extrinsic motivation; Theory Y counters that people are better and further motivated by satisfaction of their basic needs and by appeals to their sense of participation and involvement. These ideas are well known and widely used today; Drucker was a major contributor to their early development.

But Drucker is no airy theorist incapable of practical work. He is a consultant whose services are heavily sought by industry and government. He is in such demand that he can charge $1,500 a day for his services and never lack clients. He is a consultant who does not try to provide clients with an answer to their problems. Rather, he tries to point out what the proper questions are and to help the clients find the answers. In early work with a manufacturer of glass bottles, he shocked the executive committee by asking them what business the firm was in. Silence followed the question, and then the chairman replied with a hint of anger in his voice, "We make glass bottles for soft-drink makers and others." "No," replied Drucker, "your business is not making bottles. You are in the packaging business." That answer, coming from an unusual perspective, greatly altered the executives' view of the company and its problems and led to solutions never suspected by the executive committee. Drucker constantly advises his clients to build from strength, to use the abilities that each person possesses, and to structure assignments so that no manager is forced to work long in an area where she or he is weak. Managers of the old school always looked at weaknesses and worked for their correction. Drucker said, "Forget the weaknesses. Put the person in a position where his weaknesses will not matter; use and develop the strengths of each employee."

Drucker has raised the art of consulting to new heights, making practical applications of the theories of management he developed. As a writer he has been an important contributor to the practical side of management. *The Effective Executive* is full of good advice to managers, advice useful on a day-to-day basis. His later book, *Management: Tasks—Responsibilities—Practices,* has in it long sections that are intensely practical. Even his more theoretical works have a practical bent. Arjay Miller, former president of Ford Motor Company, says that *The Concept of the Corporation* was "extremely useful in forming my judgments about what was needed at Ford. It was, by considerable margin, the most useful and pragmatic publication available and had a definite impact on the postwar organizational development within the Ford Motor Company" (*Drucker: The Man Who Invented the Corporate Society,* 1976, p. 32). Peter Drucker, philosopher, theorist, and practical authority, is, without doubt, a major figure in the history of American business and a man who helped to shape and form the corporation as we know it today.

Materials for this essay were taken from John J. Tarrant, *Drucker: The Man Who Invented the Corporate Society* (Boston: Cahners Books, Inc., 1976) and from Tony H. Bonaparte and John E. Flaherty, eds., *Peter Drucker: Contributions to Business Enterprise* (New York: New York University Press, 1970). Drucker's latest book is *Managing for the Future* (Truman Talley Books/Dutton, 1992).

Keep in mind the completed version of the paper that comes out of Step 6 is *not*—repeat, *not*—the final version of the paper. Step 6 produces a rough draft, a version suitable for revision and not much else. Think of that draft as a good start, but remember that it is still a long way from completion. Use the remaining steps of the writing process in revising your draft. Wait a day or two (if possible) between completing the draft and undertaking the revision.

Follow the seven steps in the revision process (pages 308–309) to produce the best paper possible.

Step 7. Assess the Thesis of the Draft

Basic Question: Is the thesis a proper expression of your knowledge on the subject?

Strategy: Read each supporting paragraph or section of the essay individually and write a topic sentence for each one. From the topic statements produce a thesis statement for the draft. Compare it to the original thesis. If there are differences between the two, create a new, better thesis. Omit the introduction from the outline; it does not provide support for the thesis.

Paragraph 2. Drucker invented the idea of the corporation as we know it.
Paragraph 3. Drucker has written extensively and developed important concepts in management.
Paragraph 4. Drucker is more than a theorist; he is a consultant who is much in demand.
Paragraph 5. Drucker has shown managers how to apply his ideas.

These five topic sentences agree with or add up to the thesis statement as originally written and refined. The thesis statement is an accurate reflection of the information gathered in Step 3.

Step 8. Assess the Content

Basic Question: Does each paragraph or section offer genuine support for the thesis?
Strategy: Check the topic statement for each paragraph or section to be sure each one supports the new thesis. Remove and replace any paragraph or section that does not support the thesis.

All the content seems to support the thesis. No material develops an idea outside of the thesis, and there is adequate support of the thesis.

Step 9. Assess the Order of Presentation

Basic Question: Does the order of presentation provide the reader with a logical progression or pathway through the essay?
Strategy: Try different orders of presentation, shifting sections around to see if you can find a better order than the one you used for the first finished draft.

The order of the paragraphs works from theory to practice and also has some movement forward in time. Thus the order seems to be logical.

Step 10. Assess the Paragraphs

Basic Questions: Is each paragraph unified and complete? Is each paragraph developed following the best possible method of development?
Strategy: Using the topic sentences from the sentence outline, check the content of the paragraph to be sure it develops one idea and only one idea. Check the content to be sure that the paragraph contains enough specific, concrete details to make the topic statement clear to the reader. Evaluate the introduction and conclusion separately as a single unit.

Introductions serve two basic purposes:

1. They catch the interest of the reader and identify the subject.
2. They state the thesis or set the direction for the essay.

The introduction tries to catch the interest of the reader by making a connection between students of business and Drucker, a preeminent teacher, writer and consultant.

The last sentence of the introduction suggests the thesis of the essay. The conclusion closes out the essay by offering a slightly rewritten version of the last sentence of the introduction.

The paragraphs of support each develop a single idea and have sufficient detail to make the paragraph complete.

Step 11. Correct the Mistakes in the Draft

Basic Question: What errors in grammar and mechanics do I need to correct?
Strategy: Read each sentence as an independent unit, starting at the end of the paper and working to the beginning. Reading "backward" in this fashion assures that you will not make mental corrections or assumptions as you read.

- Check each sentence for errors in completeness (Lesson 13), subject–verb agreement (Lesson 22), pronoun–antecedent agreement (Lesson 23), pronoun case (Lesson 24), dangling or misplaced modifiers (Lesson 14), and the use of prepositions (Lesson 25). (**Note:** As you find errors in your papers and as marked errors appear on papers returned to you, keep a record of them—either by putting a check in the appropriate lessons of this book or by marking your reference handbook. You will soon discover whether you have a tendency to repeat certain kinds of errors, and you simplify your proofreading by checking first for these errors. In a short time, you should be able to eliminate repeat faults from your writing.)
- Check each sentence for errors in punctuation; check for missing punctuation marks *and* for unneeded marks.
- Check for errors in mechanics, capitalization, and spelling.

Step 12. Write the Final Draft

Basic Question: What form shall I use for the final copy of the paper?
Strategy: Follow the guidelines for manuscript preparation specified by your teacher, printing or typing the final copy on plain white paper. Be sure to read the final copy carefully for errors.

Progress Tests

Subjects and Verbs; Parts of Speech
(Lessons 1, 2)

NAME _____ SCORE _____

Directions: Copy the subject of the sentence on the first line at the left and the verb on the second line.

_____ 1. Our first sight of the dilapidated house depressed us.
_____

_____ 2. There was no sign of life about the farm.
_____

_____ 3. Each of the tourists carried a small camera.
_____

_____ 4. Beyond the pines grew a few dwarf junipers.
_____

_____ 5. This was only the first of a long series of interruptions.
_____

_____ 6. Close to the summer camp is a nine-hole golf course.
_____

_____ 7. He's the only one of my teenage friends with an unlisted phone
_____   number.

_____ 8. By this time next week most of the vacationers will have left the
_____   island.

_____ 9. Not one of the villagers had received the proper legal notice.
_____

_____ 10. One of the bored clerks perfunctorily rubber-stamped Jane's
_____   passport.

_____ 11. Moments later a covey of quail rose from the large patch of
_____   weeds.

_____ 12. Next on the program will be three songs by the junior-high
_____   mixed chorus.

_____ 13. Finally, shortly before midnight, the last of the guests drove away.
_____

_____ 14. On the kitchen table lay the remnants of a quick lunch.
_____

_____ 15. Behind the shed was a short row of plum trees in full bloom.
_____

Directions: Each sentence contains two italicized words. In the space at the left, write one of the following numbers to identify the part of speech of each italicized word:

1. Noun   3. Verb   5. Adverb
2. Pronoun   4. Adjective   6. Preposition

_____ 1. The *address on* the letter was almost illegible.

_____ 2. The general *addressed* the troops and urged them *on.*

_____ 3. More money will be available at *some later* date.

_____ 4. *Later, some* of the guests washed the dishes.

_____ 5. In a firm *voice,* the sergeant demanded an *apology.*

_____ 6. The teacher *voiced* the opinion that Joe's speech was needlessly *apologetic.*

_____ 7. *Beyond* a doubt, the *arrival* of the Marines saved the day.

_____ 8. *Doubtlessly* a large crowd will await the candidate's *arrival.*

_____ 9. A *lovely* park is *close* to the campus.

_____ 10. The *alert* dog guarded the prisoner *closely.*

_____ 11. The sentinel was commended *for* his *alertness.*

_____ 12. *Everyone* thinks your action deserves a *reward.*

_____ 13. *Every* member of the squad must work *harder.*

_____ 14. The children *like* an *occasional* visit to the zoo.

_____ 15. *Occasionally* Julia's practical jokes *annoy* me.

_____ 16. We consider these interruptions only a *minor annoyance.*

_____ 17. We *worked throughout* the hot afternoon.

_____ 18. You should be commended for your *enthusiastic work* on the project.

_____ 19. *This* plan sounds completely *workable.*

_____ 20. *This* improvement cannot be made *without* additional funds.

NAME _____   SCORE _____

Directions: Identify the italicized word by writing one of the following abbreviations in the space at the left:

    S.C. [subjective complement]   I.O. [indirect object]

    D.O. [direct object]   O.C. [objective complement]

If the italicized word is *not* used as one of these complements, leave the space blank.

_____   1. Next Thursday afternoon might be a good *time* for our next meeting.

_____   2. You should have looked up the correct *spelling* of the word in your dictionary.

_____   3. I can have your meal *ready* for you in half an hour.

_____   4. The truck had been standing out in the sub-zero *weather* all week.

_____   5. One in high political office must avoid even a *hint* of scandal.

_____   6. In a hard-fought eighteen-hole playoff, Jeremy emerged the *winner*.

_____   7. The injured woman could give the *police* only a sketchy account of the accident.

_____   8. You should send the personnel *officer* a list of your previous employers.

_____   9. These nitrogen-filled bags will keep the potato chips *crisp*.

_____ 10. How *old* is that noisy, gas-guzzling car of yours?

_____ 11. How many *miles* per gallon do you get from your car?

_____ 12. The children were happily making *sandcastles* on the beach.

_____ 13. Henry made *me* an attractive offer for my used camcorder.

_____ 14. A fresh coat of paint would make this dingy room more *attractive*.

_____ 15. In Chinese cooking, dried sea cucumber is an important *ingredient*.

_____ 16. When will you send *me* a bill for your professional services?

359

_____ 17. Our new state officers are taking on an awesome *responsibility*.

_____ 18. "I want every one of these windows *spotless* by noon," said the sergeant.

_____ 19. "I want every one of these *windows* spotless by noon," said the sergeant.

_____ 20. Later the picture frames will be given three *coats* of varnish.

_____ 21. In his youth he had been looked upon as the town *buffoon*.

_____ 22. How *certain* can we be of the mayor's support for our project?

_____ 23. Which of these three samples do you consider the best *buy*?

_____ 24. *Which* of these three samples do you consider the best buy?

_____ 25. During the cook's testimony the accused man appeared *worried*.

_____ 26. After a noticeable pause the umpire called the pitch a *strike*.

_____ 27. All of us wish *you* a prosperous New Year.

_____ 28. The influx of refugees brought our *city* new problems.

_____ 29. How *wide* should we make the new path?

_____ 30. How wide should we make the new *path*?

_____ 31. Susan had been putting off a *visit* to her dentist.

_____ 32. Did Mrs. Camp offer you *any* of her famous blueberry pie?

_____ 33. Did Mrs. Camp offer *you* any of her famous blueberry pie?

_____ 34. I now feel *rested* enough for the climb to the summit.

_____ 35. How *cold* do the winters get in Anchorage?

_____ 36. *Whom* has the chairwoman chosen as her assistant?

_____ 37. This dessert must be kept very *cold* until serving time.

_____ 38. First of all, someone will give *you* an aptitude test.

_____ 39. First of all, you will be given an aptitude *test*.

_____ 40. You will find the climate here quite *moderate*.

NAME _____   SCORE _____

Directions: Each of the following sentences contains one subordinate clause. Use square brackets ([ ]) to mark the beginning and the end of each subordinate clause. Circle the subject and underline the verb of each subordinate clause. Identify the clause by writing in the space at the left one of the following abbreviations:

  Adv. [adverb clause]   Adj. [adjective clause]   N. [noun clause]

_____ 1. As the chorus marched onto the stage, a small dog followed.

_____ 2. There is much merit in what you propose.

_____ 3. The scenery collapsed at the moment when Gene stepped out from the wings.

_____ 4. Have you told your family of the plans you have made?

_____ 5. Anyone as old as your niece should know the alphabet.

_____ 6. Were I you, I'd apply for the scholarship.

_____ 7. It's unfortunate that you missed the class picnic.

_____ 8. We had nothing to eat except what was left over from lunch.

_____ 9. Theodore Roosevelt did several things that restored presidential leadership over Congress.

_____ 10. According to the legend, Medusa could change a man to stone as he was looking at her.

_____ 11. The dormitory where Julie lived housed several students from India.

_____ 12. This pamphlet explains on what bases the student essays should be judged.

_____ 13. The diamond ring Alice is wearing came originally from her aunt in Holland.

_____ 14. Do you sometimes wonder if you could handle a confining job in an office?

_____ 15. Beth looks after two small children whose mother works afternoons on the campus.

_____ 16. Mark's lawyer argued that his client was not financially liable for the damages.

_____ 17. An argument that Mark's lawyer presented questioned his financial liability for the damages.

_____ 18. Mark's lawyer's argument was that his client was not financially liable for the damages.

_____ 19. Mark's lawyer's argument that his client was not financially responsible for the damages impressed the jury.

_____ 20. Some of us wonder if you would be interested in the job.

361

Directions: The italicized material in each of these sentences is a subordinate clause. In the first space at the left, write **Adv., Adj.,** or **N.** to identify the clause. Within the italicized clause the word in boldface type is a complement. Identify it by writing in the second space at the left one of the following:

    S.C.   [subjective complement]   I.O.   [indirect object]
    D.O. [direct object]   O.C. [objective complement]

———— 1. One of Jeff's difficulties is *that he is painfully* **shy** *in the presence of strangers.*

———— 2. *If you follow these* **directions,** you will avoid really heavy traffic.

———— 3. After you leave this class, I hope *that you will practice* **what** *you have learned here.*

———— 4. The letter of introduction *that you sent* **me** proved very helpful.

———— 5. The car was registered in the name of Charles Albertson, a Britisher **whom** *the FBI had been investigating.*

———— 6. Beth has as yet told no one **who** *her bridesmaids will be.*

———— 7. We are living in a period *when crises are almost daily* **occurrences.**

———— 8. I'm afraid *that I caused my* **parents** *some real embarrassment.*

———— 9. The substitute teacher devised some activities *that kept the youngsters* **busy** *for half an hour.*

———— 10. Uncle Jake sputtered indignantly *when the waiter reminded* **him** *that the customary gratuity is fifteen percent.*

———— 11. The first fish ***that*** *Laura caught* was only five inches long.

———— 12. Several friends commented on *how* **happy** *Elaine looked.*

———— 13. I am sure *that the best seats for the concert are no longer* **available.**

———— 14. I think you should tell the mechanic *that you consider his bill unreasonably* **high.**

———— 15. Although Sue has shown me *where I had been making* **mistakes,** I'm still not entirely comfortable with my new computer.

———— 16. The board approved Mr. Barnes' suggestion *that the club make Ms. Thompson an honorary* **member.**

———— 17. An actress **whom** *none of us had ever seen before* played the part of the prosecuting attorney.

———— 18. The contractor could only guess at **what** *the total cost will be.*

———— 19. Ted has been studying the pamphlet *the traffic officer gave* **him.**

———— 20. Your theme will be improved, I think, *if you make your introductory paragraph somewhat* **shorter.**

NAME ——————————————————————————— SCORE ——————————

Directions: Each sentence contains one verbal phrase. Underline the phrase and, in the space at the left, write one of the following letters to identify the phrase:

G. [gerund phrase]   P.   [participial phrase]
I.   [infinitive phrase]   A.   [absolute phrase]

———————— 1. It might be a good idea to look into the Acme Company's offer more carefully.

———————— 2. Tomorrow being a holiday, I'll probably loaf most of the day.

———————— 3. Wayne's daily chores included looking after the boss's collection of African violets.

———————— 4. Do you think that granting Larsen another extension on the loan is wise?

———————— 5. I'll send you a ten-page brochure describing this tremendous real-estate opportunity.

———————— 6. Dad would sometimes let me sit on his lap while he was steering the car.

———————— 7. Troubled by these inaccuracies, one board member demanded that new auditors be hired.

———————— 8. Hatchwood was found guilty of sending an abusive, threatening letter to the mayor.

———————— 9. Can you show me how to put this new cartridge into my printer?

———————— 10. Over the weekend I did little except review my geology notes for the midterm examination.

———————— 11. Dad has done most of the cooking this week, Mother having been called for jury duty.

———————— 12. Perhaps your client might consider buying a somewhat larger piece of property.

———————— 13. The substitute teacher's first mistake was assigning the class some additional homework.

———————— 14. Another possibility would be to rent a car at the airport.

———————— 15. Three men found guilty of espionage were deported.

———————— 16. One of Paula's unusual hobbies is collecting old theater programs.

———————— 17. Keeping the younger children quiet during the long ceremony will tax your ingenuity.

———————— 18. One of the ushers will tell you when to march to the platform for your diploma.

———————— 19. Johnson returned to Memphis, having been unsuccessful in his search for a job in Atlanta.

———————— 20. Being a charitable person, Bascom graciously accepted the apology.

Directions: Each of the italicized words in the following sentences is used as a complement within a verbal phrase. In the first space at the left, write one of the following letters to identify the phrase:

    G. [gerund phrase]   P. [participial phrase]
    I. [infinitive phrase]   A. [absolute phrase]

In the second space, write one of the following numbers to identify the complement:

    1. Subjective complement   3. Indirect object
    2. Direct object   4. Objective complement

1. You can help the committee most by providing *transportation* for the out-of-town delegates.

2. It might be to our advantage to make *Chapman* a second offer for his property.

3. There will be celebrating in Coalville this week, the local baseball team having won the league *pennant.*

4. The excited children raced to the backyard, leaving the kitchen door wide *open.*

5. These graphic pictures succeeded in making the legislators *aware* of the need for immediate action.

6. The clerk, looking extremely *annoyed* by our insistence, finally summoned his supervisor.

7. How many *signatures* were you able to get for our petition?

8. "Remember, jurors," said the attorney, "that no one actually heard my client threaten the police *officer.*"

9. Beth's aunt looked after the children yesterday, our regular sitter being *unavailable.*

10. A new regulation making students *eligible* for membership on college committees is being considered.

11. Having already sent the *bank* the February payment, Tracy was puzzled by the delinquent notice.

12. Spending time with Uncle Josh is almost as unpleasant as visiting the *dentist.*

13. Feeling *sorry* for the embarrassed clerk, Mother paid for the broken cookies.

14. Have you ever thought of becoming an airline flight *attendant*?

15. I must find a new handball partner, Jeff Toner having left *town.*

NAME _____ SCORE _____

Directions: If a sentence is correct, write **C** in the space at the left. If you find a dangling modifier, underline it and write **W** in the space.

_____ 1. In purchasing a dog for a family pet, its background is as important to consider as its appearance.

_____ 2. A boat as light as this one can be upset by sitting on the side the way you are doing now.

_____ 3. Turning the car into the driveway, my purse fell to the floor and the contents scattered all over.

_____ 4. Dad is certainly busy enough this morning without asking him to drive us to the gym.

_____ 5. Dad is certainly busy enough this morning without being asked to drive us to the gym.

_____ 6. Upon reaching nine years of age, my family moved again, this time to Omaha.

_____ 7. Having bruised her ankle while taking inventory this morning, the boss told Edith to take the afternoon off.

_____ 8. I think I'll splurge tonight and order an expensive dessert, tomorrow being payday.

_____ 9. The tapes may be used again after rewinding them.

_____ 10. The tapes may be used again after being rewound.

_____ 11. After filing away all the loose magazines and pamphlets that I have acquired this year, my shelves look quite tidy.

_____ 12. To be assured of a capacity audience, the price of the tickets must be kept low.

_____ 13. The weather having turned cold and windy, we decided to take along our parkas.

_____ 14. Exhausted after the long hours of studying, Luke's head slowly nodded and finally came to rest on the open book.

_____ 15. Notice also that, by being reversed, this coat can be used in rainy weather.

_____ 16. Notice also that, by reversing it, this coat can be used in rainy weather.

_____ 17. Notice also that, by reversing it, you can use this coat in rainy weather.

_____ 18. Meeting Lois after work, she suggested that we see a movie.

_____ 19. Yesterday, while eating lunch on the patio, a flock of crows made a raucous racket.

_____ 20. Instead of leaving the lawn mower out in the rain, it should be put away in the carport.

365

Directions: Rewrite each of the following sentences twice:
    a. Change the dangler to a complete clause with subject and verb.
    b. Begin the main clause with a word that the dangler can logically modify.

1. Having been in the army for five years, my serious reading has been neglected.

    a. _____

    b. _____

2. While mowing the grass, the long-lost gold chain was found.

    a. _____

    b. _____

3. Before applying the first coat of paint, the surface should be sanded well.

    a. _____

    b. _____

4. To be assured of a successful cake, the flour must be sifted thoroughly.

    a. _____

    b. _____

5. Having turned the horses loose, they raced for the cool, inviting stream.

    a. _____

    b. _____

NAME _____   SCORE _____

Directions: Study these paired sentences for incompleteness, misplaced modifiers, faulty parallelism, and faulty comparisons. In the space at the left, write the letter that identifies the correct sentence.

_____ 1. a. Our service department uses only factory-approved materials.
         b. Our service department only uses factory-approved materials.

_____ 2. a. One of the laboratory assistants having had enough presence of mind to rush the injured student to the infirmary.
         b. One of the laboratory assistants had enough presence of mind to rush the injured student to the infirmary.

_____ 3. a. Although a sergeant's pay is lower than a commissioned officer, an officer has several additional expenses.
         b. Although a sergeant's pay is lower than a commissioned officer's, an officer has several additional expenses.

_____ 4. a. Our company specializes in cars of conservative design and which get good gas mileage.
         b. Our company specializes in cars that are conservatively designed and get good gas mileage.

_____ 5. a. Last semester Johnny had a better grade-point average than any other fellow in his fraternity.
         b. Last semester Johnny had a better grade-point average than any fellow in his fraternity.

_____ 6. a. Gladys only approves of a movie if it has a gloriously happy ending.
         b. Gladys approves of a movie only if it has a gloriously happy ending.

_____ 7. a. What started the argument was Fran's casual remark that hers was the fastest of any speedboat on the lake.
         b. What started the argument was Fran's casual remark that hers was the fastest of all the speedboats on the lake.

_____ 8. a. Jan had to reluctantly admit that all college students are not vitally interested in modern dance.
         b. Jan had to admit reluctantly that not all college students are vitally interested in modern dance.

_____ 9. a. It was one of the greatest thrills, if not the greatest thrill, of my life.
         b. It was one of the greatest, if not the greatest thrill of my life.

367

———— 10. a. Minnesota, I have been told, has more lakes than any state in the Union.
b. Minnesota, I have been told, has more lakes than any other state in the Union.

———— 11. a. The road is wide, hard-surfaced most of the way, and very few sharp curves.
b. The road is wide and hard-surfaced most of the way and has very few curves.

———— 12. a. The survey revealed that the salaries of the janitors were equal, and in some cases higher than the beginning teachers.
b. The survey revealed that the salaries of the janitors were equal to, and in some case higher than, those of the beginning teachers.

———— 13. a. The receptionist told me to return the questionnaire to her as soon as I finished it.
b. The receptionist told me to, as soon as I finished the questionnaire, return it to her.

———— 14. a. Some of the more vocal fans, still complaining about Coach Driscoll's lack of imagination and new ideas.
b. Some of the more vocal fans are still complaining about Coach Driscoll's lack of imagination and new ideas.

———— 15. a. "I admire neither the mayor's politics nor the people he associates with," said Ms. Ames.
b. "I neither admire the mayor's politics nor the people he associates with," said Ms. Ames.

———— 16. a. The predicted rainfall will be as heavy as that of the last few days, if not heavier.
b. The predicted rainfall will be as heavy as, if not heavier than, the last few days.

———— 17. a. One unusual bit of information being that Hong Kong boasts of more Rolls Royces per square foot than any city on earth.
b. One unusual bit of information is that Hong Kong boasts of more Rolls Royces per square foot than any other city on earth.

———— 18. a. Danny managed by December to pay off nearly half of his father's debts.
b. Danny managed to by December nearly pay off half of his father's debts.

———— 19. a. The accident happened because the street was icy and the other driver was inexperienced and careless.
b. The accident happened because the street was icy and because of the other driver's inexperience and carelessness.

———— 20. a. Whose ACT scores were best, yours or your twin brothers?
b. Whose ACT scores were better, yours or your twin brother's?

NAME _____   SCORE _____

Directions: Change the italicized sentence to the form indicated in the parentheses and write the two sentences as one sentence.

1. *The Jensens were in Hawaii on vacation.* They missed the dedication of the new court-house. (adverbial clause of reason) _____

   _____

2. *The Jensens were in Hawaii on vacation.* They missed the dedication of the new court-house. (absolute phrase) _____

   _____

3. *Brush the movable metal parts lightly with oil.* This will protect them against rust. (gerund phrase)_____

   _____

4. Brush the movable metal parts lightly with oil. *This will protect them against rust.* (infinitive phrase) _____

   _____

5. The survivors were flown to Ellertown by Ben Towle. *He is a local helicopter pilot.* (adjective clause) _____

   _____

6. The survivors were flown to Ellertown by Ben Towle. *He is a local helicopter pilot.* (appositive) _____

   _____

7. *I had read the editorial.* I decided to write a letter to the editor. (adverbial clause of time) _____

   _____

8. *I had read the editorial.* I decided to write a letter to the editor. (participial phrase)

   _____

   _____

9. *I had read the editorial.* I decided to write a letter to the editor. (prepositional phrase with gerund phrase object) _____

   _____

10. With our sandwiches we drank warm ginger ale. *Our meager supply of ice had melted.* (absolute phrase)_____

    _____

Directions: Rewrite each of the following numbered items as one complex sentence; show enough of the new sentence to illustrate the construction. In each case use the italicized subject and verb for the main clause. Use a variety of the subordinating units listed on the first page of Lesson 15.

1. I knew Stan Whipple in college. He is now a successful art auctioneer. *I was surprised* to learn this. _____

_____

2. I spent five hours typing my research paper and *I was* exhausted and so I went to bed before nine o'clock. _____

_____

3. This *quilt* has been in our family for over sixty years. It *was made* by my grandmother. She was twenty years old when she made it._____

_____

4. I finished high school in June. I didn't find a job that I liked. *I returned* to summer school for a course in word processing. Word processing is a valuable skill for anyone.

_____

_____

5. The recipe called for chopped pecans. *I used* chopped peanuts instead. Chopped peanuts are more suited to my limited budget. _____

_____

6. Hank and I attended college together. That was twenty years ago. *He seemed* completely lacking in ambition. But he was intelligent. _____

_____

7. Jackson is not a very strong student, but he is a good basketball player and so *I suppose* he'll have no trouble getting into college somewhere._____

_____

8. Mother is usually easygoing. She rarely raises her voice. *She surprised* the family. She announced that this year she was not cooking a big Thanksgiving Day dinner. _____

_____

9. Duncan graduated from college with a degree in pharmacy. But now *he manages* a seed company. The company is large. It is located near Lompoc, California. _____

_____

10. Laura's uncle learned that she was majoring in journalism. *He sent* her a letter. It was stern and unequivocal. It ordered her to change her major to law. _____

_____

NAME _____ SCORE _____

Directions: In each sentence a ∧ marks a point of coordination between (1) two verbs with a coordinating conjunction, (2) two independent clauses with a coordinating conjunction, or (3) two independent clauses without a coordinating conjunction. In the space at the left, write one of the following:

    0 (no punctuation is needed)
    C (a comma is needed)
    S (a semicolon is needed)

_____ 1. "I have a new machine here," said the mechanic ∧ "in two minutes it will analyze your car's exhaust."

_____ 2. Dr. Ellis's lecture must have impressed her audience ∧ for dozens of people with questions crowded around her after she finished.

_____ 3. Many years ago Jerome had fished for bass and muskellunge in northern Minnesota ∧ in those days no one worried about polluted lakes and streams.

_____ 4. Ms. Brady's comments on student themes were sometimes cruel ∧ and did not endear her to the students in pre-engineering.

_____ 5. The living conditions of the people are improving slowly ∧ but there is little hope for significant change.

_____ 6. The party must have been rather unexciting ∧ for my roommate was home and in bed by ten o'clock.

_____ 7. The day-long meeting was routine and uneventful ∧ for the visiting students from India it must have seemed quite dull.

_____ 8. Under the new law automobile drivers over seventy years of age must pass a test ∧ otherwise their current licenses will be revoked.

_____ 9. This set of matched golf clubs normally sells for $350 ∧ but during our anniversary sale it is available for only $265.

_____ 10. This set of matched golf clubs normally sells for $350 ∧ during our anniversary sale, however, it is available for only $265.

_____ 11. This set of matched golf clubs normally sells for $350 ∧ but during our anniversary sale is available for only $265.

_____ 12. A teenager carrying a noisy boom box lurched past Mrs. Howe ∧ and sat down in the only unoccupied seat in the bus.

_____ 13. For several months General Benham had been receiving anonymous threats over the telephone ∧ but had not reported them to the police.

_____ 14. For several months General Benham had been receiving anonymous threats over the telephone ∧ but he had not reported them to the police.

_____ 15. The ill-mannered guard neither answered Marcy's question ∧ nor invited her to step inside out of the rain.

_____ 16. The ill-mannered guard did not answer Marcy's question ∧ nor did he invite her to step inside out of the rain.

_____ 17. The ill-mannered guard did not answer Marcy's question ∧ moreover, he did not invite her to step inside out of the rain.

_____ 18. This television by itself sells for $672 ∧ with its matching stand the price is $730.

_____ 19. The advertised price is $730 ∧ but without the matching stand the price is only $672.

_____ 20. Ms. Shaw has used these videos in her seventh-grade class ∧ she reports that the student response was good.

_____ 21. Ms. Shaw has used these videos in her seventh-grade class ∧ and reports that the student response was good.

_____ 22. Ms. Shaw has used these videos in her seventh-grade class ∧ the student response, she reports, was good.

_____ 23. Our special this week is the four-head VCR pictured in our advertisement ∧ we are offering it at the low price of $109.

_____ 24. You'll like its on-screen menu system ∧ and inexperienced users will appreciate its easy-to-understand panel display.

_____ 25. Ms. Stern comes to our firm well-recommended ∧ for the past four years she headed a work force of nearly seventy people.

_____ 26. Ms. Stern should go far with our firm ∧ for she is intelligent and hard-working.

_____ 27. Dean Lewis accepted the students' petition ∧ and promised that he would study it carefully.

_____ 28. *Ilex opaca* is an American holly with glossy leaves and red berries ∧ the foliage and berries are often used for Christmas decorations.

_____ 29. Juniors in this program normally take History 350 ∧ however, Dean Tate has allowed me to substitute Political Science 107.

_____ 30. A limited number of viewers have called this movie a masterpiece ∧ but many others are bothered by its ambiguities.

Progress Test 9

Punctuation: All Marks (Lessons 17–20)

NAME _____ SCORE _____

Directions: The following sentences contain fifty numbered spots between words or beneath words. (The number is beneath the word when the punctuation problem involves the use of an apostrophe in that word.) In the correspondingly numbered spaces at the left, write C if the punctuation is correct or W if it is wrong.

1. _____   (1) Had we known that the lecture would attract such a large audience; we
                  ₁
2. _____   would have scheduled it for Farwell Hall, which has three hundred seats.
                  ₂
3. _____   (2) The average tourists' equipment consists of: a camera, a raincoat, dark
                  ₃   ₄
4. _____   glasses, and a guidebook.
5. _____   (3) Geoffrey Chaucer, who wrote *The Canterbury Tales,* is known for his
                  ₅
6. _____   realism, his humor, and his accurate observation.
                  ₆
7. _____   (4) The 1928 Olympic Games, by the way, made history for competitive
                  ₇   ₈
8. _____   events for women were introduced.
9. _____   (5) Mother was not amused when she discovered that the children had made
10. _____   a snowman and had used one of her new golf balls for it's nose.
                  ₉   ₁₀
11. _____   (6) Frank Duveneck, a portrait painter who was born in Kentucky on
12. _____   October 9, 1848, eventually settled in Cincinnati where he died in 1919.
                  ₁₁   ₁₂
13. _____   (7) "I distinctly heard someone say, 'What's that guy talking about?' " said the
                  ₁₃   ₁₄
14. _____   new teacher.
15. _____   (8) If you didn't draw this hilarious caricature of me, I wonder who's
                  ₁₅
16. _____   responsible for it?
                  ₁₆
17. _____   (9) "Please remember, my dear Miss. Scroggs," said the secretary, "that a
                  ₁₇
18. _____   neat tidy appearance is one of the best recommendations."
                  ₁₈
19. _____   (10) Dark clouds crept up from the west, and the hot, sultry air was ominously
                  ₁₉   ₂₀
20. _____   quiet.
21. _____   (11) When Mr. Davis finally does resign the position will probably be filled
                  ₂₁
22. _____   by one of the boss's nephews.
                  ₂₂

373

23. _____ (12) When we lived there, the village was peaceful and restful, now it has been
23

24. _____ ruined by noisy ill-mannered tourists.
24

25. _____ (13) Mr. Oldham's assessment for the new paving on Elm Street being, in his

26. _____ opinion, too high; he protested to Ned Lane, a member of the council.
25   26

27. _____ (14) "Responsibility for the seating arrangement at the banquet will be

28. _____ someone else's, not your's," the chairperson told Edith.
27   28

29. _____ (15) A short, quite pathetic appeal was made to the mayor by an elderly
29

30. _____ woman whose property tax had been nearly doubled.
30

31. _____ (16) A fiery, political speech was made by our senior county commis-
31

32. _____ sioner who hopes to be reelected.
32

33. _____ (17) "This car seems to be pulling slightly to the left, I wonder if one of the
33

34. _____ tires is going flat?" said Marge.
34

35. _____ (18) Epictetus, a Greek Stoic who was originally a slave, taught in Rome until
35

36. _____ A.D. 90 when the emperor Domitian banished all philosophers.
36

37. _____ (19) This week you'll find real bargains at Shops-Mart in: light fixtures, paint,
37

38. _____ linens, and childrens' shoes.
38

39. _____ (20) "My briefcase isn't here in the car," said McCall; "I wonder if I could have
39

40. _____ left it in your office."
40

41. _____ (21) "We had a bad storm when I was out fishing in the bay two week's ago,"
41

42. _____ said Mark, who knew that Jo was a nervous landlubber.
42

43. _____ (22) The last bus from Lawrenceville having arrived with no passengers, Jim
43

44. _____ and Trudy walked slowly to their car and drove back to the farm.
44

45. _____ (23) "Let's drop the matter," said Anne impatiently. "After all these problems
45

46. _____ are nobody's business but mine."
46

47. _____ (24) Louisa is writing a book about her paternal grandmother who was a
47

48. _____ vigorous worker for womens' rights.
48

49. _____ (25) From the very first difficulties beset the planned expansion; finally
49   50

50. _____ resulting in the withdrawal of funds by the two principal backers.

NAME _____ SCORE _____

Directions: The following sentences contain fifty numbered spots between words or beneath words. (The number is beneath the word when the punctuation problem involves the use of an apostrophe in that word.) In the correspondingly numbered spaces at the left, write **C** if the punctuation is correct or **W** if it is wrong.

1. _____   (1) The treasurer's report was so long, so disorganized, and so dull that some
 1 2

2. _____   of the listeners dozed off at times.

3. _____   (2) At daybreak a crow parked itself outside our balcony and kept us awake

4. _____   with it's loud   raucous scolding.
 3 4

5. _____   (3) The dodo and the roc, both commonly found only in crossword puz-

6. _____   zles, are similar in some respects, and different in others.
 5 6

7. _____   (4) The dodo, a bird that is now extinct, actually lived in Mauritius   but the
 7

8. _____   roc lived only in people's imagination.
 8

9. _____   (5) Rotary International was founded in Chicago, Illinois, in 1905, it now has
 9 10

10. _____   chapters in more than seventy countries.

11. _____   (6) The Jensens sat in the airport for six long, tedious hours; their flight being
 11 12

12. _____   delayed by what was called an equipment shortage.

13. _____   (7) Your equipment should consist of: heavy hiking boots, a waterproof
 13

14. _____   tarpaulin, and plenty of warm clothing.
 14

15. _____   (8) Today I received from a travel agency a new calendar; on the cover
 15

16. _____   theres a beautiful picture of the Bay of Naples.
 16

17. _____   (9) "A team that wont be beaten can't be beaten," said Coach Wellby, who is
 17 18

18. _____   hopelessly addicted to clichés.

19. _____ (10) In the outer lobby is a huge oil portrait of the founder of the firm; his
 19

20. _____   stern   humorless face adding to the austerity of the surroundings.
 20

21. _____ (11) The midterm test will cover the following materials: the class lectures to
 21

22. _____   date and chapters 2, 3, 4, and 5 of the text.
 22

23. _____ (12) The play has received good reviews from the critics, I suppose it's
24. _____   impossible to get tickets at this late date.
25. _____ (13) "You agree with me, dont you," Jean answered, "that my suggestion was a
26. _____   reasonable one."
27. _____ (14) For most of this summer Martha has been borrowing one of my
28. _____   bikes; her's is now too old and too rusty to be safe.
29. _____ (15) Flight 723, which is scheduled to arrive here at 4:12 P.M. has been delayed
30. _____   at Topeka, Kansas, because of bad weather.
31. _____ (16) Coleman, the third baseman, threw down his glove, and screamed that the
32. _____   runner hadn't touched the base.
33. _____ (17) The art teacher, Miss. Philbrick, asked Janey if she had ever done any
34. _____   professional modeling?
35. _____ (18) Our neighbors, the Thomas's, have a new television set that has a much
36. _____   larger picture than our's.
37. _____ (19) The notice on the bulletin board announced the new schedule: breakfast
38. _____   at six-thirty, lunch at eleven-thirty, and dinner at six.
39. _____ (20) "After all my friends will help me out of this, they know that my word is
40. _____   as good as my bond," said Mr. Winther.
41. _____ (21) Julia's cousin Larry studied at Heidelberg, where he became well
42. _____   acquainted with Judge Coleman's only grandson Herman.
43. _____ (22) "Judd shouldn't have taken offense at my remark, I merely asked him if he
44. _____   was made up for a masquerade party?" said Eugene.
45. _____ (23) Dr. Andrews has written articles about child psychology but his own
46. _____   childrens' behavior in a group is far from admirable.
47. _____ (24) "The story line, the costumes, the music—everything must be changed,"
48. _____   said Cecil Burbank, the new director.
49. _____ (25) Laura is the kind of person who shops downtown until five oclock, and
50. _____   then complains about the crowded condition of the bus on her ride
                     home.

NAME _____   SCORE _____

Directions: Study these sentences for (1) the correct form of a principal part of a verb, (2) the correct subject–verb agreement, and (3) the correct tense of a verb. Underline every incorrect verb and write the correct form in the space at the left. No sentence contains more than two incorrect verb forms. Some sentences may be correct.

_____ 1. After setting in the hot sun all day, every one of the petunia plants
_____   I put out this morning has wilted badly.

_____ 2. Neither Dr. Alterton nor his assistant were able to make sense of
_____   the peculiar symbols written on the wooden slab.

_____ 3. Has either of your two roommates begun to be interviewed for a
_____   job after graduation?

_____ 4. One story that I've heard is that Judge Trowbridge payed back to
_____   the bank all of the money that his nephew had stole.

_____ 5. The mayor, along with three of her top aides, has been asked to
_____   set at the head table with the visiting dignitaries.

_____ 6. "I been hunting in these woods for fifty years but never before
_____   seen a critter like that one," said the guide.

_____ 7. Stan walked into the principal's office, laid his books on the table,
_____   and says, "I've come to the end of my rope."

_____ 8. There was only seven seconds left in the game when Pete West let
_____   fly from midcourt and sank the game-winning three-pointer.

_____ 9. A news story reports that the appearance of mysterious patterns
_____   in wheat fields have become a summer diversion in southern
_____   England.

_____ 10. After the eight-o'clock bell had rang, Mr. Towle said, "The fact
_____   that the weather is bad don't mean that we won't hold classes
_____   today."

_____ 11. I like to go to the movie with you, but I saw that show last month
_____   in Dallas.

_____ 12. Don't it worry you that the price of your shares of stock have
_____   fallen by nearly thirty percent in four months?

_____ 13. Seated behind us were a woman with four children who noisily
_____   ate candy and drunk pop during the entire movie.

_____ 14. After the other officers had given their reports, the colonel said,
_____   "The evidence has shown that neither of the two incidents were
_____   the result of equipment failure."

_____ 15. There's been so many improvements made at the Lakeside Inn
_____ that it has became one of the most popular resorts in the state.

_____ 16. As we rose to leave the auditorium, Bart remarked, "I think our
_____ speaker could have chose a livelier topic to discuss."

_____ 17. In July heat records were broke on two days, but during August
_____ the range of temperatures were normal for the season.

_____ 18. Julie had just lain down for a short rest when her neighbor came
_____ running over and tells her that there was a couple of raccoons in
her vegetable garden.

_____ 19. The Associated Press reports that the search for possible sur-
_____ vivors of the earthquake have been slowed because of repeated
aftershocks that have shaken the area.

_____ 20. The magnitude of our budgetary problems have left a shadow
_____ across the legislative process; no wonder that the confidence in
our lawmakers has sank to new low levels.

_____ 21. The advertisement announcing that our entire stock of Nature's
_____ Own Vitamins are on sale has drawn huge crowds.

_____ 22. "It's been a hectic day," said Beth. "The two-o'clock bell has
_____ already rung, and I haven't eaten a bite of lunch yet."

_____ 23. "Commissioner Bunker's standards for the behavior of public
_____ servants, including himself," the editor had written, "has always
been minimal."

_____ 24. "Neither of the two Ford trucks in our lot have been drove more
_____ than forty thousand miles," said the salesperson.

_____ 25. The number of fatal accidents at the corner of Fifth and Oak has
_____ risen alarmingly over the past two years.

_____ 26. In the lobby there is a sofa and several overstuffed chairs where
_____ patients can set and read while waiting to see the dentist.

_____ 27. The leader of the gang, along with two of his followers, were lying
_____ wounded on the floor of the garage.

_____ 28. Not one of the paintings that were taken from the museum dur-
_____ ing the robbery last summer have been recovered.

_____ 29. The girls abandoned the sinking canoe and swam safely to shore,
_____ but unfortunately their pet dog drownded.

_____ 30. Has either your teacher or the school counselor spoke to you
_____ about applying for a scholarship?

NAME _____ SCORE _____

Directions: Study the following sentences for poorly used pronouns. Look for wrong case forms, misspelled possessives, vague or inexact references. Circle each incorrect pronoun. In the space at the left of each pair of sentences, write the letter that identifies the correct sentence.

_____ 1. a. In years past, the personnel director of the laboratory would inquire about an applicant's personal life, including such things as who your associates were.
  b. In years past, the personnel director of the laboratory would inquire about an applicant's personal life, including such things as who were his or her associates.

_____ 2. a. Every guy at the dorm except Jacobs, Peterson, and me has already had his spring-term class schedule approved.
  b. Every guy at the dorm except Jacobs, Peterson, and I has already had their spring-term class schedule approved.

_____ 3. a. Four of us girls got in line for the ticket sale at seven in the morning, and then we were told that the office wouldn't open until noon.
  b. Four of we girls got in line for the ticket sale at seven in the morning, and then they told us that the office wouldn't open until noon.

_____ 4. a. "I'm supposed to ride in Phil's car," said Lew, "but, just between you and I, I'd prefer to ride in someone elses."
  b. "I'm supposed to ride in Phil's car," said Lew, "but, just between you and me, I'd prefer to ride in someone else's."

_____ 5. a. "I plan to become a forester," said Tom, "because it allows you to do your bit for saving the environment."
  b. "I plan to become a forester," said Tom, "because work in forestry allows a person to do his or her bit for saving the environment."

_____ 6. a. It said on television that the finalists, whomever they are, will meet for five games in Las Vegas.
  b. According to a television report, the finalists, whoever they are, will meet for five games in Las Vegas.

_____ 7. a. Ginny told her best friend Marge that she should lose at least five pounds.
  b. Ginny told her best friend Marge "I should lose at least five pounds."

_____ 8. a. "Dad is a dedicated fisherman, and he keeps trying to get my sister and me interested in fishing," said Mary Jane.
  b. "Dad is a dedicated fisherman, and he keeps trying to get my sister and I interested in it," said Mary Jane.

_____ 9. a. Mr. Capri's lawyer produced two witnesses who he said had been present when the alleged bribe offer was made.
  b. Mr. Capri's lawyer produced two witnesses whom he said had been present when the alleged bribe offer was made.

_____ 10. a. "All of us administrators are pleased," said Dean Powers, "that the college is attracting many adults into its Retraining Program."
   b. "The college is attracting many adults into their Retraining Program, which pleases all of we administrators," said Dean Powers.

_____ 11. a. A tourist whom we met at a filling station in Plainview told us that the highway for the next two miles is being resurfaced.
   b. A tourist who we met at a filling station in Plainview told us that they are resurfacing the highway for the next two miles.

_____ 12. a. My younger brother is a better mathematician than me, principally because he has taken several courses in it.
   b. My younger brother is a better mathematician than I, principally because he has taken several courses in mathematics.

_____ 13. a. It clearly states in the application form that you must provide a recent black-and-white picture of yourself.
   b. The application form clearly states that applicants must provide black-and-white pictures of themselves.

_____ 14. a. The person whom the Speaker of the House appoints to make this investigation must reconcile himself or herself to a thankless chore.
   b. The person who the Speaker of the House appoints to make this investigation must reconcile themself to a thankless chore.

_____ 15. a. The car ahead of our's was weaving so erratically that I didn't want to try to pass him.
   b. The car ahead of ours was weaving so erratically that I didn't want to try to pass it.

_____ 16. a. At the first pep rally the cheerleaders told we freshmen to wear our green T-shirts at every game.
   b. At the first pep rally the cheerleaders told us freshmen to wear our green T-shirts at every game.

_____ 17. a. "Is there anyone who you really think might get more votes than I in the primary election?" asked ex-Senator Wiley.
   b. "Is there anyone whom you really think might get more votes than me in the primary election?" asked ex-Senator Wiley.

_____ 18. a. The three new owners of the Busy Bee Store maintain that you can't find another merchant in town who's prices are lower than their's.
   b. The three new owners of the Busy Bee Store maintain that there isn't another merchant in town whose prices are lower than theirs.

_____ 19. a. Your brother likes to tease you. If it wasn't he who sent you the comic valentine, who do you think it might have been?
   b. Your brother likes to tease you. If it wasn't him who sent you the comic valentine, whom do you think it might have been?

_____ 20. a. "This notebook must be someone else's," said Martin. "Mine has an American flag stenciled on its cover."
   b. "This notebook must be someone elses," said Martin. "Mine has an American flag stenciled on it's cover."

NAME _____ SCORE _____

Directions: In the space at the left, write the *number* of the correct form given in parentheses.

_____ 1. I (1. couldn't have   2. couldn't of) finished typing my term paper even if I
_____   had worked on it (1. steady   2. steadily) until midnight.

_____ 2. (1. Let us   2. Let's us) put in an extra hour on this project and finish it
_____   (1. faster   2. more faster) than in the time allotted for it.

_____ 3. "(1. Where   2. Where at) can I buy some of (1. them   2. those) huge sun-
_____   glasses like the ones you are wearing?" Ms. Tower asked Letty.

_____ 4. "I have no doubt," said Mrs. Lathrop, "(1. but what   2. that) my daughter
_____   will finally select the (1. more   2. most) expensive of the two dresses."

_____ 5. Our committee got a (1. real   2. really) early start, and by noon we had
_____   addressed (1. most   2. almost) all of the political pamphlets.

_____ 6. Coach Treadwell is (1. sure   2. surely) happy about the large (1. amount
_____   2. number) of junior-college transfers who turned out for the team.

_____ 7. "Old Hank Jones (1. use to   2. used to) appear (1. regular   2. regularly) at
_____   our church functions," said Mrs. Walker, "but I haven't seen him in months."

_____ 8. Frankly, I am (1. kind of   2. rather) surprised that our girls' team did as
_____   (1. good   2. well) as they did in the regional tournament.

_____ 9. As I stood up ready to get (1. off   2. off of) the bus, a fire engine swerved
_____   around the corner and came (1. awful   2. very) close to us.

_____ 10. (1. Due to   2. Because of) his bad eyesight, Mel didn't do very (1. good
_____   2. well) on the map-reading part of the test.

_____ 11. "I know that your uncle will feel (1. bad   2. badly) if he doesn't receive an
_____   (1. invite   2. invitation) to the wedding," said Aunt Yolanda.

_____ 12. "I think (1. this   2. this here) purple scarf would look (1. good   2. well)
_____   with your new suit," said the salesperson.

_____ 13. Judged on (1. this   2. these) new and stricter criteria, Ludlow's essay is
_____   clearly the (1. better   2. best) of the two finalists.

381

_____ 14. From his report, Jack sounded (1. as if   2. like) he had a (1. real   2. really)
_____ good time on his trip to Florida.

_____ 15. I wish Professor Lynn would talk (1. more slower   2. more slowly); I (1. can
_____ hardly   2. can't hardly) take notes when he is racing to finish his lecture.

_____ 16. The thing (1. that   2. what) really surprised the firefighters is that no one
_____ was injured (1. bad   2. badly) in the spectacular fire.

_____ 17. A (1. couple   2. couple of) friends and I work out (1. regular   2. regularly)
_____ at the company's gymnasium.

_____ 18. (1. Lots   2. Many) of the native people have (1. emigrated   2. immigrated)
_____ because of the crop failures in their homeland.

_____ 19. That flower that you call an evening primrose (1. sure   2. surely) smells
_____ (1. sweet   2. sweetly).

_____ 20. The reason the deal fell through is (1. because   2. that) at the last minute
_____ the seller increased the price (1. considerable   2. considerably).

_____ 21. (1. Light-complexioned   2. Light-complected) people like you and me
_____ (1. shouldn't   2. hadn't ought to) stay out in the hot sun on a day like today.

_____ 22. (1. Because of   2. Due to) the infection in his eye, Darrell hasn't been able
_____ to study very (1. good   2. well) this week.

_____ 23. Now that he has lost weight, Graham looks quite (1. different   2. differ-
_____ ently) (1. from   2. than) the way he looks in these old photographs.

_____ 24. "I'm (1. enthused   2. enthusiastic) about my new job," said Malcolm. "It is
_____ interesting, and, best of all, it pays (1. good   2. well)."

_____ 25. By your answer to Mike's question, did you mean to (1. imply   2. infer) that
_____ you feel (1. bad   2. badly) about the election results?

NAME _____ SCORE _____

Directions: Each sentence has two italicized words or expressions. If you think that a word or expression is inappropriate in serious writing, write a correct form in the space at the left. If a word or expression is correct, write **C** in the space.

_____ 1. *Lying* at the side of the road was a plastic bag full of garbage that
_____   some tourist had apparently thrown from *their* car.

_____ 2. In this senior class there *are* only four or five people *whom* I think
                    are capable of successful work at the graduate level.

_____ 3. The reward money was divided *among* four of *we* hikers who had
_____   turned in the fire alarm.

_____ 4. The mechanic *lay* down the wrench and explained to Roger and
_____   *I* what had to be done and what it would cost.

_____ 5. We were *plenty* surprised when we learned that there *was* only
_____   one teacher and eighteen pupils in the entire school.

_____ 6. "I doubt that fellows as short as you and *me* can play basketball
_____   *good* enough to earn a letter," Al said to Jeremy.

_____ 7. No one at headquarters was *suppose to* know *who* the new agent
_____   was reporting to in Berlin.

_____ 8. Sergeant Gross did not *suspicion* that quite a few of *we* men had
_____   been sneaking off to the movies in the village.

_____ 9. A gregarious person like Andy seems able to make *themself* feel
_____   right at home almost *anywheres.*

_____ 10. By the end of the second week every freshman should have *cho-*
_____   *sen* which social club *they* will join.

_____ 11. "Who can be *enthused* about *those kind* of video games?" asked
_____   Claire.

_____ 12. Just *like* I had predicted, after the speech there *wasn't* more than
_____   three or four questions from members of the audience.

_____ 13. Dan was *sure* surprised to learn that everyone in class except
_____   Marcia Lerner and *him* would have to take another test.

_____ 14. The reason there is a critical shortage is *because* neither of the two
_____   state-supported universities *is* turning out qualified engineers.

_____ 15. The thief, *whoever* he was, had apparently left the warehouse
_____   parking lot in a small truck that he had *stolen* earlier in the day.

_____ 16. "These people speak a language that is strange to us," said the
_____   guide, "but in truth they are really not much different *from* you
                             and *I*."

_____ 17. *Has* either of the two plum trees you planted *began* to bear fruit
_____   yet?

_____ 18. *Due to* the icy condition of the roads, all of *we* latecomers were
_____   given excuses today.

_____ 19. The sale of season tickets for basketball games this year *has*
_____   declined *considerable*.

_____ 20. The missing climber's backpack was found *lying* at the bottom of
_____   a small crevasse, where it had apparently *lain* for several days.

_____ 21. Every one of the stocks that you recommended to my wife and
_____   *me* last year *has* declined in value.

_____ 22. All of us agree that *whoever* took the money from the Christmas
_____   Fund was *real* desperate.

_____ 23. The committee's choice for chairperson was Marge Bingham, not
_____   *I*, in spite of the fact that my experience is much broader than
                             her's.

_____ 24. Just between you and *me*, my parents don't approve of *me* post-
_____   poning my senior year of college.

_____ 25. *Whom* do you suppose could have written *them* insulting anony-
_____   mous letters to the superintendent?

Spelling Rules; Words Similar in Sound (Lesson 27)

NAME _____ SCORE _____

Directions: In the spaces at the left, copy the correct forms given in parentheses.

_____
_____
1. We took a cab to the auditorium, but when we arrived the (conference, conferrence) had (already, all ready) begun.

_____
_____
2. The homemade warning device, although far from perfect, is (quiet, quite) (servicable, serviceable).

_____
_____
3. The fast-talking salesman maintained that he was a (personal, personnel) friend of several New York (financeirs, financiers).

_____
_____
4. "In my lifetime I (seized, siezed) many golden (opportunities, opportunitys) but couldn't hold on to them," Mr. Caldwell answered.

_____
_____
5. "I'd hardly call this an (unforgetable, unforgettable) (dining, dinning) experience," said Sal as she set aside the bowl of luke-warm soup.

_____
_____
6. "(Neither, Niether) of your two laboratory experiments was (completely, completly) satisfactory," said the lab assistant.

_____
_____
7. The Acme Corporation has donated to the city a very (desirable, desireable) building (cite, sight, site) for the proposed convention center.

_____
_____
8. "Just to be in the (presence, presents) of such a (fameous, famous) basketball star is a great honor," said the youngster.

_____
_____
9. I haven't seen my neighbors lately; in all (likelihood, likelyhood, liklihood, liklyhood) (their, there, they're) out of town.

_____
_____
10. Some people (beleive, believe) that the city engineer will (altar, alter) the specifications in order to attract more bidders.

_____
_____
11. Remember, (its, it's) considered good manners to (complement, compliment) the hostess after a good meal.

_____
_____
12. With my two time-consuming jobs, I assure you that I have no (leisure, liesure) time (activities, activitys) to speak of.

_____ 13. "Our negotiators managed to (affect, effect) an (advantageous, advantagous) settlement with the union," said Mr. Siebert.

_____ 14. (Unfortunately, Unfortunatly), similar (incidence, incidents) are being reported to the police with increasing frequency.

_____ 15. The judge (adviced, advised) the quarreling neighbors to settle their problem (peacably, peaceably) without outside help.

_____ 16. This semester Sherwood's work in mathematics has (shone, shown) a (noticable, noticeable) improvement.

_____ 17. The (principal, principle) of the school was not (deceived, decieved) by young Thompson's outlandish story.

_____ 18. After confessing to the theft, the man (lead, led) the officers to the place in the barren (desert, dessert) where he had buried the loot.

_____ 19. "I think (your, you're) being very (courageous, couragous)," said Belinda to the young firefighter.

_____ 20. "Frankly, Alice," said Marlene, "I think that your new friend is (outrageously, outragously) (conceited, concieted)."

_____ 21. The three (attornies, attorneys) representing our competitor were much younger (than, then) I had expected.

_____ 22. The bank president rewarded the (casheir, cashier) (who's, whose) quick thinking had thwarted the holdup.

_____ 23. For her (neice's, niece's) birthday Ms. Simpson sent her a box of monogrammed (stationary, stationery).

_____ 24. "I predict that our (cheif, chief) of police will (loose, lose) his job after the next election," said Alderman Whiteside.

_____ 25. After (poring, pouring) over dozens of books in the library, I feel that I have done a (thorough, through) job of researching the matter.

NAME _____   SCORE _____

Directions: Each sentence contains two words from the first half of the spelling list. In each of these words at least one letter is missing. Write the words, correctly spelled, in the spaces at the left.

_____   1. The new dorm__tory, which will be finished by next fall, will
_____   ac__modate three hundred students.

_____   2. I am cer__n that you and your family will enjoy your tour of
_____   Great Brit__n.

_____   3. The results of most of our school's ath__tic contests for the past
_____   two seasons have been dis__pointing.

_____   4. In class were between thirty-five and fo__ty enthu__tic students.
_____

_____   5. The careless, a__ward boy accident__y broke one of the jars.
_____

_____   6. The new clerk in the office is sometimes embar__sed by his glar-
_____   ing mistakes in gram__r.

_____   7. We were dis__atisfied with the poor service and the ex__rbitant
_____   price of the meals.

_____   8. Caldwell is building a large apartment complex ac__oss the street
_____   from a large cem__tery.

_____   9. Janice is an exception__y good student of for__n languages.
_____

_____   10. Delegates are arriving for an international confer__nce con-
_____   cerned with protecting the env__nment.

387

Directions: These sentences contain thirty italicized words from the first half of the spelling list. A sentence may have no misspelled words, one misspelled word, or two misspelled words. Underline each misspelled word and write it, correctly spelled, in a space at the left.

———————————
———————————
1. *Confidentially,* Mr. Burke's resignation *dosen't* make any real *difference* in our company's long-range plans.

———————————
———————————
2. Although only an *amateur,* Ms. Davis has *aquired* a collection of early-American pewter that is *amoung* the best in the nation.

———————————
———————————
3. *Finally,* late in *Febuary,* an *eminent* retired general spoke out strongly against the proposed treaty.

———————————
———————————
4. One of the *candidates* for mayor gave the *committee* a lengthy *explaination* of his financial dealings.

———————————
———————————
5. This applicant is an *efficient* worker whose wide *experience* makes her *especialy* well equipped to replace Thornton.

———————————
———————————
6. *Apparently* the new *apparatus* will cost the county *approximately* three thousand dollars.

———————————
———————————
7. *During* your college days, ownership of an *excellent dictionary* is a necessity.

———————————
———————————
8. The visitor's harsh *criticism* of our *goverment* was, we all agreed, not *appropriate.*

———————————
———————————
9. "I *allways* went to chapel when I was in school," said Uncle James. "*Attendance,* I might add, was not *compulsory.*"

———————————
———————————
10. *Accompaning* the letter was a brochure with a *discription* of the proposed *condominium.*

NAME _____   SCORE _____

Directions: Each sentence contains two words from the second half of the spelling list. In each of these words at least one letter is missing. Write the words, correctly spelled, in the spaces at the left.

_____   1. Densmore found it nec__sary to borrow money in order to fin-
_____   ish his sop__ore year of college.

_____   2. I can rec__mend Ms. Lukens highly; I am sure that she will do
_____   the work satisfa__ly.

_____   3. After speaking to Prof__r Quigley, I felt more opt__tic about
_____   being able to finish the course.

_____   4. The secr__ry of the local chamber of commerce ordered a large
_____   quan__ty of the booklets.

_____   5. Leonard's parents lost pract__ly all of their pos__sions in the fire.
_____

_____   6. The three of us left the chemistry lab__atory and walked to a
_____   nearby rest__nt for lunch.

_____   7. The superinten__nt ordered me to return all of the books to the
_____   school lib__ry.

_____   8. The teacher said that Angela's interp__tation of the poem was
_____   highly orig__nal.

_____   9. Oc__sionally Jenny would su__prise the family by offering to
_____   plan and cook a meal for them.

_____   10. The spe__ch instructor criticized my pron__ciation of a few his-
_____   torical place names.

389

Directions: These sentences contain thirty italicized words from the second half of the spelling list. A sentence may have no misspelled words, one misspelled word, or two misspelled words. Underline each misspelled word and write it, correctly spelled, in a space at the left.

1. You must admit that our drama club has put on several *really successful preformances.*

2. Some people look upon *politics* as a somewhat *rediculous pastime.*

3. Last month I worked overtime on *Wednesday* the *ninth* and Saturday the *twelfth.*

4. In his writings one can find many *specimans* of *propaganda* that play upon racial *prejudices.*

5. The *sergeant* and I often go to the gym to exercise on the *parallel* bars to develop grace and *rythm.*

6. My lack of *preserverence* can *undoubtably* be explained in impressive-sounding *psychological* terms.

7. I *regard* it a *privilege* to interview such a prominent member of the British *Parliament.*

8. My *pardner's schedual* is so full that he never has time for more than a hurried *sandwich* at noon.

9. "I *usualy* avoid parsnips and *similiar vegetables,*" said Mr. Jefferson.

10. I *recognize* the fact that a person of my *temperment* should *probably* avoid being around small children.

NAME _____   SCORE _____

Directions: Write the plural form or forms for each of the following words. When in doubt, consult your dictionary. If two forms are given, write both of them.

1. beef _____   _____

2. child _____   _____

3. curio _____   _____

4. donkey _____   _____

5. fox _____   _____

6. graffito _____   _____

7. handkerchief _____   _____

8. hippopotamus _____   _____

9. knife _____   _____

10. mouse _____   _____

11. oasis _____   _____

12. opportunity _____   _____

13. phenomenon _____   _____

14. portico _____   _____

15. process _____   _____

16. roomful _____   _____

17. species _____   _____

18. stadium _____   _____

19. syllabus _____   _____

20. trout _____   _____

21. valley _____   _____

22. variety _____   _____

23. waltz _____   _____

24. witch _____   _____

25. workman _____   _____

Directions: The following sentences contain fifty numbered words. If a word is correctly capitalized, write **C** in the space with the corresponding number. If a word should not be capitalized, write **W** in the space.

1	2	3
4	5	6
7	8	9
10	11	12
13	14	15
16	17	18
19	20	21
22	23	24
25	26	27
28	29	30
31	32	33
34	35	36
37	38	39
40	41	42
43	44	45
46	47	48
49	50	

(1) My advisor, Professor Samuels, suggested that during my
    1
Sophomore year I take Accounting 194 and elective
    2   3
courses in Economics, English History, Sociology, and
              4   5   6   7
German.
    8

(2) On their recent trip to the East, Mother and Aunt Lydia
                               9   10   11
visited the Museum Of The City Of New York, which is
              12   13 14   15 16   17   18
on Fifth Avenue at 104th Street.
    19   20   21

(3) Bob's native American fishing guide gave him a photograph
              22
of Mount Baker, a snow-capped Mountain of the Cascade
    23   24   25
Range Northeast of Seattle.
    26   27

(4) The day after the Fourth Of July holiday, the Professor of my
                      28   29 30   31
class in American Literature tested us on our reading of Poe's
          32   33
Fall Of The House Of Usher.
    34 35 36 37   38 39

(5) Formerly a Captain in the United States Coast Guard, Linda's
              40   41   42   43   44
Father is now an assistant to Secretary Watkins of the
    45   46
Department Of The Interior.
    47   48 49   50

NAME _____   SCORE _____

Directions: If you find a misspelled word, underline it and write it correctly at the left. (Consider an omitted or misused apostrophe a punctuation error, not a spelling error.) In the column of figures at the left, circle the numbers that identify errors in the sentence. Each sentence contains at least one of the following errors:

1. The group of words is a sentence modifier.
2. There is a dangling or misplaced modifier.
3. There is a misused verb (wrong number, tense, or principal part).
4. There is a poorly used pronoun (wrong number or case form, or inexact reference).
5. There is an error in punctuation.

_____
1   2   3   4   5

(1) A car that was backing out of the restaurant parking lot had a breifcase setting on its top but when I tried to signal them they just waved and drove off.

_____
1   2   3   4   5

(2) Last Sunday, while looking out the window of my new condominium, an ugly rat come out from some bushes and ran across the lawn.

_____
1   2   3   4   5

(3) "The simple construction of the five opening lines of the poem result in an especially pleasing rythm," Professor Quigley Houston told his class of literature majors.

_____
1   2   3   4   5

(4) The boss's inability to make quick decisions, as well as her often faulty judgment, have certianly brought about most of our companys really serious problems.

_____
1   2   3   4   5

(5) The chair of the board, to use an obvious example, a person with admireable instincts and real dedication but little skill in management.

_____
1   2   3   4   5

(6) "The fact that advance ticket sales have been dissappointing don't mean that the concert will be postponed, does it," the worried young sophomore asked.

_____
1   2   3   4   5

(7) "The preformance of our defensive backs in the last three games have been less than outstanding," said our head coach who sometimes uses understatement to emphasize his points.

_____
1   2   3   4   5

(8) Trying to decide on our route, it was pointed out that the shorter one was quite hilly and winding, therefore the shorter one would very likely take more time than the longer one.

_____
1   2   3   4   5

(9) Theres not more than three or four people in this entire city goverment whom I'd say are capable of leadership in difficult times.

_____
1   2   3   4   5

(10) The three older women always arrived at the class earlier than the other students, they also managed to quickly, carefully, and throughly complete every assignment.

_____ (11) Assembling in the superintendent's office at ten o'clock, Mr.
1 2 3 4 5   Swift asked we seven freshmen if we wanted to form an honors
                     class?

_____ (12) My neighbor's oldest son, for example, who confidently selected
1 2 3 4 5   a course in engineering, in spite of the fact that his knowledge
                     of mathmatics and physics were slight.

_____ (13) Apparently the mischievous youngsters choice of companions
1 2 3 4 5   have given him many oppertunities to get into real trouble.

_____ (14) Although both Thelma and Mary Lou were named in the
1 2 3 4 5   grandmother's will neither one of them have as yet received
                     their share of the inheritance.

_____ (15) How can you maintain that this dictionery is yours when some-
1 2 3 4 5   one else's name and address is stamped on its inside cover.

_____ (16) Their delay in making shipments, in addition to their higher
1 2 3 4 5   prices, have lost business for them, they're no longer serious
                     compitition for us.

_____ (17) "Just between you and I," said Eddie, "there's to many people in
1 2 3 4 5   this elevator; let's wait for the next one."

_____ (18) The amateur entrepreneur explained to my partner and I that
1 2 3 4 5   the influx of orders from small investors have undoubtedly
                     effected the market unfavorably.

_____ (19) Bruce's face turned flaming red upon hearing that his grade on
1 2 3 4 5   the literature midterm test was higher then anyone elses.

_____ (20) I'm quiet sure that I won't get the job, I was told that to be hired
1 2 3 4 5   a person either had to be a union member or have their appren-
                     tice card.

_____ (21) The article concluded with the following sentence; "Part of the
1 2 3 4 5   credit should go to whomever supplies the restaurant with its
                     incredibly fresh vegetables."

_____ (22) People in our neighborhood are extremely dissatisfied with the
1 2 3 4 5   maintainence work of the Highway Department, there's still
                     several deep potholes in our street.

_____ (23) We were unhappily supprised to hear the mayor say, "Neither of
1 2 3 4 5   these projects, although desperately needed, have been funded,
                     our repair fund only has four thousand dollars left in it."

_____ (24) There having been, if I remember correctly, two or three pro-
1 2 3 4 5   ductions of our drama association that many in the audience
                     nearly thought were of professional quality.

_____ (25) After crossing the boundary into the next county, bad driving
1 2 3 4 5   conditions can be expected for approximately fourty miles; the
                     government having neglected the roads and bridges outrageously.

NAME _____ SCORE _____

Directions: If you find a misspelled word, underline it and write it correctly at the left. (Consider an omitted or misused apostrophe a punctuation error, not a spelling error.) Circle at least one of the numbers at the left:

1. The sentence is correct.
2. There is a dangling or misplaced modifier.
3. There is a misused verb.
4. There is a misused pronoun.
5. There is an error in punctuation.

_____
1 2 3 4 5

(1) While walking down the slippery wooden steps to the beach, a most embarassing thing happened to my escort and I.

_____
1 2 3 4 5

(2) In the margin of my theme Professor Jenkins had written this note: "You can now see, can't you, that the omission of two commas from this sentence have produced a humerous effect."

_____
1 2 3 4 5

(3) The eminent critic nearly spent forty-five minutes giving us an extraordinary explaination of one of the short poems we had read.

_____
1 2 3 4 5

(4) Clancy, a chunky, pleasant sophomore who I had known in high school, stopped me and said, "Tell me, friend, what you thought about that last test we took in mathematics."

_____
1 2 3 4 5

(5) "The usual procedure," explained the receptionist, "is that Ms. Stanton's secretary or one of her assistants are on duty until five oclock on Wednesdays."

_____
1 2 3 4 5

(6) I could hardly believe what I had just heard, the superintendent had never before ever spoke so harshly to any of we students.

_____
1 2 3 4 5

(7) The frightened little boy told Mother and me that he had become separated from his parents, had wandered away from the other picnickers, and had been chased by a fierce dog.

_____
1 2 3 4 5

(8) Beyond the village of Greenville the motorist must procede cautiously, I have been told that they are resurfacing the highway for approximately ninety miles.

_____
1 2 3 4 5

(9) If anyone tells me that any child can learn to, with patient teaching, play a musical instrument, I'll give them a real arguement.

_____
1 2 3 4 5

(10) On the last night of Homecoming Week there is usualy a banquet at which the college president or the football coach give the alumni an inspirational speech.

_____
1 2 3 4 5

(11) Apparently every guy in our dorm except you and I has already had a conference with their academic adviser.

395

_____ (12) "The *Santa Maria* wasn't Columbus's favorite ship," explained
1 2 3 4 5   Dr. Slade. "After its destruction he is quoted as saying that it was
                    'too weighty and not suitable for making discoveries.' "

_____ (13) "There's probably only three or four boys on this team whom I
1 2 3 4 5   think stand a chance of receiving college atheletic scholarships,"
                    said Coach Wills who is normally quite optimistic.

_____ (14) "I'm absolutely sure that the suspected troublemakers about
1 2 3 4 5   whom the principal of the school has been talking are not you
                    and I," Jacklin confidently told his pal Barnhart.

_____ (15) After reading the pamphlet you brought me from the library,
1 2 3 4 5   my understanding of the history, purpose and accompolish-
                    ments of the United Nations have been broadened.

_____ (16) Unfortunately, many intelligent and conscientious high-school
1 2 3 4 5   graduates lack enough funds to go directly to college, which is
                    an outrageous situation.

_____ (17) The person whom I was referred to told me that I would have
1 2 3 4 5   to only wait a few more days before learning whether I or one
                    of the other contestants have won the first prize.

_____ (18) Having paid my fine at the local sheriff's office, our next desti-
1 2 3 4 5   nation was Centerville where I understand they also have
                    extreamly strict laws relating to speeding.

_____ (19) The personnel director replied, "Our company plans to within
1 2 3 4 5   a month or so hire a new financial adviser whom we all hope
                    will solve these troublesome problems for us."

_____ (20) "Dont it seem unusual that every one of us five trainees received
1 2 3 4 5   the same letter of recommendation from the boss?" asked Stan.

_____ (21) The police sergeant approached my roommate and me, opened
1 2 3 4 5   his notebook, and asked, "Has either one of you ever before seen
                    the hammer that was found lying near the front door?"

_____ (22) Miss Perkins was a truely dedicated teacher, she seemed always
1 2 3 4 5   ready to graciously and uncomplainingly give her time to
                    whomever came to her for help.

_____ (23) The members of the planning committee have studied these
1 2 3 4 5   problems and have become convinced that neither of the two
                    suggested remedies has been satisfactorily researched.

_____ (24) This applicant has only been studying Russian for three semes-
1 2 3 4 5   ters, his knowledge of the grammar, literature, and pronounci-
                    ation are quite limited.

_____ (25) The fact that your niece's careless handling of money could
1 2 3 4 5   result in her loosing the property to the mortgage holder don't
                    seem to trouble either she or her husband.

Appendix A

Sentence Combining

Sentence combining is a simple process designed to help you write more sophisticated and effective sentences. You began to employ combining techniques in Lesson 7 and its accompanying exercises, so the following exercises ought to be familiar to you. The exercises in Appendix A begin with the simplest kinds of combining, embedding an adjective from one sentence into another sentence, thus enriching one sentence and eliminating the other. The exercises then move through the formation of compound sentences and into complex sentences, those constructed with verbal phrases and subordinate clauses.

Every set in these exercises can be done in several ways, each one correct in its own way. The first set offers a good example of the possibilities:

> The man was tall.
> He was thin.
> He walked down the street.

The simplest combined form puts the adjectives tall and thin in the sentence immediately before the noun:

> The tall, thin man walked down the street.

But it is possible to move the adjectives into more emphatic positions:

> Tall and thin, the man walked down the street.
> The man, tall and thin, walked down the street.

Each of these options is correct and each creates a slightly different sentence, a sentence that draws the reader's attention to the facts in slightly different ways.

These additional combining exercises will help your writing in two ways. First, they will remind you of different ways of expressing the same idea, and thus they will expand the range of constructions you employ in your writing. Second, the exercises will focus your attention on punctuation as you make up the combinations.

Remember that every set in these exercises can be done in several ways, all of them correct. For each set, test the various ways of creating combinations and you will make yourself a more flexible and more effective writer.

Combine the sentences in each numbered unit into a single longer sentence.

1. The man was tall.
   He was thin.
   He walked down the street.

   _____

   _____

2. The tall, thin man walked down the street.
   A woman walked with him.
   She was short.
   She was blonde.

   _____

   _____

3. The man and the woman walked down the street.
   The street was dusty.
   The street was crowded.

   _____

   _____

4. The tall, thin man and the short, blonde woman walked down the dusty, crowded
   street.
   They walked slowly.
   They walked into a cold north wind.

   _____

   _____

5. The man and the woman were very cold.
   They stopped in front of a store.
   Then they went inside.
   They went inside for a cup of coffee.

   _____

   _____

Combine the sentences in each unit into a single sentence by using compound verbs.

6. Jim walked down the hall.
   He entered the last classroom on the right.

   _____

   _____

7. Robert and the girls parked the car in the student parking lot.
   They made the long walk to the library.

   _____

   _____

8. The office building is seven stories high.
   It has a long circular drive in front of it.

   _____

   _____

9. We went to the soccer field.
   Then we walked into the picnic area.

   _____

   _____

10. Tom went to the basketball game.
    Sue went to the basketball game.
    They sat at mid-court behind the team's bench.

    _____

    _____

Combine the sentences in each unit into a single sentence by putting the items into a series.

11. Joan picked up her purse.
    She picked up her umbrella.
    She picked up a set of car keys.

    _____

    _____

12. She walked slowly down the stairs.
    She got into her car.
    She drove happily off to work.

    _____

    _____

13. Jim opened the windows.
    He turned on the fan.
    Then he began to work on the test.

    _____

    _____

14. I have lost my textbook.
    I have lost my lecture notes.
    I have lost my workbook.

    _____

    _____

15. I have called all my friends.
    I have searched the trunk of my car.
    I have even looked on my desk.

    _____

    _____

Combine the sentences in each unit into a single compound sentence.

16. The bus arrived late.
    George didn't mind waiting for it.

    _____

    _____

17. The tall boy looks like a basketball player.
    He would rather study nuclear physics.

    _____

    _____

18. I spend a great deal of time at the Student Union.
    It is a wonderful place.

    _____

    _____

19. The three little boys went to the soccer game.
    They stayed only a few minutes.

    _____

    _____

20. Thunder and lightning hit the area very suddenly.
    Both teams left the field in a great hurry.

    _____

    _____

Combine these same sentences in each unit by using adverbial clauses.

21. The bus arrived late.
    George didn't mind waiting for it.

    _____

    _____

22. The tall boy looks like a basketball player.
    He would rather study nuclear physics.

    _____

    _____

23. I spend a great deal of time at the Student Union.
    It is a wonderful place.

    _____

    _____

24. The three little boys went to the soccer game.
    They stayed only a few minutes.

    _____

    _____

25. Thunder and lightning hit the area very suddenly.
    Both teams left the field in a great hurry.

    _____

    _____

Combine the sentences in each unit into a single sentence by using participial phrases.

26. The tall, slender girl walked out of the garage.
    She moved close to a blue car.
    She inspected the outside of the car for dents and scratches.

    _____

    _____

27. The girl walked up to the car.
    She opened the door of the car.
    She checked the odometer reading.

    _____

    _____

28. The girl opened the hood of the car.
    She took a wrench out of her toolbox.
    She removed a spark plug so that she could check it.

    _____

    _____

29. The girl looked at the tip of the spark plug.
    She looked very carefully.
    She shook her head sadly.

    _____

    _____

30. She replaced the spark plug.
    She closed the hood.
    She walked slowly away from the car.

    _____

    _____

Combine the sentences in each unit into a single sentence by using adjective clauses and participial phrases.

31. The lifeguard sat in the tower.
    He scanned the water carefully.
    He was looking for people in distress.

    _____

    _____

32. Only a few people were at the beach that day.
    They sat on the sand.
    They listened to their CD players.

    _____

    _____

33. The lifeguard watched the ships.
    The ships sailed by on the horizon.
    He regularly checked two people.
    The people were swimming nearby.

    _____

    _____

34. About noon the lifeguard left the tower.
    He walked slowly across the sand.
    He was carrying his umbrella and sunscreen with him.

    _____

    _____

35. He sat quietly at the lunch counter.
    He ate a hot dog with onions and pickles.
    Then he took a short nap on a bench nearby.

    _____

    _____

Combine the sentences in each unit into a single sentence by using a variety of constructions.

36. Last night three guys came to visit Jim.
    The three guys had played on his high school soccer team.
    The four of them talked until 3:00 A.M.

    _____

    _____

37. One of them is studying accounting.
    He had been a weak student in high school.
    He now works very hard at his courses.

    _____

    _____

38. He had never enjoyed school very much.
    He finds several of his courses extremely interesting now.

    _____

    _____

39. The second guy is in the Air Force.
    He is a year older than the others.
    He is studying to be an electronics technician.

    _____

    _____

40. The third guy intends to enter the state university this fall.
He has been working in construction since he graduated from high school.

_____

_____

Make the first sentence in each of the following units a participial phrase or a gerund combined with a preposition.

41. The two men were installing a satellite dish on the roof.
They found a small suitcase on the roof of the building.

_____

_____

42. The girls were walking slowly down the hall.
They stopped to talk to the other students.

_____

_____

43. The clouds built up slowly in the west.
They brought lightning and thunder early in the evening.

_____

_____

44. The players saw that defeat was certain.
They played even harder for the rest of the game.

_____

_____

45. The teacher walked into the room.
She was rolling a cart.
The cart had a computer and an LCD projector on it.
She was carrying a laser pointer.

_____

_____

Combine the sentences in each unit into a single sentence by using a variety of constructions.

46. The woman was tall and slender.
    She was wearing a gray coat.
    She met a man.
    She met him in the lobby of the hotel.

    _____

    _____

47. The man was extremely young.
    He was poorly dressed.
    He had no important information to give her.

    _____

    _____

48. The man told the woman his sad story.
    She was disappointed.
    Her disappointment was extreme.
    She told him (two things).
    He was fired.
    He would never work in industrial espionage again.

    _____

    _____

49. In response, the man told her (something).
    He had just landed a job with IBM.
    The job was in their security office.

    _____

    _____

50. (Something) seems unlikely.
    The man was telling the truth.

    _____

    _____

Combine the sentences in each unit into a single sentence by using a variety of constructions.

51. The new office building down the street is finally finished.
    A few tenants are moving in.

    _____

    _____

52. Three lawyers moved into an office on the third floor yesterday.
    Today they installed a new phone system.

    _____

    _____

53. That building has fifty offices in it.
    Only six of them are occupied.

    _____

    _____

54. The rent for the offices is extremely high.
    Many of the offices are vacant.

    _____

    _____

55. The owners need to lower the rent.
    They might go into bankruptcy.

    _____

    _____

Appendix B

NAME _____ SCORE _____

Directions: In the space at the left of each pair of sentences, write the letter that identifies the correctly punctuated sentence.

_____ 1. a. "Whenever I try to study my class notes are almost unreadable," complained Ruth, "I must be more careful about my handwriting."
   b. "Whenever I try to study, my class notes are almost unreadable," complained Ruth; "I must be more careful about my handwriting."

_____ 2. a. Some of the stockholders are now wondering if the company has overextended itself by buying the two new ships.
   b. Some of the stockholders are now wondering, if the company has overextended itself by buying the two new ships?

_____ 3. a. Although the Perkinses live less than a block away from us, we hardly feel that we know them well.
   b. Although the Perkins's live less than a block away from us; we hardly feel that we know them well.

_____ 4. a. The following notice recently appeared on the bulletin board; "The editors of this years yearbook have decided to dispense with the so-called humor section."
   b. The following notice recently appeared on the bulletin board: "The editors of this year's yearbook have decided to dispense with the so-called humor section."

_____ 5. a. I scraped the mud and mashed insects from the windshield and Jennie sadly inspected the crumpled, rear fender.
   b. I scraped the mud and mashed insects from the windshield, and Jennie sadly inspected the crumpled rear fender.

_____ 6. a. After they had cleaned the kitchen, put the children to bed, and locked the front door, Pete and Jane looked forward to a quiet, peaceful evening.
   b. After they had cleaned the kitchen, put the children to bed and locked the front door; Pete and Jane looked forward to a quiet peaceful evening.

_____ 7. a. Some neighbors asked questions about Jim's strange friends but Mother told them that it was nobodys concern except our family's.
   b. Some neighbors asked questions about Jim's strange friends, but Mother told them that it was nobody's concern except our family's.

411

_____ 8. a. "Tryouts for the class play have been completed," Miss. Lowe, the drama coach, announced, "this year we are blessed with almost too much talent."

b. "Tryouts for the class play have been completed," Miss Lowe, the drama coach, announced; "this year we are blessed with almost too much talent."

_____ 9. a. My office mate claims to understand horse racing, but his bets every month usually cost him a week's pay.

b. My office mate claims to understand horse racing but his bets every month usually cost him a weeks pay.

_____ 10. a. The childrens' father made a good impression, the presiding judge, in fact, commended him for his handling of the matter.

b. The children's father made a good impression; the presiding judge, in fact, commended him for his handling of the matter.

_____ 11. a. Coach Stannard scheduled volleyball tryouts for February 16, 1998 and nearly two dozen eager, young women turned out.

b. Coach Stannard scheduled volleyball tryouts for February 16, 1998, and nearly two dozen eager young women turned out.

_____ 12. a. "How can we foreigners learn English," complained Carmen, "when you give different pronunciations to words like *bough, cough, dough, plough* and *slough.*"

b. "How can we foreigners learn English," complained Carmen, "when you give different pronunciations to words like *bough, cough, dough, plough,* and *slough?*"

_____ 13. a. Located 85 miles offshore, its pipelines stretching across the ocean floor, the platform well is nearly completed and will soon begin pumping oil to the mainland.

b. Located 85 miles offshore, its pipelines stretching across the ocean floor; the platform well is nearly completed, and will soon begin pumping oil to the mainland.

_____ 14. a. "You will remember, boys and girls, to give this brochure to your parents, won't you?" said Mr. Turner, the third-grade teacher.

b. "You will remember, boys and girls, to give this brochure to your parents, won't you," said Mr. Turner, the third-grade teacher.

_____ 15. a. "I commend you, Lois," said the boss, "for your suggestion, but I wonder if you've thought of the engineering problems involved."

b. "I commend you Lois," said the boss, "for your suggestion, but I wonder if you've thought of the engineering problems involved?"

_____ 16. a. In a large, antique car collection in California, we saw a one-cylinder car in running condition, it had the starting crank on one side.
   b. In a large antique car collection in California, we saw a one-cylinder car in running condition; it had the starting crank on one side.

_____ 17. a. "The attendance clerk wasn't impressed by my excuse, and I doubt that she'll find yours very convincing," said Anne.
   b. "The attendance clerk wasn't impressed by my excuse and I doubt that she'll find your's very convincing," said Anne.

_____ 18. a. "Are you aware of the fact that most of the pistachio nuts sold here, are imported from Greece and Turkey," asked Dr. Ash who is a storehouse of trivia.
   b. "Are you aware of the fact that most of the pistachio nuts sold here are imported from Greece and Turkey?" asked Dr. Ash, who is a storehouse of trivia.

_____ 19. a. The auto age for America really began in 1908 when Henry Ford, the son of a farmer, produced his Model T which was black, reliable and cheap.
   b. The auto age for America really began in 1908, when Henry Ford, the son of a farmer, produced his Model T, which was black, reliable, and cheap.

_____ 20. a. The manager smiled faintly and said, "It seems a shame, doesn't it, that a football player of Jake's ability must retire just because someone's spreading ugly rumors?"
   b. The manager smiled faintly and said, "It seems a shame, doesn't it, that a football player of Jake's ability must retire just because someones spreading ugly rumors."

_____ 21. a. It was four o'clock on a chilly, damp September afternoon, and the beach was deserted except for two bored lifeguards.
   b. It was four oclock on a chilly, damp, September afternoon and the beach was deserted except for two bored lifeguards.

_____ 22. a. My daughter pulled on her gloves and started to snip off the wilted blossoms, her expression revealing her complete lack of interest in gardening.
   b. My daughter pulled on her gloves, and started to snip off the wilted blossoms; her expression revealing her complete lack of interest in gardening.

_____ 23. a. Some of the electrical equipment failed, for nearly twenty hour's the explorers had no radio contact with the base.
   b. Some of the electrical equipment failed; for nearly twenty hours the explorers had no radio contact with the base.

_____ 24. a. If theres one thing today's students don't need; it's more critical, admonitory, or threatening advice hurled at them by long-nosed sanctimonious adults.

b. If there's one thing today's students don't need, it's more critical, admonitory, or threatening advice hurled at them by long-nosed, sanctimonious adults.

_____ 25. a. "A team that won't be beaten can't be beaten," shouted Coach Miller, who had a seemingly endless supply of clichés.

b. "A team that wont be beaten can't be beaten," shouted Coach Miller who had a seemingly endless supply of clichés.

NAME _____ SCORE _____

Directions: Each of the following sentences contains three italicized words, one of which is misspelled. Underline each misspelled word and write it, correctly spelled, in the space at the left.

_____ 1. "There are limitations on the length, breadth, and *heighth* of packages we ship, and the weight must not *exceed forty* pounds," the agent said.

_____ 2. My present was a box of fancy *stationery;* I was *dissappointed* that I didn't *receive* something more practical.

_____ 3. The food served at this rural inn is *becoming fameous* throughout Great *Britain.*

_____ 4. Lathrop sought the *advise* of an *eminent psychiatrist.*

_____ 5. This may sound *unbelievable* to you, but our city *library* has been struck three times by *lightening.*

_____ 6. Jerry is *dissatisfied* with his new *schedual* because it does not allow him time for studying *during* the afternoons.

_____ 7. In her *sophmore* year Joyce took a course in *speech* and two courses in *literature.*

_____ 8. The play had *it's* first *performance* in Hartford last *February.*

_____ 9. "An *acquaintance* of mine *reccommended* your *restaurant* to me," said Mrs. Watkins to the receptionist.

_____ 10. The applicant attempted to flatter the interviewer by saying, "You are *undoubtably knowledgeable* about the latest *technology* in our field."

_____ 11. "Your *humorous* remarks were not *appropriate* for a serious *occasion* such as this one," said the chairperson.

_____ 12. I admit that my new dog behaved *deploreably* last *Wednesday* at *obedience* school.

_____ 13. The data we get from these *questionnaires* could have an *effect* on next year's hiring *proceedures*.

_____ 14. *Reference* to a *dictionary* could have quickly settled the *arguement* the two of you were having.

_____ 15. We must all *recognize* the fact that tourism is the *principle* source of income in our quaint *village*.

_____ 16. Yesterday one of the arrested men *lead* the police officers to the place where the *equipment* stolen from the *laboratory* had been hidden.

_____ 17. A *goverment* spokesperson announced that the new *satellite* will provide weather forecasters with *indispensable* data.

_____ 18. The coach happily announced a *noticeable improvement* in batting averages, *especialy* in those of our outfielders.

_____ 19. A serious accident on the highway caused us to *loose approximately ninety* minutes of valuable time.

_____ 20. A senior *pardner* of the firm *conceded* that further meetings would very likely be *necessary*.

_____ 21. "This *pamphlet* is full of the most *rediculous propaganda* I've ever read," shouted the incumbent.

_____ 22. "*Neither* of these two small countries could withstand a long *seige*," replied *Sergeant* Lewis.

_____ 23. As he presented Enid with the award, the *superintendent* said, "Here is a young person *who's courageous* fight has inspired all of us."

_____ 24. When arrested, Elaine had in her *possession* a large *quanity* of *counterfeit* money.

_____ 25. "Serving on this *committee* has been a *priviledge* and a wonderful *experience*," said the retiring chairperson.

NAME _____   SCORE _____

Directions: In the space at the left, copy from within the parentheses the form that would be appropriate in serious writing.

_____ 1. Bert was surprised to learn that everyone in the class except Maria and (he, him) had to take another test.

_____ 2. The thief apparently had crept through the broken ventilator grill and had (laid, lain) quietly in the storeroom until nightfall.

_____ 3. Mary Ellen wasn't at the park yesterday; it hardly could have been (she, her) who tore your scarf.

_____ 4. Anyone selected for the acting presidency must prepare (himself or herself, themself, themselves) for a short and thankless term of office.

_____ 5. The reason I'm looking so pale is (because, that) my sunlamp needs repairing.

_____ 6. Some fellow who had occupied the room before I arrived had left some of (his, their) old clothes in the closet.

_____ 7. I wish someone on the school paper would write an editorial in (regard, regards) to the noise in the library reading room.

_____ 8. Just between you and (I, me), Luke shouldn't expect to get off with only a lecture from the judge.

_____ 9. You're convinced now, aren't you, that you (hadn't ought to, shouldn't) leave your garage unlocked?

_____ 10. My sister once studied the alto saxophone but never played it (good, well) enough to be chosen for the school band.

_____ 11. The robbers, (whoever, whomever) they were, must have known exactly when the workers would be paid.

_____ 12. The school's new program must be effective, for there (has, have) been surprisingly few complaints from parents.

_____ 13. Not many jobs are available, (because, being that) the government has curtailed operations at the navy yard.

_____ 14. After speaking into the microphone, Laura played back the tape and commented on how (different, differently) her voice sounded.

_____ 15. "Vote for (whoever, whomever) you think is the best candidate," answered Anita's father.

_____ 16. In a political campaign every candidate makes promises that (they know, he or she knows) cannot possibly be kept.

_____ 17. Also included in the packet (is, are) a travel guide, some special trip tips, and two exceptional bonus prizes.

_____ 18. Someone should have told (we, us) ushers that the main door had not been unlocked.

_____ 19. Do you know who the man is who is (setting, sitting) at the head table next to the guest speaker?

_____ 20. As everyone knows, neither DDT nor any other insecticide (has, have) the ability to distinguish between good and bad insects.

_____ 21. If the helicopter pilot had not dropped blankets to the men stranded on the ice floe, they probably would have (froze, frozen) to death.

_____ 22. After a few months Carrie (began, begun) to have doubts about her nephew's ability to manage her investments.

_____ 23. No one could have been more surprised than (I, me) to learn of your recent marriage.

_____ 24. The gratification resulting from working on the school newspaper and other publications (outweighs, outweigh) the demands on one's time.

_____ 25. After a person has sat for five hours in the blazing sunlight listening to this kind of music, (he or she feels, they feel) numb and beaten.

NAME _____ SCORE _____

Directions: Study these paired sentences for incompleteness, dangling or misplaced modifiers, faulty parallelism, and faulty comparisons. In the space at the left, write the letter that identifies the correct sentence.

_____ 1. a. The cotton crop this year, we all hope, will be much better than last years.
b. The cotton crop this year, we all hope, will be much better than last year's.

_____ 2. a. Because we are the parents of five active children, our washing machine is running much of the time.
b. Being the parents of five active children, our washing machine is running much of the time.

_____ 3. a. Searching the area carefully, we finally found the tunnel entrance, expertly covered by underbrush and which the other searchers had overlooked.
b. Searching the area carefully, we finally found the tunnel entrance, which had been expertly covered by underbrush and which the other searchers had overlooked.

_____ 4. a. The group's intention, surely a noble one, to constantly and relentlessly encourage the protection of the environment.
b. The group's intention, surely a noble one, is to encourage constantly and relentlessly the protection of the environment.

_____ 5. a. Believing me to be a better public speaker than anyone else in the class, my parents told all the relatives that I would be the valedictorian.
b. Being a better public speaker than anyone in the class, my parents told all the relatives that I would be the valedictorian.

_____ 6. a. Malaysia and other countries proved incapable of sheltering or unwilling to shelter all of the refugees.
b. Malaysia and other countries proved incapable or unwilling to shelter all of the refugees.

_____ 7. a. "I neither intend to withdraw from the race nor to in any degree stop pointing out my opponent's shortcomings," Ms. Hawley replied.
b. "I intend neither to withdraw from the race nor in any degree to stop pointing out my opponent's shortcomings," Ms. Hawley replied.

_____ 8. a. When seen from a distance, the white cliffs seem to resemble icebergs.
   b. When seen from a distance, one might think that the white cliffs were icebergs.

_____ 9. a. This popular young actor lives high in the Hollywood hills in a small apartment decorated with posters of auto races and bullfights.
   b. This popular young actor lives in a small apartment decorated with posters of auto races and bullfights high in the Hollywood hills.

_____ 10. a. The relatively small amount of flood water has not and probably won't cause any major damage.
   b. The relatively small amount of flood water has not caused and probably won't cause any major damage.

_____ 11. a. When we replaced the wooden shingles with a composition roof, the insurance company agreed to lower our annual premium quite considerably.
   b. By replacing the wooden shingles with a composition roof, the insurance company agreed to quite considerably lower our annual premium.

_____ 12. a. Commissioner Reed stated that our downtown streets are as clean, if not cleaner than, other cities.
   b. Commissioner Reed stated that our downtown streets are as clean as, if not cleaner than, those of other cities.

_____ 13. a. I already have a full enough schedule of work today without being asked to listen to you practice your speech.
   b. I already have a full enough schedule of work today without asking me to listen to you practice your speech.

_____ 14. a. The reason for our moving being that the security system at Elmhurst Manor is more modern than the old apartment.
   b. The reason for our moving is that the security system at Elmhurst Manor is more modern than that at the old apartment.

_____ 15. a. Sylvia Andrews is a self-sufficient and talented person who, since her parents died, has supported herself and her younger brothers tutoring students in mathematics.
   b. Sylvia Andrews, a self-sufficient and talented person who has supported herself and her younger brothers since her parents died tutoring students in mathematics.

_____ 16. a. My mother's paternal grandmother was one of the very few, if not the only, woman to study veterinary medicine in the early 1900s.
   b. My mother's paternal grandmother was one of the very few women, if not the only woman, to study veterinary medicine in the early 1900s.

_____ 17. a. You must either return these books to the library or pay a substantial fine.
      b. Either you must return these books to the library or pay a substantial fine.

_____ 18. a. I hope that the yield from these tax-free bonds will be equal to, if not more than, the yield from your stocks.
      b. I hope that the yield from these tax-free bonds will be equal, if not more than, your stocks.

_____ 19. a. Albert's plan being to, as soon as he receives his inheritance, retire to some remote island in the South Seas.
      b. Albert's plan is to retire to some remote island in the South Seas as soon as he receives his inheritance.

_____ 20. a. You will be given preferred seating only if you have donated at least $200 to the Opera Guild.
      b. You will only be given preferred seating if you have donated at least $200 to the Opera Guild.

_____ 21. a. Ellen hopes that her tax-deductible contributions this year will be equal to, if not more than, last year's.
      b. Ellen hopes that her tax-deductible contributions this year will be equal, if not more than, last year.

_____ 22. a. Pietro maintains that most people in his country are easygoing, warm-hearted, friends to Americans, and having a tolerance for the ideas and ways of foreigners.
      b. Pietro maintains that most people in his country are easygoing and warmhearted, are friends to Americans, and have a tolerance for the ideas and ways of foreigners.

_____ 23. a. Fairhaven has one of the largest airports in the state, if not the largest.
      b. Fairhaven has one of the largest, if not the largest, airport in the state.

_____ 24. a. While just getting nicely adjusted to high-school life, my family moved again, this time to Baltimore.
      b. While I was just getting nicely adjusted to high-school life, my family moved again, this time to Baltimore.

_____ 25. a. Quickly totaling the bills, imagine my dismay on discovering that I nearly owed my entire month's salary.
      b. Quickly totaling the bills, I was dismayed to discover that I owed nearly my entire month's salary.

Appendix C

Answer Key to Practice Sheets

Practice Sheet 1, page 5

1. was
2. arrived
3. were
4. goes
5. becomes
6. answered
7. hangs
8. was
9. signed
10. came
11. attended
12. (is)
13. are
14. knew
15. attended
16. pounded
17. sat
18. walked
19. seemed
20. came

Practice Sheet 1, page 6

1. one
2. space shuttle
3. assets
4. record
5. river
6. payments
7. none
8. shipment
9. several
10. bodyguard
11. lure
12. many
13. ending
14. hope
15. absence
16. developments
17. work
18. all
19. rates
20. some

Practice Sheet 2, pages 15–16

1. 5,3
2. 6,4
3. 2,1
4. 2,5
5. 2,4
6. 6,3
7. 1,4
8. 1,4
9. 1,5
10. 6,3
11. 4,3
12. 1,6
13. 4,2
14. 3,6
15. 5,4
16. 1,5
17. 2,6
18. 2,6
19. 4,3
20. 2,4
21. 4,4
22. 5,6
23. 3,1
24. 1,6
25. 1,6
26. 1,3
27. 5,4
28. 2,3
29. 2,1
30. 3,5
31. 1,4
32. 3,4
33. 2,4
34. 3,5
35. 3,1
36. 1,5
37. 3,4
38. 5,1
39. 5,4
40. 3,5

Practice Sheet 3, page 27

1. mystery
2. suspects
3. time
4. traitor
5. judgment
6. dean
7. ours
8. investment
9. necessity
10. prequisites
11. farmer
12. winner
13. power
14. pilot
15. Tuesday
16. resorts
17. help
18. highlight
19. believer
20. friends

Practice Sheet 3, page 28

1. innocuous
2. qualified
3. foul
4. ineffectual
5. rancid
6. suspicious
7. unworthy
8. undefeated
9. better
10. ready
11. uncomfortable
12. young
13. conspicuous
14. workable
15. shy
16. clear
17. tired
18. vital
19. bold
20. active

Practice Sheet 4, page 35

1. children crossed bridge
2. member applauded him
3. garlic possesses properties
4. guard keeps visitors
5. Mr. Thorpe will tolerate insolence
6. you will sweep front hall
7. we saw exhibits
8. All noticed improvement
9. Jaspar played games
10. Someone had turned light
11. Club will appreciate response
12. Dozens have cleaned lot
13. test will cover material
14. Martha plays game
15. Bob picked one
16. we saw part
17. I shall file bit
18. Rachael had read two
19. niece made impression
20. boys sampled one

Practice Sheet 4, page 36

1. One mailed I.O.
2. representatives will talk D.O.
3. teacher called O.C
4. shepherds left O.C.
5, we left D.O.
6. Aunt Louise left I.O.
7. You will hear D.O.
8. One had brought I.O.
9. I do consider O.C.
10. pep talk gave I.O.
11. talk made O.C.
12. owner showed I.O.
13. commentators interpreted O.C.
14. You have sampled D.O.
15. rioters set O.C.
16. committee names O.C.
17. One will ask D.O.
18. speaker gave D.O.
19. Grandfather brought I.O.
20. Chet made D.O.

Practice Sheet 5, pages 43–44

1. could, 3	11. must have, 1	21. will be, 3	31. has, 3
2. has been, 3	12. will, 3	22. have, 1	32. will, 3
3. have, 2	13. should have been, 1	23. have been, 2	33. might have, 1
4. could have, 2	14. have, 5	24. has, 2	34. could have, 3
5. will have, 4	15. will be, 1	25. have, 1	35. should have been, 3
6. should have 5,	16. has been, 3	26. have been, 4	36. might have, 2
7. had, 3	17. have been, 1	27. has been, 5	37. should have, 4
8. should have, 5	18. will, 4	28. could have, 2	38. will, 5
9. has been, 2	19. should, 5	29. has been, 1	39. might, 5
10. will, 3	20. should be, 3	30. should, 2	40. shoule have, 1

Practice Sheet 6, page 53

1. 3, could be seen	5. 5, are being kept	9. 5, is (not) considered
2. 4, will be allowed	6. 4, will be shown	10. 3, should have been paid
3. 3, will be met	7. 3, would be appreciated	
4. 3, is being considered	8. 4, will be sent	

Practice Sheet 6, page 54

1. What	4. Which	7. old	10. fish	13. What
2. What	5. Whom	8. Whom	11. whose	14. whom
3. people	6. money	9. Who	12. Whom	15. much

Practice Sheet 7, pages 61–62

1. 0	6. C	11. 0	16. C	21. C
2. C	7. C	12. 0	17. 0	22. 0
3. S	8. S	13. 0	18. C	23. C
4. S	9. C	14. S	19. 0	24. S
5. S	10. S	15. 0	20. C	25. 0

Practice Sheet 8, pages 73–74

1. 1	9. 7	17. 1	25. 8	33. 1
2. 3	10. 6	18. 8	26. 1	34. 10
3. 7	11. 9	19. 9	27. 3	35. 7
4. 1	12. 2	20. 7	28. 8	36. 1
5. 5	13. 3	21. 6	29. 2	37. 5
6. 9	14. 1	22. 7	30. 9	38. 10
7. 7	15. 3	23. 3	31. 7	39. 6
8. 2	16. 1	24. 1	32. 2	40. 1

Practice Sheet 9, page 83

1. bench	4. Mobile	7. old-timer	10. Jeff O'Neal	13. Larry Benhan
2. vegetables	5. concert	8. old-timer	11. tie	14. Those
3. spot	6. hat	9. Jeff O'Neal	12. woman	15. people

Practice Sheet 9, page 84

1. *flight* on which our party was booked
2. *Uncle Theo* who is usually very cautious when money is involved
3. *meat* that was served to us
4. *error* that caused our plan to fail?
5. *book* you recommended.
6. *person* who told you that story
v7. *person* whose car ran into yours?
8. *anyone* who was in the area when the fire broke out.
9. *end* of which line we saw our two friends.
10. *someone* who's trusting, greedy, and foolish.
11. *everyone* where they could observe everyone who went through the turnstile.
12. *couples* whom she had invited
13. *contribution* you can make
14. *one* of which the committee accepted
15. *decisions* that are painful to you.

Practice Sheet 10, page 95

1. S.	5. O.P.	9. D.O.	13. D.O.	17. S.C.
2. D.O.	6. S.C.	10. O.P.	14. Ap.	18. S
3. O.P.	7. S.	11. S.	15. O.P.	19. D.O.
4. D.O.	8. D.O.	12. S.	16. S.C.	20. S.C.

Practice Sheet 10, page 96

1. O.P. (how these developments will affect future students at the college)
2. S. (that almost 75 per cent of our graduates will enter some business)
3. Ap. (that the mail contained no complaints about his decision)
4. S.C. (that we left home this morning before the sun had risen)
5. D.O. (that Sue had applied for a job)
6. S. (What happened at graduation)
7. O.P. (what happened at graduation)
8. S. (what happened at graduation)
9. D.O. (that anyone you recommend will do a good job for us)
10. O.P. (whoever gets the job)
11. O.P. (whatever will reduce taxes)
12. S. (whoever takes the job)
13. S.C. (that if a player misses practice she may not play in the next game)
14. S.C. (that we should undertake a cake sale as a fund-raising project)
15. Ap (that we should undertake a cake sale as a fund raising project.)
16. D.O. (how truly awesome a single tree could be)
17. S. (what I discovered yesterday)
18. S. (Whoever called me about the apartment)
19. S. (that we can get away early for the holiday)
20. S.C. (that we are waiting for the caterer to deliver the box lunches)

Practice Sheet 11, page 107

1. O.P	5. S.C.	9. D.O.	13. D.O.	17. S.C.
2. S.	6. S.	10. S.C.	14. S.	18. S.
3. D.O.	7. O.P.	11. S.	15. O.P.	19. D.O.
4. O.P.	8. D.O.	12. O.P.	16. S.	20. O.P.

Practice Sheet 11, page 108

1. Adv	5. Adj	9. Adv	13. N	17. N
2. Adj	6. N	10. N	14. Adj	18. Adj
3. N	7. Adv	11. N	15. N	19. N
4. N	8. N	12. N	16. N	20. Adv

Practice Sheet 12, pages 117–118

1. president	11. _____	21. Cars	
2. _____	12. _____	22. _____	
3. crowd	13. students	23. brother	
4. storm	14. _____	24. Jim	
5. _____	15. Mark	25. woman	
6. boys	16. Alicia	26. Watson	
7. _____	17. Alicia	27. _____	
8. woman	18. _____	28. fans	
9. _____	19. announcer	29. _____	
10. team	20. _____	30. audience	

Practice Sheet 13, pages 129–130

1. S	7. S	13. F	19. F	25. S
2. F	8. F	14. F	20. S	26. F
3. F	9. F	15. S	21. S	27. S
4. S	10. S	16. S	22. F	28. S
5. S	11. S	17. F	23. F	29. F
6. F	12. F	18. S	24. S	30. F

Practice Sheet 14, page 139

1. B	3. B	5. A	7. B	9. A
2. A	4. A	6. B	8. A	10. B

Practice Sheet 14, page 140

1. B	4. B	7. A	10. B	13. A
2. B	5. A	8. B	11. A	14. B
3. A	6. A	9. B	12. A	15. A

Practice Sheet 14A, pages 143–144

1. B, Realizing that the streets were very slick from the rain
2. A, Being a very successful young executive
3. B, To get the maximum tax benefits
4. B, not expecting to see Mary Chase so far from home
5. A, Upon receiving the invoice
6. B, At eleven years of age
7. A, Broadcast live from the stadium
8. B, When using this powerful detergent
9. B, Before getting the camera focused
10. A, Being older and slower
11. A, Having misunderstood the assignment
12. B, Exhausted after fourteen hours of driving
13. B, Having stood in the oily marinade for hours
14. A, Painstakingly repairing the damaged web
15. B, Approaching the continental divide
16. A, Covered with the grime of centuries
17. A, To avoid overexposing the picture
18. B, Meeting Lou after geology class
19. A, If unable to attend
20. A, Seen from miles away

Practice Sheet 15, page 151

1. 5	4. 2	7. 6	10. 1	13. 7
2 1	5. 3	8. 2	11. 6	14. 4
3. 7	6. 3	9. 3	12. 5	15. 1

Practice Sheet 15, page 152

1. To have a wide choice of classes. . . . ,go
2. Finding the last of the puppies. . . . , I took
3. Raymond Larson, who is the road manager. . . .
4. If frost is predicted for tonight, you should. . .
5. With frost predicted for tonight, you should cover. . .
6. . . . . old sheets to protect the plants.
7. hours in the library looking for additional. . . .
8. . . . . Allison McGee, the president's executive assistant.
9. While you were stuck. . . . , the meeting started
10. Rolando Gomez, who is the new chairman of Jackson's re-election committee, before today.

Practice Sheet 16, page 159

1. A	3. B	5. B	7. A	9. A
2. B	4. A	6. A	8. B	10. B

Practice Sheet 16, page 160

1. B	3. B	5. A	7. B	9. A
2. A	4. B	6. A	8. B	10. B

Practice Sheet 17, pages 167–168

1. 4, 1 paper, copies,
2. 2, 3 run, fastest,
3. 5, 1, after, fall,
4. 4, 3 fall, long,
5. 1,3 today, short,
6. 4, 2 house, box,
7. 5, 1 leaving, lunch,
8. 5,3 that, overwhelming,
9. 4, 2 morning, downtown,
10. 3, 4 competent, assistant,
11. 3, 4 patched, raincoat,
12. 1, 2 photography, composition,
13. 4,1 hour, class
14. 2, 1 Spencer, Ryan,
15. 4 or 5,1 painting, new,
16. 4, 2 apartment, Jorge,
17. 3, 1 beautiful, office,
18. 4, 3, boys, long
19. 2,1 toast, breakfast,
20. 4 or 5, stood, backwards,

Practice Sheet 18, page 177

1. 2 cousin, team,
2. 4 spiders, remember,
3. 1 foreman, mechanic,
4. 5 now, fans,
5. 1 cowboy, smoking,
6. 6 earlier,
7. 1 horse, whip,
8. 4 Sam, believe,
9. 1 Mr. Jones, solemn,
10. 2 outcome,
11. 2 car,
12. 6 no, asked,
13. 1 cast,
14. 5 over, George,
15. 1 Joan,

Practice Sheet 18, page 178

Nonrestrictive clauses and phrases should be set off with commas

1. R
2. N jogging,
3. N car, neglect,
4. R
5. N Joan, severely,
6. R
7. R
8. N Mr. Smith, years,
9. N Morton's,
10. R
11. R
12. N Jim, shoulder,
13. R
14. N Ms. Thompson,
15. N Joyce,

Practice Sheet 19, page 189

1. C
2. W lots
3. W impressive:
4. W lawyer's
5. W else's
6. W delete colon after *in* men's work clothes, children's shoes
7. W, already."
8. W It's, people's
9. C
10. W everyone's
11. W Let's
12. C
13. W car's, with leather seats . . . .
14. W team's year's
15. W o'clock cake's

Practice Sheet 19, page 190

1. My brother said, "I have lost my wallet."
2. The sales manager observed, "I will need to hire two new division managers."
3. My teachers often tell me, "You are too talkative in class."
4. The policeman asked, "Do you need directions to the next town?"
5. Did she tell you, "The elevator is being repaired"?
6. The teller said to me that it would take only a minute to compute my interest.
7. My father said that he certainly appreciated all my hard work.
8. His sister answered that she did not want to go sailing in this rainy weather.
9. The salesman asked why I had selected the convertible.
10. Didn't she say that I should take the right-hand fork after the covered bridge.

Practice Sheet 20, page 197

1. C
2. C
3. C
4. C
5. C
6. C
7. W, pp. 13, vol.3.
8. C
9. W. eg.,
10. W, stay.
11. change"?
12. here' "?
13. W, etc.
14. Dr., be?
15. "Run!" shouted;

Practice Sheet 20, page 198

1. 2, 4, o'clock morning,
2. 1,2,3, hook, bait; you're
3. 1,2 don't entirely,
4. 1,2,3 fragile, it; it's
5. 2,4, excuse, yours
6. 1,3, swear, Charleston;
7. 1,2,4, open, I'd Loftus,
8. 1,3, late: Store, children's
9. 4, now,
10. 1,2,3, said, booth; there's

Practice Sheet 21, pages 209–210

1. sunk, brought
2. ran, driven
3. flew, frozen
4. lain, laid
5. took, caught
6. begun, eaten
7. spoken, climbed
8. sat, taken
9. did, paid
10. written, came
11. became, stolen
12. rose, began
13. flown, chosen
14. worn, hung
15. given, broken
16. known, ridden
17. shined, laid
18. risen, drowned
19. grown, saw
20. spent, lent

Practice Sheet 21, pages 211–212

1. saw, C
2. C, taken
3. sworn, torn
4. spoken, C
5. C, began
6. C, C
7. C, lent
8. saw, hidden
9. risen, C
10. lie, C
11. done, know
12. sat, C
13. C, run
14. C, worn
15. threw, lay
16. dragged, sank
17. drowned, came
18. crept, caught
19. frozen, C
20. left, began

Practice Sheet 22, page 221

1. makes	4. is	7. qualifies	10. is	13. takes
2. were	5. has	8. seem	11. was	14. was
3. is	6. have	9. is	13. has	15. is

Practice Sheet 22, page 222

1. lessens	7. increases	13. faces
2. show	8. has	14. C
3. has	9. C	15. exceeds
4. C	10. C	
5. has	11. seems	
6. C	12. decide	

Practice Sheet 23, pages 231–232

1. B	4. B	7. B	10. B	13. B
2. A	5. B	8. B	11. A	14. B
3. B	6. B	9. B	12. B	15. B

Practice Sheet 24, page 241

1. 1	5. 5	9. 5	13. 1	17. 3
2. 5	6. 1	10. 2	14. 4	18. 2
3. 1	7. 1	11. 4	15. 6	19. 5
4. 1	8. 4	12. 4	16. 5	20. 4

Practice Sheet 24, page 242

1. me	5. I	9. she	13. whoever	17. whom
2. I	6. he	10. who	14. her	18. she
3. me	7. who	11. who	15. whom	19. who
4. whom	8. me	12. he	16. whoever	20. me

Practice Sheet 25, pages 251–252

1. respected, adv.	6. optimistic, adv.	11. car, adj.	16. boy, adj.
2. soaring, adv.	7. Sand, adv.	12. will run, adv.	17. walked, adv.
3. hoax, adj.	8. he, adj.	13. football players, adj.	18. pattern, adj.
4. behavior, adj.	9. me, adj.	14. destructive, adv.	19. remained, adv.
5. problems, adj.	10. floors, adj.	15. are growing, adv.	20. pool, adj.

Practice Sheet 25, pages 253–254

1. happy	8. awkwardly	15. well
2. considerably	9. awkward	16. surely
3. well	10. steadily	17. badly
4. easily	11. really	18. regularly
5. incorrectly	12. sweet	19. good
6. equally	13. suddenly	20. somewhat
7. badly	14. different	

Practice Sheet 26, pages 265–266

1. infer, supposed	6. Let's, anywhere	11. way, very	16. Because of, three
2. try to, farther	7. that, among	12. as far as, very	17. think, incredible
3. May, disinterested	8. number, fewer	13. Because, should have	18. That, rather
4. surely, could have	9. very, enthusiastic	14. continuous, irritated	19. Many, angry
5. Besides, many	10. that, almost	15. very, criterion	20. ought, teach

Practice Sheet 26, pages 267–268

1. Because of, somewhere else
2. C, used to
3. Those kinds, C
4. Many, C
5. Because, way
6. supposed, C
7. C, very
8. C, where (at)
9. Ought you, among
10. C, C
11. In regard to, no comments
12. C, C
13. suspect, C
14. C, regardless
15. those, surely
16. wants to work on, C
17. that, because of
18. C, C
19. off, C
20. should have, as if

Practice Sheet 27, pages 279–280

1. equipment
2. Except
3. canvas
4. writing
5. allotted
6. extremely
7. desirable
8. advise
9. regrettable
10. preferred
11. hiring
12. its
13. incidents
14. You're
15. Their
16. serviceable
17. lose
18. descent
19. course
20. presents
21. quite
22. principal
23. council
24. unforgettable
25. shown
26. Later
27. fascinating
28. picnicking
29. affected
30. than

Practice Sheet 28, page 287

1. bases
2. biopsies
3. bistros
4. craftsmen
5. curricula, curriculums
6. data, datums
7. fleeces
8. flunkies
9. foxes
10. Joneses
11. journeys
12. memorandums, memoranda
13. moose
14. oxen, oxes
15. ploys
16. portfolios
17. proofs
18. ratios
19. reindeer
20. sons-in-law
21. spies
22. volleys
23. wharves, wharfs
24. wives
25. zeros, zeroes

Practice Sheet 28, page 288

1. W
2. C
3. C
4. C
5. W
6. W
7. W
8. W
9. C
10. W
11. W
12. C
13. W
14. W
15. W
16. W
17. W
18. W
19. C
20. C
21. W
22. W
23. C
24. W
25. W
26. W
27. W
28. W
29. C
30. C
31. W
32. W
33. W
34. C
35. W
36. C
37. C
38. C
39. C
40. W
41. C
42. W
43. W
44. C
45. W
46. W
47. W
48. C
49. W
50. W

Practice Sheet 29, pages 295–296

1. acquaintance, committee
2. irresistible, awkward
3. fascinated, equipment
4. exorbitant, environment
5. forty, interpretation
6. fundamentally, competent
7. auxiliary, continuous
8. controversial, characteristic
9. amateur, athletics
10. harass, embarrass
11. interrupt, irrelevant
12. approximately, arithmetic
13. extremely, conscientious
14. hurriedly, indispensable
15. dissipated, across
16. Apparently, arguments
17. excellent, eliminated
18. height, incredible
19. impromptu, conference
20. Association, business
21. during, aggravated
22. efficient, bureaucracy
23. Astronaut, category
24. absence, acknowledged
25. arctic, extraordinarily

Practice Sheet 29A, pages 299–300

1. legitimate, propaganda
2. Wednesday, twelfth
3. unanimous, representatives
4. misspelled, questionnaire
5. surprise, parliament
6. pamphlet, sandwich
7. proceed, schedule
8. scientific, nuclear
9. secretary, preparation
10. performance, wholly
11. recommends, repetitions
12. recognize, sophomore
13. perseverance, successful
14. maintenance, procedures
15. mathematics, satisfactorily
16. technology, supersedes
17. ridiculous, pursue
18. specimens, separately
19. practically, mischievous
20. obliged, temperature
21. privilege, superintendent
22. satellites, similar
23. precious, miniature
24. lightning, realized
25. library, liable

Index